MADMEN,
MADWORLD

Duke University Press   Durham and London   2013

LAUREN M. E. GOODLAD LILYA KAGANOVSKY ROBERT A. RUSHING EDITORS

MADMEN,
MADWORLD

Sex, Politics, Style, and the 1960s

© 2013 DUKE UNIVERSITY PRESS
All rights reserved

Printed in the United States of America on acid-free paper ∞
Designed by Courtney Leigh Baker
Typeset in Arno Pro and Trade Gothic by Tseng Information Systems, Inc.
Library of Congress Cataloging-in-Publication Data appear
on the last printed page of this book.

CONTENTS

Every scholarly work is, in some sense, collaborative, but edited volumes are particularly so. We thank first and foremost our fantastic contributors for their hard work and dedication to this project over the past two years. Our anonymous reviewers were some of the best intellectual interlocutors we had, and we thank them for their detailed engagement with this volume and the many ways they helped to make it better. We thank our editor, Courtney Berger, and everyone at Duke University Press for their enthusiasm for this book. And we particularly thank our incredibly hardworking graduate student research assistants at the Unit for Criticism and Interpretive Theory: Mike Black, Carl Lehnen, Katherine Skwarczek, and, toward the end of the project, MC Anderson and Amanda Monson.

All three of the editors of this volume share a common academic home in the Unit for Criticism and Interpretive Theory at the University of Illinois, Urbana-Champaign, but we also thank our more traditional academic homes for their support: the Department of English; the Department of Slavic Languages and Literatures; the Department of Spanish, Italian and Portuguese; and the Program in Comparative and World Literature. This project originated in a symposium in Urbana in 2010, and we are grateful to the many cosponsors and participants, including Pat Gill, Jennifer Greenhill, Diane Koenker, Michael Rothberg, and Paula Treichler. Nancy Abelmann, our associate vice chancellor for research in the humanities and arts, brought the project to the attention of the Campus Research Board at the University of Illinois, which provided generous funding for copyediting and permissions.

Many, many colleagues and friends contributed to this project—too many to mention individually—sometimes through their personal support, sometimes through animated discussions about the show, and most often through both. Jason Mittell's superb writing on seriality was an inspiration for our work. Michael Bérubé, Caroline Levine, Dana Polan, and Jeremy Varon were endlessly generous in providing expertise and illuminating thoughts at various stages of this project. They also contributed to the multi-authored series of posts for seasons 4 and 5 of *Mad Men* on the Unit for Criticism's weblog, *Kritik*. For their witty and on-the-spot blogging, we are also indebted to Sandy Camargo, Eleanor Courtemanche, Jim Hansen, Konstantine Klioutchkine, Adam Kotsko, Sanja Lacan, Carl Lehnen, Todd McGowan (whose post brought the blog and this volume to the attention of the *New York Times*), and Faith Wilson Stein. For permission to reprint Jerry Yulsman's stunning photograph of Dick Gregory and Hugh Hefner at the Playboy Club, we (and Clarence Lang) thank Barbara Woike and Tom Yulsman. We owe special thanks to Phil Abraham for his generosity in sharing his time and his insights from inside the show's production, as well as Eileen Gillooly for her kindness in making this introduction.

We thank our families and friends for their support, help, and encouragement with this project (and in particular, our parents, the real *Mad Men* generation). Mark Sammons has earned a special note of gratitude for his help with many things, not least of which was this volume's title.

Finally, a very special and sad acknowledgment of our colleague, contributor, and friend Alex Doty, who died while this volume was in production. Our condolences to his family and friends everywhere—he will be missed. We are grateful to Corey Creekmur for writing Alex's contributor biography.

LAUREN M. E. GOODLAD,
LILYA KAGANOVSKY, AND ROBERT A. RUSHING

On 16 July 2010 the *New York Times* online edition ran an interactive feature on what reviewer Alessandra Stanley, in an accompanying piece, called
a "cultural phenomenon." The occasion was the season 4 premiere of *Mad
Men*, scheduled to air nine days later. As most readers of this book know,
Mad Men is an AMC television show about Don Draper, a fictional character who is creative director for Sterling Cooper, a fictional New York advertising agency in the 1960s. What stood out in July 2010, therefore, was the
seriousness of the *Times* reportage, which interspersed photographs from
the 1960s with scenes and stills from a television drama. In a piece labeled
"Seeing History in 'Mad Men,'" the *Times* oscillated between describing the
historical 1960s and *Mad Men*'s characters (Egner). "The Korean War created Don Draper," the newspaper of record wrote, as though asserting a biographical fact. *Mad Men*, the *Times* seemed to say, was creating a window on
the nation's past through which viewers might experience America's history
in narrative form. Don Draper was not fiction but biography; *Mad Men* was
not television but a repository of the past. Pastness itself was redefined as
the past of the 1960s, the past of postwar America, a past of knowable events
about which one might read in the *New York Times*.

The *Times*'s soft spot for *Mad Men* is hardly surprising. The show, set in
the last golden age of print, appeals to the same well-heeled professionals
who read newspapers, re-creating a time before television and the Internet
supplanted broadsheet journalism as the premier venue for news and opin-

ion. Season 4 thus gave us Don announcing his withdrawal from cigarette advertising in the same venerable pages that had just proclaimed *Mad Men* a "cultural phenomenon." Such paradoxes have become common. An article on Cary Grant in the August 2010 issue of *Vanity Fair* opened: "Our story is set in the years before *Mad Men*, when Eisenhower was in the White House and America had only 48 states" (Beauchamp and Balban). What does this willful conflation of fact with fiction suggest? As the show invites its audience to look with post–*Mad Men* eyes on iconic media from the 1960s, is it reconfiguring our conception of the past?

At one level *Mad Men* has simply awakened memories of an early-1960s America that had been lost between the vintage 1950s of *Leave It to Beaver* and the late-1960s explosion of Woodstock, feminism, black power, and *The Mod Squad*. It is also clear, however, that *Mad Men* is not simply jostling memories but creating them: as the historian of the 1960s Jeremy Varon writes in this volume, "The show is more plausibly the staging of a fantasy than the rendering of history." Likewise, as Mabel Rosenheck proposes in her chapter on fashion, the show's relation to the vintage artifacts it displays is performative: an active construction that bespeaks twenty-first century representation of the 1960s. Thus media commentators on the *Mad Men* zeitgeist are not so much seeing the 1960s *in* the show as seeing them *through* it. Their doing so arguably tells us less about the 1960s than about the current desire for collective memories of the past.

By and large, the essays in this volume do not look to *Mad Men* for an accurate depiction of the 1960s, but they do explore the show's remarkable impact on how history is experienced. Americans have generally been a presentist people, seldom invoking the past beyond occasional nods to forebears. Recent soothsayers have announced "the end of history" (the title of Francis Fukuyama's bestseller of 1992), as well as technology's reshaping of the globe (Thomas Friedman's *The World Is Flat* [2005]). If *Mad Men* has seemed to put history back on the map, it is a sign of the show's groundbreaking approach to period drama: its use of the forms of historical fiction to capture and create an intense experience of the present day. In this way, phantasmatic and millennial though it may be, *Mad Men* has altered the vision of the 1960s, and of pastness itself.

The show's ability to do so, we suggest, rests on a few interrelated premises. First, despite the hype about the show's historical accuracy, *Mad Men* is as selectively anachronistic as it is showily mimetic. Perhaps never before has a television show been praised so effusively for its "realistic" qualities and painstaking attention to period details. Fan participation ritualizes this fetishism of the detail, with websites such as Natasha Vargas-Cooper's *The Footnotes of Mad Men* following each new episode with research on early-1960s artifacts and events.[1] Viewers get caught up in discussions about the books in Don's office, the clothing used to develop principal characters, and the use of nuanced interiors such as season 3's update of the Drapers' living room or season 4's creation of a new office space for Sterling Cooper Draper Pryce.[2] Paradoxically, the spotting of occasional inaccuracies (Bryn Mawr didn't have sororities when Betty would have attended; the IBM typewriters featured in the pilot, set in March 1960, weren't available until 1961; Joan quotes Marshall McLuhan's famous phrase "the medium is the message" three years before it was published) seems to intensify the show's mimetic halo, exacerbating the tendency for discourse about the show to "forget" that it is fictional.

On closer examination, however, *Mad Men*'s lovingly tended mimicry is selective and deliberately counterpoised with other features of its diegesis. Thus, as Lauren M. E. Goodlad observes in this volume, the show's over-all realism tends toward a literary naturalism associated with groundbreaking nineteenth-century novels such as Gustave Flaubert's *Madame Bovary* (1856) and Anthony Trollope's *The Way We Live Now* (1874–75)—both of which, like *Mad Men*, first appeared in serial form. By contrast, the show's *visual* aesthetic (as Robert A. Rushing notes in his chapter) takes its cues from the most glamorous cinema of the mid-twentieth century, along with glossy period magazines such as *Vogue, Playboy,* and *Ladies' Home Journal. Mad Men* thus combines naturalism's relentless exposure of social pathology with a surface allure culled from the most glittering self-representations of the era. The show's most significant anachronisms, therefore, are not the occasional errors, but the conspicuous departures from all but the façade of the period texts that *Mad Men* invokes.

THE BEST OF EVERYTHING

In "Six Month Leave" (2.9), wise-guy comedian Jimmy Barrett hails Don as "the Man in the Gray Flannel Suit," a reference to Sloan Wilson's novel of 1955 and Nunnally Johnson's film of 1956. *Mad Men* thus inserts itself into a period archive that includes Grace Metalious's *Peyton Place* (1956) and Frank O'Hara's *Meditations in an Emergency* (1957). To be sure, Don's sartorial panache, as performed by Jon Hamm, re-creates the aura of matinee idols such as Gregory Peck, Cary Grant, and Sean Connery (see Jim Hansen in this volume). Yet despite Jimmy's determination to peg Don as a Peck look-alike—"I loved you in *Gentleman's Agreement*," he tells him in "The Benefactor" (2.3)—Don is hardly the double of characters like Philip Schuyler Green in Elia Kazan's movie of 1947, Thomas Rath in *The Man in the Gray Flannel Suit*, or Atticus Finch in Robert Mulligan's *To Kill a Mockingbird* (1962). Don may be a suburban commuter with a wartime secret, but his problems have little to do with the Fordist-era conformity that Wilson saw threatening postwar America.

In a memorable scene from *The Man in the Gray Flannel Suit*, three men, one of whom is Rath, walk into a business meeting wearing nearly identical garb, an iconic statement of the "uniform of the day" (S. Wilson, 11; fig. Intro.1). As Catherine Jurca observes, "Tom Rath's renowned attire" signifies "the massification of the middle class" and "the deterioration of [its] status and privilege" (85). Wilson's answer to this engulfing corporate culture is a return to moral values: Rath saves his integrity and marriage by telling the truth about past infidelity, putting family and community before corporate ambition. Of course, deteriorating middle-class privilege—albeit of a post-Fordist and neoliberal kind—is a defining experience for *Mad Men*'s audience. But Don is hardly a likely candidate for moral redemption. Indeed, while *Mad Men* sustains identification with Don by holding out the possibility, even the hope, that he will change or grow in Rath-like manner, it also makes clear that the impulse to "believe in Don" is the ultimate sucker's bet (witness season 4's Faye Miller as a memorable reminder of the odds).

If Don cannot be Rath—if he is in fact an anti-Rath who casts doubt on the very idea of male virtue—that is partly because films like *Gentleman's Agreement*, *The Man in the Gray Flannel Suit*, and *To Kill a Mockingbird* are firm in their conviction that secular progress, however precarious, is achievable through moral agency, an expectation that naturalistic narrative tends to flummox. Thus, while Rath learns the value of being true to himself, Don hardly recognizes a boundary between self and self-invention. Though rarely unfeeling, and even quixotic, Don reflexively brings Madison Avenue to bear on the non-office world Rath holds sacrosanct. Whereas Rath defines himself *against* the limitations of his job in public relations, Don is an ad man to the roots of his Brylcreemed hair.

Here is where a second premise behind *Mad Men* becomes especially significant: although the show's investments in historical contexts are multifold, history functions first and foremost as the material fabric of an arresting aestheticism. Aestheticism explains how Don Draper—whose very name suggests the artful donning of masculine drapery—transforms the well-cut business suit into a mark of nimble self-fashioning. Thus, like much

FIGURE INTRO.1. Gregory Peck in *The Man in the Gray Flannel Suit* (1956), surrounded by colleagues in the "uniform of the day."

else in the show, the riff on the Man in the Gray Flannel Suit adopts tropes from a *pre*-counterculture 1960s to articulate experiences relevant to a *post*-counterculture twenty-first century. If this is hardly a magical time machine, like the "Carousel" Don pitches to Kodak, it represents an innovative play between mimesis and anachronism.

Then too, it is not only Don but also the show's strong female characters whose embedding in "realistic" early-1960s contexts relies on motifs abstracted from period texts. In "Babylon" (1.6), Betty and Don discuss *The Best of Everything*, Rona Jaffe's novel published in 1958 and Jean Negulesco's movie of 1959. *Mad Men* cannily borrows from the movie a template for the offices of Sterling Cooper (figs. Intro.2–Intro.3) as well as the set piece of the young woman's first day at work in a sophisticated Manhattan firm. As Dianne Harris writes in her chapter in this volume, "Location lends reality and authenticity to action." *Mad Men*'s borrowing inspiration for its ad agency interior from Negulesco's comparable set for Fabian Publishing Co. (based on Jaffe's real-life experiences at Fawcett) thus imports the topos of female clerical workers spatially and professionally ensconced by male executives (an aspect of midcentury office life that male-centered narratives like Wilson's occlude). As Harris suggests, the extensive open space in which Sterling Cooper's secretarial staff labors mobilizes "panoptic qualities that not only permit but actually produce the sexual tensions and sexual harassment" that make the show so arresting.

Like *Mad Men*, *The Best of Everything* is a tell-all tale of the midcentury working girl. As the movie opens, Caroline Bender (Hope Lange) is a young secretary starting a new job in the big city, much like Peggy Olson. Another secretary, Gregg Adams (1950s supermodel Suzy Parker), is an aspir-

FIGURES INTRO.2–INTRO.3. Office space in *The Best of Everything* (1959).

ing actress. Notably, Fabian employs a female editor, Amanda Farrow (Joan Crawford), who has chosen career over domesticity. The *New York Times* review described this genre as a cautionary tale of "the hearth vs. the desk" (H. Thompson). Behind the comic air of pink opening credits and Johnny Mathis crooning that "romance" promises "the best of everything," the film insists that young women balance the enticements of urban freedom against the hazards of premarital sex and defeminizing professional ambition.

As in *Mad Men*, the sexual double standard is everywhere on display: an older editor, Mr. Shalimar (Brian Aherne), puts his hand on Caroline's knee while offering to advance her career; Gregg ends up in the arms of a ladies' man (Louis Jourdan) who quickly tires of her; and when another secretary accidentally becomes pregnant, her boyfriend tricks her into thinking he will marry her while driving her to an abortionist. Less familiar to *Mad Men*'s audience is the depiction of career aspirations as antithetical to female nature. Thus, when Caroline, a Radcliffe graduate, begins making savvy business suggestions, the eligible executive Mike Rice (Stephen Boyd) accuses her of angling for his job. Toward the end, Miss Farrow decides to find domestic happiness with a widower, only to discover that it is "too late" for her to dispense womanly care. The movie closes with Caroline happy to restore "the desk" to her returning boss, and to embrace "the hearth" as Mike's wife-to-be.

The Best of Everything provides a number of interesting insights into *Mad Men*. As Don lies in bed reading Jaffe's novel, Betty zeroes in on Farrow—the character whom she least resembles. "Joan Crawford is not what she was," she tells Don. "Her, standing next to Suzy Parker—as if they were the same species. . . . To think, one of the great beauties, and there she is so *old*" (1.6). Betty thus refuses the proffered identification with Caroline: a well-educated, upper-middle-class blonde, much like herself, whose happy ending is marriage to a handsome executive. Instead, she idealizes the youth of the most self-destructive character, Gregg, who falls to her death from a fire escape while clinging to the heartless playboy who discards her. Fittingly, the scene closes with Betty confessing a dependence that recalls Gregg's desperate need for the errant lover who deems her "suffocating" and "possessive." "I want you so much," Betty whispers. "It's all in a kind of fog because . . . I want you so badly." When Don replies reassuringly, "You have me, you do," we know he is lying. If Betty intuits that her storybook marriage to a handsome executive is as precarious as Gregg's affair with an infamous ladies' man, the reason, of course, is that Don is playing both parts.

Here once again *Mad Men* reproduces the resplendent surfaces of Hollywood cinema while stripping out the stark moral contrasts and idealized domestic norms. This signature fusion of glamour and naturalism works quite differently from other recent retrospectives such as Todd Haynes's *Far from Heaven* (2002). In this celebrated tribute to Douglas Sirk, Haynes reconstructs the world of the 1950s—not as it might really have been, but as it was represented in Sirk's magnificent Technicolor melodramas. What viewers and critics loved about *Far from Heaven* were not only its period details and capturing of Sirk's visual richness, but also its filling in of the gaps left in his narratives. In a literal return of the repressed, homosexuality and interracial romance are made visible, while vices like cigarettes are hidden. Subtext becomes text as Haynes brings to the surface what Sirk circled around and disavowed. In doing so, Haynes seems to correct the movies he commemorates, taking his revision of midcentury narratives much further than *Mad Men's*. As many critics have noted, *Mad Men* unmasks—but does not decenter—the white middle-class narratives that dominated the period. If the risk for the show is the disturbing dissonance of a luscious mise-en-scène saturated by jarring prejudice, the risk for Haynes is a complete rupture from what made Sirk's aesthetic compelling in the first place—the social tensions that Hollywood's mainstream could not yet openly render.

"YOU'LL LOVE THE WAY IT MAKES YOU FEEL"

Consider historical fiction as it typically appears on television: *Foyle's War* (ITV, 2002–) depicts a middle-aged police chief in a small English town during the Second World War. In one episode ("Among the Few," 2.2), Foyle's son is training to be a pilot in the Royal Air Force when his squadron-mate comes under suspicion of a crime. Foyle learns that the young man is innocent of the crime but is homosexual. As most viewers would agree, in the 1940s a provincial policeman's most likely reaction to discovering that an RAF pilot was homosexual—and in love with his son to boot—would be to arrest or report him. But Foyle displays an open-minded compassion that would be unusual in such a figure even today. *Foyle's War* thus allows us to have our enjoyment and eat it, too: viewers can both warm to Foyle and the glamour of wartime flyboys *and* have them untarnished by the prejudices from which the show's feel-good heroism is abstracted.

Ironically, period shows like *Foyle's War* are rarely if ever singled out as "smug," while, for some viewers, the charge of smugness clings to *Mad Men* like the stale odor of cigarettes. Alongside profuse acclaim from every quarter, including Emmy Awards for Outstanding Drama for four consecutive years, *Mad Men* has been subject to this line of critique from several academic and literary corners. Thus, according to Sady Doyle in the *Atlantic*, *Mad Men* "affords viewers an illusion of moral superiority"; and for Benjamin Schwarz, also writing in the *Atlantic*, the show "encourages the condescension of posterity" by inviting its audience "to indulge in a most unlovely—because wholly unearned—smugness." Both writers echo Mark Greif's earlier claim in the *London Review of Books* that "*Mad Men* is an unpleasant little entry in the genre of Now We Know Better." In the most extensive critique so far, Daniel Mendelsohn argues in the *New York Review of Books* that the show's "attitude toward the past is glib and its self-positioning in the present is unattractively smug." Why is a show that lays bare the racism, sexism, and decadence of the past judged to be self-congratulatory, when more conventional historical fare spares viewers entirely from reflecting on injustice? The question points to a set of ongoing debates about *Mad Men* that this volume explores in multiple ways.[3]

To be sure, *Mad Men* does not have the mass appeal of a network hit. For some audiences the pace is unnervingly slow. Many viewers old enough to have experienced the 1960s report that *Mad Men* brings back memories they would rather forget. Similarly, some younger viewers find realistic depiction of racism and misogyny too uncomfortable to tolerate. For still other audiences, *Mad Men's* aestheticism is itself an obstacle to pleasure. As one colleague mused, "I think I may be too personally ambivalent about style to have the same response . . . as some of my better-dressed friends. I hate myself at some level if I spend too much time on clothes and décor." The assumption here is that watching *Mad Men* entails positive embrace, perhaps even emulation, of its glamorous style (although plenty of *Mad Men* watchers neither sport vintage fashion nor throw elegant cocktail parties). Then too, some male viewers find it difficult to identify with the show's spectacularly flawed protagonist. "I think Don is harder to take for men than [for] women," writes one interlocutor. "Heterosexual women can likely assume that he is hardly relationship material, and fantasize about pleasure without strings or commitment. But for men, he's a threat — someone who sinks their esteem and incurs a sense that 'life isn't fair' insofar as a mysterious lout is rewarded with his choice of beautiful women."[4] Writing on his blog, *Just TV*, the television scholar Jason Mittell wrestles with the disconnect between his critical "habitus" and his reflexive "dislike" for the show: "I fully acknowledge that it is a 'good' series. . . . It is objectively better made . . . than the vast majority of programs airing on American television. But . . . I would rather watch many programs that are less well-made, less intelligent, and less ambitious, as I find them more satisfying and pleasurable" ("On Disliking"). Such reactions not only illustrate the intense feelings the show incites, they also suggest that part of understanding *Mad Men's* strong appeal means recognizing that it is not for everyone.

Still, it is worth pointing out that none of these reactions is at all self-congratulatory. For Caroline Levine, writing in this volume, shows like *Mad Men* and *The Sopranos* (HBO, 1999–2007) give us characters who, despite their flaws, are too compelling to enable the thorough detachment that a smug attitude requires. *Mad Men* "does not invite us to displace pernicious assumptions about sexism, racism, and homophobia onto an exotic, far-off place or time," she argues, "but brings them just close enough to us to give us [a] feeling of uncanny familiarity." Following Levine, one needs to ask, Who are these smug viewers whom *Mad Men* allegedly flatters? In Greif's analysis, unexamined hostility toward the show and its cast stands in for the answer. Assessing the role of Draper, Greif writes, "[Jon] Hamm looks perpetually wimpy and underslept. His face is powdered and doughy. He lacks command. He is witless. The pose that he's best at, interestingly, is leaning back in his chair; it ought to be from superiority, but it looks as though he is trying to dodge a blow." One can appreciate the critical bravado here without being convinced by the argument it purports to confirm: Is it likely that *Mad Men* "flatters us" because its leading man looks doughy and witless?

Doyle's feminist analysis also invites questions. Disturbed that audiences do not recognize that Joan Holloway was raped by her fiancé in season 3 — not "sort of" raped — Doyle unaccountably blames the show: "our inability to identify misogyny, even on a show that presents it so melodramatically," points to the persistence of sexism. While Doyle is surely right about continuing sexism, she offers no evidence for the theory that *Mad Men* somehow obscures this reality. "We can't face [sexism] directly unless we're assured that it's behind us," Doyle claims. When she cites a female story editor who explains that several incidents depicted on *Mad Men* "come directly from experiences that I and the other women writers have had in our lifetimes," Doyle seems to think that viewers will be shocked to hear it. This presumption of a gullible audience, indulged by a show that panders to its weakness, echoes the premise embedded in Greif's title — "You'll Love the Way It Makes You Feel." Adopted from the tagline that Peggy writes for a weight-loss device–*cum*–vibrator, Greif's title likens watching *Mad Men* to masturbation. In a comparable essay, Anna Kelner of *Ms.* worries that *Mad Men* "is crafting a whole new generation of would-be Bettys (Draper's stylish wife) not Peggys (the show's ambitious 'career girl')." Yet since many viewers dislike Betty (or, perhaps, love to hate her), the commentary surrounding this much-criticized character hardly suggests that the show is inspiring female viewers to become neurotic housewives and unhappy mothers. Instead, viewers' favorite female characters by far are Joan, Peggy, and the unforgettable Rachel Menken from season 1 — all three formidable "career girls" whose stories underline the tensions between marriage and work.[5]

Condescension is also at play in Mendelsohn's critique, though to do this essay justice, many of its perceptions are accurate: *Mad Men*'s plotlines *are* melodramatic; its interiors airless and "boxed"; and the style of acting it cultivates, mannered and flat. But Mendelsohn's tack is less to elucidate how such supposed flaws produce "unattractive" smugness than to establish the viewer as rube: "That a soap opera decked out in high-end clothes (and concepts) should have received so much acclaim and is taken so seriously reminds you that fads depend as much on the willingness of the public to believe as on the cleverness of people who invent them." This critical condescension concerns characters and viewers alike: "The writers don't really want you to think about what Betty might be thinking; they just want you to know that she's one of those clueless 1960s mothers who smoked during pregnancy." This said about a character who is on to her husband's infidelity from the start, who takes out her neighbor's pet pigeons with a shotgun — a woman who is complex and frustrated enough to lure a friend into a vicarious affair while she herself has sex with a stranger in a public rest room. Can it really be true that none of this prompts viewers to ponder what Betty is thinking?

In what is perhaps his most damning criticism, Mendelsohn argues that the writing in *Mad Men* is "very much like the writing you find in ads." This interesting analysis of *Mad Men* and advertising (a topic explored in this volume by Lynne Joyrich, Lilya Kaganovsky, Lauren M. E. Goodlad, and Michael Bérubé) might be different if Mendelsohn did not accept the much-hyped premise of a show that accurately documents America's history. As several contributors to this volume show, *Mad Men* is less interested in reproducing 1960s advertising than in capturing what the late-capitalist social world surrounding advertising means to viewers watching the show today. Like the best historical fiction, the show adopts resonant material from the past to speak audibly to the present. Historical realism of this kind directly contrasts with the "capitalist realism" that Michael Schudson, in one of the most penetrating studies of the topic to date, aligns with advertising. What advertisements portray, writes Schudson, is "relatively placeless," "relatively timeless," "abstracted," and "self-contained" (211). Yet while advertisements do not depict particular realities, they strive for the illusion of reality as such. The "rich, cinematic, often crowded detail in magazine ads and television commercials" bespeaks an "obsessive attention to making every detail look 'right'" (217).

Mendelsohn's analysis is thus partly right: *Mad Men* captures the look and, at times, the feel of a 1960s advertisement; it does so, however, not to flatter us but to defamiliarize a millennial condition that is entirely our own. Mendelsohn's blind spot on the show's contemporaneity is especially striking in his analysis of Salvatore Romano's closeted gay identity. Sal's season 3 story line, he objects, "isn't really about the closet at all." Of course, the point is debatable given that Don, who discovers Sal's secret while the two are traveling together, is in a closet himself — which, as Alexander Doty shows in this volume, endows their interactions with multiple tensions. But for Mendelsohn the show fails because it diverges from accurate documentation. Noting that Sal is fired after he rebuffs the sexual advance of the firm's most important client, Mendelsohn protests: "That's not a story about gayness in the 1960s . . . it's a story about caving in to power, a story about business ethics." He may be the only writer today who thinks that Americans should not be watching more television stories about business ethics.

Similarly, Greif thinks he has found the smoking gun when he points out that "It's toasted," the slogan Don produces in "Smoke Gets in Your Eyes" (1.1), was "first used by Lucky Strike not in 1960 but in 1917." The scene pivots on Don's need to surmount the daunting marketing problem cigarette advertisers faced in 1960, after facts about smoking and cancer began to spill into the popular press. Whereas all advertising contends with the need to differentiate brands that are virtually indistinguishable, tobacco advertising peddles products that are indistinguishably toxic. Seizing on a toasting process that all cigarette manufacturers employ, Don articulates a special instance of the marketing strategy that Rosser Reeves, the legendary executive at Ted Bates, called the "unique selling proposition": the elevation of a particular feature (such as chocolate that melts in your mouth, not in your hands) to the status of a brand's inimitable raison d'être. Thus when Don's tagline replaces a pernicious universal ("Everybody else's tobacco is poisonous") with an abstracted particular ("Lucky Strike's is toasted"), it shows how advertising disarticulates an illusory freedom of choice from the actual constraints and perilous addictions of consumer capitalism. Since the show is dramatic fiction, it no more matters that Lucky Strike used this slogan long before the proven cancer link than that "Smoke Gets in Your Eyes" is borrowed from a song written in 1933. Greif goes on to point out that in the 1950s and '60s, advertisers were "eager to believe in a Svengali model of mass persuasion. The black-magic prestige of professional psychology was at its height." It never seems to occur to him that the writers of *Mad Men* mute this midcentury scientism, with its strong echoes of *The Man in the Gray Flannel Suit*, in order to engage in deliberate anachronism.

IT'S NOT A SCIENCE

It is not just any anachronistic account of advertising that *Mad Men* constructs, but a rich one that over-layers the Brave New World of midcentury behaviorism with a story about countercultural cooptation told by Thomas Frank in *The Conquest of Cool: Business Culture, Counterculture, and the Rise of Hip Consumerism* (1997). The advertising of the 1950s and early 1960s, Frank explains, was of a piece with a business culture known for "soul-deadening conformity" and "empty consumerism" (7). Guided by leading lights, such as "Father of Advertising" David Ogilvy, the agencies of this period viewed their work as a science, adopting the bureaucratic hierarchies and managerial style of the Fordist corporation. Under Reeves, Ted Bates's ads favored repetitious taglines and scientific endorsements. Advertising, Reeves claimed in *Reality in Advertising*, does not need copywriters who indulge in a "solipsist universe," like Tennyson's "Lady of Shalott," but rather, professionals under "the strict discipline of attaining a commercial goal" (121–22). Likewise, Ogilvy subjected the creative process to time-tested rules, scientific positivism, and managerial control. Critical of any approach that smacked of "the mystique of the Bauhaus," he warned in *Confessions of an Advertising Man* that "aesthetic intangibles do not increase sales" (121). In such a context, books like Vance Packard's *The Hidden Persuaders* (1957) could describe a manipulative ad industry that used psychological research to "probe our everyday habits" (12). Packard's argument was part of a growing anticorporate critique that included David Riesman, Nathan Glazer, and Reuel Denney's *The Lonely Crowd* (1950) and William H. Whyte's *The Organization Man* (1956), as well as fiction such as Wilson's *The Man in the Gray Flannel Suit* and Richard Yates's *Revolutionary Road* (1961). Sixties counterculture was, in this sense, the fruit of rebellious energies defined in opposition to business and advertising.

Thomas Frank, however, rejects this simple contrast between corporation and counterculture. He argues that business culture not only coopted the storied rebellions of the 1960s but also anticipated and in some ways fueled them. The epicenter of this corporate insurrection was an advertising industry that had burst the bonds of Fordism and liberated its inner hipster. By the end of the decade, Frank writes, "advertising would . . . transform itself from a showplace of managerial certainty" to a "corporate celebration of carnivalesque difference" (49–50). This was, in effect, to demote researchers, account executives, and upper management in favor of the copywriters, artists, and creative directors whom Ogilvy had dismissed as "the Bauhaus brigade" (124). As ads began to mock and ironize the bromides that Madison Avenue had once proudly blazoned, the end result was commodification of the counterculture and the rise of a "cool" consumerism.

Although this transformation extended into the 1970s, the first major salvo came in 1959 when Doyle Dane Bernbach's (DDB) Volkswagen ads "altered the look, language, and tone of American advertising" (Frank, 55). Bill Bernbach, the leader behind this coup, would become an "enfant terrible" and "hero among creatives" (Twitchell, 193; Schudson, 57). With an almost Wildean flair for aphorism, Bernbach declared that advertising was an art, that rules were meant for artists to break, and that "the real giants

FIGURE INTRO.4. Harry and Sal discuss the Volkswagen "Lemon" ad
("Marriage of Figaro," 1.3).

have always been poets, men who jumped from facts into the realm of ideas"
(qtd. in Frank, 57). By the late 1960s, agencies were increasingly following
DDB's example: they dethroned management, assembled charismatic creative teams, and even argued with clients. Advertising, for a time, became
"anti-advertising," a proto-postmodern ironization of consumer capitalism
(Frank, 68).

Of course, the Sterling Cooper depicted in the first three seasons of *Mad
Men* is precisely the kind of white shoe agency that preexisted DDB's rise
to prominence in the early 1960s. Whereas rising stars like Bernbach and
the Volkswagen copywriter Julian Koenig were Jewish, Sterling Cooper's
lone Jewish employee works in the mailroom. In "Marriage of Figaro" (1.3),
Sterling Cooper's writers nervously eye the Volkswagen "Lemon" ad (fig.
Intro.4). In "Babylon," when a representative from the Israeli Tourist Board
declares her intention to compare Sterling Cooper's "traditional" offerings
to DDB's, Don tartly replies that "Sterling Cooper doesn't like to think of
itself as traditional." Moreover, Ken Cosgrove and Pete Campbell recall
Rosser Reeves in nurturing literary aspirations. That is, the same utilitarian
technocrat who exhorted admen to "believe only what they can weigh, measure, calculate, and observe" had another side to his character (Reeves, 153).
Reeves would go on to write a semiautobiographical novel about a poet-hero
who leaves behind millions to become the kind of Greenwich Village bohemian with whom Don cavorts in season 1. Indeed, Don himself considers a
comparable escape into the hedonism of California in season 2.

While *Mad Men* thus dramatizes the tensions between research, accounts, and creative, the overall effect is historical composite, not reenactment of the DDB-led creative revolution. Set in 1960, the pilot already constructs Don as creative impresario and aligns market research with the professorial Dr. Greta Guttman, whose Freudian shibboleths seem out of touch. It is not until season 4, by which point Sterling Cooper Draper Pryce is a fledgling start-up, that Dr. Faye Miller represents a sophisticated form of market research in tension with creative instincts. When Faye's focus group suggests that Peggy's idea for a cold cream ad centered on self-indulgent rituals will be less successful than a campaign promising matrimony, Don insists that advertising's job is to invent ideas consumers have not yet imagined for themselves ("The Rejected," 4.4). Pete illustrates the ascendency of this Bernbachian ethos when he shows off Sterling Cooper Draper Pryce's up-to-date Creative Lounge. Pointing out the youthful ambience to prospective clients, he says, "We can't tell you *how* it happens, but it does happen *here*" ("The Chrysanthemum and the Sword," 4.5). Meanwhile, the ever more irrelevant Roger, a product of the Reeves generation, pens his risible memoir, *Sterling's Gold*.

Advertising thus provides a structure for exploring the moral quandaries of a corrupting world. Although this is not a documentary portrait of Madison Avenue in the 1960s, it captures resonant features of the zeitgeist while using specific campaigns to shape story worlds in multiple ways: for example, the brilliant Kodak "Carousel" pitch discussed in Irene Small's chapter. Turning "surface into depth," according to Small's masterful reading, the pitch provides a fitting close to season 1's narrative of mounting despair, just as season 3's "Limit Your Exposure" ad underlines the continuing theme of closeted identity (Doty, this volume). In her chapter on "Maidenform" (2.6), an episode named after a brand, Kaganovsky shows how an advertising campaign subtends *Mad Men*'s sophisticated play with gendered spectatorship.

Some of the most memorable accounts, such as season 1's Nixon campaign and Israeli tourism bid, do not culminate in scripted pitches but instead percolate into the show's narrative substrate. In 1963 when the Kennedy campaign hired DDB, they signaled their attunement with the changes that led to the creative revolution. But the point of making Sterling Cooper Nixon's choice, according to Michael Szalay, is to isolate Don's embodiment of the ascendant "hipness" that structures the show's depiction of race ("Mad Style"). Thus, according to Szalay's chapter in this volume, the adman-artist is a Maileresque "hipster manqué" and Don, a symbolic black

FIGURE INTRO.5. Ann-Margret in *Bye Bye Birdie* (1963) ("Love among the Ruins," 3.2).

man (like his silhouette in the credits) trying to pass for white. Likewise, in Goodlad's reading, Don's resistance to selling Israel as a global commodity reveals his ambivalence toward a position of Judaized exile and otherness. In all of these ways, *Mad Men* uses advertising to glimpse the structures that make 1960s history palpable in our own day.

Still, while *Mad Men* has not yet scripted ads in the DDB style, the show itself is frequently self-referential, metatextual, and ironic. As Don says to the hapless client he manipulates in "The Hobo Code" (1.8), if advertising is not a religion, it's also "not a science." Like Don making his pitch, *Mad Men* understands very well that it is putting on a show, constructing the fetish of the magical time machine. Indeed, the show underscores its artifice, reminding viewers that they are watching a "remake" of the 1960s that should never be taken for the original.[6] To see this self-referential aspect at work we need go no further than advertising (of course): for example, Sal's failed Patio commercial. "Love among the Ruins" (3.2) opens with the first bars of "Bye Bye Birdie," and when the screen fades in from black, we are watching George Sidney's film of 1963 (fig. Intro.5). When the scene cuts from the actress to reaction shots from the Sterling Cooper boardroom, viewers do a double take as they find themselves caught within the mise en abyme world of fictional representation. The client's idea for Patio, a new diet cola, is to replicate the opening sequence of *Bye Bye Birdie* "frame for frame." "Is it just a knock-off?" Peggy asks. "Are we allowed to make fun of it at least?" But while Peggy thus gestures toward the ironic stance that was making DDB's ads all the rage, the men in the room cannot see past Ann-Margret's charms. Although Sal's remake is a technical success, both the ad men and the clients recoil from it, as if they are seeing an uncanny double. Ken and Don point out that the commercial is "an exact copy, frame for frame" and *exactly* what the clients had asked for, but the two clients insist that there's something "not right about it." As Roger sums it up, "It's not Ann-Margret."

The problem is not simply that we have a copy in place of the original. As Slavoj Žižek suggests, "the more formally identical the remake, the more palpable the difference between original and copy." "Sameness" underscores the "uncanny difference" particular to each version's "underlying libidinal economy" (*Enjoy Your Symptom*, 234–35). Thus as Sal's wife, Kitty, watches him reenact the *Bye Bye Birdie* scene, she realizes the "truth" about Sal's sexuality. Sal's "exact copy" of Ann-Margret is a kind of "drag" which produces an ambivalence that gets coded in the ad as "pretend" or "off." The ad is not queer because Sal is, it is queer because there is an added layer of meaning that the viewer (both inside and outside the show) cannot help but understand, which adds something to the original and decenters it.[7] *Mad Men* repeats the opening scene of *Bye Bye Birdie* five times over several episodes, and the uncanny repetition points to the problem of the "remake" as a whole, which in trying to produce sameness always ends up with difference. In this way, *Mad Men* has some fun with its own fetish for period accuracy as it "remakes" the 1960s.

THE FOG

Historically, the 1960s marked the last great expansion of middle-class prosperity and the crest of U.S. prestige; but globalizing currents were already under way that would make borders more porous and place transnational capital beyond the reach of the nation-state's regulatory oversight. Paradoxically then, the same revolutionary trends that enabled hip consumerism to thrive on the growing cultural and economic power of women, students, African Americans, Catholics, Jews, and other minorities, eventually promoted the so-called free market as the perfect arbiter of every need and desire, constituting neoliberalism as we know it. For several contributors, the secret to *Mad Men*'s appeal is Don's ability to figure this unassimilable doubleness.

The point of such readings, however, is not to posit *Mad Men* as a utopian text. Writing in this volume, Dana Polan notes that the show does not take its meditation on "madness" from pioneering media like Joseph Heller's *Catch-22* (1961) or Stanley Kubrick's *Dr. Strangelove* (1964), which saw madness as a source of revolutionary political potential. Leslie J. Reagan's chapter makes a comparable point about *Mad Men*'s depiction of reproductive practices: while the show portrays Peggy's gynecological exam with painstaking accuracy, its engagement of abortion rights is less radical than the television show it cites—the groundbreaking episode of *The Defenders* aired in 1962 from which *Mad Men*'s "The Benefactor" (2.3) borrows its title. This deliberate distance from a counterculture that is always imminent but never quite born is one of the several ways through which the show engages a present-day neoliberalism that handily channels revolutionary energy—an impasse that shapes the Mad World that *we* know. Nevertheless, such fidelity to a post-1960s–as–pre-1960s stance on the *longue durée* is bound to strike some commentators as an acceptance of what *is*.

Although some readers may disagree, we think it unlikely that *Mad Men* spurs nostalgia for the 1960s housewife. Indeed, given the vogue for male protagonists with fascinating secret lives—a feature integral to *The Sopranos*, *Breaking Bad* (AMC, 2008–), and *Dexter* (Showtime, 2006–)—*Mad Men* stands out for its reliance on strongly developed female characters. By contrast, even a profoundly novelistic show like *The Wire* (HBO, 2002–8) focuses primarily on relationships between men. Katie Roiphe may declare that *Mad Men* incites the "tiniest bit of wistfulness" for the prefeminist era ("On 'Mad Men'"). But as the historian Claire B. Potter argues, Roiphe seems to miss the show's point: "The retro fashion and perfect sets only provide a brittle frame for a fraying heteropatriarchal culture." Like Potter, we think that viewers recognize the difference between midcentury aesthetics and prefeminist inequality, distinguishing readily between the *sexy* and the *sexist*.

We also agree with Potter that the show is not "sexist and racist" but rather "provides a forum for pondering sexism and racism." And yet we are not surprised that the determination to provoke reflection by rendering white middle-class America in all its glaring privilege and insularity (what Kent Ono in this volume calls "demographic realism") causes consternation for some viewers, including contributors to this book.[8] Thus Latoya Peterson argues that *Mad Men* is "afraid of race," refusing to "engage" the world of minority characters like Carla (the Drapers' housekeeper) and Hollis (the elevator operator in Sterling Cooper's office tower) ("Afraid"). Clarence Lang's chapter in this volume proposes a different view. When Hollis tells Pete that African Americans have "bigger problems to worry about than TV," the interaction, Lang notes, does more than accurately depict the inequality between the two men. Rather, the scene in "The Fog" (3.5) "acknowledges the sea change occurring in U.S. race relations" as blacks like Hollis began to gain power as consumers. Lang goes on to describe a blues-oriented "cool" in dialogue with the era's black freedom struggles, arguing that *Mad Men*'s story world would be enriched if hipsters of color made their mark beyond the suggestive credits sequence. Jeremy Varon concludes on a similar note, urging that social movements of the 1960s remain crucial because of the "moral imagination and impulse for change" that they display—examples of which *Mad Men* might also inspire in its viewers.

In what is perhaps the most nuanced theoretical take on *Mad Men* and race to date, Ono argues that the show is symptomatic of *postracism*, a cultural condition "premised on the assumption that race and racism are . . . passé." Thus a character like Carla is there to signify "*Mad Men*'s self-conscious awareness of the fact that racism existed in the 1960s." By not showing more, however, the show not only demonstrates "the irrelevance of her personal life to white people in the 1960s" but also "objectionably produces the irrelevance of her personal life to television viewers now." While this is the strongest critique of *Mad Men* and race in the volume, the desire to see Carla rendered more fully is shared by several contributors and doubtless many viewers. By contrast, Bérubé's afterword argues that the impulse to wish that *Mad Men* "follow Carla home" is mistaken. Although it would be pleasurable "to transcend the Drapercentric worldview," to insist on it is to demand that the series "accommodate more of What We Know Now by letting us see what the white inhabitants of Mad World neither knew nor cared about." Bérubé thus joins Ta-Nehisi Coates in judging the strategic focus on white perspectives to be "incredibly powerful," an important "statement on how privilege, at its most insidious, really works" ("Race").

We do not propose to settle this debate, but we do wish to highlight its complexity and significance. If criticism of *Mad Men*'s white perspective often reproduces a familiar plaint about the limitations of realism, there is clearly more to say: both about the value of unvarnished depictions of white racism and about the formal capacities of naturalistic realism. As rendered in the first four seasons of *Mad Men*, Carla (Deborah Lacey), without a last name or a home we can see, is nonetheless a powerful presence whose facial expressions, body movements, and careful speech convey more than mere measure of her time onscreen suggests (fig. Intro.6). Confuting the pernicious trope of the Good White People who enable racial progress (Bérubé, this volume), Carla equally evades the opposing trap of the "magic negro"— the pitfall to which *Far from Heaven*'s idealized African American gardener

FIGURE INTRO.6. Carla's silent presence ("The Chrysanthemum and the Sword," 4.5).

arguably succumbs.[9] Yet while we share Coates's view that the show's white vision "works," we also find it interesting that *Mad Men* director Phil Abraham thinks that a glimpse of Carla's family would be "cool" and consistent with the show we know (see appendix A). From Abraham's perspective, if *Mad Men* "fears race," it is because the creators do not wish their white progressivism to overwrite the exclusions of the past.

Taken as a whole, the essays in this volume suggest that there is no single formula to explain what *Mad Men* gets right or wrong about race. The device of embedding story lines in the ebb and flow of history works at different levels and with different degrees of success: brilliant, for example, when the breakdown of the Draper marriage plays out against the "thirteen days" of the missile crisis; far less so when excerpts from "I Have a Dream" provide the background for Don's pursuit of Sally's teacher. A minor black female character may work well to support Paul Kinsey's pompous variation on the Good White Person and less well in a plotline about a British expat's predilection for "chocolate." Resisting the charms of an attractive "Asian waitress" may make sense in a scene about Don's guilty capitulation to corporate imperatives, whereas portraying Honda's executives as hapless dupes, caught in their Japanese culture, seems downright un–*Mad Men*–like.

It is testimony to *Mad Men*'s status as a "cultural phenomenon" that in introducing a collection of essays on the topic, one finds much to say before discussing the series as a television show. *Mad Men* surely belongs to the elevated category of *quality television*, a term denoting the kind of writerly cable drama that entered the scene with HBO's now classic series *The Sopranos*.[10] While *The Sopranos* is an obvious forerunner for *Mad Men* in being the show Matthew Weiner helped to produce in the years before launching his own series (see Szalay, this volume), there are various ways in which *Mad Men* connects to other "quality" series.

One of those ways is audience. *Mad Men* has grown steadily more popular: from the one million viewers who watched the premiere in 2007 to the three and a half million viewers for the fifth-season premiere in 2012 (Kondolojy). If these are not especially large numbers by network television standards, they are respectable for a cable drama.[11] Moreover, like *The Sopranos* and *The Wire*, *Mad Men* is a prestigious critical success that singlehandedly established AMC as a destination for quality TV. Although *Breaking Bad*, with a similar size audience, is also acclaimed, it is *Mad Men* that explores its position as the flagship series for a network attempting to make its mark (see Joyrich, this volume).

Mad Men's viewership is also considerably larger than the audience for each broadcast. In 2010 it was the number-one show among the "time-shifted" viewers who watch a show after it airs on recording devices such as TiVo (*Nielsenwire*, 2). Moreover, digital recording is only one form of time-shifting. *Mad Men* viewers who dislike commercial interruption may download a "Season Pass" from iTunes and watch digital files at their leisure. Then too, a whole set of additional viewers watches the show months or even years later on DVD.

If *Mad Men* attracts fewer viewers than the most popular network shows, the viewers it attracts are notably affluent. According to the *Hollywood Reporter*, more than half of the households that watch *Mad Men* earn more than $100,000 per year, making these "the wealthiest fans in all of cable TV land." Such viewers can afford cable, DVR, iTunes, and possibly even the BMWs frequently advertised during the series' season premiers (Armstrong). One might also hypothesize that *Mad Men*'s viewers are more media-centered than other viewers. The cinematic character of quality TV is enhanced by uninterrupted viewing, or by viewing the show as an "event" (for example, the numerous *Mad Men*–themed parties that accompany each season's opening installments, including one in Times Square, New York, for the third-season premiere).[12]

According to *Advertising Age*, liberals are 124 percent more likely to watch *Mad Men* than conservatives (Bulk).[13] Although we found no firm data to support it, our impression is that most viewers of the show are at least thirty years of age (many of our graduate students watch *Mad Men* but only those undergraduates with interest in topics such as film studies or fashion do). It therefore seems safe to surmise that the show's viewers are relatively wealthy, politically liberal, and technologically "plugged-in." Although there is no hard data on the racial demographics of the viewership, popular imagination has the show's fans as white (*Mad Men* appears as number 123 on the satirical blog *Stuff White People Like*, just below Moleskine notebooks).

Of course, while *Mad Men* viewers may often be white, they need not be Americans or residents of the United States. That is, *Mad Men* is not only *about* globalization but also a product of it: a quintessential American cultural export in telling a story about the height of U.S. hegemony that speaks to Britons, Czechs, Danes, Finns, Hungarians, South Koreans, and Ukrainians, among others. (When the show aired in Turkey, it was fined for excessive onscreen smoking.) Receiving an award in Cologne, after watching himself and Elisabeth Moss (Peggy Olson) dubbed into German, Jon Hamm told reporters, "It seems incredible that something that seems so specific to a particular time and place in America . . . can reach an international audience" (Roxborough). But the fact is in many ways predictable. *Mad Men*'s Madison Avenue is a hub in a global network, an industry that produces ad campaigns for Hilton Hotels, Rio de Janeiro, and Haifa alongside public relations campaigns for the new Penn Station. Stylistically, the show illustrates a high-modernist chic that resonates even in places where Ossining, New York—the original Draper family hometown—has never been heard of. Will *Mad Men* one day air in Bangalore, Beijing, Johannesburg, or Kuala Lumpur? We do not know, but we imagine that it is already playing on iPads and DVDs in these and many other global nodes. The show's aestheticization of the alienation to which globalization gives rise seems to translate into many languages.

Mad Men's audience ranges from occasional viewers to those for whom the show is "destination TV." There are also relatively intense fans who meet for live discussion, stage *Mad Men*–themed parties, and even produce original art or fiction set in the world of *Mad Men*—all typical fan rituals. In one of the best-known iterations of such activities, *Mad Men* enthusiasts created the Internet application MadMenYourself.com, which was eventually incorporated into AMC's website. The site enables users to design their own *Mad Men*–inspired icons to match their gender and appearance, complete with vintage fashion and hair. Blogging on the show on *Just TV*, the television scholar Jason Mittell invokes the category of the "acafan," or academic fan ("On Disliking"). Although none of the editors of this book is likely ever to own a BMW, we think it fair to acknowledge that some readers may judge the writing of scholarly articles and books to constitute a fan ritual all its own.

While AMC invites *Mad Men* fans to call themselves "Maddicts," *Saturday Night Live* ridiculed fans as "Mad Mennies" in a skit hosted by *Mad Men* actor January Jones in November 2009. The piece depicted fans as obsessed eccentrics, dressing like characters and memorizing the dialogue. When Jones opined that such fans are "like Trekkies," the "Mad Mennies" invoked the narcissism of small differences: "Trekkies are losers who live with their parents and pretend they're in space. *We* live with our parents and pretend we work in advertising—much cooler!" Of course, *Saturday Night Live* can hardly claim immunity to the malady: Hamm's three SNL appearances include two parodies of his performance as Don that have been viewed on the Internet thousands of times. Meanwhile, cast and crew members from *Mad Men* have been interviewed on the National Public Radio show *Fresh Air* no fewer than four times—another indication, like Frank Rich's admiring columns in the *New York Times* or even our own Unit for Criticism and Interpretive Theory series of *Kritik* blog posts on the last two seasons—that *Mad Men* enthusiasm is taken seriously in some quarters.[14] There is perhaps a fine line between participating in these relatively elite forms of appreciation and the kind of fandom SNL simultaneously ridicules and perpetuates.

Many scholarly studies (e.g., Bacon-Smith; Jenkins, *Convergence Culture*; Penley) argue that fan activities resist dominant models of passive consumption, constructing "practices of everyday life" that creatively reuse the culture industry's materials (de Certeau). More recent studies (e.g., Sandvoss) suggest that fan activities simply represent the minimum amount of "play" necessary for consumerism to function. *Mad Men* fans offer some evidence for both views. On the one hand, some fan activities appear to be disconnected from consumer tie-ins such as the Banana Republic campaigns in which huge placards of the show's stars are plastered on city streets and shopping mall windows. In contrast to such corporate fare, *Mad Men* fans have produced, for example, cakes that incorporate images of the show's stars or official logos, but not always in ways that reproduce AMC's interests.[15] Likewise, *Mad Men* fan fiction runs the gamut from tame drabbles such as Mary Jane Parker's tale of Sally helping Joan in the office ("The Name on the Door"), to elaborate narratives about the sexual lives of the show's characters such as "Portrait of a One Night Stand" by kasviel in which Don "punishes" Pete for revealing his alter ego—with spanking and sex.[16] Such fan activities generate new objects for private consumption that are unlikely to appear on AMC's website. If such "resistance" is clearly limited, it does take *Mad Men* fan participation beyond the passive consumption of imitation 1960s furniture, cocktail shakers, and Brooks Brothers knock-offs of vintage fashion.

That said, *Mad Men* enthusiasts do use fan communities to talk about products they would like to buy. For example, *Basket of Kisses*, a popular *Mad Men* blog focused on discussion of the show, features a "What to Buy" link displaying products such as dolls, cufflinks, and DVDs. The website has asked its readers, "What props from *Mad Men* do you covet? It can be furniture, highball glasses, a cigarette lighter, anything. Do you adore mid-century styling? . . . 'Fess up" (Lipp). What is, perhaps, unusual about *Mad Men*'s fandom is that its mainstream demographic—affluent fans of an award-winning series and subject of much NPR and *New York Times* chatter—must still "'fess up" to desiring common objects like a set of highball glasses. This suggests that media fandom and consumption may be mutually sustaining. Indeed, there may be an extra thrill for the purchaser of that midcentury cigarette lighter who not only acquires a coveted object but also does so for reasons that are socially suspect (his or her "embarrassing" media fandom) and potentially libidinally charged (think of Sally Draper watching *The Man from U.N.C.L.E.* [4.5]).

TOMORROWLAND

If *Mad Men* is "cinematic" television at its finest, it is television nonetheless. As Lynne Joyrich emphasizes in this volume, television, unlike the movies, is characterized by *flow*: the fragmentation of the viewing experience through segmentation, commercial interruptions, and so forth.[17] Television also differs in its address (we go to the movies, but television lives with us). Yet perhaps the most important televisual feature for *Mad Men*, like many other quality shows, is its seriality. As Mittell observes, the first decade of the twenty-first century was remarkable in terms of the transformation in American television, not least because of the "spread of serial narrative across a wide range of fictional formats" ("Serial Boxes").

As Sean O'Sullivan notes in an essay on *Deadwood* (HBO, 2004–6), serial formats foster special kinds of audience engagement because they "exist at the crossroads between the old and the new." Unlike stand-alone novels or films, serial dramas constantly offer the "promise of the new," often introducing "a new plotline or character that will change everything." Moreover, given their "leisurely unfolding," serials draw us "into the past, as old characters appear and disappear . . . or old episodes of a program burrow into our memory, creating a history commensurate with our lifespan unlike the merely posited past of a text we can consume in a few hours or days. Every reading, or every watching, requires a reconnection of old and new, an iteration of past and present; and within a week or a month what was new will get funneled into the old" (117). As O'Sullivan further observes, Victorian novelists such as Dickens understood these lived aspects of the serial form and crafted their fiction accordingly.

The same is true of shows such as *Mad Men* that combine serial temporality with the writerly features of well-crafted novels. Indeed, the advent of quality shows packaged in box sets confers the prestige of publication on a medium once characterized by ephemeral broadcasting. The DVD box set highlights a new narrative complexity that aligns television with classic multiplot fiction while providing a physical object that can be displayed on a shelf like the works of Flaubert or Trollope (Mittell, "Serial Boxes"). As Phil Abraham says in this volume, he actually thinks of *Mad Men* as a novel, an idea he shares with Matt Weiner and others who work on the show. In this way, *Mad Men* is much more like a nineteenth-century novel than is *The Sopranos*, which often challenged the tight diachronic arc of realist narrative by including "stand-alone episodes" (Polan, *Sopranos*, 32).

These novelistic features heighten the serial audience's engagement. Recorded formats offer viewers the ability to "immerse" themselves in the spectator experience: "binging" on multiple episodes and reviewing particular scenes at will (Mittell, "Serial Boxes"). Just as Victorian readers of serial fiction published reviews, commentaries, and letters to the press, so today's TV viewers discuss their favorite shows at the workplace, on new social networks, on blogs such as Alan Sepinwall's *What's Alan Watching?*, and in the comments section for online media from *Salon* and the *Huffington Post* to the *Los Angeles Times* and the *Wall Street Journal*. Cable television's reinvention of the novelistic serial thus demonstrates the potential to summon a public in which viewers take part even if they never attend a *Mad Men* theme party.[18]

This communal effect is enhanced by the regular intervals of waiting between serialized installments that encourage a daily routine of reflection and anticipation (Mittell, "Serial Boxes"). Indeed, according to Robyn Warhol, serial narratives are "devices for structuring what bodies do in time and space," their resistance to closure a means of prolonging the relation between audience and text (72). Whether by reading a novel published in monthly parts or viewing a television narrative that airs weekly, audiences of serial media cultivate rituals of enjoying new installments followed by interludes of contemplation, discussion, and expectation—developing a serial habitus. The most striking effect of the serial temporality is the generation of feelings at once more "familiar" and "intense" than those elicited by nonserial media (Warhol, 72).[19]

As the editors of this project, we have experienced these intervals of contemplation, discussion, and expectation. In preparing this book, we have become highly attentive to the impact of serial forms. Indeed, as we conclude this introduction to a volume begun after *Mad Men*'s third season, we are especially conscious that many readers will have seen more of the show than we have right now (as we write in November 2011, the fifth season of *Mad Men* is expected to air in March 2012). Thus, although our book is finished, *Mad Men* still exists "at the crossroads between the old and the new." Throughout this introduction we have spoken of history, pastness, and the *longue durée*; but the situation necessitates our concluding in a different tense.

Mad Men's pattern so far has been to slightly outpace the real time between seasons: from its debut in July 2007 to the fourth-season finale in October 2010, the show's calendar advanced from March 1960 to October 1965. Will the show continue to move incrementally through the 1960s? Or will it surprise us by leaping ahead or even taking us back to the years before Don met Betty? Will Betty's story become ever more distantiated from the twin focal points of Don and advertising? Will Don age into the 1970s, still a dandy but sporting wide lapels, graying sideburns, and the "dry look"? Will Harry like *Star Trek*? We are not foolish enough to venture any guesses, though we recognize that the nature of serial narrative is to orient us toward an unforeseeable future.[20]

"Our worst misfortunes never happen, and most miseries lie in anticipation," wrote the serial maestro Honoré de Balzac—an aphorism that *Mad Men* has paraphrased twice.[21] In *The Sense of an Ending*, a book he collected from lectures delivered in 1965, the literary critic Frank Kermode speculated that human beings turn to fiction to escape from the emptiness of time. "The clock's 'tick tock'" suggests the stories we call "plots," which are vehicles for "humanizing time by giving it a form" (45). That is, by providing us with the meanings we grasp from "the sense of an ending," fictions seem to redeem us from time. (As Don might say, fictions provide a special kind of solace from the overwhelming perception that "the universe is indifferent" [1.8].) For the ancient Greeks, whose preferred form was drama, the sense of an ending came from tragedy. But serial forms do not promise the sense of an ending: to the contrary, their special illusion is that they will never end at all. Instead, the attachments we cultivate to the temporality of the episode, the season, and the intervals in between give us a different way to humanize the clock. Serial narratives, premised on the perpetual possibility of the new, intuit this fact; they know that audiences lead serial lives poised between what has already happened and what cannot yet be foreseen.

As *Mad Men* embeds its characters in a stream of events that viewers recognize as the historical past, the effect it most often creates is not tragedy, with its powerful sense of an ending, but dramatic irony, with its intimation of lessons learned and resolutions still to come. We glimpse, for example, in season 3, an invitation to Margaret Sterling's wedding, realizing that the day will be ruined by a terrible event. We watch the action unfold before characters who, unlike us, do not know what they are about to encounter. Then too, sometimes *Mad Men*'s savvy writers have fun with their audience, inventing fictitious figures to send fact-finding fans to their search engines in vain.[22] Sometimes the irony works in both directions. When Joan's husband joined the army to complete his medical training, many anticipated that the not-so-good doctor was heading for Vietnam. "The guy is toast," viewers opined on cell phones, blogs, and message boards. Will Dr. Harris outlive their speculations? Perhaps by now, reader, *You* Know Better.

The "promise of the new" is irresistible to us because our greatest hopes (like our worst fears) lie in anticipation. Advertising knows this too and tempts us to believe that the next great experience will come through some novel purchase. As a show *about* advertising, *Mad Men* shows us how frequently our fond expectations of the future disappoint us. In this way, an insistent dramatic irony runs through the series. In "Ladies Room" (1.2), for example, the agency works on an ad for an antiperspirant in a newfangled form: the aerosol can. The irony here is how quickly today's hot product becomes tomorrow's environmental hazard. Who knew? Not, in this instance, Paul, who is ready to label the product "space-age": "It's from the future — a place so close to us now, filled with wonder and ease." Don, however, is skeptical: "Some people think of the future and it upsets them. They see a rocket and they start building a bomb shelter." Yet in season 3 their roles are reversed. When Paul barely contains his contempt for a client who plans to raze Penn Station, a magnificent Beaux Arts structure from 1910, Don saves the day with a vision of a *new* New York as a "city on a hill" (3.2).

Even if this pitch did not include a glowing reference to California, Don's words would be an ironic prelude to the protagonist of season 4's finale, "Tomorrowland" (4.13). A Disney exhibit filled with midcentury visions of space-age travel like the TWA Moonliner, Tomorrowland is the destination for Don's visit with his children and his secretary, Megan. Perhaps we could have guessed that the man who lost the Hilton account because he couldn't deliver "the moon" would never make it into the space age. Instead, Don finds his future in an uncanny repetition of the past. The closing music for the episode is "I Got You Babe," the pop hit by Sonny and Cher from 1965 — the same song that greets Bill Murray every morning when he wakes up in the movie *Groundhog Day* (1993), in which Murray plays Phil Connors, a narcissistic weatherman trapped in the events of a single day.

In *Groundhog Day*, the sense of an ending comes when the protagonist becomes a better person. Connors hankers for his producer (Andie MacDowell), and when he finally transforms into a man she can love, he wakes up beside her and knows that Tomorrowland has come. Like *Groundhog Day*, *Mad Men*'s fourth season posed the question of whether a man thoroughly devastated by mistakes of his own making can change. Of course, change is a loaded idea for *Mad Men*: while the show is a modern-day realist narrative, it has never yet been a bildungsroman in which the narrative trajectory coincides with the protagonist's moral growth. Rather, Don is an antihero — albeit one who convinces us that he is somehow better than the world that made him. We must believe in Don's nobler instincts and thrill to his moments of transcendence even while knowing that if he ever sustained them, he would no longer be Don, and we would no longer be watching *Mad Men*. This is the irony of our serial viewership: watching Don reinvent himself in the face of a new challenge, inspiration, or object of desire, we somehow forget that *We* Should Know Better.

Yet for all their evasion of the sense of an ending, even the longest-running serial narratives eventually end. To be sure, some television forms extend over a seemingly endless period of time: *General Hospital* (ABC) has aired since 1963, and *M*A*S*H* (CBS, 1972–83) lasted eight years longer than the Korean War. *Mad Men* is now poised to continue for as many as seven seasons. But whereas soap operas occupy the diurnal temporality of their broadcast and *M*A*S*H* elongated a particular historical span, a historical fiction such as *Mad Men*, which moves forward into a knowable stream of events, has a harder creative burden to bear. What will *Mad Men* be like if, advancing into the decade, it no longer pivots on the premise of looking at the pre-counterculture 1960s from a post-counterculture vantage point? *Mad Men* will then have to do what so far it never has: tell us what it thinks about *those* 1960s. It will need to open itself to newly empowered voices—voices either excluded from or marginalized in a mise-en-scène that was first imagined as a vehicle to articulate white male privilege and insularity.

Perhaps some new character development will emerge that changes the show's center of gravity (an aggressive Megan? a teenage Sally? a renegade Pete? A civil rights or anti-war narrative?). But so far *Mad Men*, when not about the Draper marriage and its adulterous satellites, has made the dialectic of Don and Peggy its emotional center. Indeed, Don could not have been so compelling a character were he not also Peggy's mentor and (usually) supporter. Don's words at Peggy's hospital bedside (taken up in Rushing's chapter); Peggy's bailing Don out of the lockup; Don's telling Peggy he would spend his life trying to hire her; and, in season 4, Peggy's taking Anna's place as the one person who understands Don are among *Mad Men*'s most memorable moments. If the show were about the sense of an ending, there could be plenty to say about a Peggy ready to move on from her apprenticeship and take the leading role in her own Peggy-roman. But can Peggy thrive in the world of advertising, the quintessence of alienated creativity in the show's symbolic economy? Is the young woman Don helped to rescue from the stigma of unwed motherhood destined to become another version of Don?

And what about Don? The show pulls us toward him because he only very partially embodies the fantasy of a resilient masculine will-to-power. Paradoxically, Don works as a serial character because again and again he manages to be just one step away from the abyss into which we see him drop in the opening credits; and because the fallen world over which he walks his tightrope feels so palpably real. Don, in other words, is imbued with the sense of an ending, but it is an ending that viewers want to defer. We know Don will fall, but we do not want him to—yet.

NOTES

1. See http://www.theawl.com/tag/footnotes-of-mad-men (accessed 21 May 2011).

2. On the books, see *Vulture*; on the living room, see Grad. On "Mad Style," see Tom and Lorenzo's series of blog posts at http://www.tomandlorenzo.com/category/television/mad-men. According to the *Times*, only HBO's *Deadwood* generated comparable discussion about the "authenticity of its language" (Zimmer).

3. Compare *Mad Men* to a show that unabashedly condescends toward the past:

Life on Mars (BBC, 2006–7; remade in the United States for ABC in 2008–9). The conceit of a present-day detective trapped in the 1970s of his childhood enables the protagonist's contrast between his own enlightened ethics and the sexism and corruption depicted as endemic to the 1970s. See also Michael Bérubé's discussion of *Pleasantville* in this volume.

4. Emails to Lauren Goodlad, 10 September 2010.

5. Discussion of Betty's being one of the worst mothers in media history can take on misogynistic overtones or the reverse. Blogger Kevin Fitzpatrick ranked Betty twenty-third in a list of "TV's most undeniably horrible mothers," describing her "as one of the most universally reviled characters on television." Yet in response to "Betty Draper: Is She as Bad as She Seems?," a post by Amy Graff on the *San Francisco Chronicle* blog *The Mommy Files*, one respondent wrote, "She married a guy who swept her off her feet, started pumping her full of children and then rarely showed up at home. It's really hard raising kids alone. Then she finds out he's using an assumed name, has been married and has been sleeping with most of the women on the East Coast behind her back. . . . No adult in the show cares about her, and she was trained to keep her troubles to herself" (lovescats789, 29 July 2010).

6. While critics often see self-referentiality as distinct from the character-driven, naturalist narrative we have so far described, we think realism's capacity for irony and self-referentiality is underestimated.

7. As the feminist critic Gail Finney points out, the current usage of "queer" reflects its development from the Low German for "oblique or off-center" into the contemporary German *quer* ("diagonally, sideways, or against the grain") and the English *queer* ("strange, odd, deviant"). Finney, 122.

8. However, for additional reflection on *Mad Men* and race in light of season 5, see Goodlad and Levine, "You've Come."

9. On the "magic negro," a simple black character who exerts extraordinary impact on white lives, see, for example, Hughey. In Haynes's version of the trope, the character is more sophisticated, though still fundamentally "magical."

10. On earlier uses of the term with reference to prestige comedies like *The Mary Tyler Moore Show*, see Feuer, "MTM Enterprises."

11. The 11.9 million viewers who tuned in for the finale of *The Sopranos* in 2007 represented a "historical feat" for cable; the 5.1 million viewers drawn three years later to the season 3 premiere for HBO's youth-oriented *True Blood* are cited as the next-best showing for a cable station (*Associated Press*; Andreeva). This makes *Mad Men*'s 3 million viewers considerable even if numerous commentators rightly suggest that the show's "buzz" exceeds its viewership or ability to attract advertising.

12. For a video of the event, which featured the broadcasting of the premiere on Times Square, see "Mad Men on the Street," *New York*, http://videos.nymag.com /video/Mad-Men-On-The-Street;Drunk-Men (accessed 29 May 2011).

13. The study, however, defined "social liberals" somewhat questionably as those

who "disdain moral authorities and believe children should be exposed to moral dilemmas and allowed to draw their own conclusions" (Bulk).

14. The *Fresh Air* interviews were originally broadcast on 9 August 2007, 22 September 2008, 26 July 2010, and 16 September 2010.

15. One cake altered the iconic Draper silhouette to show a woman's hairdo and the logo "Mad Mom"—a Mother's Day gift for a *Mad Men* fan. See Masket.

16. "Drabbles" are probably named after a Monty Python sketch featuring a game called Drabble in which whoever writes a novel first wins. "Portrait of a One Night Stand" is an example of "slash fiction" in which mainstream, heteronormative media culture is repurposed to show a homoerotic romance.

17. Although some recorded formats remove the evidence of flow, it remains part of the DVR experience even for viewers who fast-forward through the interruptions.

18. Michael Warner's notion of the counterpublic summoned by the circulation of print thus applies to the serial television text.

19. For Mittell, the asynchronous and potentially solitary viewing of the DVD-watcher inhibits "communal engagement" ("Serial Boxes"). This effect may be more typical of a forensic show such as *Lost* (ABC, 2004–10) than a neonaturalist and highly novelistic narrative such as *Mad Men*. That is, *Mad Men*'s community of engagement seems to integrate participation of late-coming DVD-watching viewers alongside those who keep up with the latest episodes.

20. As this volume goes into production in July 2012, the editors of this volume have viewed (and blogged on) season 5—but we retain our concluding comments as they were written in 2011. It turned out that Betty did indeed become more and more distanced from the show's focus; and it was Paul, not Harry, who became a *Trek* fan.

21. In "Out of Town" (3.1), Sal condenses it to "Our worst fears lie in anticipation," and Don says the same in "The Fog" (3.5).

22. For example, the pointed reference to "Dr. Lyle Evans" in "The Chrysanthemum and the Sword," a subject of much Internet chatter as viewers developed a consensus that the man did not exist.

PART ONE
MAD WORLDS

MADDENING TIMES

Mad Men *in Its History*

LANE PRYCE: [*looking at the newspaper
for a movie to go see with Don Draper*]
"It's a Mad, Mad, Mad, Mad World."

DON: Yes, it is. — "The Good News," 4.3

Mad Men: it's a pretty nifty title. Obviously and efficiently (and aided by the consonance of those monosyllabic words), it puns on Madison Avenue and on that location's key role in the development of postwar advertising culture ("ad men"). And it taps perhaps into a general if intangible anomie, frustration, and even anger that these men in gray flannel suits sometimes feel toward the way of life they're caught up in (and caught in), and that we, the spectators, are typically supposed to feel that men in the popular culture devoted to life in Madison Avenue corporations are supposed to be feeling.

But it's here — in the reference to "men" — that the title already reveals an incompleteness: clearly, *Mad Men* has been as much about women, and their own desires and dreads, as they confront the fraught historical period referenced over the course of the series. Just as it was easy to forget the plural in Matthew Weiner's previous series, *The Sopranos* (HBO, 1999–2007), and imagine it as being centrally and even primarily about Tony Soprano's "issues," it is tempting to see *Mad Men* as another installment in the on-going saga of popular culture's representation of a "masculinity in crisis" (and here the show would be doubly invested in that representation as both a show about men in the 1960s and a show made in the newer representational moment of the first decade of the twenty-first century—which has brought its own sense of the imputed crisis of masculinity to bear on the subject matter).

Obviously, *Mad Men* is not *not* about an overbearing, omnipresent, and (to its own view, at least) omnipotent masculinity. One could even suggest that the incompleteness of the title is ironic and contributes to the series' ongoing depiction of the way these men themselves confront the incompleteness of their masculine hold on their world. If the very end of the very first episode serves as a sort of punch line to suddenly reveal that Don Draper has a suburban life complete (or incomplete in its own way) with suburban housewife (this after much of the episode has shown him cavorting with a beatnik woman from Greenwich Village), it is one consequence of later episodes to fill in that other world, and give perspective and voice to the wife (and to other women characters) in a manner often apart from Don (and from other male characters). Of course, that the women are sometimes given their own scenes and their own points of view independent of male presence does not mean that they in any way *become independent*. Not for nothing, if the series title focuses on masculinity, is a season 4 episode that focuses on the women overall named "The Beautiful Girls" (4.9), picking up the sort of patronizing phrasing that we might imagine the ad men to use, precisely, to pigeonhole the women in their work and leisure lives.

In this respect, if, from the very partiality of its title to the course of its narrative over the seasons, *Mad Men* bears an incompleteness to its representational project, it is as possible to argue that the representation of such incompleteness *is* its project, rather than a failing *within* it. In other words, it might be that the series uses the partiality of the worlds it depicts—such as the world of "men" in the corporate demographic—to dramatize limitation and the forms of narrative struggle against it. This is not a total or totalized picture of the times as they were but a deliberately partial and incomplete picture of how some people lived some parts of those times and, in some cases, groped toward other ways of living them. The issue of incompleteness then becomes less a question of accuracy—does, for instance, the title "correctly" sum up the series?—than of representational function: How does *Mad Men* use incompleteness in the service of its dramatic project and to what ends?

In this respect, just as we can see as ironic or deliberately limited the emphasis in the series' title on "men," it is worth noting that the qualification of them as "mad" seems incomplete in its own right. Notions of being "mad" run rampant through the 1960s, but *Mad Men* invokes them only indirectly. Again, the issue is not one of accuracy. And the point is not just to catalogue the absences but to clarify how their nonpresence is often a deliberate choice and has constitutive effects on what the show prefers instead to show of its times. In 1966 the French philosopher Pierre Macherey analyzed gaps in a cultural text's representational coverage as what he termed "structuring absences," and it is the way in which valences of the "mad" hover around *Mad Men* even as it chooses other representational projects to explore that serves as the impetus for this chapter.

For instance, Mutually Assured Destruction (MAD), the doctrine of always trying to outdo the enemy in nuclear firepower so that the would-be belligerent will blink and back down from first-strike actions, is nowhere mentioned in the show, but it is there implicitly in continued references to the Cold War threat (for example, in season 1, one elevator conversation is about how absurd it is that the French, too, now have the bomb; in seasons 2 and 4, the agency flirts with a defense contract and all that it entails in terms of security clearance; and season 2 ends with the Cuban missile crisis).

Likewise, *Mad Men* offers little awareness of that sense of the absurdity of war that is summed up in the last line of *The Bridge on the River Kwai* (1957), "Madness! Madness . . . madness!," and that increasingly filters into 1960s popular culture with works like Joseph Heller's *Catch-22* (1961) — where Yossarian's feigned madness is outdone by the military's real insanity — only to then move beyond representation into reality with the Vietnam war. Even though by season 5 of *Mad Men* we are past the midst of the decade, there is little mention of the war's increasing escalation and media visibility (Joan's one-time husband, a doctor, serves in Nam, but we get minimal glimpses of the war [most often through brief news reports on TVs in the background of scenes], and certainly no assertions of any absurdity to it). More generally, *Mad Men* eschews that 1960s reversal of values so well depicted by Heller or by Stanley Kubrick, Peter George, and Terry Southern in their screenplay for *Dr. Strangelove* (1964), in which it is institutions of control — like the military, but also, by extension, schooling, medical establishment, government, and so on — that are seen as insane, and the seemingly crazy or damaged people they are processing as so much fodder who are seen as having a visionary sanity beyond institutional recognition. (As Hot Lips Houlihan puts it in *M*A*S*H* [1970], "This isn't a hospital; it's an insane asylum!" In the cult classic *King of Hearts* [1966], a soldier on mission [Alan Bates] falls in with the inmates of an actual asylum and comes to find their company preferable to the absurd and deadly insanities of military command.)

True, Sterling Cooper's founder Bert Cooper is presented as somewhat not quite right in his love of abstract painting (always a giveaway in mainstream popular culture) and in his insistence on going barefooted. There is something a bit off at the top of the corporate world. But Bert's eccentricities are presented generally as amusingly benign (both to the workers at the office and to us spectators), and there is little sense of a generalized institutional insanity that has dire consequences for the lower-echelon inhabitants of this world. It would be hard to argue that *Mad Men* is using the advertising agency as in any way a metaphor for the madness of institutionalized power in the manner that *Catch-22* does for the military.

Similarly, the 1950s and '60s are the moment in which that great symbol of what-me-worry irreverence, *Mad Magazine*, flourishes, but *Mad Men* doesn't have much of that publication's wacky, even sick humor aspect to it. Perhaps the moment from the episode "Guy Walks into an Advertising Agency" (3.6) in which, during a wild party, one of the secretaries, on a demonstration lawnmower out of control, runs over the foot of one of the executives and mangles it, comes close in its morbid yet comically zany weirdness, but the moment is ultimately just that — a moment, a single instant pulled from the flow of the show (and given special narrative explanation by the fact that the accident happens at a party that got out of control). *Mad Men* is wicked and sardonic, but rarely in the consistent and committed scandalous way that *Mad Magazine* was.[1]

To take a different notion of "mad," the series does, as noted, seem to tap into a common, even stereotypical, figure of the postwar nine-to-five male as consumed by an anomie that can render him anywhere from frustrated to cantankerous to, at times, downright angry. But being "mad" would then seem to connote something so variable (in frequency, in reach, in quality and intensity, and so on) that it would seem too vague to be a serviceable concept.[2] This seems to be the case no matter which contemporary valences of being mad we choose to look at. For instance, the discontent of the "mad men" on the show very rarely converts into that excessive anger that drives, say, Bobby Dupea (Jack Nicholson) to explode at a waitress in an iconic scene from *Five Easy Pieces* (1970), a film at the very end of the period, or that pushes Howard Beale (Peter Finch) in *Network* (1976) to declare as his infamous motto, "I'm as mad as hell, and I'm not going to take this any more."

And for all the obsession of the period with psychiatric and antipsychiatric conceptions of madness as mental disorder — reflected in the popular culture in such titles as *The Mad Woman of Chaillot* (1969) or *Diary of a Mad Housewife* (1970) or *A Fine Madness* (1966) — *Mad Men* itself offers few representations of a vibrant nuttiness. The most literal case of mental dysfunction in the series is that of Betty Draper's father, Eugene, who is suffering, in quite ordinary and realistic fashion, from senility. There is little here of the energetic madness that takes over 1960s figures in *Marat/Sade* (1967) or *Morgan: A Suitable Case for Treatment* (1966) — to reference two films from the decade in which madness is seen as an inspiration in a generalized rejection of social norms. And although Betty herself sees a psychiatrist in season 1, in this case the series' flirtation with the psychiatric establishment ultimately peters out: Betty discovers that her husband, Don, is being given updates on her treatment by the psychiatrist, and she uses the information against both of them, a triumph that basically causes the plotline to drop away.[3] (This often seems to happen with Betty's accomplishments in the course of the series: when she does something affirmative, she scores an immediate, local point, but then the show offers no follow-up, as if her achievements have no lasting impact.) To the extent that Betty is indeed a character consumed by anomie, it is worth noting that by season 4, this has manifested itself not just as rage (her misguided dismissal of the nanny who has been with her children from the beginning) but as its opposite: a descent into a passivity little different from inertia. The fourth season's last image of Betty Draper is of her curled up in veritable fetal position in her bed. In pointed contrast, 1960s madness in the popular culture of the moment was often an uplifting, invigorating leap into action: for example, "Charlotte Corday" (Glenda Jackson) in *Marat/Sade* is an inmate with sleeping sickness who rouses herself both to act the killing of Marat and, more important, to participate in the lively revolution of the inmates over the aristocrats that ends the film. What many viewers of the fourth season saw as the increasing rendition of Betty as a horrid harridan (one piece I came across ranked her as one of the worst moms of all time, along with Medea and Joan Crawford!) was also the increasing framing of her as powerless to the point of inconsequentiality (followed by her frequent absence from the episodes of season 5). From Thomas Szasz, to David Cooper and R. D. Laing, to Foucault and Guattari, the 1960s were all about finding revolutionary potential in madness, but this is not a historical path that *Mad Men* thus far has chosen to venture into. (Sally Draper may be one exception, but I will reserve discussion of that for the last paragraphs of this chapter.)

Nonetheless, it is worth returning to the question of accuracy for a moment, since one particularity — and perhaps peculiarity — of *Mad Men* is that in addition to being seen as an example of "quality TV," it is somehow taken to be, and admired as, *a document* or even *documentary* of upper-middle-class suburban life in the late 1950s and into the 1960s. Viewers assume it offers a picture of the way things were in those times. The paradox here is that a series appreciated as an aesthetic accomplishment—that is, as a construct whose value lies precisely in its creative divergence from reality (which we might take to be one mark of quality TV)—is also appreciated as an accurate picture of its time. Among the quality shows, *Mad Men* may be unique in this respect: *The Sopranos*, for instance, might often end up being about ordinary issues (family, work, relationship, moral choice), but it would be difficult to imagine that its comic Mafia was in any way to be taken as a deep document of "real" Mafia life.

Maybe there is something in the long sweep of the postwar period in America—from the clichés of a 1950s that is simultaneously conformist and about rebels without a cause into the impression of the 1960s as the period in which rebellion becomes wholehearted—that generally tempts us to take aesthetic representations of this cultural moment as veritable documentations of it. These years are ones we feel we know well, and any cultural work that offers even minimal iconic markers of that knowability can become elevated into an accurate portrayal of the times. In particular, the 1950s, we might say, seem directly sociological: that is, there is an ongoing representation of the period that invests in a set of common tropes and motifs to make us feel that we have a clear picture of what 1950s society was all about. Significantly, the most common picture of the period is built up not only from fictional works (from contemporaneous examples such as *The Man in the Gray Flannel Suit* [both the novel of 1955 and the film adaptation of 1956] to recent ones like *Mad Men* itself) but in the critical accounts of it which themselves play on recurrent iconography and narrative stereotypes. One has only to read virtually any scholarly study on the 1950s to come quickly across references (often quite similar from text to text) to sociologists of the time such as William Whyte or C. Wright Mills or David Riesman or even Vance Packard, as if they summed up the period and can still easily be referenced for doing so. The writings of these figures are adduced as symptoms of the time but also as accurate analyses that can still be used for their evidentiary, explanatory yield (thus, for instance, Riesman's notion of the "outer-directed" American is somehow taken to indicate that Americans in the period were overwhelmingly outer-directed in point of fact). Even as the classic sociologists from the time talk about how the decade witnesses the hardening of identity into sociological categories, their own writings participate in the very same process of reification and of constraining categorization. It is as if people in the 1950s were direct embodiments of abstract laws.

It is an easy step, then, to go from this seductive impression of the categorical knowability of the average American to the sorts of stereotypes on display in a film such as *Revolutionary Road* (2008), which came out after *Mad Men*'s second season: a shot of men in gray flannel suits getting off a commuter train and then marching in veritable unison is all the viewer needs to feel in the presence of a familiar set of themes (alienation, the white-collar worker as cog in the machine, etc.) and to believe that this is the way it was back "then." Such works of popular culture so become conventionalized symbols of a time that they then start to be taken as reference points for other works that come after them (in other words, conformity to their vision is taken somehow to be conformity to the historical times they claim to be representing). Thus, in 2010, when *Variety* reported on plans by the BBC to develop a television series that would be about "sexual tension against the backdrop of the ruthless, male-dominated world of 1950s mass media," the industry journal could offer as its single commentary, "Sound familiar?"— obviously suggesting that the show sounded a lot like *Mad Men* (Clarke).

Now (and the reader may have been itching to remind me of this salient point), it is in fact the case that *Mad Men* is only marginally about the 1950s specifically. The first season pointedly begins the story in the first months of 1960 as the agency gears up for an advertising campaign for Richard Nixon's presidential run, and it ends at Thanksgiving of that year. By season 3 we are well within the 1960s, past the Kennedy assassination (November 1963). By the beginning of season 4, it is Christmas 1964, and by the end we have had the Beatles and the more foreboding side of the British Invasion in the form of the Rolling Stones in 1965. Season 5 ends in 1967. The astuteness of *Mad Men* is to choose to be a show not about the 1950s but about the ostensible departure from that decade to something else—something that often comes into the show as mere glimpse, unassimilated foreshadowing, vague premonition, and the transient allusion to new worlds and ways of life that threaten the stable, conventionalized meanings of the 1950s. This is true both for the characters in the series and for the viewers who have to keep revising their sense of what they are watching as the episodes keep "progressing" in historical time (I put that term in quotation marks since although the dates advance, it is often a question of the characters' ability to seize the day and move forward with a history that is in motion all around them). This, then, is one source of the incompleteness that I have suggested is integral to the representational project of the show.

If in common convention the 1950s are fixed into stereotypes, the 1960s are about all of that seeming to come undone. Part of what seems so particular about *Mad Men* in the history of serial television is that it is not merely about the narratively internal changes that happen to its fictional characters as they interact with each other but about how a real, extratelevisual history is seen to be impacting them. The show is filled with real events and registers how the characters register them. It is, like certain novels of the nineteenth century to which it is sometimes compared, a work of "historical fiction" (see, e.g., Goodlad, this volume).

Take, as a contrast, Matthew Weiner's previous television effort, *The Sopranos*, for which he was a writer, producer, and sometime director: that show is set in a recognizable time, but except for a few references to 9/11, there is little sense of weightier, larger events pushing in on this enclosed Mafia world. (Of course, at the broadest level, as Tony Soprano admits, and as the title of the series' final episode, "Made in America," implies, the story of these latecomer Mafiosi does bear a connection to the larger story of late capitalism: as Tony explains early in episode 1 of season 1, he has the feeling of coming in at the end of something.) Or take, as another point of contrast, another recent work of quality TV, *The Wire* (HBO, 2002–8): as numerous commentators have noted, *The Wire* does have ambition of showing a city in all its urban complexity and interconnection. And there is a sense of history here (for example, the decline of the white dockworkers as social force), but it is still one pitched at the broadest level of the long-durational changes in late capitalism rather than in the impingement of immediate historical events on the lives of the fictional characters.

Some of what we might call the historicism of *Mad Men* is about getting the surface details right: this is a show very much about the look of clothes, the clink of drink glasses, the wafting up of cigarette smoke, and all those other markers that help contribute no doubt to the impression that somehow the series is serving as documentation of the times. But *Mad Men* also enters into its times through a concern with large-scale punctual events: political (e.g., presidential campaigns, elections, and assassinations; the suicide of a presidential mistress [Marilyn Monroe]), cultural (e.g., contemporary movies and songs, the Beatles invasion), and social (e.g., the increasing struggles of African Americans for visibility and agency in society). The workers at Sterling Cooper (and later Sterling Cooper Draper Pryce) may be rooted in a very specific place, the space of their office, but the show is all about opening them up to other spaces—for instance, the road trip that Don takes with young druggies in "Seven Twenty Three" (3.7) and in which he gets mugged by them, the journey downtown to wild Greenwich Village that Peggy goes on in "The Rejected" (4.4)—including, pointedly, the space represented by the presence of the electronic medium of television, which brings seemingly faraway events into the proximity of the fictional characters.

There are the historical events, and then there are the reactions of the fictional characters to them and what they do with them. Even though Don Draper is the seeming protagonist of the series, it is noteworthy how often he is shown to be on the wrong side of history, supporting in his professional work causes that are either doomed to failure (Richard Nixon for president! Don even declares, "I am Dick Nixon," as a point of identification) or promised success in the immediate present only to go down in the longer annals as errors of moral judgment (the demolition of Penn Station). The show wants us to recognize that Don often gets it wrong. And not only in his professional life: for instance, he bets on Sonny Liston in his infamous ill-fated match with Cassius Clay ("The Suitcase," 4.7), and he dreads the Beatles concert he is taking his daughter Sally to ("Hands and Knees," 4.10). *Mad Men* needs from us this recognition of the characters' fallibility in history because it is key to the way we watch the show from our historical present and reflect back on fraught lives such as Don's and the mistakes he (and others around him) often make as they grope toward a new world for which they are only partially prepared. It is telling that in a very early episode ("Marriage of Figaro," 1.3), we see the Sterling Cooper admen, including Don, confused by the success (and great acclaim in advertising history) of Volkswagen's campaign engineered by the ad firm Doyle Dane Bernbach in which it ironically referred to its own car as a "lemon": despite their acumen in the business, these "experts" don't get hipness and irony and are at a loss to understand the new cutting edge despite their own frequent desire to be part of it.

Of course, against all the fixities of 1950s life, Don Draper offered his own form of attempted liberation by changing his identity and trying to build his life anew. On the one hand, this is very *1950s* in its own way—the man who goes "on the road" to new worlds of discovery. But it is also key in *1960s* culture, where dropping out of the existence one has been given to try to make something new of one's self is a common theme. (It receives a nightmare version in John Frankenheimer's film *Seconds* [1966], in which a discontented white-collar New Yorker has his life reinvented for him by a secret corporation only to discover that he is in a trap from which death is the only escape.)

Like Bobby Dupea in *Five Easy Pieces*, a key cinematic swan song to the 1960s, Don Draper moves between different levels of the American class hierarchy, trying out different ways of being. Draper finds none of them without their own dead ends. *Five Easy Pieces* in contrast opts for an open-ended ambiguity typical of 1960s and early 1970s films, where the film terminates in nondecision: here, Bobby simply goes off—to the future but also directly off-frame. One could perhaps imagine the multiyear run of *Mad Men* ending that way: Don simply vanishing on one more of his trips west (as he almost seemed to do toward the end of season 2, only to return readily to the advertising way of life). But it is as likely that Don will dig deeper into the business way of life he has chosen for himself.

In fact, if Don's change of identity somewhat resembles that dropping out that was so much an aspiration of 1960s youth, it matters that his choice to begin again is ultimately, if I can put it this way, to "drop in": that is, by throwing off his original life, Don does not so much reject the establishment as create conditions in which he can more wholeheartedly embrace it. It is not insignificant that "Don" began on a farm but finds his new life in the city, the place of corporate success: his trajectory is the opposite of that romanticized journey back to the land that characterized so many 1960s dropouts. (One episode, "Waldorf Stories" [4.6], is filled with flashbacks about his eager-beaver desire to enter into the advertising business and show that he has what it takes.)

And it matters too that Don had his conversion of identity long before the 1960s (during the Korean War, in fact). By the time Don gets to the 1960s, he is already in many ways fixed in who he is now, and there is little room for additional openness to radical change. Thus in "Blowing Smoke" (4.12), where his colleagues at Sterling Cooper Draper Pryce might view as a willful act of self-destruction of their firm Don's decision to write a *New York Times* op-ed piece against the ways other ad firms shill for big tobacco, Don's dramatic act is, we might say, a lateral move within the corporate world, rather than a rejection of it. Don is shaking things up not to destroy his professional world but to find a new path *within it* (we know he's not sincere about the moral high ground he's taking since we see him puffing away at a cigarette as he writes his screed against smoking and advertising's support of it; as the episode's title tells us, he is "blowing smoke"). By the 1960s Don can act impetuously, but generally he does so in the service of career building, rather than any sort of anti-establishment large-scale revisioning of fundamental values and identity. At the end of season 4, fans might have been blogging vociferously about whether Don's sudden desire to propose to his very composed and, in all things professional and domestic, competent secretary Megan was "crazy," but whatever the advisability of his move, it has little of that radical rejection of establishment identity that characterized inspired acts of identity change in the hipper realms of 1960s culture. On the one hand, as his own staff (especially the women such as Peggy and Joan) note cattily, Don is simply performing to type (the boss involved with his secretary, as happened earlier to his colleague Roger Sterling and legions of other men in the business world), rather than somehow dramatically breaking away from corporate typecasting. On the other hand, in Megan, Don is gaining both a domestic goddess (she is a woman who knows how to handle his children, unlike his ex-wife, Betty) and a professional whose perceptive assessment and ambition in the corporate world is no less endorsing of that world than Don's.

A key figure in 1960s popular culture's valorization of madness was the independent free spirit who became involved with a more uptight person, who through this relationship opened up to new, unconstrained modes of being. In some couples, the figure of mad inspiration might be the male (as with the corporate slave–turned–grand iconoclast played by Jason Robards in *A Thousand Clowns* [1965] who tries to bring the by-the-books social worker played by Barbara Harris out of her shell), but it was more often a hip, even hippie, woman who in the typical plot took it as her veritable life's mission to bring the male out of his establishment trap. There is now even a newly minted moniker for this special character across the history of cinema: she is, the Internet instructs us, to be known as the "manic pixie dream girl," with Wikipedia's entry quoting one definition of her as "that bubbly, shallow cinematic creature that exists solely in the fevered imaginations of sensitive writer-directors to teach broodingly soulful young men to embrace life and its infinite mysteries and adventures."[4] Harking back to screwball comedies such as *Bringing Up Baby*, of 1938 (in which Katharine Hepburn teaches the repressed paleontologist Cary Grant to embrace the wacky side of life), narratives of mad, enlightened inspiration by a zany hippie chick proliferate through the 1960s. (This setup even occurs in the fluffy TV series *That Girl!* [ABC, 1966–71], in which fun-loving Ann Marie [Marlo Thomas] has to keep trying to get emotion out of square Donald [Ted Bessell], leading some spectators to wonder why she even wasted time on him in the first place.)

In *Petulia* (1968), for instance, a staid and conventional doctor (George C. Scott) is given the chance in a San Francisco that has already experienced the "Summer of Love" to catch up on life's new possibilities by the fun-loving title character (played by Julie Christie). All the uptight male has to do is witness the pixie (often in silhouette as, arms outstretched, she romantically embraces the whole world) and he is ready to turn his back on his old way of life (see, for instance, Peter Sellers's extravagant conversion to San Francisco hippie life in *I Love You, Alice B. Toklas* [1968] when he meets up with free-spirited Leigh Taylor-Young, who became a veritable icon of such a role). The dire paranoid conspiracy film *Seconds* confirms how widespread the convention was, since it is able to use its seeming familiarity to subversive ends. Here, the corporate executive who has been given a new identity by a mysterious corporation is about to give up on his new way of life until, walking on the beach one day, he sees a barefooted, flowing-haired vision of a woman who fully draws him over to her way of being when she runs madly into the surf and cries, "Ocean, I love you!" with her arms outstretched. Only later does he discover that the corporation has assigned her to seduce him into accepting his new identity (as a Malibu artist).

In *Mad Men*, Don Draper comes close to meeting his own free-spirited dream girl in the form of Miss Suzanne Farrell (Abigail Spencer), his daughter's schoolteacher with whom he has an affair in season 3. In typical pixie fashion, Miss Farrell appears to Don in a dreamlike moment: outside with her class, she dances around magically, her hair wafting poetically, as Don looks on at this vision of inspiration. But their adventure is short lived and seems to inspire Don to no major rethinking of the coordinates of his existence. In keeping with his 1950s nature, what matters to him is the fulfillment of sexual conquest rather than finding himself opened up to a new, life-altering experience. Don likes to think he is in love with some aspect of these idealized women that he doesn't find in Betty, but there is something in him that prevents him from moving forward with that love (just as he has trouble moving forward with broader history). When he unexpectedly (for the viewer as well as characters in the series) proposes to his secretary, Megan, at the end of season 4, it might well seem that Don is making a break to a new way of life, a new mode of being, although it is more than tempting to see Megan as simply the better version of the 1950s he wishes he could hold onto (Megan attracts him because she does so well with his children; she promises — in his starry eyes, at least — to be the perfect suburban housewife that Betty never could be).

With exceptions like Miss Farrell, most of the women Don has affairs with across the show's seasons bear strong connections to his work world (for example, Rachel, a client; Bobbie, a client's wife; Faye, a consultant; Megan, his secretary) and thereby cement his connections to that way of life rather than zanily suggesting any sort of alternative to it. They are all business women, just as he is a business man. Perhaps Midge (Rosemary DeWitt), a beatnik artist that Don sees on the side in the first season, might have represented another version of the inspiring hippie pixie (and she comes close to the role when, as Don looks on, she nonchalantly tosses her television set out of her upper-floor apartment window). But from the start Midge seems to represent for Don no more than a superficial flirtation or casual experimentation with an alternative way of life (and Don's lack of interest in embracing her way of life is confirmed for him—and for the spectator—when he meets the kinds of beatnik friends Midge hangs with and finds them aggressive and pretentious).

Of course, although Don Draper is at the center of *Mad Men*, the series is an ensemble work, with multiple character arcs and story lines, and other characters on the show have their own flirtations with the romantic, alternative possibilities of 1960s cutting-edge culture. For example, as the seasons of the show progress, Peggy has a series of intriguing encounters with the 1960s promise of new ways of living. It is important to note, though, that in chronicling Peggy's forays into bohemian culture, the show is not somehow suggesting that Women as a general demographic are being given chances that the (perhaps more entrapped) men are not. Clearly, for instance, Joan is not entering the 1960s in the same way as Peggy. Peggy is *not* a symbol of a general condition of woman, and what matters is the specific biography she is given and how she develops in relation to it. In particular, it matters that from the very first episode of the very first season, the spectator is made to think that Peggy is stuck in a rut—somehow prudish, somehow repressed, and somehow screwed up (her way of dealing with her own prudishness is to sleep with the wrongest man and then, in a later episode, to vamp up in the wrongest way). The spectator is, I think, manipulated by the show into wanting Peggy to change but also, eventually, into realizing that some changes are just not right for her.

Here, in contrast to what I just suggested, gender does start to matter—but in another manner: in the earliest episodes, it is easy to want Peggy to not be so frumpy, but the way in which the other office workers keep advising her to show off more of her legs becomes a first sign that not every alternative to frumpiness is a liberation. In other words, to become more of a sexy vixen than a seemingly repressed frump offers an alternative—for Peggy herself, for her colleagues who deal with her, and for the spectator who watches her—but it is not clear that this is really the desirable outcome. The spectator has to learn what might be appropriate choices for this 1960s woman, and enticing clues of at least one other possible path toward that begin to appear in season 4 when Peggy encounters new sexualities and new political commitments. As Jim Hansen has noted in a perceptive blog about "The Rejected" ("Coolest Medium"), we see Peggy at a crossroads (between corporate professionalism and bohemian adventure), and she more than any other character comes to represent the possibility for change even if the outcome of that is not yet apparent, even by the end of season 5. In fact, just as there are many indications that Peggy could be receptive to 1960s counterculture, there are equally as many hints that she will remain as steadfastly committed to career and advancement: for instance, she may decide in "Chinese Wall" (4.11) to make the somewhat radical Abe her "boyfriend," as she proudly declares to a copywriter colleague (already there are hints that this new lover is not as great a radical as we might imagine), but she seems almost as much as Don to be interested more in simply getting good sex from the encounter than in letting herself be seduced into her companion's lifestyle. Earlier, in "The Beautiful Girls," when Peggy tries out Abe's integrationist ideas at a corporate meeting only to see them quickly shot down, she appears to realize she wants to put career ahead of liberal political commitment and drops her efforts at consciousness raising among her colleagues.

Again, the issue is not one of accuracy—were commitments to change in the 1960s as fraught and fickle as all that?—but of the show's own aesthetic and political choices in representing the decade as it does. And the choices it makes are clearly pointed. Thus, if in the first season bohemian Midge might seem to represent a new style of hipness so unlike the seemingly cool but really uptight world of the suited sophisticates from Madison Avenue, her reappearance in "Blowing Smoke" in season 4 confirms just how much of a dead-end the bohemian lifestyle would turn out to be for so many burned-out denizens of the 1960s lifestyle. (And in any case, her world has been shown to be sanctimonious and silly from the start, so one should not have expected much in the way of revolution there.) Midge offers to prostitute herself, and is encouraged in that by her ersatz husband, in an episode that began by suggesting that Madison Avenue work is itself a form of pimping—the Heinz man says to the desperate pitches of an overeager Don, "I bet I could get a date with your mother right now"—and thereby implies a connection between these two worlds of selling out by selling out one's self. Likewise, Midge's heroin addiction is in its own way a form of nonprogressing cyclicity (you shoot up only to have to do it again), not some revolutionary strike for the future, and it bears comparison as an unbreakable, filthy habit to Don's incessant smoking as he writes his supposedly virtuous missive about the dangers of cigarettes.

In turning his back on any further involvement with Midge, Don is turning his back on a certain promise glimpsed in a bohemian 1960s lifestyle. And, it might be said, *Mad Men* itself is turning its own back in similar fashion through its willed refusal to imagine the experimental and artistic culture of the decade as anything but a dead end driven by the same instincts of self-satisfaction and self-interest as the squares it was supposed to offer an alternative to. There is nothing inspired, nothing madcap, about Midge's mode of being as we last see it.

In respect of the series' general foreclosure of mad inspiration as an acceptable radical alternative, for us and for the characters, it might well be appropriate that one of the very few actual uses of the term *mad* in *Mad Men* comes in Lane Pryce's mention of Stanley Kramer's *It's a Mad, Mad, Mad, Mad World* (1963), quoted in the epigraph to this chapter. No doubt one shouldn't overinterpret the quick, inconsequential allusion to what now seems itself an inconsequential piece of movie history (in fact, Lane and Don choose not to see the film). But it is intriguing to note that the one bit of "mad" behavior from the 1960s that *Mad Men* references in this case has to do with a story about money grubbing by a motley crew of competitors, most of whom are played by a venerable guard of old Hollywood stars and stand-up comic icons including Ethel Merman, Spencer Tracy, Sid Caesar, and Mickey Rooney. On the one hand, this is not "madness" as poetic inspiration of, say, a beat sort: the madness that impels these would-be gold diggers is sheer greed and self-interest, precisely the sort of materialism that beat madness would come to disavow ("Moloch whose blood is running money!" as Allen Ginsberg famously puts it in *Howl*). Rather than point to the new communal values that the 1960s would hold out as an ideal, however unrealized in actual practice, *It's a Mad, Mad, Mad, Mad World* looks back to a world of everyone-for-him-or-herself where rivalry and backstabbing are the order of the day. (Even the shared laughter that unites all the failed competitors at the end of the film is a vicious laughter, expended at the expense of a character who has injured herself.) On the other hand, but also in a bow, perhaps, to the same competitive world, the film itself seems resolutely to want to refuse its historical time in its insistence on using so many actors who are from previous decades and who can only seem square and even anachronistic faced with the new cinema of the 1960s (the wackiness alluded to in the title is to an older tradition of comic shtick). Like Kramer's later Spencer Tracy outing, *Guess Who's Coming to Dinner* (1967), *It's a Mad, Mad, Mad, Mad World* seems resolutely and even polemically a call to support an increasingly dated mode of cinematic entertainment in the midst of a world that is changing and has its cinematic forms changing along with it. Kramer's film is an ode to old-fashioned cinema in everything from style to content, and it tries to strike a moral blow against emergent directions in the culture of the decade.

It is interesting, then, that *It's a Mad, Mad, Mad, Mad World* offers its own image of 1960s hipness but only to subsume the energies of the counterculture within the general race for pecuniary self-interest. Famously, there is an abrupt cut early in the film to a beatnik shack (complete with far-out sculpture) in which a wild hipster, Sylvester (played by a vibrant Dick Shawn), wearing only the briefest of brief red bathing trunks, dances frenetically around a hip chick in a black bikini. The phone rings incessantly as Sylvester boogies around the girl, whose dancing is energetic but robotic and who pays her partner no heed as if she is absorbed in her activity to the point of zen ignorance of the world around her. When Sylvester answers the phone, it is his mother (Ethel Merman) summoning him to the chase after the buried fortune, and he immediately drops the business at hand to go help her. The would-be hipster is here just an easily infantilized mamma's boy (at least that's not Don Draper's problem!), and his hip chick is no obvious fount of poetic inspiration (the more he dances around her, the less reaction he gets). As with *Mad Men*, *It's a Mad, Mad, Mad, Mad World* offers glimpses of a less bridled mode of 1960s existence but closes it off as a real option for its characters.

It is always risky with quirky, cutting-edge television series that are still producing new seasons to make predictions as to where things are going to end up. No viewers, for instance, seemed to have anticipated that Don would propose to Megan at the end of season 4. Indeed, as an anecdotal, minor sign of the show's unpredictability, when I first conceived this chapter I was struck by the lack of dialogue including the word *mad* in a series that nonetheless referenced the term in its title: I had planned then to cite Kramer's *It's a Mad, Mad, Mad, Mad World* as one example of "mad activity" from the period that, typically, was not referenced by the show. I was taken aback when the series did end up making pointed, if passing, reference to the film. This is a series that can keep one guessing.

There is always the possibility that some character in the series will have a substantial, life-altering encounter with madness or at least with inspiring madcapness. Indeed, when I discussed earlier the ways in which Betty Draper and her father both have bouts of psychiatric disorder, I could have completed the lineage with the important—but highly ambiguous and, at this point in the history of the series, open-ended—case of Betty's daughter, Sally. Sally is, quite simply, one of the most vexed or fraught characters on *Mad Men*, and she is exceedingly difficult to figure out (by both the characters in the series and we the viewers of it). In a strong way, Sally does exhibit many of the forms of madness that the 1960s became so invested in: she is unpredictable (in a manner that sometimes approaches psychosis, as in her raggedly cutting her hair in "The Chrysanthemum and the Sword" [4.5]), she is adventurous and experimental, she is unruly and rebellious, she is unhappy and searching for pleasures undreamed of (including sexual ones). In Sally, the 1960s senses of madness as mental malady and as liberatory anger merge.

Sally might, like so many other characters, turn back from the promise of the period and opt for conventionality. She does, after all, seem to fall into patterns of passivity and obedience as much as her mother has. In some way, it seems appropriate that on the Internet, Sally's rage has been turned into one of the most popular animated GIFs (graphic interface format) — clips from media that have been tinkered with to make a single action repeat over and over again in uncanny and hypnotic fashion. The GIF of Sally takes the moment in "The Beautiful Girls" when she falls down in the hallway of her dad's agency as she tries to run away, and it replays the instant of enraged upset into a disturbing and yet absorbing infinity. The GIF combines anger and endless impotence in one endlessly revolving gesture.[5]

Of course, the looping GIF is a viewer's emendation imposed on the TV series rather than something that was scripted into *Mad Men*'s original narrative world. Nothing in the show thus far confirms that Sally will remain in a narrative limbo. True, the move to a new home that her mother forced on the family at the end of season 4 means that some avenues are closed off to Sally (for instance, it would increasingly be harder for her to develop her complicated bond with Glen [Marten Weiner]). But nothing requires the restless Sally to stay put. If one calculates the historical timeline, Sally would be a young teenager when the Woodstock Festival takes place in 1969. Maybe she will be one of those 1960s runaways who ends up there or somewhere else in the fractured landscape of the period. Perhaps, in the guise of Sally, *Mad Men* will discover through some plot twist that, as another 1960s figure raging against but also beholden to parental authority, Norman Bates, puts it in *Psycho* (1960), "We all go a little mad sometimes."

NOTES

1. A friend of mine refers to the lawnmower scene as "Lynchian" — along with a moment in which Betty suddenly throws up after learning of Don's infidelity with Bobbie Barrett and the episode abruptly ends on that action ("The Gold Violin," 2.7), and the memorable moment in which from a striking angle we see Betty shooting a rifle at a neighbor's homing birds (in the aptly titled "Shoot," 1.9). The point is that it is recognized that *Mad Men* has special moments, viewable as weird but iso-

latable as moments specifically, and that these have a particular and partial cultural provenance (the branding of them as "Lynchian").

2. It is the very imprecision of the notion of being "mad" that an inspired parody of *Mad Men* on *Sesame Street* in 2009 exploits (thereby confirming how much the children's show is simultaneously for the parents in the room). The Don Draper puppet meets with two assistants ("sycophants," as he directly terms them) to work on the Happy Honey Bear account. Sketches they have come up with of bears missing out on honey make the ad men mad and then sad. Finally, they come up with a sketch of a joyous bear eating honey, and this makes everyone happy. It's been an emotional roller coaster, declares Don: they've been able to go through a gamut of feelings in such a short time.

3. Similarly, Peggy Olson, a copywriter, is almost institutionalized when anomie she feels because of a pregnancy she is unaware of is misdiagnosed as mental disorder. But Peggy is quickly pulled from the world of the mad and returned to Madison Avenue.

4. "Manic Pixie Dream Girl," *Wikipedia*, http://en.wikipedia.org/wiki/Manic_Pixie_Dream_Girl (accessed 6 December 2010). The source quoted is Nathan Rabin, "The Bataan Death March of Whimsy Case File #1: *Elizabethtown*," *My Year of Flops*, A.V. Club, 25 January 2007, http://www.avclub.com.

5. See the Gif Party website, http://gifparty.tumblr.com/post/1159425316/.

MAD SPACE

DIANNE HARRIS

Life takes place. Everything we do, everything we experience, happens in a spatial field, in a physical location, against a material backdrop that is now almost always configured, at least to some extent, by people. Whether they are produced for the stage or the screen (large or small), scenic design and sets are essential: they describe and define spaces, they are crucial actors in the production of the viewer's experience, and they are likewise necessary to the production of forms of knowledge that are specific to the carefully crafted viewing experience. Location lends reality and authenticity to action; sets provide a sense of place and therefore of credibility and reality. Although these statements may seem remedial to some, they bear articulation because the spaces of television production—as with those in which we daily live our lives—can so easily become invisible, like the air we unconsciously breathe. I use the term *invisible* here not in its literal sense; spaces are, of course, visible, seeable. But vision, like space, is socially constructed, socially produced. We see what we are acculturated to see, our gaze directed by a range of cultural forces that shape what is and is not cognitively available in the visual field. Because space (and by extension here, sets) remains largely unseen and unexamined in quotidian life, it can appear both natural and neutral, preordained and even (in the case of landscapes) God-given. As such, and because of this very invisibility, space is among the most potent of ideological devices. It conveys meaning without appearing to do so because it is so often presumed to be without content. Nothing could be further from the truth, and nothing can therefore be more consistently and pervasively persuasive as space. It does what it does silently, at the periphery of our attention, just as it inescapably surrounds and influences us. Through a myriad of often subtle iconographic and semiotic cues to which we are highly attuned if often inattentive, spaces tell us who we are and are not; they tell us where we do and do not belong; they are fundamental material artifacts in the construction of personal, family, national, and state identities.[1] Sets designed for both stage and screen are meant, to some extent, to disappear, to fall away from our foreground consciousness so that actors and dialogue can become the focus of our attention. But like the built world we inhabit, sets are nevertheless constant, if silent, actors contributing to the formation of character, action, and plot. Space shapes culture whether it is real or fictive.

Architectural historians have seldom examined television as an archive whose evidence can be used toward the fabrication of spatial histories.[2] There are important studies of cinematic depictions of architectural and urban spaces, such as those produced by Nezar AlSayyad and Dietrich Neumann, both of which advance the notion that film can be an important medium or tool for spatial analysis. AlSayyad writes, for example, that "urban theory and theories of modernity may be greatly enhanced by using cinema as a critical medium of experience" (4), and he questions whether "our understanding of the city [can] be viewed independently of the cinematic experience," since our knowledge of many global locations is almost entirely informed by celluloid (and now digital) representations of urban spaces that many of us will never have the opportunity to visit (15; see also Lamster). Following his logic, we might similarly ask whether it is possible to view postwar spaces of labor and of domesticity outside the semiotic and representational influence of televised depictions of those spaces? And what can be learned from looking at the spaces so scrupulously and fastidiously designed and constructed as sets for *Mad Men*?

In this chapter I examine two spaces seen recurrently in seasons 1–3 of *Mad Men*—the Sterling Cooper offices and Don and Betty Draper's home—to elucidate the significance of specific architectural forms and styles to plot development. I selected these two spaces because they appeared most frequently in episodes from the first three seasons, and as such, their plot significance is most fully articulated. In consequence, these two spaces also permit a more robust examination of the ways in which gender, race, and sexuality intersect with the delineation of office and home in *Mad Men*. Space matters on *Mad Men* as it does everywhere, and it is nearly always interior spaces that matter for this show. With a very few notable exceptions, such as the fantastically gasp-producing moment when the Drapers go on a picnic and toss all their trash out into the landscape without even a hint of the ecologically induced guilt we would experience today, *Mad Men* relies on interior spaces to assist the writers who seek to probe characters' inner and often hidden lives that lurk beneath the polished and superbly period-costumed surfaces of nearly everyone in the cast.[3] *Mad Men*'s spaces perfectly produce a set of relationships that are, not surprisingly, plot-essential. As numerous critics and viewers have noted, the show's design and the almost fetishistically accurate sets and costumes play a significant role in attracting viewers whose love and nostalgia for midcentury design and material culture equal that of the show's producer, Matthew Weiner. Weiner himself has been quoted as stating, "The design is not the star of the show. . . . I don't want to be distracted by it" (Witchel). Nevertheless, the design is *a* star, if not *the* star of the show. It is certainly an essential supporting actor. In asserting this, I follow recently published works by Pamela Wojcik and Merrill Schleier, who have respectively demonstrated the necessity of the space of the apartment and the skyscraper as narrative devices—as plot essentials—in the formation of cinematic experience and cultural knowledge. Indeed, as Wojcik has urged, the spatial dynamics of all films (and by extension television shows) deserve consideration in order to determine "how space sets the parameters for the plot, themes, and ideology of not only individual films but also genres. . . . Like props, characters, and other semantic elements, space and place are more than just one lexical choice among many; they are imbricated in signifying structures that are historically determined and that carry tremendous connotative and ideological weight related to issues of sex, gender, class, race, the body, individuality, family, community, work, pleasure, and more" (6–8). In what follows, I hope to demonstrate the necessity of both office and domestic space to the creation of the highly gendered and sexualized—and also racialized—plots developed for *Mad Men*.

The Sterling Cooper offices are located in an International Style high-rise, its exterior depicted among numerous similar high-rise buildings that provide the backdrop for the black, silhouetted figure's free fall in the show's opening credits and that are on display through the windows of the offices occupied by the male executives (fig. 2.1). The term *International Style* was first coined in 1932 for an exhibit curated by Henry-Russell Hitchcock and Philip Johnson at the Museum of Modern Art, New York, and it was intended to describe a universalist architecture that was considered suitable for any part of the world for a variety of uses (including residential), and

FIGURE 2.1. International Style buildings seen through the windows of an office at Sterling Cooper.

whose volumes and forms were determined primarily by the materials of twentieth-century industrial mass production: concrete, steel, and glass (fig. 2.2). Some of its original adherents in architectural practice also imagined this new architecture as the material manifestation of a social and political movement, one that could erase the particularities of class difference by creating an architecture suitable for everyone, everywhere; by establishing minimum housing criteria for the masses; and by advocating collective policies for town planning that would redistribute land in a more just and equitable fashion. Many of the architects who participated in the first Congrès International d'Architecture Moderne (CIAM) in 1928 therefore held a decidedly leftist social and political orientation, and they imagined the modernist architecture that just four years later was named International Style to be socially, politically, and economically transformative. Given the venue, however, it is not surprising that the MoMA exhibit emphasized style, form, and aesthetics over a social or political vision, and after 1932, International Style modernism became increasingly associated with — even symbolic of — the objectives of corporate capitalism.[4]

Manhattan is, of course, composed of an eclectic collection of high-rise buildings that date from a range of periods but that were largely constructed after 1900 and therefore present a range of architectural styles since archi-

FIGURE 2.2. The Lever House at 390 Park Avenue, New York, a well-known example of International Style architecture. Architect: Gordon Bunshaft for Skidmore, Owings, and Merrill, 1952. Photograph courtesy of Nathaniel Robert Walker.

tectural fashions shifted fairly rapidly in the first five decades of the century. That the view through the Sterling Cooper offices should focus on other International Style buildings is not inevitable. Indeed, the poster that advertises season 4 shows Don standing inside what appears to be an empty International Style office space but gazing out toward a Manhattan skyline that includes a somewhat more diverse range of building styles, perhaps signaling other changes to come (fig. 2.3). But the selection of the International Style for the Sterling Cooper offices is a particularly apt one considering that despite some of the earliest efforts by architects to connect this modernist form to revolutionary social ideals, it was rapidly coopted by corporate culture and is ideally suited to capitalist modes of production. Sleek glass-and-metal façades known as "curtain walls" hang like a skin off the building's structural system and rely on materials and technologies that at least appear "of the moment" (in this case, the early 1960s, even if most of those materials and their applications predate that era by several decades). The style's

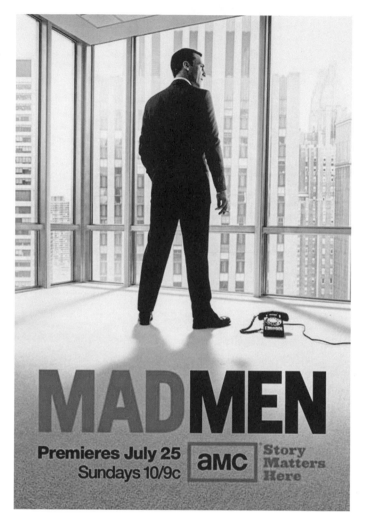

engineering and materials afford the vast, open plan of the secretarial pool
with its modular and uniform coordination of furnishings that could be arranged and rearranged at will according to an internal grid echoing that of
the building's structural system—a grid that implies the interchangeability
of the human as well as the furnished office components, and that visually
dominates in *Mad Men* through the doubling effect of the seemingly endless grid of fluorescent ceiling lights (fig. 2.4). The hierarchically arranged
outer-ring offices with their views indicate status, the promise of organizational efficiency, and by 1960, clear associations with elite culture. The International Style office set thus produces a visual environment in which uniformity, precision, order, and control prevail.[5]

FIGURE 2.4. The grid of ceiling lights in the Sterling Cooper offices enhances the viewer's perception of the secretarial grid.

But perhaps more important, the modernist spaces of the Sterling Cooper offices allow two things: an extensive open space for the secretarial pool with panoptic qualities that not only permit but actually produce the sexual tensions and sexual harassment that keep us glued to the screen, and a visual freedom that creates an antithesis to the intense claustrophobia of the domestic Draper spaces. The Drapers' home would not seem nearly so confining, dark, and oppressive without the sweeping spaces of the "bull pen" (as the AMC website labels the secretarial space), with its high-wattage lighting, its seemingly endless rows of uniformly distributed workstations, and its spaces that seem to open out from the edges into unknown parts of the agency's physical world. Daylight floods the offices men occupy at Sterling Cooper through the ample, if rigidly fixed, glazing of the window walls, and glowing translucent panels ensure that the office spaces retain their spacious, modern appearance even if office doors are entirely closed (fig. 2.5). Spaciousness remains one of the key signifiers of architectural modernism, but also of modernity itself since it implies freedom of mobility and the forms of social dominance that pertain to that freedom (Isenstadt). It is therefore especially important that the outer offices maintain an open quality even though they are enclosed. With their windows to the outside world, the outer executive offices at Sterling Cooper seem far less confining than the seem-

FIGURE 2.5. Translucent panels permit a continuous glow of light in the outer-ring offices at Sterling Cooper.

ingly unrestricted spaces of the inner open plan of the secretarial pool. An interesting architectural inversion is at play here such that the partitioned (and therefore architecturally traditional) world of the outer offices appears to be part of a progressive, male-dominated world, whereas the inner office incongruously retains its adherence to traditional gender boundaries despite the modernity implied by the open plan. The spatial inversion is a subtle one, but it heightens the tensions at play within the Sterling Cooper workplace.

In her study of gendered spaces, Daphne Spain has referred to women's jobs as "open floor" and to men's jobs as "closed door," an organization that is perfectly reflected in the Sterling Cooper office arrangement. Women's open floor jobs disallow privacy just as they inhibit women from partaking in decision-making activities and restrict their access to specific forms of executive knowledge. As Spain notes, "Spatial arrangements in the workplace reinforce status distinctions partially by providing more 'closed door' potential to managers than to those they supervise" (211, 215). The ability to withdraw to private, external offices continually reinforces the existence of a domain of white male privilege in *Mad Men* just as the lack of that ability reasserts the lower status of the women in the secretarial pool. Joan and Peggy eventually attain their own offices, but neither is afforded the full privacy that would elevate their status as fully commensurate with the men. Peggy's office walls do not reach to the ceiling, and she uses the flimsy construction to eavesdrop on conversations in the adjacent office; Joan's season 4 office sits in the middle of the Sterling Cooper Draper Pryce floor plan, and we observe her frustration at being frequently intruded upon.

In fact, the spatial freedom permitted by the office's open plan is only ever fully available to men. With the single exception of Peggy, only the male employees can move easily between secretarial pool, common spaces, and their own private offices. And the open space of the secretarial pool houses a complex social dynamic, since the panoptic supervision it allows can be by turns liberatory, comforting, and stifling. The latter derives from the absence of privacy in the central pool that serves as a self-regulatory space (in the Foucauldian sense) in which the women confine their actions to those that can safely be observed by anyone whose gaze might happen upon them. But that same space can offer comfort, even a sense of safety, compared to the concealed world of the outer offices. Women enter the outer office ring only when invited to do so, and once behind those closed doors, they sacrifice the limited autonomy afforded to them by the security of the very panoptic supervision that can also stifle (think, for example, of some of the coerced and even forced sexual encounters that take place in the outer-ring Sterling Cooper offices). Joan, who is arguably the most powerful and respected woman in the office, lacks a precisely prescribed or assigned location (although her location in the office becomes more fixed in seasons 4 and 5), but her authority derives from her ability to "know her place" even if it is not precisely mapped in spatial terms. The freedom of mobility she enjoys stems from her ability to read and decipher the fine-grained boundaries she negotiates (and continues to negotiate as her power increases in season 4). She never oversteps, even when she literally does so by crossing a threshold into the male, outer-office domain, and eventually, in season 5, into the boardroom as a voting partner—a position she gains only by prostituting herself to a powerful client. The open plan of the central office space amplifies these conditions so that viewers can easily perceive the freedom of male movement, of male creative thought, through contrast with the more restricted movements of the female employees.

Furthermore, the open plan of the secretarial pool may be seen as inciting a release from sexual mores not only for Sterling Cooper's male executives but also for its female staff. Leslie Salzinger has written about the ways in which "a given workplace evokes particular sexual subjectivities in managers and workers alike" to create what she calls "shopfloor sexuality" (68). Although Salzinger's subject is the maquiladora shop floor of factories located on the U.S.-Mexican border, her analysis brilliantly conveys the ways in which panoptic spaces like Sterling Cooper's secretarial pool "directly, if unintentionally," create a kind of "extreme sexual-objectification of the workforce." The space is designed "as a machine that evokes and focuses the male gaze in the service of production . . . an architecture that controls through visibility . . . that is ultimately as much about fostering self-consciousness as it is about the more mundane operations of super-vision. . . . The enactment of managerial practices based on men obsessively watching young women creates a sexually charged atmosphere, one in which flirtation and sexual competition become the currency through which shopfloor power relations are struggled over and fixed. In this framework, women are constituted as desirable objects and male managers are desiring subjects" (70). Thus this space, which is so central to *Mad Men*, itself becomes a rather complicated actor that subtly shapes our expectations of possible action, dramas that at some level, we know will unfold even before they do so, and perhaps even before they are written, because those spaces are already inscribed in our experience.

Finally, with its emphasis on surfaces and skin (curtain wall, window wall, flat planes, rectilinearity), the International Style provides a perfect visual echo of the characters themselves. *Mad Men* repeatedly invites its audience to contemplate the reality that lurks below the polished surface each character presents. Just as the exterior of an International Style building appears as a reflective surface and therefore as visually impenetrable by day — its clean solidity standing for a corporate rectitude and impeachability that twenty-first-century viewers may regard with nostalgia — so too *Mad Men*'s characters maintain polished exteriors that belie the complicated lives concealed beneath their fashionable clothing, their perfectly coiffed hair, and their own unblemished and beautifully styled bodies.[6]

If the Sterling Cooper offices create the perfect setting for early 1960s corporate ad men, the Drapers' suburban house seems, on first impression, to be strangely outmoded, *retardataire*. With their family of four (five in subsequent seasons) and with their need to project conventional family life, the pre-divorce Drapers could not be urban apartment dwellers like Pete and Trudy Campbell; Betty, like so many housewives of the period, would see urban life as unhealthy for her children, and city schools as too old and (what is certainly worse) integrated. In the first three seasons, before the Draper divorce, viewers experience primarily the counterpositioned spaces of the urban office and the suburban residence. It is only after Don and Betty dissolve their marriage in season 4 that Don moves into an urban apartment. Despite the dominant and widely documented postwar movement of middle- and upper-middle-class whites to suburban locations that offered individual houses on privately owned lots, many Americans continued to live in cities. Apartments offered alternative living spaces that held appeal for many, but as Wojcik has noted, they came to hold very specific symbolic connotations when deployed as the setting for television and film plots. Instead of signifying the space of white, heteronormative family stability, apartments conveyed alternative identities for occupants, but they were most obviously and repeatedly used as settings imagined as appropriate for single, nonmarried occupants. Likewise, hotels serve as the setting for illicit trysts and (on one occasion) for a homosexual liaison. But when they appear, the hotel and the apartment are important counterfoils to the social stability and conformity of the suburban house and the corporate office. The alternative spaces of hotel and apartment reinforce the viewer's expectations about the assignment of specific behaviors to specific spaces, underlining the correlative value of space to plot. It is telling that Don begins to occupy an apartment only after his concealed identity is revealed to his wife. His urban apartment is the locus in which he unravels, becomes an alcoholic, and hyperventilates with fear when he imagines further exposure of his secrets. By contrast, the suburban house and the season 3 Sterling Cooper offices remain spaces of containment, even after Don's secrets are revealed within their walls.

Millions of other young families of Don's and Betty's age during the postwar period became first-time homeowners in brand new houses in equally new developments, and so we might have expected to see Don and Betty living in such a location. After all, the period between 1945 and 1960 saw the mass construction of some of the largest housing developments in U.S. history; more than eleven million houses were built in suburbs nationwide between 1950 and 1960, with considerable help from the Housing Act of 1949 (G. Wright, 167). Communities such as the Levittowns (Long Island, Pennsylvania, and New Jersey); Park Forest, Illinois; and Lakewood, California, came to epitomize the built manifestation of a government promise made to returning GIs that was likewise dependent on a series of government-backed subsidies and loan programs administered through the Federal Housing Administration (FHA) and the Home Owners Loan Corporation (HOLC). The financing from those agencies fueled a suburban construction boom that was meant to satisfy an enormous pent up demand for housing that resulted from the stagnation of residential construction caused by the Great Depression and U.S. involvement in the war. The earliest houses constructed in those developments after the war ended followed minimum FHA standards and were therefore very small. Some of the earliest houses built in Levittown, Long Island, contained less than one thousand square feet of living space, but they also cost less than $8,000 and required a very small down payment for those who could take advantage of the GI Bill—namely, working-class and middle-class white Americans who came to view ownership of such homes as a ticket both to citizenship and to a white, middle-class identity.[7] Before 1957, the Levittowns in Long Island and Pennsylvania were all-white communities whose residential demographic was maintained through the enforcement of restrictive covenants that were not unlike those found in many similar developments nationwide. And the whiteness of suburban living mattered in these developments, as it had in more upscale suburban locales, for decades.[8]

Despite the midcentury stereotype of young families living in mass-produced, homogenous developments such as those that inspired Malvina Reynolds's song "Little Boxes" about "ticky tacky" houses that "all look just the same," Don and Betty Draper do not live—could not live—in a Levittown-like development. Instead, their suburbia is in bucolic, staid, and economically comfortable Ossining in Westchester County, a town with a history that dates back to the early nineteenth century. It is a suburb with a well-recorded past—a residential requirement for a man who has erased his own. By association, if Ossining has a history, its residents must possess one equally respectable and tranquil. As a suburb, Ossining is more like the locales described in some of John Cheever's short stories: upscale, leafy, established, white except for the hired help. As in "The Housebreaker of Shady Hill" (1958) or "The Swimmer" (1964), those Arcadian locales hide the pathologies of deceit, infidelity, alcoholism, mental illness, and criminal behavior.[9] Moreover, Ossining's apparent suburban tranquility is disrupted by the presence of the Sing Sing Correctional Facility, one of the most infamous prisons in New York State. *Mad Men*'s producer selected a town that perfectly reflects Don's persona, since it contains an ominous space (the prison) within what appears to be an otherwise idyllic setting.

Instead of a stylishly modern postwar house—and despite their California-ready appearance, many of these were constructed in the Westchester County region where Don and Betty reside—the Drapers' Ossining home is staid and conservative in appearance, more like *Mr. Blandings Builds His Dream House* (1948) than like anything that was being promoted in the architecture and design literature of the 1950s or early 1960s (figs. 2.6–2.7). Matthew Weiner must have recalled that Mr. Blandings was a copywriter for an advertising agency, a man who earned his professional reputation by in-

CARY GRANT and MYRNA LOY
starring in the timely new hit
"MR. BLANDINGS BUILDS HIS DREAM HOUSE."
an RKO Radio Production — a Selznick release

FIGURE 2.6. The house featured in the film *Mr. Blandings Builds His Dream House* (1948).

FIGURE 2.7. The Draper home. Photograph courtesy of Lindsay Blake, www.iamnotastalker.com.

venting a slogan for a laxative. And like Don Draper, Mr. Blandings suffers a crisis of conscience, except that his derives not from the maintenance of multiple identities and a series of lies and infidelities but instead from a lack of career fulfillment and an abiding sense that his advertising job is itself dishonest (Fox, 203).

As with Cheever's houses, the refined, colonial-style exterior of the Draper residence signals affluence, comfort, respectability, and most important, a solidly white, upper-class identity. Despite Don's extramarital fascination with the bohemian lifestyles and fashions of Greenwich Village (where his lover Midge resides in season 1), or with the forward looking and modernist designs of the products he promotes at Sterling Cooper, he daily returns to a house that was, by 1960, exceedingly conventional in its style and design. Despite the clever connection to Mr. Blandings, it is not an inevitable choice. As with many locations throughout the United States, Westchester County provided the possibility for living in a newly constructed, one-of-a-kind, architect-designed house of substance. Indeed, the very magazines in which Sterling Cooper advertisements would have appeared—popular and shelter magazines such as *House Beautiful, House and Garden, Life* magazine, and *Ladies' Home Journal*—all featured upscale homes designed by architects for moneyed clients like the Drapers. Designed with open-plan configurations, large areas of glazing, sliding or accordion-fold walls, centrally located family rooms, separate wings for parents and children, abundant built-in storage, an emphasis on spaciousness, indoor-outdoor connections that facilitated specific lifestyles of leisure, and plenty of new appliances and gadgetry, such homes were designed to appeal to young families of means. Priced between $28,000 and $45,000, they were perhaps best represented in *House Beautiful*'s annual selection of a "pace-setter" house, a residence from which the editors expected most readers could take one or two design ideas but for whom the house itself was likely beyond their financial grasp (fig. 2.8).

Houses such as these possessed the cachet of having the cultural stamp of approval of the design intelligentsia and marked their owners as progressive, learned, and modern. What they lacked, significantly, was a clear symbolic association with a solidly white identity. And as a figure that Michael Szalay characterizes as "passing" ("Mad Style"), Don Draper has a great deal at stake in the game of identity formation and self-fashioning. Don's assumed identity forces him to hide his roots (rural and impoverished), his bastard status, his prostitute biological mother, his alcoholic and abusive father—all of his "Tobacco Road," hillbilly, white-trash origins. Don's history marks

The American Style
in a Pace-Setter House

*Here is a Pace-Setter House that combines our
three BIG ideas for 1950—Climate Control, Privacy, and
the American Style. It proves that you can have all
these aspects of better living at moderate cost—if you
know what to look for and don't give up till you find it*

Edwin A. Wadsworth
Architect

Germano A. Milono
Associate architect

Thomas D. Church
Site planting and landscaping

Warde Corley
W. & J. Sloane, San Francisco
Decoration and furnishings

William Manker
Color stylist

David D. Bohannon Organization
Community developers and builders

Climate Control in this house meant, primarily, wind control. Without it, comfortable outdoor living isn't practical. Here, mass of house itself is designed to act as wind screen deflecting steady winds up over sunny, enclosed patio.

This house is remarkable because it offers better living than many twice as costly. It's remarkable because it was built by a regular merchant builder as one of a whole series that will sell complete, without fuss or feathers, for $25,000. Solidly it! It typifies the emerging American Style by its emphasis on comfort and convenience, by its lack of ostentation and insistence on good design. Yet see how economically those qualities are achieved. The house, which stands on a 70-ft. lot, has a floor area of only 1,600 sq. ft. It is built of standard materials, available anywhere in the U. S. The really valuable ingredient is good design which gives the house privacy and a garden that's nice to look at, pleasant to live in, easy to maintain.

FIGURE 2.8.
"Pace-Setter House"
(*House Beautiful* 92
[June 1950]).

him as decidedly off-white, more like the Jewish Rachel Menken than like his wasp coworkers at Sterling Cooper or like Betty and her family. His whiteness is not quite pure, slightly tainted, an incomplete project, much in the same way that assimilating Americans who sought to erase at least some traces of ethnicity or their "white trash" backgrounds were understood as impurely or incompletely white.[10]

Similarly, and despite its frequent association with white walls, the iconography of architectural modernism — both the high-style modernism of the International Style and the "soft modernism" of postwar housing designed by architects such as A. Quincy Jones, Fred Emmons, Harwell Hamilton Harris, John Yeon, Hugh Stubbins, Harris Armstrong, O'Neil Ford, and many others—was itself off-white, not understood as necessarily WASP or gentile.[11] With so much at stake, Don could never consider purchasing a new house of modernist design, not because they lacked history (as does Don), but because of modernism's ambiguous range of symbolic associations. In his famed publication *The Status Seekers* (1959), Vance Packard articulated a number of widely held notions about the symbolic associations linking the spare, clean lines of modernist architecture and design with specific class and racial identities. He wrote that "genuine eggheads," whom he defined as intellectuals and culture producers possessing higher education diplomas and a generally higher income level, were likely to live in a "contemporary" home, and that they were the sort to "carefully measure distinctions in the design of eating utensils considered most appropriate for such a home" (Horowitz, *Selections*, 49). According to Packard, the upper classes "favor the primly severe, the lower class the frankly garish. . . . The high-status people preferred a sofa with simple, severe, right-angle lines." Eggheads, he wrote, "have enough self-assurance so that they can defy convention, and they often cherish the simplicity of open layout" (61). While Packard found that those of Italian and Polish backgrounds preferred "lots of goop in their houses," and homes that were "very garish, with loud, screaming colors," Jews were more receptive than any other group to "contemporary architecture with its openness and modernity" (64). The connection between a modernist aesthetic and a Jewish identity was flexible, however, since modernist designs and furnishings could also signal affluence and education. Packard's essentializing study appears dated today, yet numerous historians and sociologists have arrived at similar conclusions that correlate a preference for modernist, contemporary, minimalist design to white-collar employment and higher levels of income. Indeed, as Shelley Nickles has noted, midcentury consumer research indicated that the upper-middle-class preferences held by designers and by the producers of design culture for the reduced forms and quiet hues of modernist simplicity stood in contrast to the tastes and preferences of working-class consumers who preferred bulk, embellishment, shiny surfaces, and bright color. These preferences, Nickles asserts, were widely held and understood, so that everyday purchases came to signify important indications of class and ethnicity (604).

Accordingly, then, the Drapers might well have purchased such a sleek, modernist house; Don certainly desired the appearance of well-educated white-collar affluence. What he could not afford, however, especially in what would surely have been an all-white and very likely all-WASP neighborhood, was even the slightest possible taint of a Jewish identity. In 1958 the sociologist James Davis of the University of Chicago conducted a study in which housewives were shown a series of photographs of four distinct living rooms and asked to identify the possible occupants of each. One of the photographs was of Davis's own, contemporary-style, living room, and it showed floor-to-ceiling bookshelves along one wall, a wall with large windows, a butterfly chair, and a sleek coffee table covered with magazines. Many of Davis's study participants identified his room as belonging to Jewish occupants—for them, the modernist furnishings and interior space and the shelves of books signaled a non-WASP identity. If such subtle cues could "taint," it is certain that postwar Americans who were anxious about their identity could ill afford such an aesthetic risk. The stakes for ordinary Americans were high: anything other than a solidly white identity could mean exclusion from the housing market altogether. For a character such as Don Draper, who is "passing," the stakes are even higher. The staid colonial, then, was the only logical choice for *Mad Men*'s producers, the only domicile to which Don could possibly return to confirm his created sense of himself at the end of each day.

Moreover, the forced congeniality demanded by the open plan found in a modernist house would never work for Don and Betty. Sadly, their congeniality is forced even within the privacy afforded by the traditionally programmed and divided spaces of their colonial house. The walled sequence of rooms they occupy symbolically enhances the representation of a marriage that we are meant to see as tragically bounded by the sealed emotions of the intimate strangers who inhabit both the house and the relationship. Don and Betty's marriage drama requires rooms that both reify the gender boundaries defining and confining their lives and simultaneously conceal their many secrets. Thus the rooms of the Draper home are traditionally configured and, for a wealthy couple with a substantial home, are shot to appear small, cramped, confining, and claustrophobic. In contrast to the brightly lit, spacious, open office, the Draper house seems always to be cast in twilight; the dark, knotty pine paneling of the kitchen dims the morning sunlight and makes the walls appear closer than they actually are, and the heavy draperies in the living room and kitchen cast a necessary gloaming, if not a gloom, over their domestic lives (fig. 2.9). Draper family dreams are confined within the walls of a conventional house that resists and therefore creates a tension with what we are meant to see as the unconventional lies of Don and Betty's marriage. In appearing almost hypernormal but being a space within which abnormal lives and lies are played out, the house heightens the contrast and enhances the drama. As it does so, it recalls the tropes associated with suburban

FIGURE 2.9. Betty Draper in her dimly lit, confining kitchen.

fiction and film in which the utopian appearance of suburban perfection is disrupted by family dysfunction that transforms the residential setting into a profound dystopia (again, recalling Cheever's Westchester County house-breaker or his unhinged swimmer, or the tragic Frank and April in Richard Yates's *Revolutionary Road* [1961], to cite some midcentury examples). It is not insignificant that some of Don's most shocking departures from his marital vows and family ties — the episode in which he disappears to Palm Springs and has an extended affair with a young woman, Joy — take place in a sunlit, modernist house with glass walls, an open plan, and doors that seem not to lock (there are morning intruders in the bedroom) (fig. 2.10). The occupants of that house live as upper-class bohemians who seek to discard their conventional identities to attain sexual and other freedoms, and the Palm Springs modernism of their retreat provides the perfect liberatory set-ting for their (and for Don's) multiday escape/indulgence. When he leaves that sun-drenched house — after a detour along the California coast — Don returns home to the dimly lit, carefully delineated rooms of his home and marriage, a spatial contrast that viewers hold in mind as they watch Don's dalliance with alternative possible futures and identities.

As noted here and elsewhere, *Mad Men*'s creator is obsessed with period detail, with "getting it right" in every episode, and with avoiding anachronism

FIGURE 2.10. Don and Joy in a Palm Springs modernist house.

(to the best of his ability). Yet architectural modernism itself was not "of the moment," not strictly of the late 1950s and early 1960s, although it continued to evolve in those decades. Indeed, as a stylistic category, architectural modernism was already half a century old by the time Don Draper would have begun to occupy his Madison Avenue office. Nevertheless, it provides a perfect foil, the ideal spatial "actor," for the show's story lines, even — perhaps especially — when it is absent, and *Mad Men's* producers, writers, directors, and designers use it to brilliant effect. What their slavish attention to the details of space and of material life shows us is that, as Dell Upton has asserted, "the self is always a self in space" ("Sound as Landscape," 24). And Mad Men are likewise best viewed, and understood, in Mad Space.

NOTES

1. For a more complete analysis of the social construction of vision and its relationship to the spatial realm, see D. Harris and Ruggles, "Landscape and Vision." On space as a powerful ideological tool, see Mitchell.

2. Although the houses portrayed in such 1950s and early 1960s programs as *The Donna Reed Show* (1958–66), *Father Knows Best* (1954–60), *Leave It to Beaver* (1957–63), and *The Dick Van Dyke Show* (1961–66) are indelibly imprinted in the conscious-

ness of the U.S. baby boomer population, those sets have received little scholarly analysis from architectural historians. For examples of such analysis, see Bennett; Friedman; and Hayden.

3. Although there was a growing ecological awareness in some U.S. locations during the late 1950s, a watershed moment might be the initial publication of Rachel Carson's book *Silent Spring*, in September 1962.

4. For good introductions to the history of International Style architecture, see Curtis; and Frampton. On CIAM, see E. Mumford.

5. The use of the grid to organize spaces was certainly not new to the postwar era in the United States. See Upton, *Another City*, 150–51.

6. On modernism's focus on surfaces and skin and its connection to corporate capitalism, see G. Wright, 158.

7. For general histories of postwar suburbia, see Hayden; K. Jackson; and Longstreth. On the historic links between homeownership and citizenship in the United States, see Freund.

8. On the history of racially restrictive covenants in the suburban United States, see Fogelson. On the whiteness of Levittown, see Sugrue, "Jim Crow's."

9. See *The Stories of John Cheever* (1978). "The Swimmer" is explicitly referenced in the season 4 episode "The Summer Man" (4.8).

10. On Jews as not quite white, see Brodkin. On definitions and analysis of the meanings associated with the term *white trash*, see Wrayle and Newitz. On Don as a secret Jew, see Goodlad, this volume.

11. On "soft modernism" or "everyday modernism," see Treib.

REPRESENTING THE
MAD MARGINS OF THE EARLY 1960S

Northern Civil Rights and the Blues Idiom

CLARENCE LANG

Mad Men conjures New York City in the early 1960s to engage contemporary questions about American identity, gender, ethnicity, sexuality, and the family. The early 1960s was a time of rapid flux in black-white relations, and "Negro rights" was the leading domestic issue of the day. Yet on *Mad Men*, African Americans are notable for their visibility only on the far margins of the drama (Coates, "Race"; Peterson, "Doesn't"). The depiction of African Americans largely as working-class laborers is not necessarily problematic: viewed sympathetically, it reflects some truth about the occupational limits most black men and women faced before the watershed 1964 Civil Rights Act. More troubling for a series that sensitively foregrounds the hidden interiors of its white characters is the black characters' curious lack of such depth. Of the black characters in the show's first four seasons, only one — Sheila White — is even granted the courtesy of a surname, underscoring her middle-class status. The postwar civil rights struggle, which was then in its epic "heroic" phase and would transform society in the United States, is relegated even further to the margins (P. Joseph, 6). Framed in the distant South, the movement is functionally disconnected from the everyday lives of *Mad Men*'s imagined New Yorkers.

When African Americans do appear, they issue pithy comments freighted with meaning (Merritt; Schwarz). Such quiet nobility, however heavy handed, at least portrays black characters as more than set dressing. Indeed, read benignly, *Mad Men*'s marginalization of black characters offers a reconstruction of a past in which African Americans were seldom seen by whites and even less seldom heard. Ta-Nehisi Coates, for example, discerns in *Mad Men* an ironization of the dominant white male standpoint; the rendering of black invisibility as a "beautiful, lovely, incredibly powerful omission" ("Race").

I cannot quite agree. The unexamined inner lives of black characters and the framing of the early civil rights upsurge as an exclusively southern phenomenon strike me as a historical amnesia that contradicts *Mad Men*'s fetishization of historical detail. Because the aesthetic gaze is never reversed, and because African Americans are always presented in isolation from one another, the show naturalizes a black quietude that did not actually exist. Further, by counterpoising an era of black invisibility to a present in which a black family resides in the White House, the show implicitly lays the past to rest. That is, because the series has not (or has not yet) dramatized the social contestation that enabled the changes it indirectly celebrates, and because the action centers on white characters, it reflects an American exceptionalist myth of gradual, inevitable progress toward racial democracy (Singh, 32, 42). As Kent Ono also argues in this volume, the creators of *Mad Men* presume a transcendence of the racial past without actually addressing race in any consistent manner.

Despite these shortcomings, *Mad Men* offers enough to make one imagine how much could be done with a show that interweaved the narratives of a black social movement with the more mundane patterns of black working-class life. Greater attention to black characterizations could foster a deeper, more meaningful commentary on the casual inequalities of gender, race, ethnicity, and class that the show takes seriously, but whose dimensions so far have been limited to white cast members. A show this preoccupied with the masks people don in plain sight has much to gain aesthetically from plumbing the depths of the black experience and teasing out the interplay of African American resistance and accommodation. This would entail presenting black characters not only as vividly sentient outside the presence of whites but also as deeply knowledgeable about the ways of the white characters looking past them.

Common to the poet Paul Laurence Dunbar's declaration "We Wear the Mask" (J. Braxton, 71), the historian Robin D. G. Kelley's apt admonition that "we are not what we seem" (35), and the scholar Darlene Clark Hine's description of black working-class women's "culture of dissemblance" (912) is the recognition of African Americans' expertise in sustaining individual and collective lives behind the proverbial veil of exclusion. As the novelist and essayist James Baldwin (*Notes*, 28) and intellectuals such as bell hooks (165) and David Roediger have argued, the veil was not just a mechanism for deflecting the white gaze (through strategies such as feigning ignorance or smiling when angry), but also a lens through which to critically view and evaluate whiteness. The muffled voices and sideways glances, and the emotionally intense interiorities they reflect, are perfect for the show's mode of storytelling. Moreover, in the early 1960s, African American cultural accommodation was expressed through the practice of "cool." Pivoting on the popular idioms of jazz and black observational humor, cool sprang from a blues-oriented outlook on modernity characteristic of the urban black working class. Could *Mad Men* be cool (or perhaps "cooler") by providing a better key to the show's articulation of white and black characters alike? I suggest that the blues, as a way of perceiving and living in the world, could be energizing and, yes, cool for *Mad Men*.

DISTANCING THE CIVIL RIGHTS MOVEMENT

Mad Men portrays the freedom struggles African Americans waged during the early 1960s in a casual, sporadic, and arguably dubious manner. In "The Fog" (3.5), as the account executive Pete Campbell attempts to convince his clients at Admiral TV to advertise to an expanding "Negro market," he references the black-owned Johnson Publishing Company. Although both the Admiral and Sterling Cooper executives balk at the idea, Campbell's pitch nods to the rising black postwar purchasing power that buoyed mass demonstrations against segregated public accommodations and other barriers to black participation in capitalist markets (Cohen; Green, 129–77; Walker; Weems, 70–79). Pete's interest in black consumers prompts him to interrogate Hollis, the black elevator attendant, about his television-buying habits (fig. 3.1). The conversation is initially tense. Hollis, taken aback and unsure of Pete's intentions, is guarded. Pete responds by manually halting the elevator car and pressing Hollis further, prompting the latter to finally declare, "We've got bigger problems to worry about than TV, OK?" When Pete insists that "everyone is going to have a house, a car, a television—the American Dream," Hollis looks at him with cold skepticism before restarting the elevator car. The scene dramatizes the unequal relationship of power between

FIGURE 3.1. Pete interrogates Hollis on the elevator ("The Fog," 3.5).

the two men. Yet, notwithstanding Hollis's doubtfulness about Pete's gospel of postwar abundance, the scene acknowledges the sea change occurring in U.S. race relations by drawing attention to the elevator operator's identity as a consumer, an equal participant in the cultural marketplace, and, hence, a citizen.

It is no coincidence, therefore, that the most accomplished black character on the show, Sheila White, is the assistant manager of a supermarket, a quintessential institution of postwar consumption (Peterson, "Doesn't"). Paralleling Johnson Publishing, Sheila embodies an advocacy for the black material success and comfort that the market is believed to supply and which would benefit advertising agencies and their corporate clients. African American "freedom" thus becomes conflated with the exercise of individual consumer initiative, overlooking how the "free market" failed to deliver postwar prosperity to most African Americans (Saul, 12–17). In fact, when black freedom activists employed acts of civil disobedience at lunch counters, they did so as a means toward realizing broader group-based, state-protected social democratic rights (Baldwin, Price, 265; Singh, 32). In part, the elevator scene plays as a moment of Pete's self-actualization, allowing him to recognize Hollis as neither simply the "help" nor a handy market research subject, but also a man with whom he might share a common American Dream. This typifies a pattern in the series in which the issue of "Negro rights" becomes a window into white outlooks, preferences, and conflicts.

One of the means through which *Mad Men* decontextualizes the experience of black characters is by banishing the civil rights struggle to the South. Events in Mississippi and Alabama are mentioned in passing by characters on the show or viewed on television screens. "I don't know why people keep stirring up trouble," the media head Harry Crane comments in "The Jet Set" (2.11). "It's bad for business — just another reason not to watch TV." Apart from ironizing Harry's preoccupation with advertising revenue, the remark indirectly frames the tumult as a *southern* inconvenience to Madison Avenue from afar. In "Wee Small Hours" (3.9), Betty Draper tells Carla, her housekeeper, that the nation may not yet be "ready" for the rights southern Negroes are demanding. "I hate to say this," she says, referring to the infamous Sixteenth Street Baptist Church bombing of 1963 that claimed the lives of four black Birmingham girls, "but it really made me wonder about civil rights. Maybe it's not supposed to happen right now." While the point is clearly to expose Betty's self-serving view of herself as more racially enlightened than her southern counterparts, such critical gestures do not counter the show's overall identification of the South as the place where black struggles happened.

References to southern black insurgency also loosely frame the short-lived romance between the copywriter Paul Kinsey and Sheila White. Significantly, the middle-class Sheila is the only African American character who is outspoken with regard to civil rights activism, suggesting that common laborers such as Carla or Hollis would have lacked the assertiveness, or the economic and social independence, to take part in, much less lead, political struggle. Is it possible that Sheila's upwardly mobile status, mirrored in her political boldness (and perhaps also her relationship with Paul), is what entitles her to a surname — "White," no less? Appearing first in "The Inheritance" (2.10), she convinces Paul to join her in the Freedom Rides in support of southern civil rights (a plotline that shows Paul to have privately preferred a business trip in California to "making history") (fig. 3.2). However, two episodes later ("The Mountain King," 2.12), Sheila has dumped him and makes no further appearances. Once again we are left with the impression that black freedom activism is something that took place below the Mason-Dixon line.

RECOVERING THE NORTHERN "NEGRO REVOLT"

Were *Mad Men*'s creators to depart from the misperception of an exclusively southern civil rights movement, an altogether different picture might emerge. New York City, home to over a million African Americans in the

FIGURE 3.2. Harry and Sheila argue about the Freedom Rides ("The Inheritance," 2.10).

1960s, was a flourishing center in the struggle for "Negro rights" (Biondi). In *The Negro Revolt* (1962), journalist Louis E. Lomax opined that "the current crisis in American race relations could well come to a head somewhere outside the South" (54). Lorraine Hansberry's *A Raisin in the Sun* (1959) and Claude Brown's autobiographical *Manchild in the Promised Land* (1965) captured the racism and angst faced by black northerners. Moreover, grassroots activism was common to cities such as Philadelphia, Milwaukee, Chicago, Detroit, Oakland, and St. Louis (Theoharis and Woodard; Countryman; P. Jones; H. A. Thompson; Sugrue, *Sweet Land*; Self; Lang, *Grassroots*). These Northeast, Midwest, and West Coast struggles were also peopled, and frequently led, by working-class African Americans (K'Meyer; Levy).

As a result of northern black electoral influence, two African Americans had, by the 1960s, served for decades in the U.S. House of Representatives: William L. Dawson, of Chicago, and Adam Clayton Powell Jr., of New York City. Chosen to chair the powerful Education and Labor Committee in 1961, Powell championed the expansion of black civil rights (Hamilton, 329–39). Activists in the early 1960s lobbied for access to skilled working-class jobs and white-collar professions, including in advertising (Collins; H. Hill). As Jason Chambers argues in *Madison Avenue and the Color Line* (113–56), demands for black employment in advertising were issued in tandem with calls to alter African American images in the ads themselves. Another northern-based organization, the Negro American Labor Council (NALC), lobbied for a similar black freedom jobs agenda and promoted social unionism and racial equality within the ranks of organized labor. Initiated by A. Philip Randolph, president of the all-black Brotherhood of Sleeping Car Porters and the nation's most prominent black labor spokesman, the NALC was pivotal in organizing the 1963 March on Washington that provides the backdrop to the season 3 episode "Wee Small Hours" (J. Anderson; Pfeffer).

In February 1964 protests on behalf of black and Puerto Rican children culminated in a one-day boycott of the New York public school system (Ransby, 153; C. Taylor, 121). In 1962 organizers associated with the Brooklyn Congress on Racial Equality (CORE) spearheaded a campaign to improve sanitation services to the Bedford-Stuyvesant community where most of Brooklyn's black population lived (Purnell, "Taxation," 62). Activity around this issue paralleled protests against the dislocating effects of slum clearance and urban renewal on working-class African American neighborhoods. At the 1964 New York World's Fair, members of Brooklyn CORE coordinated disruptive traffic "stall-ins" to demonstrate their overarching opposition to American racism (Purnell, "Drive Awhile," 46). At the same time, activists were challenging the housing policies that fostered white racial homogeneity in communities such as Ossining, New York, the suburban Westchester idyll where the Drapers reside during the show's first three seasons.

International politics were also on the radar of the black New Yorkers on the margins of *Mad Men*. Many would have idealized the Cuban Revolution and celebrated Fidel Castro's visit in 1960 when he took up residence at the Hotel Theresa in Harlem. Inspired by a visit to Cuba that same year, black New Yorkers such as the beat poet LeRoi Jones (later Amiri Baraka) and the cultural critic Harold Cruse became representatives of a strengthened black nationalist consciousness. The central figure behind this shift was Malcolm X, minister of the Nation of Islam's (NOI) Temple Number Seven in Harlem. By the early 1960s Malcolm had attracted a range of grassroots black adherents beyond Harlem and the NOI's membership (Goldman; Lincoln; Malcolm X). It is hard to imagine how Malcolm's renown can have escaped the consciousness of the fictional Hollis, the kind of young black working man to whom the NOI's assertively masculine stance might have offered an alternative (Estes, 88–91). Yet it is not until the season 4 episode "The Rejected" (4.4) that Malcolm's existence is even acknowledged, when Peggy Olson, one of the show's white characters, casually refers to his assassination.

Granted, as Michael Bérubé suggests in his afterword to this volume, it would be unfair to expect the show's main characters to possess an early twenty-first-century historical consciousness. Many white northerners were doubtless unaware of or indifferent to the black freedom struggles happening in their cities. But it does not seem unreasonable to expect the show's creators to research the social dynamics of this period as carefully as the white-dominated façade—to make the black political ferment in New York City part of *Mad Men*'s historical common sense.[1]

UNCOVERING BLACK GRASSROOTS ACCOMMODATION

So far I have suggested that *Mad Men*'s quest for authentic representation of racism has led to an overemphasis on southern activism, which scholars have begun to thoroughly reevaluate. But it would also be a mistake to overemphasize political resistance as the major feature of the black working-class imaginary. "There is much more to [African Americans'] living than simply resisting white supremacy," asserts the scholar Eddie S. Glaude Jr. He avers that "if [black] lives are reduced simply to struggle and our stories presume an understanding of black agency as *always already* political, then the various ways [black people] have come to love and hope are cast into the shadows as we obsess about politics, narrowly understood" (78–79). Wage-earning African Americans did not just march, demonstrate, mobilize, and build movement organizations. They also *lived*, which entailed daily accommodations that culturally conditioned the diffusion of grassroots black movements.

It is at this more intimate level of interpretation that the show might have easily drawn us closer to *Mad Men* characters such as Carla and Hollis, portraying the stories behind their public masks. The challenge would be to better understand what cultural critics such as Ralph Ellison, James Baldwin, Albert Murray, and Glaude have identified as the "tragic sensibility" underlying black working-class life—the ability to avoid despair, and even achieve elegance, while confronting a world fraught with danger and contingency. This blues-oriented approach to modernity, Ellison explains, is "an impulse to keep the painful details and episodes of a brutal experience alive in one's aching consciousness, to finger its jagged grain, and to transcend it, not by the consolation of philosophy but by squeezing from it a near-tragic, near-comic lyricism" (*Shadow and Act*, 78). For Murray, the blues idiom constitutes the ability to "maintain the dancer's grace under the pressure of all tempos" (25), while for Glaude it invokes the "beauty of black life and struggle" (11). From this standpoint, strategies of accommodation amounted to neither hopelessness nor capitulation to the structures and logic of white racism. Rather, the blues revealed black workers' ironic tenacity, as Baldwin would frame it in *The Fire Next Time* (1964), in making a way out of no way.

This blues sensibility tantalizingly appears at the edges of *Mad Men*. Consider, for instance, Hollis's oft-cited remark during the elevator ride with Pete Campbell, "Every job has its ups and downs" (3.5). Though the comment is lost on the self-absorbed Pete, it is meant to register with the audience as Hollis's acknowledgment of the nature of his job—a statement that he is resigned to this work but not defeated by it. In an earlier episode, when Peggy ponders how a celebrity like Marilyn Monroe could have been lonely enough to take her own life, Hollis responds, "Some people just hide in plain sight" ("Six Month Leave," 2.9). The comment might be read as an allusion to Ellison's novel *Invisible Man* (1952), capturing Hollis's own sense of black experience in a white-dominated society. The blues philosophy of Ellison's nameless protagonist was never cynical about such circumstances. A Hollis cast more deeply in this mold would, like Ellison, embrace hope for the possibility of a "humanity . . . won by continuing to play in the face of certain defeat" (*Invisible Man*, 498–99). Although Hollis spends his days riding "in a box on a rope in a pit" (Whitehead, 5), the sense of his life beyond some negative void could and arguably should have been developed.

Carla also shows the hint of a blues mode of accommodation. In her study of representations of black domestics in African American literature, the scholar Trudier Harris identifies two major figures: the typically southern "mammy" who identifies entirely with her white employers, compromising her connections to the black community, and the northern "militant" who violently rejects white paternalism (24). Between these two categories are the blues-oriented "transitional northern maids," such as the protagonist of the novelist Alice Childress's *Like One of the Family* (1956), who exhibit neither acquiescence nor outright resistance. Such characters "realize that straightforward political action . . . is unavailable to them yet refuse to merge their personalities completely with those of the white women for whom they work" (T. Harris, 87). This is a fitting description of Carla. Reserved but not timid, she has a maturity that contrasts starkly with Betty Draper's childishness. Although plainly dressed, she wears no uniform, a signifier of the black domestic's inferior status (Katzman, 237). This sets her apart from Viola, the black domestic who works for Betty's parents. Carla's dress thus symbolically narrows the social distance between her and her employers while gesturing toward an autonomous life outside the Draper residence.

Carla tends to the Drapers' children and household, allowing Don and Betty to maintain the façade of normalcy as their marriage collapses over Don's infidelity. Yet in "Six Month Leave," Betty's suffering prompts Carla to violate the guise that she is invisible, that she cannot see her white employer

FIGURE 3.3. Carla moves from cautious silence to overt conflict ("Tomorrowland," 4.13).

except as her employer wishes to be seen. Observing Betty's deteriorating state, Carla warily volunteers the information that she has been married for nearly twenty years. Betty at first rebuffs the invitation to dialogue, then acknowledges the obvious fact that she and Don are separated. "You know what helps?" the housekeeper says. "Splash cold water on your face and go outside. You'll notice things are right where you left them."

Unlike Viola, Carla here does not play the part of Betty's nurturing "mammy." Instead, she tacitly challenges Betty to step outside her immediate anguish to gain a fuller perspective on her circumstances. Carla is simply one woman speaking candidly to another. Yet she is also all too aware of the economic risks of getting too deeply enmeshed in the lives of her employers. Indeed, at the end of season 4 ("Tomorrowland," 4.13) Betty callously fires Carla when the latter allows Sally, Betty's daughter, to visit Glen, a young male friend. Like the "transitional maids" Harris discusses, Carla maintains firm control of her mask. It is only when Betty abruptly dismisses her, compounding the act with a disparaging comment about Carla's (unseen) children, that the housekeeper comes close to challenging her (fig. 3.3).

Carla's overall comportment speaks to the "culture of dissemblance" that, according to Hine, black working-class women developed to project openness while shielding their inner lives from white scrutiny (912, 915). The concept applies equally to the women's restroom attendants, seen briefly in an early scene involving Betty and Mona, the wife of Roger Sterling. In "Ladies Room" (1.2), one of two black attendants, sizing up the high-fashion accessories of the white women on whom they rely for tips, observes, "Those purses get any smaller, we're going to starve." Significantly, it is perhaps the only instance in the entirety of *Mad Men*'s five seasons in which two black characters interact with each other out of the hearing of whites. As with Carla, the women's invisibility is at least partially self-imposed, providing a veil behind which they privately fulminate against racism, sexism, and class exploitation without surrendering their cultural identity or succumbing to self-hatred.

Although these moments give some voice to a blues ontology, they occur largely through glimpses of black characters at work, spaces in which they are isolated from other blacks and almost always under the surveillance of whites.[2] Were the camera instead to pan to the homes of women like Carla and the ladies' room attendants, the audience might learn how black working women's cult of secrecy on the job allowed them to carry out their duties effectively and "to bear and rear children, to endure the frustration-born violence of frequently under- or unemployed mates, to support churches, to found institutions, and to engage in social service activities, all while living within a clearly hostile white, patriarchal, middle-class America" (Hine, 916). In these northern black spaces, life was that "mixture of the marvelous and the terrible" (Ellison, *Shadow and Act*, 20). Working-class African Americans sustained beauticians' associations, Elks lodges, and block clubs while facing the hardcore joblessness that followed automation and deindustrialization. On their coffee tables, copies of the King James Bible, *Muhammad Speaks*, and *Ebony* and *Jet* were laid side by side, their eclecticism revealing black workers' ethos of self-cultivation, and their political and intellectual heterogeneity.

The closest that the series comes to showing African American domestic life is the scene in "Flight 1" (2.2) in which Paul Kinsey throws a party at his apartment. As Pete and Trudy Campbell are shown entering a worn-looking hallway, Trudy assures her husband that she has "no problem with Negroes" but is "just worried about the car." Pete's evident astonishment at the loud revelry at a nearby party, along with Trudy's fear of black criminality, immediately establishes the viewer's sense that Paul lives in a predominantly black (or at least heavily integrated) urban neighborhood whose denizens are engaged in play. Following the sound of loud music and laughter to Paul's apartment door, the two find his party in full swing with rhythm and blues music, drinks, and marijuana on hand. As the white guests from Sterling Cooper eschew the black guests and mainly mingle with each other, the camera never leaves the white regulars.

A similar moment occurs in "The Beautiful Girls" (4.9), when Roger and Joan find themselves accidentally strolling at night through a declining part of town. Joan's anxiety proves well founded when a wild-haired black man, obscured in shadow, robs them at gunpoint and flees. During the tense exchange, Roger instructs Joan to avert her eyes from the gunman's face—an understandable and even wise response. Aesthetically, however, the moment is an ironic reinforcement of black invisibility. The robber wields the power of life and death, but Roger and Joan retain the power not to see him. The encounter leaves them shaken as well as sensually awakened by having survived; they respond by having desperate sex in a semi-hidden walkway. Like the party at Kinsey's, the scene fastens a connection between black criminality and heightened sensuality within the aesthetics of the show.

IDENTIFYING A WORKING-CLASS BLUES IDIOM

By identifying African American vernacular solely with the dangerous and carnal, *Mad Men* misses the antinomies inherent in the "blues matrix" (Baker, 1–14), as well as the nuanced treatment of everyday black life, either or both of which might have informed the show's approach to a mass culture that black vernacular heavily shaped. For example, the New York City beat subculture that Don engages through his affair with Midge Daniels possessed a large African American and Puerto Rican presence (Smethurst, 43–44). The beats' music of choice, jazz, was solidly grounded in the cadences of black working-class life. Alongside rhythm and blues, and soul, it commanded an expansive audience in northern black working-class communities in the early 1960s. In *Blues People* (1963), Amiri Baraka maintained that one could interpret African Americans' evolving ways of thinking about the world by assessing the blues-based musical forms present at a given historical moment (152–53, 211). The evolution of hard bop and soul jazz from the late 1950s to the mid-1960s thus paralleled northern black freedom struggles and African liberation movements, representing black cultural assuredness, desire for individual self-mastery, and yearning for group fellowship and "collective deliverance" (W. Martin, 48–60).

Epitomizing a blues idiom of accommodation and psychic flexibility amid the crises of an early Cold War society teetering between peace and atomic annihilation, "cool" was, as Baraka describes, the ability "to be calm, even unimpressed, by what horror the world might daily propose" (Jones, 213). Notwithstanding the powerful presence of black female jazz voices such as Abbey Lincoln and Nina Simone, cool was, further, a distinctly *masculine* stance, basing a great deal of its prestige on the sexual mastery of women (Porter, 149–90; Saul 63–72). Appropriated by mass media, cool was often deployed as a romanticized racial primitivism by novelists and essayists who regarded blackness as the model for a white heterosexual male virility. Unable to afford "the sophisticated inhibitions of civilization," Norman Mailer noted in his controversial essay "The White Negro" (1957), African Americans possessed a nihilistic "morality of the bottom" that freed them to live in pursuit of immediate pleasure (*Advertisements*, 341, 348). In *On the Road* and other works, the beat novelist Jack Kerouac sentimentalized African Americans as well, though he did so in a more pastoral and feminized vein: black people were more authentically "American," of the soil, and thus worthy of emulation (Nicholls, 533). For both, jazz was the key artifact of black authenticity and white "Negritude" (see also A. Levine).

Mad Men touches on this theme through Don. He is not "hip" in the manner of Paul Kinsey, who pretentiously disavows postwar white bourgeois society. Rather, Don's outward cultural conformity is belied by his unconventional private behavior. At various points in the show's first season, he visits his paramour, Midge, in her Greenwich Village environment, listens to Miles Davis, and smokes marijuana with her and her beatnik friends. At dinner with Roger and Mona Sterling, Don skillfully resists efforts to lure him into discussing his past, tacitly evoking a blues "culture of dissemblance." Late in season 2, during a business trip to Los Angeles, he "drops out" to take up residence among an elegantly decadent group of international jet setters. Earlier in the season, he and his fellow ad execs visit an illegal gambling parlor, where they encounter the black heavyweight champion Floyd Patterson and the (fictional) insult comic Jimmy Barrett. This setting is significant given that "ethnic" entertainers along with black athletes, musicians, and hustlers were imagined as part of the same "hip" cultural underground (Early, 7). The scene not only conveys Don's sense of ease among the hipster crowd but also communicates the idea that ad men as a group were fully part of this subculture. The point is reinforced through the ad men's recurring references to themselves and each other as prostitutes and pimps supplying clients with fine meals, good liquor, music, and access to young women. The disrepute of this lifestyle is hammered home by Pete's wealthy father. "Wining and whoring," he comments disdainfully. "No job for a white man" ("New Amsterdam," 1.4).

Don's bearing, appearance, and social status closely resemble what Gerald Early describes as an urbane white corporate "code of masculine cool" (8), expressed through clothes, cars, women, and other objects of consumption glamorized in *Playboy* magazine (Bryer, 106–7). Suitably, then, in "Hands and Knees" (4.10), Don joins business partner Lane Pryce on an outing to New York's Playboy Club. Don does not manifest the "psychopathy" that Mailer contends aligns his "white Negro" with African Americans (339; also A. Levine, 63). Still, the fact that Don trades his rural underclass background for another man's identity places him in close proximity to Mailer's archetypical rebel. Unlike Mailer's "white Negro," however, Don moves from the obscure margins to a life of bourgeois ease and consumption. Rather than unshackling himself from the pretense of cultural conformity, Don hides within it, adopting an elaborate masquerade. This volatile character symbolizes both the "Man in the Gray Flannel Suit" and the antiestablishment (see the introduction to this volume).

Since *Mad Men*'s main exposition of cool occurs through Don, constituting him as an outsider within, whiteness is the normative prism through which the series treats marginality and "otherness" on matters of race. *Mad Men* thus misses the chance to better unpack the period's cool by showing the working-class black public that fostered it. The audience loses the opportunity to explore how, in contrast to the simplicity and spontaneity imaged by Mailer and Kerouac, the blues idiom of cool was disciplined as well as improvisational, grounded as well as spontaneous, and most important, cerebral as well as earthy. The blues, as Baldwin described it, was also anchored in historical memory, unlike the selective forgetfulness that characterizes Don, or Mailer's "white Negro" more generally (*Notes*, 6; *Fire Next Time*, 18–19, 111).

Nor was the culture of hard bop and soul jazz the only carrier of postwar cool. Audiences faced the absurdities of racism, and the pain and beauty of modernity, not only through edgy music but also through socially incisive humor. This had long been part of the tradition of black working-class self-preservation and transcendence that *Mad Men* refracts. As the performer Nina Simone remarked, "The music and the comedy, the jazz and the politics, it all went together" (67–68). One of the individuals who best personified this stance was the popular nightclub comic Richard Claxton "Dick" Gregory, whose performances before integrated audiences brought black comedic voices from "chitlin' circuit" venues to a contested space in the cultural mainstream (Gregory, *Nigger*; Lorts, 200–231; Saul, 139). Gregory had, in the early 1960s, become one of the nation's highest-paid black standup comedians. A freewheeling participant in northern and southern black freedom struggles, he hobnobbed with Adam Clayton Powell Jr., Martin Luther King Jr., Malcolm X, and the militant activist Gloria Richardson of Cambridge, Maryland (Gregory, *Up from Nigger*, 45–46, 92–93). Only recently removed from the poverty into which he had been born, Gregory viewed the world squarely within the working-class blues idiom, as when he pointed to the irony of making a handsome living riffing on the ways of white folks, in front of white crowds. "When I left St. Louis I was making five dollars a night," he observed. "Now I'm getting $5,000 a week—for saying the same things out loud I used to say under my breath" (*From the Back*, 21).

Laid-back, dressed in a plain suit and tie, and with a cigarette always in hand, Gregory addressed audiences in a deft manner that soothed as well as stung (Saul, 33, 45). Deadpanning about segregation, African American working-class life, the southern black revolt, and the cold realities of racial and economic oppression in the North, he exhibited both the erudition of the black working-class public and the relaxed intensity of a jazz player. Ridiculing the postwar abundance that eluded most African Americans, he remarked: "You gotta realize, my people have never known what job security is. For instance, comes another recession and the economy has to tighten its belt—who do you think's gonna be the first notch?" (*From the Back*, 59). "You know why Madison Avenue advertising has never done well in Harlem?" he quipped; "We're the only ones who know what it means to *be* Brand X" (*From the Back*, 59). On the occasions when an irate white audience member heckled him with the epithet "nigger," he donned a clever mask of accommodation (*Nigger*, 144). "According to my contract, I get fifty dollars from the management every time someone calls me that," he would retort (*From the Back*, 18). Gregory is relevant to *Mad Men* because he spoke about race, class, and power in a manner unavailable to many black laborers in their workaday lives. He accomplished for black men like Hollis what the acerbic comic Jimmy Barrett does vis-à-vis the show's recurring treatments of anti-Semitism and interethnic prejudice among whites. Having obtained his first major break at Chicago's posh Playboy Club in early 1961, Gregory is evidence that the *Playboy*-oriented environment that *Mad Men* recreates amounted to more than a loosening of sexual mores (Gregory, *Nigger*, 142–45). *Playboy*'s editor and publisher, Hugh Hefner, himself a former advertising copywriter, used the magazine to generally celebrate the "good life"—a state of being rooted in the consumption of expensive goods and commitment-free pleasure (Bryer, 26, 187; Fraterrigo, 19). In the process, Hefner helped to sanctify an advanced capitalist economy driven by the rise of Madison Avenue. His sponsorship of the 1959 Playboy Jazz Festival in Chicago, the proceeds of which were donated to the local Urban League, was one of his many initiatives in support of black freedom struggle. Yet, as the

FIGURE 3.4. Toni is introduced to Lane's father and Don at the Playboy Club ("Hands and Knees," 4.10).

historian Marjorie Lee Bryer comments, "Hefner's promotion of civil rights and his use of integration as a marketing tool also *generated* a significant amount of his celebrity and wealth" (299). The swank *Playboy* lifestyle was facilitated by social policies that fostered black structural unemployment as production was displaced by a financial economy (Foster and Magdoff, 18, 128), and that demolished black neighborhoods to make way for sleek bachelor pads and office buildings. Although Gregory praised Hefner as a benefactor, his onstage observations implicitly challenged the market-driven narcissism that his patron defended.

To the extent that Hefner's Playboy enterprises made visible black freedom and culture, they were equated overwhelmingly with manhood. Black women were largely excluded from the magazine's discourse as voices of political and cultural analysis, and during this period they were equally absent within its sexual iconography as centerfolds and "bunnies" (Bryer, 190–91, 342). From this standpoint, the brief appearance of Toni, a black Playboy Club waitress in *Mad Men*'s fourth season, becomes exceptional, though she is only the passing love interest of a supporting character (fig. 3.4).

Gregory's *From the Back of the Bus* contains an intriguing photograph likely taken at the Playboy Club in Chicago (98; fig. 3.5). Interpreted in a particular vein, the image speaks to the underexplored aspects of *Mad Men*'s historical setting that this essay has addressed. Hefner is pictured standing in the foreground, flanked by two women recognizable as Playboy bunnies. All three are in deep silhouette. Hefner, holding his signature smoking pipe,

FIGURE 3.5.
Dick Gregory
and Hugh Hefner
at the Playboy
Club. Photograph:
Jerry Yulsman.
Reproduced with
the permission of
Barbara Woike.

projects self-assuredness in a suit and tie. With his hair cut short, neatly combed and shiny with pomade, he is the pseudo-hipster media mogul dabbling in nonconformity while upholding the essential values of the status quo. He could easily be a prototype for Don Draper: like Don, who is the sum of a constructed identity, Hefner carefully crafted and enacted his persona as an urbane gentleman of leisure. Close in the background but slightly out of focus, a similarly well-dressed Gregory stands on the stage, simultaneously spotlighted and shrouded in shadow. Present but not sharply defined in the image, he is situated, in a manner similar to a Hollis or a Carla, as a half-seen and artful critic of performances of white male bourgeois hegemony. For the *Mad Men* writers, Gregory might suggest the enormous power of this role.

CONCLUSION

In this chapter I have tried to indicate what a more sustained and creative consideration of African Americans' role in the cultural and political landscape of the early 1960s might have yielded—or might yet yield—for *Mad Men*. In presuming a black northern quietude that did not exist and denying access to the domestic and private lives of its black characters, *Mad Men* indulges in a selective forgetfulness. Yet, paradoxically, one of the show's strengths has been to figure black laborers as dormant representations of a working-class culture from which the blues idiom sprang—circling back into the show through the cultural undergrounds that the Mad Men enjoy. Because blacks have been left on the margins, though, the series portrays the social inequalities of the past in order to render them as spectacles for a complacent post–civil rights present.

I suggest that even a sympathetic look at *Mad Men* must recognize that the show's self-aware limits on black representations distort the racial landscape. This is perhaps most true of the present day, when the achievements of postwar black freedom movements remain targets of opposition. Indeed, moving further into the 1960s, the show seems less concerned than ever with expanding access to black characters. Given the new office setting in a building with automated elevators, viewers no longer see Hollis or any other character who might replace him. The Draper divorce makes Carla less visible, and her dismissal at the end of season 4 all but ensures her absence from future episodes.[3]

These omissions are regrettable for *Mad Men*'s white as well as black characters. After all, the blues exemplify an indigenously "American" form of existentialism (Baker, 12; Ellison, *Shadow and Act*, 17, 29; Murray, 58). When Glaude argues that a blues-oriented sense of tragedy requires one to "constantly choose between competing values and to live with the consequences of those choices without yielding to despair" (19), he raises a point that could have as much meaning to Don and Betty Draper as to Carla and Hollis. A more fully developed blues idiom could add shading to the Drapers' alienation and deadening individualism. It could provide another way of looking at the collaborative freedom and creative fellowship that Don and his coworkers achieve in the sequence of events that gives rise to Sterling Cooper

Draper Pryce at the end of season 3. It might even provide some needed context for the infamous scene in which Roger Sterling, wearing blackface makeup, serenades his new bride, Jane ("My Old Kentucky Home," 3.3). Dislodged from any developed context and with race treated in a glancing manner, such images only baffle and offend. Perhaps as *Mad Men* moves into its remaining seasons it will discover the tragic blues traditions of adaptation not only as social movement but also as a way of humanizing life—which might also enrich the world of alienated white executives and their unhappy wives.

NOTES

I thank the following for helpful comments on this work: the editors, Davarian Baldwin, Kent Ono, David Roediger, Dianne Harris, Mark Leff, James Kilgore, Bill V. Mullen, Pat Gill, David Goldberg, and Natasha Zaretsky. This chapter also benefited from exchanges I shared as a 2009–10 Illinois Program for Research in the Humanities Faculty Fellow. I am indebted to the other fellows with whom I participated in conversations on the theme of "representation."

1. This does occur in the season 5 premiere, "A Little Kiss" (5.1), which opens with a sidewalk civil rights protest for fair employment on Madison Avenue. In a scene based on a real-life event, a group of young ad men splash the black demonstrators with water-filled paper bags, setting into motion events that end with the firm hiring its first black secretary, Dawn Chambers (yet another African American character whose upwardly mobile status is signified by a known surname). The episode's concluding scene, in which the cast regulars find themselves face-to-face with a roomful of silent, dignified black job applicants, is a pivotal moment in the series. But such scenes of northern black freedom protest have been the exception proving the rule in terms of the show's treatment of the movement. Proponents of a "long" civil rights movement have challenged the conventional 1955–65 timeline as well as the southern regional focus of the movement. See Hall; Lassiter and Crespino; and Theoharis. For a critical approach to the "long" movement thesis, see Cha-Jua and Lang, 281; and Lang, "Between Civil Rights."

2. A notable departure from this norm occurs in season 5's "Mystery Date" (5.4), when Peggy discovers Dawn asleep in the office afterhours and invites her to spend the night at her apartment. The possibility of friendship is undermined by Peggy's clear ambivalence about leaving her purse unattended in Dawn's presence. Yet the scene at Peggy's apartment is remarkable as the show's most intimate encounter between black and white coworkers, who come the closest to interacting on an equal basis—even though the secretarial work Peggy has left behind is a hard-won employment opportunity for Dawn.

3. Dawn offers the possibility of filling this void, though at the end of season 5 she appears to be merely the latest in a chain of thinly sketched, tertiary black characters.

AFTER THE SEX, WHAT?

A Feminist Reading of Reproductive History in Mad Men

LESLIE J. REAGAN

After the sex, what? If you watch *Mad Men*, you know the answer to that: a smoke, a drink, or both. Perhaps a phone call—and sometimes in the middle, unfortunately, a fire alarm. Sex is a central theme in *Mad Men*, as are the power dynamics and aftereffects of sex, including pregnancy, childbirth, and children (or not). "After the sex" in my analysis encompasses not only the "after" but the "before," the thinking and planning, contraceptives, and conversations about sex and its consequences—in other words, the reproductive ideologies, practices, and technologies of the show.[1] My longer time frame is also historical: I look at *Mad Men* in relationship to the period that it remembers for its viewers today while analyzing the meanings of the show's representations in the present.

As *Mad Men* shows its viewers, a central part of a woman's reproductive history consists in her encounters with gynecology and obstetrics. Like traditional television doctor shows, *Mad Men* has produced accurate medical scenes (see Turow); but more important, it has dared to reveal male supremacy as a problem in medicine. The show's creator, Matthew Weiner, and its writers clearly respect history and understand sexism and gender construction. That gendered awareness helps attract viewers to the show. At the same time, however, by focusing solely on the reproductive lives of its white, elite, and rising middle-class characters, *Mad Men* produces a partial and therefore partially misleading picture of gender roles, the rise of feminism, and the urgent reproductive issues of the period. In *Mad Men*'s rendition of history, the issue of reproductive control in general—and abortion in particular—appears to concern only white women who either want to be career women or do not "need" an abortion because of their privileged situation. As a result, the audience misses how race and class figure in the larger reproductive history of the 1960s. That picture would include the use of abortion among women of color, as well as the political work of black and Puerto Rican women in New York and elsewhere around sterilization abuse and the rights to have children, to be single mothers, and to receive welfare support for their children. The ramifications of this show's representation for feminism and reproductive justice are significant. Given its discussion of gender and reproductive politics, *Mad Men* is a show that feminists may want to both embrace and rewrite.

Mad Men has worked extraordinarily hard to place itself in a specific time—to be accurate and believable as it tells the interwoven stories of office and home, political and civil rights events, and especially gender revolution. DVD sets of the series include time capsules and minihistorical documentaries that detail the research behind the show while also demonstrating Weiner's interest in educating his audiences. Features for home viewing include "Birth of an Independent Woman" and "Time Capsules" on the "historical events of the 1960s"—all recognizable as educational documentaries with historical footage, narrators, professional historian "talking heads," and an objective viewpoint.[2] These extratextual components indicate the care the show's producers have taken to ensure accuracy in the medical scenes. Television historically has committed itself to using accurate terminology and sought the endorsement of medical societies, and, early on, it showed physicians in an exclusively positive light. *Mad Men*'s realistic representation of physicians and their female patients is in keeping with the drive for accuracy, but also with the post-1970s depiction of doctors as less than perfect (see Reagan et al.; Turow and Gans-Boriskin).

Mad Men is unusual and emotionally gripping—especially for its female viewers—when it depicts gynecological and obstetrical scenes as moments of blatant and often coercive male medical authority. Together with scenes focused on birth control, childbirth, and infertility, the depiction validates women's complaints about medicine and men, and shows why the women's health movement of the late 1960s and '70s arose to create women's health centers across the country, demand legal abortion, and insist on female physicians, midwives, and home births. These story lines capture the audience's attention and illuminate a world (now mostly unfamiliar to younger generations) in which contraception and abortion were hard to get and against the law.

In *Mad Men*'s first episode ("Smoke Gets in Your Eyes," 1.1), the "new girl," Peggy, is introduced to the office, eyed by all, and immediately told by the young ad man Pete Campbell, "It wouldn't hurt if you showed some leg around here." She is sent off on errands by the head secretary, Joan, to get what turn out to be office supplies: chocolate and roses for the telephone operators whom she needs to woo. Viewers also see her go to a "Midtown Medical Building." It is 1960. Later, viewers will understand that this too is an errand for an essential office supply: birth control. When we next see Peggy, she is in the doctor's office—which is painted a lima-bean green like nearly every clinic or hospital at that time—reading a pamphlet titled *It's Your Wedding Night. What Every Bride Should Know.* Dr. Emerson walks in. "Joan Holloway sent you over. She's a great girl," he remarks as he lights a cigarette.

This scene is gripping—one can see and feel Peggy's anxiety as well as her perfect gendered understanding about how she needs to perform in order to succeed in obtaining what she wants: the contraceptive pill. She does not respond when the doctor jokes about Joan's sexuality while simultaneously admonishing Peggy about her own sexual behavior and marriage prospects. What most of us today would see as not only inappropriate and rude but also sexist—a term that did not yet exist—was normal in 1960. The fact that Peggy is single and searching for methods to avoid pregnancy means that jokes can be made and she has to endure them, for only a doctor could prescribe the new pill or a diaphragm. Doctors had all the power, and many would refuse a woman like Peggy's request: birth control was still illegal in some states. The U.S. Supreme Court decisions that overturned state laws and made contraception legal are, for the characters in *Mad Men*, still in the future.[3] In 1960 someone like Peggy would have no legal right to contraception.

Jokes about gynecology, breast examination, and women and their bodies were ever-present in medicine in this period. Barron Lerner, who has researched the history of breast cancer, found sexual jokes and mean remarks about women—as patients, colleagues, and wives—throughout the medical literature, and in minutes of professional meetings. Students today are often shocked when they encounter this material, finding it hard to believe that such remarks can be found in print. But no one at the time was trying to hide it. This sexist banter held the male world together and, importantly, made it acceptable for men to specialize in obstetrics and gynecology.

FIGURE 4.1. Peggy at the gynecologist's office ("Smoke Gets in Your Eyes," 1.1).

Few women objected directly; they lived with it. Peggy's exam is the only popular film or television picture of a gynecological exam that I can think of that gets it right in its atmosphere and emotional resonance. Peggy is in a vulnerable position, alone with this male doctor, without a nurse for comfort or implicit protection against male sexual coercion or rape (fig. 4.1). The doctor smokes and says, "Try to make yourself comfortable. Relax," at the precise moment that he pulls down the stirrups. The smoking underlines the doctor's power, marking the office as a space designed for his comfort, not for hers. (The smoking itself would have been a violation of a norm. Doctors did not typically smoke when seeing patients, although illegal abortionists sometimes did; see Reagan, *When Abortion*.) And no one finds those stirrups comfortable. The examination table and stirrups, like the space, are designed for the doctor's ease in looking, not for the patient's comfort. She is prone, knees open — in a position that girls learn from a young age is immoral and dangerous. As the feminist health scholar Terri Kapsalis observes about the gynecological exam, the doctor talks to the woman's vagina, not to her (see also C. Lewis).

As Dr. Emerson begins Peggy's exam, he continues to talk — not about the exam, but about her marital status and about sex, explaining that he is not "here to judge," and yet judging nonetheless. The combination of familiarity, sexualized language, paternalism (a tone expected from doctors of the time), moralizing, and threat, from a man who is not much older than Peggy and may have slept with Joan himself (or wanted to), underscores that all the power is on his side. Peggy is in no position to argue and has to pay the price for trying to gain some control of her sexuality and reproduction. While we as viewers might be aghast or shouting at our TVs, Peggy calms herself by emotionally leaving the scene and immersing herself in the image of a placid lake advertised in a calendar on the opposite wall. She replies, like the good Catholic girl she is, that she is "a very responsible person." She understands quite well what is required of her in order to secure the prescription. She does not challenge the patronizing and rude doctor; she remains polite and subordinate.

In the end, Peggy receives a prescription for Enovid for $11 per month. As a secretary, Peggy earns $35 per week making the pill almost 10 percent of her income. In today's dollars, that would be about $80 per month—a pretty hefty amount for a single working girl.[4] Today's well-meaning future MDs often find it hard to understand the strength of the women's health movement of the 1960s and '70s and the vehement anger at the medical profession that it expressed. It seems so unfair, so aggressive. Yet this scene from *Mad Men* captures a sense of the patronizing, demeaning, embarrassing, and simply thoughtless behaviors that provoked the women's health movement to demand patients' rights (see K. Davis, 20–23, 28). Indeed, this scene could be valuable in medical education today to exemplify poor historical practices and serve as a starting point for discussion of respectful treatment of patients.

Peggy's first day at her new job ends when she is woken in the middle of the night by knocks on the door from the very ad man who insulted her that morning, Pete Campbell. Pete has left his bachelor party and come to her house because, as he tells Peggy, he "had to see her." She brings him into her room. She is armed with a prescription, and viewers might think that she is "protected" (although the pill is not effective instantaneously, and Peggy may not even have started taking it), or the audience might not think at all about protection, since most contemporary television never concerns itself with the issue. That is day one at Sterling Cooper for Peggy and day one for *Mad Men*: the naive new girl is quickly learning the ropes.

The final episode of the first season, "The Wheel" (1.13), also ends with a surprise about Peggy as it follows through on the consequences of her decisions in the pilot. Doubled over with pain, Peggy rushes to the hospital (again with green walls) only to be told by the emergency room doctor that she is pregnant. "That's impossible," she replies. Offscreen, Peggy gives birth to a baby boy. When the nurse brings him to her room and asks her if she will hold him, she refuses. As viewers, we see her sadly looking at the wall, an image reminiscent of her strategy for managing the gynecological examination nine months earlier: imagining herself elsewhere.

In denial. Perhaps that is the quick analysis of Peggy.[5] She may seem like one of the obese women who do not realize they are pregnant until they go into labor, seen on shows such as *I Didn't Know I Was Pregnant* (TLC, 2009–), or like young women who appear in news stories today who give birth in bathroom stalls because they are in denial about their pregnancies.[6] Yet more than anything, Peggy's situation suggests how the stigma surrounding sexual activity and pregnancy can lead some unmarried women to refuse to believe the truth. Many more tried to hide it through abortions, adoption arrangements, and quick marriages.[7]

Peggy says, "I don't understand," but it seems likely that she understands all too well what pregnancy means for her. Observant viewers as the season aired picked up hints of Peggy's pregnancy from fleeting scenes of her vomiting at work and gobbling extra sandwiches, or comments about her expanding waistline. Ignorance and denial do not fit Peggy's character. She does not wear baggy clothing to cover up and hide; she is not obese. She wears structured clothing that covers her shape well. As she says, her pregnancy is "impossible," referring to a biological impossibility, to disbelief, or simply to social reality. It is impossible for Peggy to be "expecting," to show, to bear a child, to be a mother in this society as a single woman, as a working woman, as a Catholic daughter. As a pregnant daughter, she might be kicked out of her home; as a single mother, she could lose her job, have to turn to welfare, and come under state surveillance and bed checks; she could lose her child. As a single mother she would be a stigmatized and shamed woman rather than a respectable one (Pleck; Solinger). Her condition is, as Peggy states so clearly and bleakly, impossible.

Peggy's pregnancy takes the rest of *Mad Men's* characters, and took its audience, by surprise—as planned. What was happening to Peggy's body over the course of the season was a closely kept secret between Matthew Weiner and the actress Elisabeth Moss. In DVD commentary, Weiner and Moss report that the cast and camera crew were "shocked" when Peggy went into labor on the set. Fans blogged about their surprise. This carefully plotted story worked well—the season ended dramatically, leaving viewers waiting for next year's offering. But it also avoided engaging the issue of abortion and the dilemmas that a young woman like Peggy would face in 1960—or in 2007. By having Peggy "not know," *Mad Men* circumvented any controversy that might have arisen from airing a Catholic woman considering or going through with an abortion.

In season 2, Betty Draper echoes Peggy, both physically and emotionally ("Meditations in an Emergency," 2.13). When Betty's doctor confirms that she is pregnant, she says, "I can't believe this. Dr. Aldrich, I *can't* have a baby right now." Betty is the beautiful wife of Don Draper, *Mad Men*'s handsome leading man and increasingly remote husband. The Drapers have two school-age children; they live in a clapboard house in a wealthy white suburb; every day, Carla, their black housekeeper, comes to their home to cook and care for their house and kids until late in the evening.

Peggy and Betty both declare their pregnancies impossible. Yet while Peggy doesn't "understand" that she has gone into labor, Betty, still very early in her pregnancy, understands quite well and can consider doing something about it. As her doctor quickly grasps, she is thinking about the possibility of abortion, though neither of them uses that word. In fact, the word *abortion* is used in a previous episode ("The Benefactor," 2.3), reminding viewers of its controversial status, then and now. In that episode — which references and replays a segment of a television show from 1962 about the subject — *Mad Men*'s audience learns that in the 1960s this word was taboo and that advertisers ran away from it.

Betty says emphatically that she cannot have a baby. Her spotting was not caused by horseback riding, her doctor tells her. His comment provides a subtle explanation for her increasingly frenzied horseback riding, a sport believed to cause miscarriage. Although this was an old idea dismissed by most doctors, desperate women continued to try riding (as well as tennis, swimming, and driving on bumpy roads) as a way to terminate pregnancy (M. Davis, 66). If a woman failed to induce a complete miscarriage, she might hope to induce her doctor to finish an incomplete one. Standard medical procedure to complete a miscarriage entailed performing a dilation and curettage (the same procedure as an abortion). A sympathetic physician might also perform a "D and C" to prevent infection when the real intention was an abortion. Betty neither has a miscarriage nor is bleeding enough — or desperate-sounding enough — to convince her doctor to perform an abortion.

Viewers might assume that a privileged white woman could easily get an abortion, but in fact Betty's options are limited. Her doctor reprimands her and tells her she will be happy soon, and not to worry about her figure. He does not offer her a referral, saying instead, "Mrs. Draper, if we're having the conversation I think we're having, there are alternatives, obviously. But . . . I find it hard to believe that as a married woman of means you would even be considering that. *That* is an option for young girls, who have no

FIGURE 4.2. Betty Draper at the doctor's examination table ("Meditations in an Emergency," 2.13).

other option." Private doctors or nurses often did give patients the name of a reliable doctor, but Betty's does not. Though less crass than Peggy's doctor, Dr. Aldrich is also patronizing and dismissive. When he walks out of the room, the camera moves away from Betty, once again leaving her alone, perched high and still at the end of an examination table. Fully clothed in a dark dress and heels, her skirt arrayed across the table, she is a black monument memorializing a death. It is a funereal portrait (fig. 4.2).

American women in 1962—and other years—did get illegal abortions, and some were able to get quite safe or even legal abortions from doctors in hospitals. There were high-end physicians who performed abortions if one knew how to locate them. A ladies' man like Don could surely find and pay for a safe abortion provider, and there was the option of going to Puerto Rico as many New Yorkers did (although, as Betty's friend Francine dryly notes, Puerto Rico would not have been a good option during the Cuban missile crisis). A rich couple like the Drapers could have flown to Mexico, Japan, or England, where safe abortions were available (Reagan, "Crossing the Border"; Reagan, *When Abortion*). But for someone like Betty, a married mother of two acting alone and in secret, flying out of the country would be out of the question. She could go to Albany, another alternative suggested by Francine, and be back in a day with Carla watching her children. Locating the abortionist, paying for the procedure, and covering it up would not be impossible for a woman like Betty, but it would take great determination. Betty's friend, like her doctor, tells her it will be okay, that sometimes it's better to just not think — exactly what Peggy does in the first season. Betty is ambivalent. She adjusts. She conforms.

Women more desperate than Betty did drive long distances, scrape together the money, or induce their own abortions. Class and racial discrimination were inscribed into access, safety, and danger. When women arranged for an illegal abortion, many were told to wait alone at a street corner, where they were picked up, blindfolded, and driven around the city before being given an abortion in an unknown apartment or hotel by an unseen practitioner (often a doctor). Some abortionists took advantage of their clients' vulnerability and demanded sex in exchange for an abortion; others raped them. The poorest women used their own methods — orange sticks, Lysol, chemicals, and other means. They frequently ended up bleeding, infected, and dying in hospital emergency rooms. Cook County Hospital in Chicago, for example, had an entire ward devoted to septic abortion cases; nearly five thousand women came in every year. Some women died. In New York City, rates of death due to abortion were four times higher among Puerto Rican and African American women than among white women. By the 1960s, illegal abortion (usually self-induced) had become the primary contributor to maternal mortality in the United States, accounting for 40 to 50 percent of these deaths. Abortion had become a pressing public health problem. Public health authorities knew that these deaths were preventable. The hemorrhaging and infected patients profoundly affected the doctors who treated them, repaired their torn uteri, abdomens, and intestines, and held their hands. By 1969 those medical experiences led the majority of doctors in the U.S. to support the legalization of abortion (Reagan, *When Abortion*).

Earlier in season 2, as mentioned, "The Benefactor" foreshadows Betty's dilemma by referencing a 1962 episode of *The Defenders* (CBS, 1961–65).[8] *The Defenders* was a father-son legal show known for its progressive politics, and the episode referenced in *Mad Men*, also titled "The Benefactor," made a stir by openly featuring abortion: sponsors pulled their advertisements; it came up in FCC investigations into censorship by advertisers; and some CBS affiliates refused to air it because, as the Sterling Cooper ad men learn in *Mad Men*, the word *abortion* is used "thirty times." In fact, the controversial episode not only uses the word *abortion*: it also opens with an abortion mid-operation.

"The Benefactor" was part of an emerging public discussion about the nation's criminal abortion laws — one that physicians and attorneys had begun in the late 1950s. In 1959 the prestigious American Law Institute proposed a standardized model law on abortion that states began to consider. Such model laws, or reform laws, would enable doctors to grant legal abortion to preserve the woman's health, in cases of rape or incest, or when the fetus was damaged. Of course, such laws would not have permitted women like Betty or Peggy to have legal abortions. Nor would they have helped most of those who had illegal abortions at the time. Although there was both strong support for and opposition against this legislation, the number of people it would affect was quite limited.

Popular support for reform laws did not arise because of women like Betty and Peggy, or even because the public believed rape victims should have access to legal abortions. Instead, it was the threat of serious birth defects from thalidomide and the German measles epidemic that suddenly made abortion reform more salient to Americans in the 1960s. Thalidomide, an ingredient in cough syrups and sleeping pills in Germany and England, caused babies to be born without arms or legs. When pregnant women caught German measles in early pregnancy, the virus caused fetal heart defects, deafness, blindness, and mental retardation — or all combined. The German measles epidemic threatened every pregnant woman because there was no way to know if one had caught it, no test, no vaccine, and no way to avoid the contagious children blamed for spreading it. Many women and doctors felt that if they faced these kinds of terrible "deformities," the obvious thing to do was to have an abortion and avoid the apparently inevitable outcome of having a "deformed" baby (Reagan, *Dangerous Pregnancies*).

As married, middle-class, white women began to talk bravely about their need for abortion, they changed the picture of the aborting woman from deviant to decent. The specter of respectable women in agony over a potentially damaged pregnancy permitted the first conversation in the United States that listened respectfully to women about abortion. Hitherto, journalistic representations of abortion had focused on deadly abortion or had represented the abortionist as a sleazy gangster and his female client as psychologically sick. Such representations of criminal abortion were racialized as well: abortionists were often depicted as "colored," and the "sick" (white) women who had abortions were often in sexual relationships with men of color (see, e.g., J. Martin).

The *Defenders* episode did important cultural work in 1962 and contributed to a more respectful conversation about abortion. Although the young women depicted in "The Benefactor" are more like Peggy than like the married women concerned about damaged pregnancies, the television show managed to spur conversation by making the abortionist a respectable (and paternalistic) white male doctor who refuses to accept money, and by making his patients sympathetic white characters.[9] In addition to speaking about and representing an abortion in progress, "The Benefactor" challenged the reigning stereotypes by showing a woman who survives her abortion without harm and by offering a depiction of sworn expert testimony before a judge about the facts of abortion. Indeed, in the eyes of television critics and viewers, the show advocated abortion law reform. CBS defended its show, promised to air it without sponsors, and then ran it later than originally planned with a new sponsor. *The Defenders*—and this episode in particular—is remembered by scriptwriters and television historians as particularly significant for challenging sponsors and raising questions about television censorship and prudery. The show continued to take on controversial subjects. Yet even at the time, at least one observer noted that the episode still took a safe route by portraying an unlikely abortionist: a physician who refuses any payments as atonement for his own daughter's death from an illegal abortion (Gould, 43).

Today's audiences would find the original "Benefactor" dated and paternalistic, but they might also see its relevance to current reactionary efforts to recriminalize abortion and state laws that require women under the age of eighteen to notify or obtain consent from their parents in order to have an abortion. In the original show, police enter and raid the doctor's office, finding a young woman on the operating table. *The Defenders* accurately depicts law enforcement at the time: the woman caught in the raid of the abortionist's office is made to testify in court. Seeing an opportunity for a scoop, one reporter violates the norm (described by the judge in the episode) of keeping the names of female witnesses out of the papers to protect them from the shame and stigma of abortion. When the witness's father sees the headlines, he is enraged. He yells at his meek daughter, who shrinks against the wall. Then he slugs her. The scene vividly depicts exactly why some young women, then and now, do not tell their parents about their pregnancies or abortions: they fear paternal shame, rage, and violence (see Joffe, 72–77).

In paying homage to its 1962 predecessor with its title and diegesis, *Mad Men*'s "The Benefactor" implicitly indicates its support for legal and safe abortion, opposes censorship of brave scriptwriters, and, perhaps, suggests that it too would like to be known for breaking social and television taboos. Yet *Mad Men* is less daring than the show that it tips its hat to. In today's climate, *Mad Men* is unusual for having a married woman consider abortion and for giving the topic an accurate and sensitive historical depiction. But it fits with its own times, at least through season 4, in that while an abortion may be considered on television, none is actually depicted. In the opening episode of season 4 ("Public Relations"), viewers learn that Joan has already had two "procedures"; later in the season she visits the office of an abortionist with the intention to terminate her pregnancy, although it becomes clear that she does not follow through. In the past twenty-five years or so, when the question of abortion has come up on television and in the movies, women rarely take that path. Clearly, the preferred "choice" (my quotation marks indicate how problematic many feminists find the term) is for female characters to have a baby. For example, in the movie *Juno* (2007) and the TV hit *Glee* (Fox, 2009–), abortion serves as a plot device: a complication for women and couples who end up choosing the presumably "harder" option of having babies over having abortions (see also Bellafante, "Abortion"; Weinman). Abortion is thus represented in a simplistic way as a simple solution. Somehow abortion no longer renders fascinating stories about the emotional, intellectual, or life development of a woman or a couple—a trend from which *Mad Men* departs only partly. Today's entertainment writers may, on the one hand, think that the abortion story line is already known and that they are writing a more interesting one. On the other hand, they also carefully avoid what they know will be the more politically dangerous narrative.

The Defenders constituted a public space in which the social and sexual issues of the time could be talked about, debated, and then talked about again in other civil spaces, both informal and formal: in media outlets, at dinner tables, at bars, in churches, and in political institutions. This courtroom show addressed many controversial topics, including race relations, infanticide, and consequences of the Holocaust. But only this one episode about abortion resulted in lost sponsors and airtime; eleven stations across the United States refused to broadcast it, and Canada banned it (*Los Angeles Times*).

It is worth noting also that *The Defenders* courageously challenged racial hierarchies in hiring and casting before the advent of antidiscrimination lawsuits, deliberately challenging racial segregation at a moment when the civil rights movement was hotly contested. The show purposely cast black actors in unexpected roles. They did not appear in "strictly Negro parts but as judges, policemen, teachers, etc." (*Sunday Gazette Mail*). Indeed, in "The Benefactor," the jury's foreman is a black man. Putting a black working man in this position of authority and in a position to pass judgment on a white doctor reversed the typical race story in real courtrooms that placed black men as criminals and whites as victims, juries, and judges. When asked by a reporter about the "habit" of hiring black actors for unexpected roles, the actor Robert Reed, who played the younger attorney, responded, "I'm proud of it. We do it as much as we can." "We get complaints from Southern stations," he admitted, "but we expect them. I think they're wrong—dead wrong." Reed revealed that even he, a white celebrity, experienced something of what the "complaints" meant: "I was in Atlanta recently and it was pretty ugly at one point. When you're face to face with bigotry it's a little hard to take" (*Sunday Gazette Mail*). His remarks also repeated the common view among white northerners that racism against African Americans was located in the South, where they did not live.

Almost fifty years later, even as *Mad Men* admirably makes visible the prejudices and racism of the 1960s, it perpetuates the idea that racism was a southern ugliness (see Lang, this volume). The "strictly Negro parts" that viewers expected to see African Americans playing in the early 1960s meant parts such as janitors, elevator men, cooks, and maids—precisely the roles that African Americans play on *Mad Men*. The series conforms to early-1960s expectations, even though it could depict the era accurately while simultaneously challenging the racial consciousness of its viewers as *The Defenders* did. Much could be illuminated about New York and the United States in the 1960s if the show moved its cameras and followed Carla home to watch her life after work and see how she managed her problems in her own social world. Who took care of her children while she watched those of the Drapers?

Part of *Mad Men*'s claim to authenticity, and its audience appeal, lies in its period design, historical accuracy, and story line of gender inequality and revolution. The producers present *Mad Men*, as well as the documentaries included as DVD extras, as both entertaining and educational. That *Mad Men* is so often accepted as a meticulously accurate account of the past is deeply problematic, because it represents the recent history of reproductive rights in a specific classed and raced light: as middle-class and white. In so doing, it obscures the painful experiences and political organizing of women of color and poor women. Women's historians have written a different history, feminists have struggled in alliances, and women of color have developed their own arguments, agendas, and organizations for reproductive rights (see, e.g., Silliman et al.).

Carla's story would complicate and illuminate the women's reproductive histories I have so far discussed by adding new class and racial dimensions. In *Mad Men* as we know it, Carla is understood only through the eyes and needs of the Draper family. By moving away from the perspective of the Drapers, the series could give viewers the pleasure of knowing more than the Drapers do about Carla (just as viewers know more than Betty does about Don's life and more than he does about hers). Developing Carla as a character whose emotional and intellectual depth is rooted in a family and neighborhood would offer new perspectives on the other characters, and a more complex and accurate depiction of the intersectional history of women, race, reproduction, and sex. As the legal scholar Dorothy Roberts contends, "reproductive politics in America inevitably involves racial politics" (9).

Mad Men does not produce happy families. When Peggy "gives away" her baby, it is not a choice. She is an unmarried Catholic woman; a child will bring shame and social rejection to her family. Only with social or family support could she rear a child as a single and working mother. Marriage was a common solution to a premarital pregnancy, but Peggy does not want to marry (at least, not Pete). And she does want to work. She must either give away her child and try to forget, or have an illegal abortion. A warm and helpful response to her and her newborn, along with the expectation that she would continue to work, would have been completely unimaginable to someone like Peggy.

Yet these were white patterns. African American responses to premarital pregnancy were usually different. Since black women were by and large excluded from special homes for pregnant single women, the middle-class black families who wanted their unmarried daughters' pregnancies and babies hidden had fewer options. The black community as a whole tended to regard children outside of marriage in a different light than did their white counterparts, and to embrace rather than reject such children and their mothers (Petchesky; Solinger).

Betty's delivery of an unplanned third child enables the show to depict the kind of hospital delivery that almost all American women experienced at the time ("The Fog," 3.5). After Don rushes Betty to the hospital, suitcase in hand, the nurse bluntly tells him his "job is done" and sends him to wait in the fathers' room — out of the way of the staff. The scene is a perfect rendition of the hospital fathers' room and the gender segregation that was drawn into architectural blueprints and built into hospitals. Don, isolated and bored, smokes cigarettes and drinks. His relative ease as a father of two contrasts with the anxieties of a new father-to-be who shares the waiting room with him. As Judith Leavitt has shown, few hospitals of the 1960s allowed husbands to enter private labor and delivery rooms. As a well-to-do couple in the New York City area, the Drapers could have found a hospital that permitted husbands to attend their wives during labor—massaging their backs, giving them ice, and reminding them to breathe—a privilege the Drapers seem unlikely to seek. Sharing labor and the experience of birth intensified intimacy, which the Draper marriage lacks. Instead, Don shares intimate moments and a bottle of whiskey with the young man in the fathers' room, while Betty cries out for her husband, wondering where he is and with whom he is sleeping. Don's inability to be by her side during delivery is highly structured: the nurses, the rules, and the building itself will not let him out of his space and into hers. The scene is a metaphor of their life together—they cannot get past the structural barriers of homes and offices or the poor communication that such gendered norms ensure.

As Betty calls out for her husband, the nurse acts as an enforcer. When she cries in pain, "I *can't* do it," the nurse sternly responds, "Either you can do it, or we will, but it's going to come out some way." Injected with Demerol, Betty enters a dreamlike state in which she finds her parents in her kitchen along with a bloody Medgar Evers (whose recent murder haunts the episode). Betty's view shifts and we see her mother in a housedress standing next to a suited black man who is sitting at the kitchen table with his head bent: "Elizabeth, shut your mouth," she says; "You'll catch flies." Obediently, Betty tightly closes her mouth. Then she says, like a child reporting a mistake, "I left my lunch box on the bus and I'm having a baby." Her mother scolds her: "You see what happens to people who speak up?" Finally, her father dismisses her: "You'll be okay. You're a house cat. You're very important and you have little to do." Betty wanders back to the hospital and wakes to find herself sitting up in bed with a baby wrapped in a blanket in her arms and Don standing at the foot. In this typical birth of the postwar period, medications have taken away both the pain of childbirth and its memory. Handed her swaddled newborn, Betty looks down and says softly, "She's beautiful." "It's a boy," Don corrects her.

Instead of having awareness of her own body during childbirth, Betty ponders, in her unconscious mind, the state of her marriage and the possibility of death. She hears her parents' warning: she should accept her circumstances, be happy, and keep her mouth shut. Speaking up and acting out—as the black man's dead and bloodied body demonstrates—are fatal. *Mad Men* uses a black body to give a message to its white characters: the murdered black man expresses the emotional and social dangers of deviating from the marriage norm of silence and subordination. In this dream state, Betty wrestles over whether she will accept her situation as her parents advise, or endure the stigma and disapproval that go with divorce. The death Betty fears initially appears to be from childbirth, but the dream warns her of a social death if she speaks out. The pains of childbirth have been muffled; the pains of her married life come to the surface. The Drapers may appear on the outside to have it all, but their marriage is dying, marked by falsehoods, affairs, and alienation. Fittingly, the birth of their third child happens to each of them separately.[10]

Mad Men viewers dart in and out of another waiting room as Pete tries to catch the news about Trudy and their baby ("Chinese Wall," 4.11). Pete seems as disempowered as a woman in labor—others control his visits and knowledge. In this waiting room, it is Trudy's parents who stay and wait and who tell him that he cannot see her. They, like the nurses in the earlier scene, are gatekeepers and regard the birthing woman's husband as a nuisance. It is Trudy's father who gives first-time father Pete some man-to-man advice: "You need to calm down. I was at a baseball game when Trudy was born. Go about your business!" Trudy's father quickly reminds his son-in-law to keep business and family separate when Pete brings up work worries at the hospital. Later Don turns on Pete and blames the firm's loss of an account on Pete's excessive interest in his wife and the baby on the way. Pete has crossed a gender line with his girlish interest in babies and cervical centimeters. He gets the point, gets back to work, and, in the end, learns about the birth of his child from a secretary's note.

MAD MEN'S SCENES OF gynecological examination, pregnancy, childbirth, marriage, and childrearing demonstrate the social enforcement of gender, heterosexual marriage, and the nuclear family. When the Drapers bring their new baby home, he cries in the night. Betty hears him and attends to him—shoulders bent and weary—alone. The episode ends with her back to the viewer, head and shoulders sagging, moonlight through curtains casting lines on her back ("The Fog"; fig. 4.3). Weiner has encapsulated Betty Friedan's *Feminine Mystique* (1963) in this mise-en-scène: Betty is imprisoned in her big house with her inattentive, adulterous husband and a new, demanding baby. (Naming Mrs. Draper "Betty" may even be a deliberate allusion to Friedan.) In many ways, Weiner has produced a show that successfully depicts the widespread frustration among white women in the early

FIGURE 4.3. Betty responding to her crying newborn ("The Fog," 3.5).

1960s with their lot as subordinates and sex objects. In addition, he demonstrates men's frustration at masculine gender roles and limited connection to their children.

I admire the many ways in which this show gets the depiction of power right—from Peggy's gynecological exam in the show's first episode to Joan and Peggy's developing friendship in the season 4 finale as coworkers who observe male power and their own exploitation with disgust. Once again they rage as, in a familiar pattern, Don marries his twenty-five-year-old secretary and the firm collectively celebrates, while taking Peggy—who has won the firm's first new account—for granted ("Tomorrowland," 4.13). Likewise, Joan's essential work is recognized with more duties and a new title—but no raise. In the same episode, Betty impetuously fires Carla and refuses to give her a reference. Her power as the upper-class white woman employer could not be more clear. All of these moments point to the producers' and writers' historical awareness of the many forms of inequality, and the show's ability to speak to multiple audiences.

But at the same time *Mad Men*'s rendition of history is stuck in history itself. It is limited to a specific white, middle-class view of the time, one famously promulgated by Friedan, which accidentally ignores or deliberately erases how race and class produced differences among women, including different political demands (Friedan; Horowitz, *Betty Friedan*). At the time that this show takes place, activist women of color organized in greater numbers for welfare rights and against forced sterilization. Working women of all races fought for equal pay, for better-paying "men's" jobs in construction and mining, and for workplace health and safety. Gerda Lerner, one of the founders of women's history, was dedicated to putting black women and class at the forefront of the emerging field of women's history (*Black Women; Majority Finds*). A minority of radical scholars like her understood that Friedan and the mainstream portrait of 1960s feminism whitewashed a more complex history. Since then, feminists, womanists, activists, and historians have developed a rich literature documenting these histories and reinterpreting the white portrait of 1960s and 1970s feminism. Women's history and reproductive history are more complex when race along with class, sexuality, religion, age, (dis)ability, and other characteristics are taken into account. Doing so is essential for dismantling the notion that white, middle-class Americans are the norm — the "real" Americans. The stories and perspectives of white, middle-class Americans should neither set the terms of political and policy debates nor dominate historical memory.

NOTES

1. Clearly this is a normative heterosexual perspective, although gay women and men had children before the "gayby boom" of the 1990s. Gay parents in the 1950s and '60s, however, were closeted, passing, and living in heterosexual marriages, just as they appear to be in *Mad Men*'s first four seasons.

2. *Mad Men: Season 2*, DVD (4-disc set, Lionsgate, 2008); special features on discs 2 and 3.

3. In 1965 *Griswold v. Connecticut* found that married couples had a right to privacy, and contraceptive practices were protected. The rights of the unmarried to birth control were not recognized until 1972 with *Eisenstadt v. Baird*.

4. On Peggy's salary, see Lipp and Lipp. On the history of the pill, see, for example, Marks.

5. Comments on blogs analyze Peggy as being "in denial," and all of the commenters appear to be surprised. See "Ten Most Shocking Moments in Mad Men #2: Doctor Tells Peggy She's Pregnant," http://www.amctv.com/mad-men/videos /2-doctor-tells-peggy-she-is-pregnant (accessed 3 July 2012).

6. On *I Didn't Know I was Pregnant*, see Calhoun.

7. Most women who have late abortions today do so following bad news about fetal health, or are poor and thus their pregnancies progress as they raise money or seek help arranging reduced fees (see Joffe).

8. Print held at the Wisconsin State Historical Society.

9. Both are unmarried. One is a victim of rape; the other is a wealthy model who expresses her gratitude for the doctor's refusal to perform an abortion when he perceives that she really wants a child. In this, the show hardly represented typical abortion cases but, rather, dramatic and sympathetic stories.

10. In later episodes of season 3, Don is more frequently alone with his children. Further, Betty immediately leaves him to enter a new marriage with a wealthy man, thus bypassing the issue of single motherhood.

THE WRITER AS PRODUCER; OR, THE HIP FIGURE AFTER HBO

MICHAEL SZALAY

> Before I ask: how does a literary work stand in
> relation *to* the relationships of production of a period,
> I would like to ask: how does it stand *in* them?
> —Walter Benjamin, "The Author as Producer"

Inspired by *The Sopranos*, and created by Matthew Weiner just before he joined that show, *Mad Men* was, Weiner would later recall, "obviously written for HBO." Weiner twice offered his show to the network but "never got a straight explanation for its pass" (Edgerton, "Selling," 6). Ultimately the series was picked up by AMC, a commercial cable network. All the same, Weiner shot it in the production studios used by *The Sopranos* and, with the blessing of the *Sopranos* creator David Chase, employed directors, cinematographers, line producers, and production designers who had been *Sopranos* regulars. All this to visible effect: *Mad Men* wears on its immaculately tailored sleeves its debt to the "quality" drama pioneered by *The Sopranos*, whether in its distinctive visual style and high production values or in its nuanced story arcs and three-dimensional characters. But in this chapter I argue that in addition to being influenced by HBO drama, *Mad Men* is also about what it means to write for, produce, and market a quality series—despite its focus on advertising in the golden age of broadcast television. As we watch Don Draper manage his copywriters and negotiate his creative vision with clients and account executives, we watch an instance of what

John Caldwell calls "industrial reflexivity," one that expresses a fantasy about what it means for writers to become the creators and showrunners of their own quality projects (*Production Culture*, 1).

David Chase was hardly the first to create, write for, and produce his own television series; he was preceded by the likes of Norman Lear, Aaron Spelling, Steven Bochco, Chris Carter, Aaron Sorkin, and many others. In *The Producer's Medium* (1983), Horace Newcomb and Robert Alley termed these typically male figures, long considered the *auteurs* of television, "creative artists." More recently, that role has involved becoming a "showrunner." The work demanded of this position far exceeds that traditionally required of producers and includes everything from managing production workforces to marketing "transmedia franchises" that, in the words of Denise Mann, "successfully mobilize a host of ancillary revenue streams, engender merchandising opportunities, and spawn a multitude of spin-offs, including digital content and promotions for the web" (99).

In the case of quality drama especially, these heterogeneous responsibilities transform each other such that it becomes impossible to distinguish between the showrunner's creative and executive functions; the result is a paradigmatically neoliberal vision of the writer and his labor. To borrow from Gérard Duménil and Dominique Lévy, the showrunner is "top management," and constitutes "the *interface* between ownership and management" (14). As Duménil and Lévy have it, "the reliance on top management has been a prominent feature of neoliberalism from its inception," and has required weaning top management of "sectional behavior" that is born from its identification with lower workforce echelons (14, 8). That reliance has been particularly important to HBO, in part because, as Toby Miller explains, the network has long "wished to avoid the tight nexus that broadcast television had with a unionized workforce and job security." Miller argues that HBO "represents the disorganized, decentralized, flexible post-Fordism of contemporary cultural capitalism. It relies on a variety of workers, many of whom do not have tenure and benefits, who are employed by small companies even when they sell their labor to the giant corporation of Time Warner" (x). HBO showrunners are the nexus of this reliance: they supervise their contingent labor force on behalf of Time Warner, even as they themselves works as temporary employees, albeit exceptionally well-compensated ones. It's worth asking whether they prove themselves worthy of this position, and of the financing that comes with it, by proposing series that advertise their willingness to participate in a predatory management structure.

As Caldwell points out, all scripts are, in their first instance of viability, business plans and branding opportunities; the earliest story sessions and producers' meetings for television projects will invariably include personnel from the financing, marketing, coproduction, distribution, merchandising, and new media departments of the network in question. Discussions at such meetings do not sacrifice art at the altar of commerce in any simple sense, at least not in the case of quality drama. There is good reason to believe that HBO, for example, takes seriously the artistic ambitions of figures like David Simon, who, in his introduction to a book on *The Wire*, calls the series a "visual novel" akin to *Moby Dick* (25). But a showrunner is not an author in a literary sense; a salaried employee, he or she manipulates for profit "the relationships of production," to recall Walter Benjamin, *in* which he or she stands, and revises literary precedents accordingly. I am interested in *Mad Men* because its industrial reflexivity revises the novelistic realism to which critics such as Lauren Goodlad and Caroline Levine (both writing in this volume) see it indebted: even as it seems absorbed in its historical milieu, even as it seems, pace Georg Lukács, to anatomize the "not immediately perceptible networks of relationships that go to make up society" in the early 1960s ("Realism," 38), it references a network of relationships particular to the television industry and, more specifically, the production and marketing of *Mad Men* itself.

Quality dramas like *The Sopranos* and *Mad Men* depict charismatic leaders — Tony Soprano, the "don" of New Jersey, and Don Draper, a successful "creative" — whose capacity to earn while navigating complex labor relations suggests Chase and Weiner's ability to do the same. At its inception, *The Sopranos* was to be about a TV producer, not a mobster (Lawson, 211). Echoes of that idea remain: in the first season, Chris Moltisanti, frustrated that he is not yet a captain, sets out to write a screenplay titled "Made Men." One of Chase's made men, Matt Weiner made good on Moltisanti's ambition while riffing on his title. Weiner's show, moreover, analogizes Draper's position as the creative director of Sterling Cooper to his own as the showrunner of *Mad Men*. Draper never functions as the true showrunner of Sterling Cooper or (in season 4) Sterling Cooper Draper Pryce — jobs that surely belong to Joan Holloway. Nor does he have any desire to run his firm's accounts (a role he explicitly disavows after the Hilton fiasco in season 3). But he does serve as an extension of the Matt Weiner brand insofar as he derives his creativity from — and not in conflict with — the managerial functions required of him. A successful creative executive, Draper embodies the fantasy that creating a show and running it require the same kinds of labor.

And yet the terms *creator* and *showrunner* indicate different relations to a productive process that both *Mad Men* and *The Sopranos* understand as inherently exploitative and self-alienating. A "labor leader" who extorts local unions, Tony Soprano extracts value from his equally predatory captains. "You're supposed to be earners," he tells his team. "That's why you've got the top-tiered positions" ("For All Debts Public and Private," 4.1). Chris Albrecht, the HBO executive who developed *The Sopranos*, might have directed these words to Chase, as Chase might have to anyone on his team, including Weiner. By the logic of these shows, Chase is most like a creator when hearing similar words, and most like a showrunner when speaking them. Tony Soprano is divided in what we might think of as an analogous fashion. As a character, he manages a workforce. But he is also the product that Chase sells to ownership. A fetish, he allows us to witness management relations within HBO being transformed, to recall Marx, into "the fantastic form of a relation between things" (*Capital*, 165). We might say, in this respect, that Soprano captures the manner in which industrial reflexivity is always also reification — a form of structurally required forgetting. If Soprano's relations with his captains represent Chase's "interface" between ownership and management, the character himself represents the site at which Chase's labor, along with the labor of his workforce, disappears into something subject to ownership by HBO. However, that labor only partially disappears: it lingers in the show's compensatory fantasy that the right kind of creativity and management might somehow transcend inherent contradictions between the interests of labor and capital.

Don Draper is a particularly reflexive instance of this commodity fetishism, insofar as *Mad Men* understands him as source of labor and, also, as a brand, as the product that he and his team must create and sell. He is, in fact, a contradictory fetish that taps into and reworks an ignominious cinematic precedent. I want to suggest that Draper's contradictory relation to management takes shape, to borrow from Michael Rogin, around "the surplus symbolic value of blacks, the power to make African Americans represent something besides themselves" (14). In Rogin's account of early Hollywood cinema, "blackening up and then wiping off burnt cork" functioned for Jews in the film industry as "a rite of passage from immigrant to American" (38, 5) — one in which the performance of blackness cleansed Jews of their ethnicity and humble class origins and left them able to pass as white. If, as Goodlad argues (this volume), *Mad Men* codes Draper as "virtual Jew," it does so in a pointedly self-aggrandizing fashion. For ultimately, Draper's interstitial racial identity indicates his ability to navigate workplace relations that—in Weiner's self-pitying design—render the firm's creatives akin to black labor serving white ownership. Draper holds in abeyance the contradictory demands of labor and management (and functions, thereby, as both a writer and a producer) by seeming both black and white and, at the same time, neither—by seeming, in the lingo of the early 1960s, a hipster, a "white Negro." *Mad Men*'s famous style, in other words, inheres in more than just the cuts of its suit lapels, the clean lines of its midcentury modernist furniture, or the "American décor" that Weiner associates with Jackie Kennedy. It inheres also in the fetishistic racial fantasy with which Weiner asserts his own ability to create, produce, and market quality drama.

IT'S NOT TV, IT'S HIP

Don Draper's thinly veiled contempt for small-minded clients and pandering account executives reflects Matt Weiner's frame of mind when he conceived the series. Draper articulates the "rage and resentment" that Weiner felt while writing assembly-line scripts for the CBS comedy series *Becker*. "Who could not be happy with this?" Draper asks in the second episode of the series, "Ladies Room," trying too hard to convince himself that he has arrived. Weiner says those sentiments were his, and explains them in light of the fact that while writing for broadcast television he enjoyed a handsome paycheck but felt unfulfilled. And so we must understand Draper's surreptitious breaks from the office to view art-house films or read Frank O'Hara as a version of Weiner's own longing for a more creative enterprise; a longing made suddenly coherent, he recalls, when he first watched *The Sopranos* and felt all at once "less alone" (Edgerton, "Selling," 6).

Cinema and poetry are crucial insofar as they represent what Weiner felt was missing from his *Becker* job but saw on offer in Chase's show. As Dana Polan notes, *The Sopranos* crystallized "a discourse of television quality" that imagines "television achieves aesthetic value precisely when it starts to look like something other than television—particularly, the established visual arts" (*Sopranos*, 87). And yet Weiner's appreciation of the show's profitability suggests why it mattered that *The Sopranos* was, in fact, television: "There was such depth and complexity to the show," he recalls, "and at the same time it was so commercially successful" (Edgerton, "Selling," 4). Rather than confirm any trade-off between the demands of art and commerce, *The Sopranos* suggested the necessary interrelation of aesthetic and commercial success. According to Weiner, quality "is a commercial decision," and is enabled by having to make commercial decisions. "I am of the persuasion," he has said, "that budget constraints are very, very good for creativity" (Edgerton, "Selling," 8, 13). In this account, so congenial to ownership, "creativity" inheres, ultimately, not in the product made, but in the managed relations that govern production.

The question at the heart of a range of other quality dramas, I would add, is not whether or not to sell, but what and how to sell, and to whom. From this perspective, *Mad Men*'s interest in advertising distinguishes it from dramas on both pay and advertising-dependent networks whose claims to quality involve not just seeming as if they were "not TV," in the words of HBO's advertising slogan, but as if they were unlike the mainstream commodities sold on TV. In fact, many of these dramas are about the production or supply of illegal substances and services: heroin and cocaine in *The Wire*, marijuana in *Weeds*, vigilante justice in *Dexter*, crystal meth in *Breaking Bad*, munitions in *Sons of Anarchy*, vampire blood in *True Blood*, alcohol in *Boardwalk Empire*, and prostitution in *Hung*.

Preoccupied with contraband, *The Sopranos* is the touchstone for this trend and begins to explain why the organized supply of illicit consumables—as opposed to the kind sold on *Mad Men*—should speak to a dramatic form pioneered by a pay television network. For decades HBO has offered material beyond the purview of the Federal Communications Commission (FCC), which no longer exerts strong regulatory control over cable programming. In 1977 HBO convinced the U.S. Court of Appeals for the District of Columbia that the FCC had exceeded its authority in regulating cable industry programming. Central to the ruling was the notion that because cable TV was purchased and not "freely distributed" like radio and broadcast TV, it was, in essence, like newspaper publishing and thus subject to First Amendment protection (Santo, 21, 25). That ruling was pivotal to the evolution of pay television and finds repeated expression within *The Sopranos*. Toward the beginning of the show's pilot, we see Tony picking up a newspaper at the end of his driveway, an action he will repeat throughout the course of the series, often while suspiciously glancing up and down the block as he scans for government agents. Securing lines of communication and distribution beyond federal jurisdiction is important to both the character and the network: circumventing the FBI is as central to Tony's fortunes as circumventing FCC regulations was to HBO's. Quality dramas produced in the wake of *The Sopranos* recognize as much when they understand themselves as responses to the reality, expressed by Vincent Rizzo on the second episode of *The Sopranos* ("46 Long"), that "as long as the human being has certain appetites for gambling, pornography, whatever, someone's always going to surface to serve these needs, always."

In the media business, underground products require underground content. HBO has tended, when not telling stories about industry insiders (*The Larry Sanders Show, Curb Your Enthusiasm, Entourage*), to take as its dramatic subjects those who are alienated, not fully enfranchised, or living in varying degrees of conflict with the mainstream: prisoners (*Oz*); mobsters (*The Sopranos*); closeted morticians (*Six Feet Under*); outlaws (*Deadwood*); circus freaks (*Carnivàle*); polygamists (*Big Love*); and vampires, werewolves, witches, and fairies (*True Blood*). Even a drama about the police in Baltimore would become, in *The Wire*, a drama about the marginalization of one police unit within a larger system of relations ultimately hostile to its goals. No doubt *Mad Men* seemed, to Weiner, an appealing project for HBO because it begins on the threshold of the 1960s, the decade singularly associated with the explosion of the marginal into the mainstream. Draper is a cool-hunter before the letter: an alienated white-collar executive who prowls New York's bohemia, he works for an industry that would begin to package and sell subcultural styles to conventional consumers in the 1960s — as HBO has done since the 1990s. Of course HBO might have thought, in turn, that Draper appeared too unapologetically on the wrong side of these developments, too smugly invested in the status quo, and that *Mad Men* was, as a consequence of its commitment to his ultimately hegemonic subjectivity, insufficiently "hip."

Hip is not "a marginal fillip but a central current in American culture," John Leland reminds us (288). Remarkably elastic, that current today polices the boundaries of countless cultural forms, fashions, and lifestyles — calibrating distinctions between the authentic and the ersatz and calculating degrees of proximity to the fountainheads of significant change. The particular hip I have in mind, however, provides the ultimate horizon for all aspirations to underground status within the United States, and is a variant of the peculiarly American tradition of blackface minstrelsy. In Eric Lott's formulation, minstrelsy was a "theatrical practice, principally of the urban North, in which white men caricatured blacks for sport and profit" (3). A "clumsy courtship" animated by complex motives, minstrelsy allowed white men to negotiate the "panic, anxiety, terror, and pleasure" attendant upon their identification with black men (50, 6). To Lott, that courtship persists: "Every time you hear an expansive white man drop into his version of black English, you are in the presence of blackface's unconscious return"; the legacy of blackface "is so much a part of most American white men's equipment for living that they remain entirely unaware of their participation in it" (5, 53).

Hip culture was certainly part of the equipment for liberal novelists writing at the end of the 1950s and the start of the 1960s, whether they were purveyors of serious fiction like Norman Mailer, Ralph Ellison, and John Updike, or pulp novelists like George Panetta and John Schneider, both of whom chronicled the advertising industry in terms that prove remarkably germane to *Mad Men* (in *Viva Madison Avenue!* [1957] and *The Golden Kazoo* [1956], respectively). These writers, I argue elsewhere, participated in a "coalition culture"—evident most famously in the period's jazz, rhythm and blues, and rock and roll—that militated on behalf of new unions between black and white voters and, in particular, the institutional needs of a changing Democratic Party (*Hip Figures*). Arbiters of hip for readers who were not, these novelists branded the liberalism of their moment. HBO works with this same model. As Avi Santo points out, citing the critics Mary Kearney and Jim Collins, networks like HBO are "designed to build coalition audiences" (30). HBO unites those audiences under the aegis of a hip house style, inaugurated in 1984 by its CEO Michael Fuchs and long central to the network's ongoing efforts, to understand itself as a kind of edgy and sophisticated MTV for adults. AMC unites its audiences in a similar fashion: its efforts to emulate HBO involved adopting the slogan "Long Live Cool."

One audience has always mattered more than others. As Jane Feuer has argued, quality television has long been addressed to "quality demographics": affluent and white consumers between the ages of eighteen and forty-nine ("MTM Enterprises," 4). But we might add that HBO-style drama understands the typically white members of that demographic as themselves internally divided coalitions, each of them constitutively ambivalent about his or her "quality" and therefore possessed of a paradigmatically hip double consciousness. A familiar conceit in this drama involves the protagonist who straddles two lives: one pedestrian and conventional, the other racy and dissident. There is the pot-dealing suburban mom in *Weeds*, the meth-producing high-school teacher in *Breaking Bad*, the serial-killer husband and father in *Dexter*, the gigolo high-school coach in *Hung*. Each of these series caters not to true outcasts, but to affluent whites who long to be both inside and outside the mainstream. Chase differentiates *The Sopranos*, the godfather of these shows, from the "corporate fascism" of broadcast television, which reverently depicts "authority figures" who are "looking out for us," such as doctors, judges, lawyers, and cops (Lawson, 214). But Chase's series was remarkable because Tony Soprano was the mob boss *as* husband, father, barbequing suburbanite, and therapy patient: at once radically out-cast and wholly representative of HBO's law-abiding viewership. In just this way, Soprano was both white and off-white. On one occasion, he complains to his analyst Jennifer Melfi about "Wonder Bread wops" who are as boring as "your average white man." She asks, "Am I to understand that you don't consider yourself white?" His reply: "I don't mean white like Caucasian" ("A Hit Is a Hit," 1.10).

It was David Simon, and not Chase, who would fully elaborate hip as racial discourse and thereby extend HBO's inaugural brand, first consolidated in its global broadcast of the "Thrilla in Manila," the title bout between Joe Frazier and the ever-hip Muhammad Ali in 1975. According to Ishmael Reed, *The Wire* exemplified the network's tacitly racist desire to seem hip, not simply because it was "tawdry," "one-dimensional," and "riddled with clichés," but because it aimed to offer affluent whites a portrait of what life is really like in black inner cities and thereby advance the career of its creator, Simon (30, 31). There is much more to say than this about *The Wire*'s treatment of poverty and race, but it is undeniable that the show's urban anthropology provided white liberals, in addition to many other things, an opportunity to slum from their living rooms. And Reed, who considers Mardi Gras a deca-dent Confederate pageant, would no doubt find as much evidence of min-strelsy in Simon's next project, *Treme*, an extended love letter to the black musical traditions of New Orleans. *Boardwalk Empire*, created by Terrence Winter, who also worked on *The Sopranos*, is of a piece with *The Wire* and *Treme* in the relish with which it makes African Americans the mascots of an à la mode Jazz Age consumerism able to satiate illicit desires and unify the otherwise diverse constituencies — ethnic whites, women, blacks, and WASPs — that its protagonist struggles to appease. Indeed, like *Mad Men*, *Boardwalk Empire* depicts blackface performances.

My goal is not to adjudicate Reed's dispute with HBO, but rather to dem-onstrate how series like *The Wire*, *Boardwalk Empire*, and *Mad Men* encode the conditions of their production and consumption by deploying "the sur-plus symbolic value of blacks." For Winter and Weiner especially, African Americans symbolize the double body of the commodity: at once concrete and abstract, they conjoin labor power and exchange value. Put more specifi-cally, they represent the downward mobility of the workforce that the suc-cessful showrunner must manage even as they underwrite the aspirational hip of the market that the series aims to reach.

The very first scene of *Mad Men* invokes African Americans as a test mar-ket (echoing an analogous scene in F. Scott Fitzgerald's *The Last Tycoon*

[1941]). The camera pans toward Draper's back, and moves over his right shoulder, reproducing the line of sight in the series logo, whose black and white tones prefigure the conversation Draper here strikes up with a black waiter in a segregated bar. At ease with the worker in a way that seems exceptional to a racist white supervisor at the same bar, Draper tries to discover what it would take for this man to give up his preferred Old Gold brand of cigarettes and switch to Lucky Strike, the account on which Draper is then at work. The worker won't be budged; he will remain loyal to his brand ("Smoke Gets in Your Eyes," 1.1). Ultimately, over the course of the series, Draper will convert to *his* brand. But his conversion is only stylistic, for this resolutely white series is not really interested in winning black viewers. Rather, it means to chronicle Draper's historically inevitable conversion to the period's liberalism, and the corresponding acceptance, among Draper's class fragment, of hip sensibilities — such that it will seem utterly unremarkable in season 4 when Draper's firm, which worked for the Richard Nixon campaign in season 1, hires as its art director a countercultural photographer who helped the Lyndon Johnson campaign dramatize the southern resurgence of the Ku Klux Klan. At no point will that acceptance require that Draper become overtly preoccupied with the fate of the African Americans who surround him and provide the labor on which he unthinkingly depends. Nor will it require him to become overtly committed to explicitly black styles. The point is rather that he will prove able and willing to consume those styles, in derivative form, as he does when he slums in an integrated Greenwich Village.

In the Greenwich Village scenes in season 1, Draper is not exactly what Norman Mailer called a "white Negro": he disdains the ethos of the Village and makes no effort to understand or identify with black culture. But he is something of a hipster manqué during these surreptitious visits to the New York underground. The Jewish heiress Rachel Menken suggests that he is as alienated from WASP society as she is; in response, he spouts sentiments straight from Mailer's essay: "You're born alone, you die alone, and this world just drops a bunch of rules on top of you to make you forget those facts. . . . I'm living like there's no tomorrow," he says, "because there isn't one" (1.1). As Mailer made clear, existential gestures like these deracinated the hipster's more overt stylistic affectations, insofar as they likened the plight of whites worried about the bomb to that of blacks faced with racial violence. Such gestures render "authenticity" both authoritative and subject to exchange. They obliquely invoke racial characteristics even as they decouple race from its ostensibly literal moorings and suggest that it is, instead, something performed: a mantle to be assumed or discarded, a way for members of one group to become members of another and yet remain themselves, a figurative rather than a literal means of seeing color.

These stylistic gestures were of great value to a changing Democratic Party: they offered white male suburbanites a low-cost way to view themselves as simultaneously inside and cast out from the center of political power — in short, as possessed of both white and black skin and thus as both like and unlike the African Americans who were then joining the party in record numbers. No doubt similar gestures remain valuable to the professionals and managers who watch *Mad Men*, especially those eager to overlook the disciplinary nature of their class position. These viewers, we might speculate, would forget that they belong, in the words of Barbara Ehrenreich and John Ehrenreich, to a group of "salaried mental workers who do not own the means of production and whose major function in the social division of labor may be described broadly as the reproduction of capitalist culture and capitalist class relations" (12). *Mad Men* negotiates these class relations by adumbrating a particularly American vision of capitalist culture, one in which the white mental worker's blackness signals, in contradictory fashion, his creativity on the one hand and his vulnerability to mechanization and replacement on the other. For the professional-managerial class, relations strain at the point of their hyphenation: a class comprising both professionals and managers must necessarily demonstrate how and why professionals (typically governed by guild-bound strictures) and managers (typically governed by organizational efficiency) can form a single interest group. Draper's ideological function is to demonstrate, against all indications to the contrary, that far from being in tension, these commitments are one and the same thing; he proves capable of executive creativity by teaching his creative team how to be, and how not to be, black.

SOMETHING MORE THAN SHOESHINE

Written by Matt Weiner, the season 2 premiere, "For Those Who Think Young," depicts Draper at loggerheads with Herman "Duck" Phillips, the head of accounts at Sterling Cooper. Phillips wants Draper to hire younger, hipper creative personnel and wants individual accounts worked by small collaborative teams of writers and artists. Anticipating Draper's resistance to his autonomy as writer and creative director, Phillips approaches Roger Sterling, who urges Phillips to talk to Draper directly. "Look," Roger says, "Don is talent. You know how to deal with that, don't you? Just assume that he knows as much about business as you do. But inside there's a child who likes getting his way." Draper will resist Phillips because of his own child-like propensity to "think young." Phillips wants young creatives because he thinks they think young in the way that the young consumers he hopes to reach think young. But as Draper tells Sterling, "Young campaigns don't necessarily come from young people."

This is a version of the logic behind the historic Pepsi campaign to which Draper dismissively refers: as Stanley Hollander demonstrates, that campaign sold an ideal of "youthfulness or what might be labeled youngness" to young and old alike (Leiss et al., 319). Writers, Draper thinks, are labile. "Stop writing for other writers," he tells Paul Kinsey. Writers should instead write for themselves, since they contain multitudes. "*You* are the product," Draper later instructs Peggy Olson, "you feeling something." Lynne Joyrich (this volume) reads this line as a recognition of the fact that for broadcast television, "the viewers themselves—not the programs, nor even, exactly, the objects in ads—have always been the true commodities: the industry operates by selling audiences to advertisers." On this view, Don's advice articulates the difference between the "first-order commodity relations" and the "second-order commodity relations" at work respectively in subscription-based and commercial television. In essence, subscription TV sells programming directly to subscribers, while commercial TV uses programming to sell its imagined viewers to advertisers (Rogers et al., 46). But Joyrich's reading does not make full sense of the context in which the line is spoken. Draper admonishes Olson to understand herself as essential to the business and account execs who do not sufficiently value her creativity. The complaint he levels at Sterling when asked to think young, which he will repeat elsewhere, is that "clients don't understand." Draper's vision of creativity aspires to first-order commodity relations: he would sell directly to consumers whom he ostensibly understands better than clients or account men like Duck. Of course Draper is not urging Olson to preoccupy herself with those consumers; his point is that she is true to consumers when true to herself and her work. This is the credo of the professional: heed your craft and its requirements and the rest will take care of itself.

And yet Draper is not Olson. She writes the copy for Mohawk Airlines while he supervises her efforts. Draper does not enjoy an ownership stake in the ad agency that employs him until the end of season 3; but already, here, his executive position complicates his account of creativity. Weiner's DVD commentary likens Draper's supervision in this instance to that of a show-runner overseeing a writing team. In fact Weiner likens Draper to David

FIGURE 5.1. The break room or an office? Joan decides where to place the Xerox copier ("For Those Who Think Young," 2.1).

Chase; he observes that he once enjoyed the same mentoring that Draper is here providing Olson. And on another occasion, Weiner recalls that Chase spoke of the television writer just as Draper does to Olson: "David viewed himself as the audience and the people in the [writing] room" (Edgerton, "Selling," 6). Chase's capacity to view himself as both the audience and a staff writer indicates not his recognition that his audience is the true object of sale (*The Sopranos* depends on first-order commodity relations), but his willingness to understand himself as both the creator and consumer of a product that is, ultimately, him. His is the brand that HBO sells, just as Draper's is the brand that Sterling Cooper sells to prospective clients. Olson can never truly be the product: like all the other copywriters, she works for Draper, selling *his* brand.

The episode "Think Young" understands these labor relations in racial terms. At one point, two black deliverymen wait for Joan Holloway to decide where to place the Xerox copier they have just delivered (fig. 5.1). Those standing about greet her first thought, the break room, as an intrusion of work into leisure. But her second thought—somebody's office—is still more ominous, and makes plain that the instrument of mechanical reproduction and the black labor that delivers it together capture the obsolescence that threatens the older "copy" writers, who worry they are about to be replaced with younger, newer models of themselves.[1] At the conclusion of the first creative meeting of the episode, we cut to Carla, the Drapers' black domestic worker, cleaning dishes. "Carla, Bobby's turning blue out there," Betty Draper observes with her usual hauteur. Black and blue: the episode likens Betty's authority over Carla to Don's over his team, and Bobby's change of color suggests that those team members (who have just called themselves "the little ones") are in the process of becoming black. After Draper interviews a very young creative team ("He's such a hipster," Weiner says of one of them in his DVD commentary on the scene), we cut to a black and a white mover with Joan and the copy machine, now in the hallway. The interracial movers are different from the first two, and the message is clear: the black workers are as replaceable as the older copywriters.

The secretaries who will operate the new machine share the most with its working-class movers. Olson has only recently left this clerical workforce and is, as a consequence, especially proximate to black labor. That proximity is the buried message in Draper's exhortation that she imagine herself "the product." After evaluating a mock-up for Mohawk Airlines that Olson and Sal Romano have produced to his specifications, Draper declares himself "uninvolved." The ad's racy appeal is too "obvious." Olsen confidently counters, "Sex sells." Draper replies, "Says who?" The question is singularly odd, because Olson's assertion reproduces almost verbatim Draper's earlier claim to the same effect: Draper is who. It is as if, in this moment, as he evaluates the product of his own oversight, he cannot recognize that part of him that created the ad. He continues: "Just so you know, the people who talk that way think that monkeys can do this. They take all this monkey crap and just stick it in a briefcase completely unaware that their success depends on something more than their shoeshine." It is at that point he tells her that her feelings are what sells, "not them" and "not sex. They can't do what we do, and they hate us for it."

Draper's conceit blackens the worker alienated from his labor. "Monkeys" code "African Americans": the product of the copywriter's labors becomes "monkey crap" and then "shoeshine," a word that might refer either to the act of polishing a shoe (labor then associated with African Americans) or to the polish itself (then associated with blackface routines). Self-alienating labor is black labor; Olson risks becoming a monkey when she reproduces the assumptions of a production regime that would understand her work as mechanized and easily reproduced. Appropriate, then, that upon leaving this meeting, she returns to her office, where Joan has decided to place the copying machine. Lest we miss the implications of Joan's decision, we cut to

Draper standing next to a black elevator operator and riding to street level. The scene captures the racially inflected downward mobility that threatens Olson and, by extension, the firm's copywriters, male as well as female.

From one perspective, everybody at Sterling Cooper faces the threat of downward mobility. Pete Campbell's father insists upon the advertising industry's intimacy with blackness. Mrs. Campbell is a member of the blue-blooded Van Dyke family, which once owned all of the land north of what is now Manhattan's 125th street. The Dyke has burst: this land is now Harlem, which is presumably why Mr. Campbell seethes that his son is moving too far north up the island. Mr. Campbell's objections to advertising are more explicit. Dripping contempt, he lampoons his son's work on Madison Avenue. "Wining and whoring," he spits; "no job for a white man" ("New Amsterdam," 1.4). *Mad Men* understands this claim in contradictory fashion. Paul Kinsey, Sterling Cooper's most conspicuously liberal copywriter, extols the wonders of the market to Freedom Riders: the consumer has no color, he announces to his disbelieving black companions. Back north, Kinsey dates a black woman and writes a short story about a night he spent in Jersey City "with all these Negroes." "We all got along," he brags. "Can you imagine how good that story is?" ("5G," 1.5). But Kinsey falls prey to his own hipness: he supplies the names of young talent to Sterling without realizing they are on offer as his replacements.

Draper, in contrast, rises to the heights that he does because he transmutes his proximity to black labor and overcomes the self-alienation implicit in it. Identified throughout the first season with blacks (as well as Jews and gays), he lives in terror of being outed as a deserter and the illegitimate son of a poor farmer and prostitute. At the end of season 1, Campbell discovers these secrets and relays them to Bert Cooper, who later uses it to blackmail the once proudly unfettered Draper into signing a contract with the firm. But in time, that firm will become synonymous with Draper. The season 4 premiere, "Public Relations," dramatizes that ascension: "We are all here because of you," Olson tells him. "All we want to do is please you." In a metadiscursive conceit that drives this home, Olson and Campbell service the Sugarberry Ham account: they strategize how to sell "Hamm," the star around whom they are arrayed. "There's always a name in every partnership that defines who they are," a reporter from the *Wall Street Journal* tells Draper, in an interview that marks his overdue acceptance that he must sell himself for the good of the firm. Embracing this role, Draper channels his proximity to black labor into market magic: his interview ends the episode, and his voice dissolves into the song "Tobacco Road," performed by the British Invasion

FIGURE 5.2. Roger in blackface ("My Old Kentucky Home," 3.3).

band the Nashville Teens. Erskine Caldwell's Depression-era novel about white tenant farmers living alongside African Americans is transformed here into a power-pop hit: "Bring that dynamite and a crane, / Blow it up, start all over again." In this context, Draper's humble origins are less a liability than a condition of his success, a condition almost conjured, we might speculate, by the product upon which his firm is centrally dependent: tobacco.

Draper's hip creative destruction requires breaking down distinctions and absorbing them. It is his idea to start a new firm at the end of season 3, and he facilitates his plan by kicking down the door of the art department. In his commentary for "Think Young," Weiner describes the comingling of writers and artists on creative teams as an overcoming of segregation. He might also have described the creative and accounts departments at Sterling Cooper as segregated—so insistently does *Mad Men* associate copywriters with blacks and account executives with WASPS—and Draper's overcoming of that segregation as an incipiently hip act of racial integration. This dynamic assumes its most properly symbolic form in the third-season episode "My Old Kentucky Home" (3.3), as we cut between an exclusive country club and the Sterling Cooper offices. At the club, Roger Sterling sings in blackface to his young wife Jane, as Campbell, Cooper, and Draper look on (fig. 5.2). At the office, Kinsey and Olson smoke pot. Draper attends the country club but calls the increasingly enfeebled and ridiculous Sterling "foolish" at the end of the party. In "Think Young," Phillips describes Sterling as "the bridge between accounts and Don." But Sterling's power wanes as Draper's waxes. Draper, and not Sterling, will bridge creative and accounts, and he will do so less by assuming Sterling's responsibilities and style than by recasting them in an appropriately hip idiom. Sterling performs his minstrel routine "with a little shoe polish" (3.3), but Draper embodies a different kind of polish: Sterling's polish reappears, dematerialized, as Draper's deracinated racial style.

Sterling's blackface figures the embarrassing and outré manner in which Sterling endeavors to think young and, by extension, mediate between creative and accounts. Draper will learn to mediate between departments as a creative, though a creative with a clarified sense of his role. In "Public Relations" (4.1), when he is confronted with his reluctance to sell himself to a reporter, Draper asks the partners, "Who gives a crap what I say anyway? My work speaks for me." But it does not speak the way he thinks it does. Bert Cooper replies, "Turning creative success into business *is* your work. And you have failed." He succeeds, the episode makes clear, when he sells the work of others as his own, a process that will require him — in a manner that reworks Sterling's blackface — to be simultaneously white and black. He has already refused to acknowledge Olson's contribution to his award-winning commercial for Glo-Coat floor wax (in a plotline that subtly revises Weiner's own troubled relationship to Kater Gordon).[2] But this episode finds him polishing his image and transforming himself into a marketable brand in ways that revisit the racial metaphor with which he described the labor of creatives to Olson. When, alone in his apartment, Draper shines his shoes while watching this commercial, the echo of "Think Young" is pointed: he has become one of those who "take all this monkey crap and just stick it in a briefcase completely unaware that their success depends on something more than their shoeshine."

Olson's labor disappears into Draper's shoeshine: burnishing his own image at the expense of hers, he symbolically arrogates to himself the status of both black worker and white owner. Advertising copywriters sell their labor for a wage to advertising firms, which extract surplus value from that labor by reselling it as "creative work" to corporations that generate surplus value, in analogous fashion, by reselling at a profit the congealed labor of those who manufacture their products or provide their services. Similarly, writers for commercial television sell their labor to production companies that resell that labor as creative work to networks, which sell airtime to corporations lured by the prospect of reaching those viewers who consume the creative work in question. Draper closes the loop. The agent as well as the

FIGURE 5.3. Meet Don Draper (end of the opening credits).

recipient of the shine, he extracts surplus value from Olson, and yet experiences it as the extraction of value from himself: in this, the comforting self-delusion of the professional-managerial class.

The instrument of his own dispossession, he is, polish in hand, implicitly in blackface. As Susan Willis reminds us, blackface functions as "a metaphor for the commodity. It is the sign of what people paid to see. It is the image consumed, and it is the site of the actor's estrangement from self into role. Blackface is a trademark, and as such it can be either empty or full of meaning" (189). Draper is self-estranged and trapped within the commodity form. But *Mad Men* understands that self-estrangement as both the cause and effect of his capacity to become a creative executive: symbolically black, he is exploited, but possessed of an outsider's purchase on the fantasies of white Americans; manifestly white, he converts that perspective into capital. As Ta-Nehisi Coates remarks in an article titled "The Negro Donald Draper," Draper is, "in the parlance of old black folks, passing." Coates is quick to add, however, that "the irony that animates *Mad Men*" is the fact that Don's "double consciousness," derived from being symbolically black, "makes him, indeed, doubly conscious, doubly aware. Don Draper sees more."

That double vision, which would convert alienation into empowerment, finds expression at the start of every episode. Wolfgang Haug describes consumers lured in by shimmering and promissory phantasms that drift "unencumbered like a multicolored spirit of the commodity into every household." These phantasms, Haug maintains, promise consumers a "second skin" (50).

The opening credits of *Mad Men* depict something like this scenario, but in reverse, as the interior of a room opens outward into a world of multicolored spirits. A silhouetted outline of a man walks into an office, stares at his desk, and places his briefcase on the floor. The camera lingers on that briefcase, which is as pitch black as the man himself and which, at least by the start of the second season, will figure as black the creative labor that white executives convert to capital. Somehow heavier than the man who carries it, the briefcase falls through the floor first as the office dissolves, just before the man too falls downward, past barely outlined buildings adorned with the alluring images of women used to sell products. The buildings then dissolve as well, until the camera falls straight through a title that reads, "Created by Matt Weiner." Having passed this symbolic threshold, the falling figure emerges from his vertiginous descent in easy possession of his space, sitting casually, smoking, somehow liberated by the white collar that seemed before to constrain: meet Don Draper, showrunner, brand, and trademark, at once empty and full of meaning (fig. 5.3).

NOTES

1. These issues were pressing: "For Those Who Think Young" aired months after the conclusion of the 2007–8 Writers Guild of America strike, during which writers risked replacement while pressing employers to grant them a greater revenue share from DVDs, and other electronic "copies" of their work.

2. Gordon was Weiner's personal assistant before he promoted her to staff writer. The two earned an Emmy for cowriting the season 2 finale, but he fired her before the start of the third season.

PART TWO
MAD AESTHETICS

THE SHOCK OF THE BANAL

Mad Men's *Progressive Realism*

CAROLINE LEVINE

The pleasures of popular culture have long been a target of attack. Where up-holders of high culture have worried about the seductions of lowbrow sensa-tionalism and violence, Marxists have argued against the profitable industry that produces mind-numbing entertainment to fill the hours not committed to deadening and dehumanizing labor. Both conservatives and radicals have bewailed the passivity of a mass audience lulled into a mindless stupor by frivolous amusements.[1] And it is precisely pleasure, according to theorists of the Frankfurt School, that distracts us from the possibility of resistance. Theodor Adorno and Max Horkheimer write, "To be pleased means to say Yes" (144). Television and media scholars have worked for decades to un-settle knee-jerk objections to popular pleasures, but the media itself con-tinues to circulate dire warnings about the consequences of enjoying mass culture too much.[2]

In a brilliant study of nineteenth-century theories of novel reading, Nicholas Dames makes the case that the suspicion of media pleasures has remained relatively constant for the past two centuries, but its targets have shifted. In our own time, Dames argues, philosophers including Richard Rorty and Martha Nussbaum have held up the nineteenth-century novel as a model training ground for democratic citizenship, contending that the absorbed attentiveness demanded by long realist texts provides an anti-dote to the lazy pleasures of television and the Internet. Ironically, however, nineteenth-century thinkers often understood absorption in the novels of their moment in precisely the opposite terms, as producing habits of indo-lence and inattention, distracting readers from the other, more important as-pects of social existence. The strange fact that the same readerly experience can be cast as a virtuous, arduous attentiveness and as a listless automaticity masks a crucial continuity: for more than a century critics have persistently valorized active labor over lazy pleasure (Dames, 18–20, 98).

I begin this way because I want to draw attention here to a technique of televisual pleasure that I call the "shock of the banal." I associate this plea-sure with three of the great, critically acclaimed television serials that have hit the screen in the postnetwork age: *The Sopranos* (HBO, 1999–2007), *The Wire* (HBO, 2002–8), and *Mad Men*. And it is *Mad Men* that puts this plea-sure to the best political use. Critics have roundly condemned the show for inviting its viewers to feel smug and self-satisfied. I suggest, however, that this critique takes part in a long tradition of presupposing the evils of popu-lar pleasures, rather than engaging in a genuine analysis of the work that they do. For all its pleasures, the shock of the banal has potentially progressive — even radicalizing — effects.

While on first glance *The Sopranos*, *The Wire*, and *Mad Men* may seem dif-ferent from one another in mood and focus, they share a dedication to a ver-sion of realism that surprises us, ironically enough, with ordinariness. Long defined by their concern with the quotidian, realist representations are not often associated with the goal of startling their audiences. And if they do err too much in the direction of thrilling plots or surprising characters, they risk losing their claims to verisimilitude. "All this is very exciting," wrote a reviewer of the sensation novel *Lady Audley's Secret* in 1863, "but is also very unnatural" (*Living Age*). Thus it may seem strange — even paradoxical — to insist on joining shock to banality. But it is the peculiar achievement of *The Sopranos*, *The Wire*, and *Mad Men* that they all generate a jolt of surprise from precisely the most humdrum of experiences.

Take the premise of *The Sopranos*, for example: a Mafia boss suffers from panic attacks and has to learn from weekly therapy sessions to let go of the dream of total control. We could of course read this opening allegorically, as a symptom of the Mafia's breakdown, or even of the collapse of a whole na-tion's confidence (see D. R. Simon); but the literal yields its own pleasures: the surprise of seeing the typically glamorized figure of the ruthless Mafia don reduced to the condition of the most mundane of bourgeois circumstances. As Tony struggles to convince his mother to enter a nursing home, and his son, A.J., is diagnosed with borderline attention deficit disorder, the criminal mind startles us most not by a willingness to commit violence or by a struggle to maintain power, but by its entanglements in the commonplace. As Chris Albrecht of HBO puts it: "[Tony has] inherited a business from his dad. He's trying to bring it into the modern age. He's got an overbearing mom that he's still trying to get out from under. Although he loves his wife, he's had an affair. He's got two teenage kids. . . . He's anxious, he's depressed, he starts to see a therapist because he's searching for the meaning of his own life. . . . The only difference between him and everybody I know is he's the don of New Jersey" (qtd. in Delaney).

The Wire makes a comparable set of representational moves. If at first we expect a conventional face-off between lawful cops and lawless robbers, we soon realize that the police department and the underworld drug business share a similar set of organizational hierarchies and pressures. The business of drugs turns out to produce the same kinds of pecking orders, promotions and demotions, incentives for good work, quality assessment, and business mergers as official institutions.[3] Stringer Bell's borrowing of *Robert's Rules of Order* for his cross-Baltimore drug consortium is perhaps the most elegant example of the spread of mundane forms.

At times the show makes the similarities between official and unofficial organizations explicit. In the beginning of season 3, for example, the detectives Jimmy McNulty, Lester Freamon, and Kima Greggs target Drac, a garrulous mid-level drug dealer in Proposition Joe's hierarchy (fig. 6.1). Drac reports to Lavell Mann, a "soldier" who is unlikely to inform on Prop Joe. "But if we take [Lavell] off," Freamon explains, "They gotta promote *someone* to replace him." "What makes you think they'll promote the wrong man?" asks Police Commissioner Burrell. "*We* do it all the time," responds Lieutenant Daniels. Burrell laughs, but it is worth noting that he also uses this point to turn the conversation to the question of Daniels's own promotion, telling him that his wife's run for office is prompting the mayor to hold up Daniels's position ("Time after Time," 3.1). Throughout its five seasons, *The Wire* involves the shock of recognizing that the supposedly sensational criminal underworld is uncannily like the most humdrum bureaucracy: subject to bad management, ineffective organizational plans, and a frustrating absence of qualified personnel. It shares much more with the workaday world of the mass of middle-class viewers—including academics—than conventional cop dramas have taught us to expect.

Mad Men does not dwell on the workings of a criminal underworld, but

FIGURE 6.1. The mid-level drug dealer Drac in *The Wire* ("Time after Time," 3.1).

given its creator Matthew Weiner's frequent participation as a writer for *The Sopranos*, it is not surprising that the AMC show bears some resemblance to its HBO forerunner. "Both are alien and amoral worlds in which people do terrible things," writes Anna McCarthy in *The Nation*, "and both shows draw us in by exposing the vulnerability of the monster" (*"Mad Men's"*). But even beyond these thematic concerns, I would argue that AMC's show offers a remarkably similar pleasure in the shock of the banal. As the first season serves up three-martini lunches, car travel without seatbelts, pregnant women smoking cigarettes, and confidential conversations between a woman's husband and her psychiatrist about what she has said in therapy sessions, we are invited to dwell with surprise on the vast distance our own culture has traveled in a mere fifty years. "The recent past," we learn, "is a different world" (McCarthy, *"Mad Men's"*). We are startled less by sensational plot twists or characters' hidden depths, in other words, than by the recognition that eating raw eggs or smacking a neighbor's child across the face used to be so awfully ordinary.

All three shows prompt a pleasure that lies, at least in part, in recognizing everyday assumptions just far enough removed from us to feel distant while remaining strangely familiar. But *Mad Men* is in some ways an inversion of the other two. The ordinariness of *The Sopranos* and *The Wire* is astonishingly similar to the ordinariness of the contemporary middle class but occurs in circumstances that are exotic—the murderous underworld of Mafia and drug trade. The ordinariness of *Mad Men* is remote but occurs in typically bourgeois homes and offices. The HBO shows surprise us with the banal in extraordinary places, while *Mad Men* startles us with extraordinary practices in the most banal of places.

These models of familiarity-in-strangeness and strangeness-in-familiarity probably bring to mind Freud's notion of the uncanny. For Freud, the *un* in *unheimlich* refers to the negation of the experience of feeling "at home," which produces discomfort and unease. But since the sensation of uncanniness emerges from desires that have been repressed, and since those desires begin in the self, they are in some sense *more* intimate and private—more *heimlich*—than the experience of feeling "at home." For Freud, then, the unheimlich necessarily tacks back and forth between familiarity and strangeness.

And yet these three extraordinary television serials do not offer us a strictly Freudian version of the uncanny. If there are infantile feelings to be censored in *The Wire* and *The Sopranos*, they are those that are most out in the open to viewers: violence, vengefulness, and greed. Thus the usual experience of the uncanny is turned upside down: what return, unbidden, are the routines of ordinary life, their very mundaneness producing our frisson of surprise. The role of the repressed in *Mad Men*'s version of the uncanny is subtler still: when the Drapers, at the end of a picnic in an idyllic scene, dump their garbage on the grass and leave, or when the children run around the house covered in dry-cleaner bags (fig. 6.2), these startling actions gesture not to the fulfillment of certain frightening and shameful desires but to another, fully functioning regime of thoughtless habits, different from our own but equally routinized and automatic. What has been repressed is another system of repression. That which, in Freud's terms, "is familiar and old-established in the mind and which has become alienated from it only through the process of repression" (241) is a cultural-historical past instead of an individual psychic one. And this version of the uncanny produces affective results very different from our usual accounts: not feelings of anxiety or a desire to subdue foreign elements, but rather a kind of comic pleasure.

It is of course this particular pleasure that has drawn the most persistent critique of *Mad Men*. From the beginning, critics have charged that the show invites us to feel smug about ourselves. Mark Greif wrote in the *London Review of Books* in 2008:

FIGURE 6.2. Sally wearing an "uncanny" dry-cleaner bag ("Marriage of Figaro," 1.3).

Mad Men is an unpleasant little entry in the genre of Now We Know Better. We watch and know better about male chauvinism, homophobia, anti-semitism, workplace harassment, housewives' depression, nutrition and smoking. We wait for the show's advertising men or their secretaries and wives to make another gaffe for us to snigger over. "Have we ever hired any Jews?" — "Not on my watch." "Try not to be overwhelmed by all this technology; it looks complicated, but the men who designed it made it simple enough for a woman to use." It's only a short further wait until a pregnant mother inhales a tumbler of whisky and lights up a Chesterfield. . . . *Mad Men* flatters us where we deserve to be scourged. As I see it, the whole spectacle has the bad faith of, say, an 18th-century American slaveholding society happily ridiculing a 17th-century Puritan society—"Look, they used to burn their witches!"—while secretly envying the ease of a time when you could still tie uppity women to the stake.

Similarly, Melissa Witkowski in the *Guardian* argues that *Mad Men* offers "an attractive fantasy that creates an illusion of distance between our past and our present," and so flatters the contemporary viewer: "The expected, self-congratulatory response is: 'Look how far we've come!'" (see also Schwarz). The presumption here is that we take pleasure in the remoteness of a historical past that was characterized by injustice and ignorance, which allows us to feel distant and superior.

But there is a crucial element to *Mad Men* that this critique overlooks.

The shock of the banal would not work in a representation that merely distanced us from the world represented: it must offer us the play of familiarity in strangeness. As with *The Wire* and *The Sopranos*, the series gives us characters compelling and familiar enough that we cannot thoroughly detach ourselves. This is part of what makes *Mad Men* a pleasurable and popular drama, but it is also what always and necessarily undermines the position of easy superiority. Unlike *The Sopranos* and *The Wire*, however, *Mad Men* also uses the shock of the banal to train our attention on the fact of rapid historical change. That is, it repeatedly reminds us that a familiar, recognizable world of home and office has been transformed within a short period — much briefer than an average lifespan. "Look how far we've come" must surely be followed by "and in such an incredibly short time!" Thus *Mad Men* does not invite us to displace pernicious assumptions about sexism, racism, and homophobia onto an exotic, far-off place or time, but brings them just close enough to us to give us that feeling of uncanny familiarity — of being both at home and not at home.

Part of what irritates *Mad Men*'s critics is precisely the series' emphasis on social transformation: the notion that it persuades us that we have come farther than we actually have, that it prompts us to believe we are beyond racism and sexism and homophobia, living in an enlightened present. This irritation depends on the presumption that there has in fact been very little social change since 1960. While I would be the first to agree that our society continues to be structured by racial, economic, and sexual inequalities, I would also argue that *Mad Men* does something far more important, politically, than to show us difference where there has in fact been sameness. It confronts us with the reality of social change; it compels us to face the fact that social worlds can — and do — undergo transformations, both large and small. That is, if there have been even minor shifts in the texture of ordinary experience, from habits of smoking and drinking, to childbirth, to routine assumptions about divorce and women in the workplace and gay male sexuality, to definitions of rape and the relaxed acceptance of casual racism and anti-Semitism, then how on earth have these changes come to pass? From episode to episode, *Mad Men* actually gives us very little reason to leap to the conclusion that we are now postrace and postgender, but it does give us a strong incentive to entertain the serious and radical political questions: Is change possible? And if so, how does it happen?

Here, I think, is where *Mad Men* is actually far more progressive than any other show on television. The show reminds us in all kinds of ways — from the passing mentions of civil rights to Kurt's casual coming out — that the radical social movements of the 1960s are looming on the horizon. Critics have sometimes charged that these moments in the series are too marginal, and that a better show would have made them central (see, e.g., Peterson, "Doesn't"). But while it is certainly true that the series has so far failed to treat such figures as civil rights activists or feminists in any detail, *Mad Men* does make them *historically* pivotal: it conveys an elite social world that, all unknowingly, is about to come under attack by a powerful set of movements that will change it for good. And this is rare in contemporary popular culture. Since the Reagan years, it has been commonplace in the United States to show contempt — if not outright hostility — for the movements of the later 1960s. From Allan Bloom's *Closing of the American Mind* (1987) to popular resentment against affirmative action, welfare, and the "permissive society," the 1960s has been vilified as the source of a range of contemporary ills. But *Mad Men* never suggests that this was either a naively idealistic or a misguided moment: to the contrary, we feel the social movements of the later 1960s approaching, and they are on the verge of unsettling and transforming the world of *Mad Men*, making it strange to us now. Thus it is the political activism of the 1960s that makes it possible for us to experience the shock of the banal at all.

I would go so far as to say that the series makes us long for the 1960s. Its three major women characters — Betty, Peggy, and Joan — all have powerful moments of yearning for fulfilling professional work. Joan's may be the most moving: after her success with a daytime television soap campaign in "A Night to Remember" (2.8), Harry abruptly thanks her for filling in as a reader of television scripts and asks her to train a replacement — a man, of course. Joan's disappointment in the moment is compelling (fig. 6.3), though she quickly reasserts her composed professional façade and even tells Peggy that she would not trade places with her if she could. But Joan's brutal and unequal marriage belies her blithe confidence in the happiness she imagines will come to her from her femininity alone, and her accomplishments as a script reader have suggested that she has the talent and enthusiasm to go far in a professional career. However ambivalent Joan is herself, the show puts us squarely on the side of women at work. And while the women achingly imagine themselves in successful careers, Don Draper gives us ample time to consider the feelings of purposelessness, alienation, and emptiness that come from career success divorced from other, more personal kinds of satisfaction. Thus *Mad Men* prompts us to yearn to overcome the separation of workplace and home life. In our own moment, conservatives routinely argue that such integration is impossible, and blame the 1960s for the demise of the

FIGURE 6.3. Joan when told that she is being replaced ("A Night to Remember," 2.8).

family: we might think of popular figures such as "Dr. Laura" Schlessinger, whose best-selling book *In Praise of Stay-at-Home Moms* (2009) insists that women should be the primary caregivers of children and explicitly targets "Alice Walker" feminists as the problem (15; see also Schlessinger, "Mommy Wars"). In this context, *Mad Men* is a valuable counterweight, intent on provoking viewers' desire for precisely the kind of feminist activism that conservatives have habitually disparaged.

Even what might seem like trivial signs of change in *Mad Men* have serious political implications. In "The Gold Violin" (2.7), after the Drapers have finished a picnic in the woods, they prepare to leave by dumping their garbage on the ground (fig. 6.4). Don casually tosses his beer can into the woods. This blithe disregard for the landscape feels startling in our own historical moment, but our visceral objections to littering come from somewhere. We can trace them to the concerted efforts of such figures as Lady Bird Johnson, whose campaign for national "Beautification" became highly visible when she helped to engineer the passage of the Highway Beautification Act in 1965, resisting powerful corporations that insisted billboards were essential to the economy. Changing the traditionally passive character of the first lady into an activist role, she also orchestrated publicity for the conservation of national parks, for urban renewal, and against pollution and littering, ushering in the green movement and making the case for its importance not just as a matter of cosmetic beauty but as an economic and social problem with wide-ranging implications: "a total concern for the physical and

FIGURE 6.4. The Drapers litter after a picnic ("The Gold Violin," 2.7).

human quality of the world we pass on to our children" (qtd. in Carlin, 288). *Mad Men* is silent on all of these details, but what the picnic scene makes starkly clear is that the mainstream of a national culture has shifted from one set of entrenched routines and expectations to an equally automatic but strikingly different set of norms in less than fifty years. On first reading, then, the littering scene may seem a mere comic effect—at best laughable, at worst self-congratulatory—but the environmental implications are arguably significant indeed. Much of the debate about climate change today revolves around the question of whether or not we can change our habits, and whether we can do so quickly enough to avert an ecological catastrophe; *Mad Men* reminds us that we have changed them before, and with surprising speed. And yet the show does not distance us from this past altogether, but always and significantly maintains the play of sameness and difference: after all, the impulse to exploit and vandalize the natural world remains strong, and thus the uncannily tranquil, relaxed, familiar feeling of this scene may serve to evoke at once our own ecological habits and the ones we have left behind.

As for the other shocks of the banal, they too point us to a variety of activist campaigns. In 1962 the Consumers Union, along with the Association for the Aid of Crippled Children, sponsored a conference on "passenger car design and highway safety," which led to the passage of a new federal law in 1964 mandating that all passenger vehicles except buses be fitted with three-point seat belts. The real difference in seat-belt use came in the 1980s, however, in the wake of the huge Traffic Safety Now campaign, ironically sponsored by automobile manufacturers who were trying to resist legislation promoted by Elizabeth Dole, then secretary of transportation, to require air bags in all cars (Conley and McLaren, 118–20). On a larger scale was the major event of the Civil Rights Act of 1964. Title VII of this law concerns workplace discrimination, prohibiting "employment discrimination based on race, color, religion, sex and national origin," and it allows employees to file suits when they have been subject to "unwelcome sexual advances, requests for sexual favors, and other verbal or physical conduct of a sexual nature."[4]

But the law has not been the only site of change since 1960. Among the most striking cultural transformations we see in *Mad Men* are the practices and expectations around childbirth. "The Fog" (3.5) shows Betty Draper undergoing the extraordinarily alienated process of a thoroughly medicalized birth. Thrown into a nightmarish, drugged "fog" during labor, she awakens to find herself holding a baby whose sex she does not know. Don, of course, is not allowed to attend the birth, and he drinks with another expectant father as they wait. Already in the 1940s women had begun to show dissatisfaction with the medicalization of childbirth, and for the next two decades the work of the obstetricians Grantly Dick-Read and Ferdinand Lamaze, advocating natural childbirth, appealed to an assortment of audiences, from Catholics such as the founders of the La Leche League, who wanted to promote an ideal model of Marian motherhood, to counterculturalists who embraced the body in its natural, uncorrupted state (see Umansky, 52–76; Ward). By the early 1970s many feminists had added their critical voices to the arguments against "twilight birth" and other medical interventions, understanding the rise of the male doctor and the decline of the female midwife as a sign of the breakup of communities of women by masculinist models of science. Grassroots organizations—from the International Childbirth Education Association, which grew from 9 to 160 chapters in the United States between 1955 and 1975, to small local groups such as Birthday in Boston—offered women an array of alternatives to what an early edition of *Our Bodies, Ourselves* called the "condescending, paternalistic, judgmental, and non-informative" medical model of childbirth (qtd. in Wolf, 144). Our experience of medicine is no less alienating today—it may in fact be more so, thanks to the complexities of health insurance, the vastness of the pharmaceutical industry, and the medicalizing of new areas of our experience, such as sex drives and attention spans. But that only reinforces the double experience of the uncanny: the alienating encounter with hospitals and doctors remains painfully familiar, but the particularities of our experience have altered, and in some ways radically.

From civil rights to seat belts and from dry-cleaner bags to childbirth, the shock of the banal in *Mad Men* persistently points to the fact that ordinary life has changed quite dramatically in fifty years. It therefore makes clear that social, cultural, and legal transformations are possible. And while we may marvel at how far we have come, *Mad Men* does not offer the unmixed pleasures of easy superiority. To the contrary: the historical uncanny in AMC's remarkable series persistently invites us to feel both near and far, both at home and not at home. It also invites us, in its own subtle way, to honor the social movements of the late 1960s, which rise up between our present and the past represented, creating the shock of historical difference. Of course, there is no question that much still needs to change. On poverty and on race the United States has shown few if any strides since the early 1960s, and some entrenched social inequalities have grown deeper. Smugness on the question of racial inequality in particular is a very real danger in the wake of Barack Obama's election as president. But the austere, even punishing, imperative never to take pleasure may be taken too far. If it is politically dangerous to get too comfortable with the progress we have made, it is surely far more dangerous to insist that we have made no progress at all.

NOTES

1. For a wonderful collection of the whole range of views, see Rosenberg and White.

2. Among the landmark texts by television and media scholars in this tradition are Coward; Fiske; and Radway. A defense specifically of televisual pleasure can be found in Caldwell, *Televisuality.* For the dire warnings, see, for example, Clark; McWhorter; and Stein.

3. As Mark Bowden puts it, "The heads of both organizations, official and criminal, wrestle with similar management and personnel issues, and resolve them with similarly cold self-interest. In both the department and the gang, the powerful exploit the weak, and within the ranks those who exhibit dedication, talent, and loyalty are usually punished for their efforts."

4. Title VII of the Civil Rights Act of 1964 (Pub. L. 88-352); for the language of sexual harassment, see the Equal Employment Opportunity Commission: http://www.eeoc.gov/facts/fs-sex.html (accessed 19 June 2010). The Equal Pay Act of 1963 (Pub. L. 88-38) is also worth noting here.

MOD MEN

JIM HANSEN

> Truth is entirely and absolutely a matter of style.
> — Oscar Wilde, "The Decay of Lying" (1891)

DON DRAPER, BUNBURYIST

Season 4 of *Mad Men* begins with an episode titled "Public Relations." The episode features a journalist from the magazine *Advertising Age* who publishes a profile of Don Draper, the creative golden boy of the newly formed Sterling Cooper Draper Pryce ad agency. The article describes Don as "a handsome cipher," noting, "One imagines somewhere in an attic, there's a painting of him that's rapidly aging." This reference to *The Picture of Dorian Gray* (1890), one of Oscar Wilde's most famous works, makes explicit what has been implicit throughout the run of the show: not only do Don's carefully constructed identity and style appear false, but their falsity has a strangely Wildean character. After all, from the earliest episodes of the show we learn that there is something counterfeit about Don's life, something superficial about his persona — that, like Dorian Gray, Don has a few skeletons in his closet. Indeed, this is the second reference to Wilde in the series, though the first one is easily missed: in "Nixon vs. Kennedy" (1.12), when "Don Draper" in a flashback brings home the body of "Dick Whitman," we hear the train conductor announce "Bunbury" just as the train pulls into the station. "This is us, lieutenant," the captain tells "Don."

To define someone as a superficial corporate shill today we often refer to him or her as "a suit" or "an empty suit."[1] But *Mad Men* reminds me of the words that Wilde's Lord Henry Wotton speaks near the beginning of *Dorian Gray*. "It is only shallow people who do not judge by appearances," Lord Henry assures us, for "the true mystery of the world is visible, not invisible" (32). *Mad Men* is not merely all style. It is a show about how deep the surface is, about the malleability of what Wilde might well call our culture's "visible symbols." As Wilde also claims in the marvelous, paradox-laden preface to *Dorian Gray*, "All art is at once surface and symbol. Those who go beneath the surface do so at their peril" (17).

That is why those moments in *Mad Men* when we watch Don Draper looking into a mirror are always discomfiting. When a character gazes at a mirror in a film—as, for example, Jake LaMotta does at the end of Martin Scorsese's *Raging Bull* (1980)—the action generally represents an attempt to "go beneath the surface," to confront a deeper self. In *Mad Men* we often glimpse Don shaving, combing his hair, and in the most general sense, polishing and reshaping his image. Such moments often end with Don staring intently at his own face in the mirror. Unlike many of us, however, Don appears to be completely aware of the fact that he stares at his image—his *imago*—and not at a thoroughly coherent, true, or deeper self. As Jacques Lacan pointed out, an imago attaches the human being to his or her reality, allows the individual to misrecognize him- or herself as a coherent, autonomous subject with at least the potential to control its surroundings (96). Yet Don does not seem to misrecognize himself as a subject in the same way that, say, I do when I wash up and ruminate on my daily responsibilities. Don constantly engages in the act of making himself up in both the cosmetic and narrative senses. He knows that his image is not that of the "true" Don Draper. He knows that he is not an entirely unified subject. By episode 3 of the first season, we viewers all know this as well. Don often seems painfully aware of his lack, but his incisive acts of self-recognition remain uncanny because they allow him a more fluid sense of his own autonomy. He does not need to imagine himself as a unified subject to imagine that he has autonomy. He always prepares a face to meet the faces he will meet, but he rarely concerns himself with the deeper truths behind them. He recognizes identity itself as an illusion. Like any artist, he shapes an illusion in order to produce the effects he seeks. By manipulating surfaces, Don proves himself to be the master of public relations.

This may be why the image of Don staring into a mirror in the episode "Seven Twenty Three" (3.7; fig. 7.1) remains even more unsettling than his

FIGURE 7.1. Don gazing in the mirror ("Seven Twenty Three," 3.7).

other moments of apparent self-recognition. The episode opens with the image of Peggy Olson, in many ways Don's female counterpart, lying in bed. Then we glimpse Betty Draper fainting onto a couch. Peggy has just slept with Duck Phillips. Betty is dreaming of Henry Francis. Finally we move to Don lying on a hotel room floor. His hair appears disheveled and his typically spotless clothes, the sartorial armature of his public identity as an advertising executive, show all the signs of a difficult night. He rises, rubs his head and neck, and walks to the mirror. The Don Draper he gazes upon in the mirror appears significantly different from the one we have seen throughout most of the other episodes.

With blood crusted around his nose and his eye slightly swollen, Don looks less like the icon of flexible self-sufficiency, less the continual reshaper of his own imago, than like a beaten, friendless man. The sequence, sexualized by Betty's fantasy and Peggy's affair, depicts the show's master seducer as isolated, outwitted, and left very much the worse for wear by whatever transpired in his room the previous night. By the third season of *Mad Men* we have grown accustomed to Don's skillful command of the world that surrounds him, his nearly effortless capacity to comprehend and bend social codes to accommodate his desires. He dresses for success in all things. Seeing his face beaten and bloodied, seeing him taken by surprise, feels unsettling. Don's reconstructed, 1960s-era masculine dandyism, which might draw comparisons to Cary Grant's Roger O. Thornhill of *North by Northwest*

(1959) or Sean Connery's James Bond of *From Russia with Love* (1963) and *Goldfinger* (1964), has a peculiarly modern feel to it. This dandified, potent subjectivity seems all but inaccessible to most of us. When faced with overwhelming opposition, this kind of dandy combines charm with force, and so provides us with an avatar of vigorous, aesthetically conscious self-control. We feel anxiety when that avatar emerges as beaten or sullied.

Of course, the dandy has always been a figure in disguise, an adept manipulator of surfaces, a symbol maker who conceals a particular secret. As a literary figure associated in the English-speaking world most closely with Oscar Wilde, the dandy also remains linked to effeminacy and illicit desire, and to those varied loves that appear at once luridly ostentatious and enigmatically unnamed. The dandy is always passing, always closeted. Wilde's own dandies, from the tragic Dorian Gray to the dandy par excellence Algernon Moncrieff in *The Importance of Being Earnest* (1895), thrive on disguise, concealment, and misdirection. But the split between the dandy's carefully constructed exterior and the concealed riddle that composes the core of his inner being remains central to his character today. That nearly uncanny capacity to maneuver back and forth between the superficial detail and the sensational mystery appears to be the dandy's defining attribute, his true art. The dandy is finally constituted for us neither by his veiled secret nor by his refined surface, but by the radical split between the two.

In Wilde's most perfectly executed comedy, *The Importance of Being Earnest*, Algernon explains that the modern world of commerce and commitment renders false identities necessary. "The Truth," he explains, "is rarely pure and never simple. Modern life would be very tedious if it were either" (326). For Algernon, social and financial responsibilities form a kind of prison. Modern man, as Algernon sees him, has internalized this carceral space and called it identity. But to pursue his desires and develop new interests, the modern man must develop the capacity to mislead, to wear masks, to live a double life. "I have invented an invaluable permanent invalid named Bunbury, in order that I may be able to go down into the country whenever I choose," he explains to his friend Jack, who has himself invented a younger ne'er-do-well brother named Ernest to impersonate whenever he is "in town" (326). Algernon dubs this act of duplicitous masquerade "Bunburying." The play revolves around Algernon and Jack as they move dexterously between apparently "true identities" that limit them and the Bunburying masquerades that liberate them. As does *Mad Men*, *The Importance of Being Earnest* generates anxiety about the possibility that two separate worlds might somehow collide, that the mask of one identity or another might slip off. Pivoting between identities constitutes nearly all of the plot work, tension, and humor of Wilde's play.

The Importance of Being Earnest works to break down the distinction between truth and falsehood. Imagined identities, Bunburying masquerades, transform nearly all of the supposedly authentic selves in the play into wholly flexible, syncretic characters. These dandies wear personas like clothing, and they remain scrupulous in their attention to the details of their vibrantly reimagined personas. In a sense, the Wildean dandy appears to us as a playwright within a play, an aesthete-*Übermensch* whose comprehensive grasp of the context in which he lives allows him to rewrite his own part — and often the parts played by others — at will. By refusing a unified identity, the dandy can revise himself and his desires. Oscillating craftily between surface and depth, the dandy reshapes both. Like Don Draper, Algernon and Jack can revise the worlds that they inhabit. Despite their astounding capabilities, however, all of these characters remain firmly *inside* of those worlds.

The dandy's capacity to contain personal and aesthetic innovation within the confines of accepted convention makes him a markedly insightful reader of social codes. But the dandy never destabilizes social narratives, nor does he constitute a radical or progressive force. The capacity to manipulate cultural conventions, to understand a social context so deftly that one can dress oneself for success in all things, finally works to reify those conventions. The codes that the dandy manipulates and accepts are still the dominant ones. Wilde sums this up very succinctly when he has Basil complain to Lord Henry in *The Picture of Dorian Gray*, "You never say a moral thing, and you never do a wrong thing" (4). The dandy points to and often embodies sociopolitical crises, but he never truly overcomes them. Neither does the dandy represent a mere force for social stability. Rather, the dandy gives form to several of the economic and political antagonisms present in bourgeois social formations, but as Theodor W. Adorno explains, "giving form to antagonisms does not reconcile or eliminate them" (249). In "Paris of the Second Empire in Baudelaire" (1937), Walter Benjamin insists that the dandy, as "a creation of the English, who were leaders in world trade," has the "gift of pleasing" (60). According to Benjamin, as capitalism changed in the era of industrialization that marked the mid-nineteenth century, the dandy's "gift of pleasing," his capacity to smile calmly at arguing businessmen and sneering aristocrats alike, helped to alleviate anxieties about social and financial changes and the inevitable economic tremors that accompanied these changes. Like Don, the nineteenth-century English dandy grasped that communal codes and the aesthetics of persona could be studied and manipulated, that the clever man in the age of capital was always selling an image of himself. For Benjamin, the dandy never emerged as a simple force for social stability. Instead, dandies masked social conflict. They moved between worlds and identities. In signifying neither revealed surface nor concealed truth but rather the radical split between the two, the dandy also comes to represent the fissure in the historical reality that gave birth to him.

THE DANDY AND THE COMMODITY

In *Materializing Queer Desire*, Elisa Glick argues that the dandy's identity remains paradigmatic of the cultural antagonisms engendered by capitalist social formations. In *Capital*, Marx explains that the fetishism of commodities actively generates a culture of secrecy and concealed truths. In the textbook Marxian example, the ideological superstructure hides the economic base. Cultural concerns like clothing design, celebrity, and art conceal the fact that laborers work behind the scenes to make bourgeois life possible. While the bourgeoisie focuses on surface details like style, workers sweat away in the mills to produce shoes and suits. In foregrounding exchange value we also conceal or neglect use value. Hence we often judge a suit of clothing not by its use as clothing but by its price tag and its label. The laborers who actually put the constituent parts of the suit together are concealed behind a manufacturer's name brand. Who attached the buttons and sewed them to the cloth seems, for lack of a better expression, immaterial if the suit is a Brooks Brothers. Capitalist societies revolve around the manipulation of revealed surfaces and concealed essences. The commodity structure forces us to look to surfaces and forget the concealed labor or use values behind those surfaces. Those concealed and repressed truths are, nonetheless, present, and Marx warns us that they will not remain hidden forever.

Glick makes the now familiar argument that since the commodity form determines our lives, the bourgeois subject revolves around a radically split "contradictory subjectivity that is constructed around the opposition between public and private, outside and inside" (18). The split engendered by the commodity structure forms modern subjectivity. We all reveal certain surfaces. We all conceal certain secrets. Furthermore, we often tend to believe that the commodity itself, some mystical "thing," will fulfill our desires, satisfy our secret lack. The commodity form promises us the possibility that we can have or be whatever we want. According to Glick, the dandy embodies the split produced by the commodity form. In representing the radical split directly, in embodying both the carefully crafted surface and the private depths, the dandy symbolizes capitalist subjectivity. The antagonism between the revealed and the concealed, public and private, that constitutes the dandy's identity signifies the historical realities of a subjectivity determined by the commodity.

I am tempted to imagine that only with the Wilde scandal and the subsequent reinterpretations of *The Picture of Dorian Gray* did the dandy emerge for us as a radically divided entity whose persona revolves around the binary of concealed and revealed secrets. Wilde might easily be read as the ne plus ultra of the split between a dandified surface and a veiled truth. But while the public image of dandyism has evolved in fascinating ways over the years, even before Wilde, the dandy had always been a reflection of irreconcilable social binaries. As early as 1859 Charles Baudelaire noted in "The Painter of Modern Life" that "dandyism appears especially in those periods of transition when democracy has not yet become all-powerful, and aristocracy is only just beginning to totter and fall" (28). In *Sex and Suits: The Evolution of Modern Dress*, Anne Hollander traces the history of the dandy from its genesis in the writing and style of the Regency-era sartorial icon George Bryan "Beau" Brummell—who is often credited with the invention of the modern men's suit—through to contemporary formulations of dandyism. Although educated at Eton and Oxford and a friend of the prince-regent, Brummell was not a nobleman, and his role as the leading authority on male dress represented a sort of fissure in the rigidified class structures of early nineteenth-century England.

Following the Reform Act of 1832, middle-class men were given the right to vote, and a series of parliamentary acts altered the ways that banks, factories, and railways could do business (C. P. Hill, 176). These reforms strengthened the development of "joint stock" companies, those business, economic, and industrial concerns with multiple shareholders that had already come into being during the eighteenth century (C. P. Hill, 111). This was compounded by parliament's passage of limited liability legislation in 1855, which made companies liable directly to creditors and shareholders, and hence made it much easier for the general public to establish corporations. In *Making a Social Body*, Mary Poovey argues that the passage of the 1855 legislation demonstrated that the social classes in England were changing, that "the aggregate—and problematic—social body had begun to dissolve into its constitutive members" (24). The landowning gentry, along with the concept of single-family ownership of large properties or of businesses, began to recede. The new industrial, legal, and financial changes resulted in a bourgeoisie that commanded vast economic power. With more money at its disposal, this bourgeoisie could mingle more openly with shareholders from the noble and aristocratic classes. Aristocratic privilege in England was transformed into—if not purchased by—economic privilege over the next century and a half, but this transformation was a sluggish, uneven one, and an interstitial space of identity seems to have developed that reflected precisely the concealed fissures in this uneven development.

During the rise of Regency England, as Parisian fashions were overshadowed by the political turmoil following the French Revolution and the Napoleonic Wars, British tailoring became the dominant style of men's clothing in Europe. As Hollander explains, the ideal male form was reconceived by Brummell and Regency-era English tailors. No longer dressed in the flowing silks and wigs of the eighteenth-century aristocracy, the modern man, the English dandy, was "part English country gentleman, part innocent natural Adam, and part naked Apollo the creator and destroyer. . . . Dressed form was now an abstraction of nude form, a new ideal naked man expressed not in bronze or marble but in natural wool, linen, and leather, wearing an easy skin as perfect as the silky pelt of the idea" (92). Form-fitting coats and pants accompanied by cravats and vests were quickly replacing the excessive late-rococo styles of the previous century.

As the public male body transformed from a flowing, silk spectacle into the more overtly eroticized, muscular Apollonian one sought after by the modern subject, it also signaled an emphatically polarized identity. Spurred on by economic changes, the dandy came to embody the height of Regency fashion. Like Don Draper, however, this figure was no longer fully at home with the working and mercantile classes and acted as something of an interloper in aristocratic circles. The Regency dandy always passed for someone else, always deployed what Benjamin calls "the gift of pleasing," to fit into any social environment. In *Mad Men* we often see Don isolate himself from his upper-middle-class social circle and gaze at the old photos from his youthful life as the son of a farmer and a prostitute. Like Don, the Regency dandy belonged to both worlds and to neither. Furthermore, as creator and destroyer, natural innocent and worldly gentleman, Apollo and Dionysus, the dandy personified the distinction between surface and depth. The highly charged, sexualized, robust masculinity that the dandy's bodily form came to represent following the rise of the English suiting industry was balanced by the dandy's cold and distant character. As Christopher Breward explains in "The Dandy Laid Bare," the sartorial philosophy offered by Brummell made "casual effortlessness" the "central desideratum of the new dandy creed" (224). This modern masculine code of dress was less frilly and more Hellenic than its eighteenth-century predecessor. Rather than constituting a marker of social station, men's clothing had transformed into a symbol of self-sufficiency, of austere composure, of visible autonomy.[2]

For Baudelaire, "the specific beauty of the dandy consists particularly in that cold exterior resulting from the unshakable determination to remain unmoved; one is reminded of a latent fire, whose existence is merely suspected, and which, if it wanted to, but it does not, could burst forth in all its brightness" (29). The dandies discussed by Benjamin and Baudelaire came into being in Regency England, but since his emergence, the dandy has taken quite a few forms. In "Decadent Heroes," Drew Todd argues that a dandified hero reemerged in the Hollywood films of the 1920s and '30s. "Contrary to most representations of aesthetes in American popular culture," Todd says, "this version was a masculine ideal in the highly designed universe of popular Art Deco movies. His 'classlessness,' coupled with his imperatives of leisure and consumption, made him a timely hero in Depression America" (168). Figures such as William Powell's Nick Charles in *The Thin Man* (1934) and Fred Astaire's Jerry Travers in *Top Hat* (1935) dressed stylishly, drank heartily, and walked—or in Astaire's case, danced—between the gritty world of the street and the aristocratic world of parties and champagne. By the late 1930s, as the Second World War began, the martini-sipping dandy played by Powell was being superseded by the tailored, world-weary, hard-drinking film noir protagonist played most memorably by Humphrey Bogart in *The Maltese Falcon* (1941) and *The Big Sleep* (1946). This cold, distant, noir-style antihero signaled a definitively forceful yet self-sufficient form of masculinity.

Although adding an actor like Bogart to the list certainly alters the terrain of any discussion of dandyism, strangely enough it is Bogart's version that resonates most fully with Baudelaire's conception of the dandy as a possessor of some "latent fire," a man determined to remain "unmoved." And like the dandies of the generation before, Bogart's hard-boiled detective moved between the world of the aristocrats for whom he worked and the working class with whom he drank and fought. Bogart's vigorous, assertive, less flamboyant sartorial masculinity constitutes the missing link between the flashy Wildean dandy and the reconstructed masculine dandyism of the late 1950s and early 1960s.[3] Most important, in all of his incarnations, the dandy appears to achieve the apotheosis of capitalist masculine subjectivity. He can be whatever he wants to be. He walks wherever he chooses to walk. He conceals whatever he chooses to conceal. He communicates between worlds. The dandy provides us with the fantasy of a capitalist subject as virtuoso Bunburyist, a subject who, like Don Draper, manipulates the various masks provided by modern society. But what effect does our cultural fantasy have on the dandy whose vaunted autonomy and flexibility we all appear to crave?

RED HERRING OR HANDSOME CIPHER

Popular culture had imagined a Mad Man before the retro-incarnation of Don Draper.[4] Alfred Hitchcock ended the 1950s and opened a window into the style of the early 1960s with *North by Northwest*, his film about Roger O. Thornhill, a Madison Avenue ad executive who wears what Todd McEwen calls the "best suit . . . in the movies, perhaps the whole world" (119). Played by Cary Grant, that embodiment of midcentury male charm and beauty, Thornhill, like Draper, becomes a man caught between two identities (fig. 7.2). During the course of the narrative, Thornhill is forced to take on an identity as government agent George Kaplan in order to survive in a world that has grown hostile to his hopes, desires, and everyday life. As played by Grant, Thornhill is as much a manipulator of style and a master of cultural codes as Jon Hamm's Don Draper. He finds his way out of every dilemma, and he does so with great panache. Like Roger Sterling, Don's supervisor, Thornhill wears a gray suit during most of his screen time.

Thornhill's ensemble is so striking that most of the other characters in *North by Northwest,* including James Mason's villainous Phillip Vandamm, Eva Marie Saint's Eve Kendall, and Martin Landau's Leonard, feel compelled to comment on it at some point during the film. The various characters refer to Thornhill/Kaplan at separate moments as "polished," "well-tailored," and an agent with "taste in clothes." In fact, watching the suit survive its many Hitchcockian perils remains one of the most distinctive pleasures of the film. The suit was designed by the famed British Savile Row tailors at Kilgour.[5] Its simple, slender cut, thin lapels, and pleated pants were imitated in the decade-defining Conduit-cut suits designed by the Savile Row tailor Anthony Sinclair and worn by Sean Connery in the first four James Bond films. At the end of the 1950s, an era when America, as McEwan explains, was "a white-shirt-and-black-suit nation," Grant's Kilgour, with its tie a touch lighter and socks a touch darker, remains a spectacle in shades of gray. Style might well be shallow, but its role in our visual and cultural imaginary invariably complicates the social world.

In *Mad Men*, as in Hitchcock's film, stylistic surfaces determine identity. The surface tells the truth, but one has to determine how to read it. *Mad Men* makes this problem explicit by dressing Don to project the image of an urbane, empowered, masculine sophisticate, while he remains a construct

FIGURE 7.2. The "best suit in the movies": Cary Grant as Roger Thornhill (*North by Northwest*, 1959).

of pure style, an imagined man. The intersections between *Mad Men* and Hitchcock's film become quite intriguing here. Roger Thornhill wears his tailored suit throughout the film until he is knocked unconscious by the police, who remove his shades-of-gray Kilgour and replace it with a store-bought white shirt, black pants, and loafers. Once he has been interpellated into the system—and renamed George Kaplan—he moves from being an individual with style to an agent of the government without it. He moves from *useless* Mad Man to *useful* agent. In contrast, Dick Whitman moves from being a private in the army, who has a state-recognized name and wears the clothes provided by the government, to an individual defined by his style. We would do well to recall that in "The Soul of Man under Socialism" (1891), Wilde argues that "the State is to make what is useful. The individual is to make what is beautiful" (1088). In the case of both Don/Dick and Kaplan/Thornhill, the surfaces are quite compelling because they provoke our desires. Both characters draw us to and help us to identify with supposed corporate shills who often speak on behalf of others. But the carefully crafted surfaces that define both men also illustrate the artistry and ingenuity that go into being a dandy. They imagine and then play identities extraordinarily effectively. Moreover, as Madison Avenue ad men, Thornhill and Draper are "suits" whose jobs entail manipulating our hopes and desires.

The distinctions between *Mad Men* and *North by Northwest* seem equally compelling. Although *Mad Men* is a show about the manipulation of façades, a show about a creative stylist who knows how to seduce both women and men, it has also been committed to revealing secrets, to the idea that everyone conceals certain truths. The show about style and surfaces remains obsessed with concealment and revelation. The ad men at Sterling Cooper know that there is something "closeted" about Don. A signal moment where the show acknowledges this comes in "Seven Twenty Three" when Bert Cooper, the agency's cofounder, convinces Don to sign an exclusive contract with the firm by asking, "After all, when it comes down to it, who's really signing this contract anyway?" (The contract is dated 7/23/1963.) Bert knows Don is not wholly or only Don. The episode that begins with a standard film trope, the beaten man looking into a mirror and apparently seeking answers, ends by acknowledging the fungibility of identity itself. Like Don, most of the characters at the agency know that a unified and singular identity is a fiction, but they all remain obsessed with keeping their various secrets, with concealing their supposed truths. The terrain of the show is a thoroughly postmodern, suspicious one. No one ever really confronts a symbolic "big Other" here. No one seems to fully control the ideological forces of this world. The characters exist in a social structure they have neither made nor fully accepted. By providing us with Don as a locus for this radically split identity and then going on to demonstrate how Peggy, Joan, Betty, Sal, and the other characters are likewise engaged in the act of moving between different performed identities, *Mad Men* represents both the seductive allure and the powerful limitations intrinsic to bourgeois social economies, to economies that appear to offer great social mobility while demanding rigid social codes and definite kinds of façades and performances.

Conversely, although Roger Thornhill seems compelled by accident and

FIGURES 7.3–7.4. Two suits in sunglasses: Roger Thornhill and Don.

by state power to transform into George Kaplan, he remains committed to the idea of a singular, unified identity. He believes himself to be a victim of circumstance who must deploy style, charm, and force in order to rescue himself. A government willing to sacrifice the welfare of its citizens, even its prettiest, most charming citizens, readily fills the role of big Other here. *North by Northwest* renders all identity subject to the whims of powerful ideological forces. Where *Mad Men* appears committed to a dramatic Foucauldian critique of life under bourgeois capitalism, *North by Northwest* operates on a more overtly psychoanalytic register. As with Wilde's dandies, however, the figures in *North by Northwest* and *Mad Men* remain firmly inside the confines of accepted cultural conventions. Draper and Thornhill ultimately gain a modicum of control over their own lives by embracing the fact that they are, to borrow the Lacanian term, constituted by lack. They realize more desires by embracing lack than they ever could as subjects who pursue stable, unified, or singular identities (figs. 7.3–7.4).

Like Wilde's Algernon, Thornhill and Draper oscillate between two identities. They exist *between* a supposedly false surface and an allegedly true self. Roger Thornhill never truly becomes George Kaplan; he exists and moves between his Thornhill and Kaplan identities. Likewise, Dick Whitman never truly becomes Don Draper; he exists and moves between his Whitman and Draper identities. Although he ponders and remembers his past, he mostly works to conceal it. Finally, the dandy shuffles between two fake identities but never between a "real" self and a "fake" mask. He juggles two masks, neither of which can be said to constitute a "real" identity.

Grant's dual role as Thornhill/Kaplan has become such a symbol for his own identity that even Marc Eliot's 2004 biography of him begins by describing a scene from *North by Northwest*. For Eliot:

> Kaplan's faked murder two-thirds of the way through the film forces the question of whether he actually is who others believe him to be, someone entirely separate—Roger O. Thornhill—or whether he really ever exists at all. Out of this question a larger one emerges: is Kaplan the creation of the Hitchcock-like CIA operative (Leo G. Carroll) who has, thus far, remained largely unseen while cleverly directing the either/or/neither Kaplan/Thornhill's every move? Or is he someone, or something, else, an externalized elaborate fantasy, perhaps, of Thornhill's most repressed desires for an idealized life of exciting adventure, of romance, of meaning? (1)

In arguing that the Thornhill/Kaplan split be read as a symbol for Grant's own identity, Eliot asserts that Grant must have found the dual role appealing because it so obviously reflected his own lifelong effort to balance his public persona as a suave leading man with a troubled, sexually ambiguous private life (2). Married five times and by most accounts at least bisexual, he existed between his public celebrity as the superlative Cary Grant and his private life as the tailor's son, Archibald Leach.

The critic Edward Buscombe argues that with "his beautifully cut grey suit, matching grey silk tie, [and] white shirt with discreet cufflinks . . . Cary Grant's late-1950s elegance appeals to women, straight men and gays" (201). This kind of statement has become an oft-repeated mantra about Grant, who has come to personify one of cinema's supreme objects of desire. Women wanted him, and those men who wouldn't admit to wanting him would at least confess to wanting to be like him. In her classic *New Yorker* piece on Grant from 1975, Pauline Kael calls him "the Man from Dream City," and in claiming "it makes us happy just to look at him," Kael sums up what many filmgoers had been thinking since Grant first appeared onscreen in the mid-1930s. Grant provides a kind of fantasy, an example of how style and elegance work together to create the illusion of a fully autonomous individual. During his lifetime his image became such an objectified fantasy that he once told an interviewer: "Everyone wants to be Cary Grant. Even I want to be Cary Grant" (qtd. in Eliot). Don plays a similar role: the women want him, the men want to be him. And vice versa. The autonomy that we imagine the dandy to have so elevates him beyond the realm of real human relations that it becomes impossible even for the dandy himself, even for Don Draper, or Cary Grant.

In reimagining Lacan's discussions of *Das Ding* from *The Ethic of Psychoanalysis*, in his essay "Courtly Love, or, Woman as Thing," Slavoj Žižek discusses how certain objects can be spiritualized and so rendered unattainable. For Žižek such an object is attainable only "by way of an incessant postponement, as its absent point of reference." This action elevates the object, as Žižek explains, to "the dignity of the Thing" (95). For Lacan, the Thing constitutes an unreachable, primordial, nearly transcendental object of desire. The Thing functions as an empty space around which the subject's desire is structured. The Lacanian Thing, like the commodity form, promises something as it allows us to imagine that our desires will be fulfilled. Commodities, but also people, can occupy the role of Thing for us. When we seek a stand-in for the Thing, though, and most particularly when that stand-in is a human being, we transform that stand-in or subject into an object to be manipulated. We erase its autonomy. Draper and Thornhill might represent "empty suits," but we have emptied those suits and filled them up with our desires. The dandy—as embodiment of the commodity form—represents the antagonisms of late capitalist society. As he becomes the Thing around which we shape our desires, the Thing we want and the Thing we want to be, he transforms into a subject without autonomy, a suit emptied of all will, into a persona without real self-sufficiency.

The dandy transforms into his exact opposite, into a nearly lifeless object, obliged to move in a phantom zone between identities, obliged to imagine which mask people want him to wear. When Thornhill finally confronts the CIA operative who has been pulling his strings and transforming him into an object desired by others, he angrily cries out, "Now you listen to me: I'm an advertising man, not a red herring!" Actually, he's both. The dandy is a survivor and manipulator of social codes, but never a fully self-determined subject. The autonomy that capitalist society fantasizes about never comes into being at all. If the dandy embodies the radical split of the commodity form, if the dandy must move between two identities, then his supposed desires are conditioned by that split, that movement. The episode "Seven Twenty Three" finds Don caught between the young thieves who drink with him and then beat and rob him, and Conrad Hilton, the CEO who demands that Don imagine a new personality for his hotels. He is desired by the wealthy and the poor. He walks in their respective circles, but he is there to provide them with something that they want. The man who looks into the mirror and signs the contract in "Seven Twenty Three" may call himself Don Draper, but like the dandies who preceded him, he remains the embodiment of a radically divided identity, a red herring, a handsome cipher.

NOTES

1. The *Oxford English Dictionary* cites the novel *Glitter Street* (1979), by Tim Sullivan, as the first published usage of the word *suit* to denote a business executive.

2. As Hollander explains, the dandy's "heroism consisted only in being thoroughly himself" (92).

3. Moreover, as in "Seven Twenty Three," *Mad Men* often deploys noir-style flashbacks to fill in the gaps about Don's past. Of course, Bogart as dandy would have to stand alongside Clark Gable's cultivated cad Rhett Butler in *Gone with the Wind* (1939).

4. Tom Rath of Sloan Wilson's novel *The Man in the Gray Flannel Suit* (1955) remains the most important and obvious forerunner to Don Draper; see the introduction to this volume.

5. According to Edward Buscombe, six identical suits were made for the film.

SWING SKIRTS
AND SWINGING SINGLES

Mad Men, *Fashion, and Cultural Memory*

MABEL ROSENHECK

In the season 1 DVD special feature "Establishing *Mad Men*," the producer Scott Hornbacher says that "accuracy to the period is of paramount importance to all of us, because if it's wrong it's embarrassing . . . and it compromises the ability for people to suspend their disbelief."[1] "Behind the Scenes" videos on the AMC website and ancillary media accounts also regularly detail the show's meticulous reproduction of everyday life in the 1960s. There is the eBay bidding war for authentic TWA pilot's wings, and issues of *Time*, *Life*, and *Playboy* recreated for momentary onscreen appearances (Keane and Lewis).[2] Highlighting costumers, prop masters, set designers, and the perfectionist auteur-creator Matthew Weiner, these explorations assure us that *Mad Men* is what the early 1960s really looked and felt like. The show's proclaimed historicity is then distinguished from the vague and nostalgic "past-ness" of movies like *American Graffiti* (1973) and television shows like *The Wonder Years* (ABC, 1988–93).

While *Mad Men* can thus be constructed as an archive of material history, the public promotion of the show reveals a more performative aspect to the text and its twenty-first-century representation of the 1960s. Before the season 3 premiere, AMC publicized the show through the slogans "The World's Gone Mad" and "New York's Gone Mad." A week of promotional events in

New York City culminated in a public screening of the premiere in Times Square. AMC's website invited fans to "watch the Season 3 premiere on the big screen and come dressed in your swankiest sixties attire to enter our pre-screening costume contest" (Oei). The AMC blog *"Mad Men" Fashion File* and magazines such as *Elle* and *Marie Claire* also encourage the live performance of *Mad Men*'s historical fictions, telling readers "how to dress like a *Mad* woman" (Krentcil, "How to Dress"; Krentcil, "The Frills") and where to find high-end lookalike pieces (Aminosharei and Joseph; *Marie Claire*). Other examples include Brooks Brothers' collaboration with the costumer Janie Bryant to release a *Mad Men* suit, and Banana Republic's *Mad Men*–inspired lines and window displays (fig. 8.1).[3]

With marketing that emphasizes historical accuracy, and promotions that encourage viewers to extend the show from screen to street, *Mad Men* provides an opportunity to examine television's representation of the past in terms of what the performance scholar Diana Taylor calls the "archive" of material artifacts and the "repertoire" of performed cultural memory. Performance highlights not only the movement from archive to repertoire but also the movement between past and present, including the meaning of the past in the present day. In this chapter I examine *Mad Men*—and in particular the show's 1960s fashions—as a contemporary negotiation of past and present and a representation of the performance of cultural memory. Though the discourse surrounding the show stresses historical accuracy and an authentic archival look, the embodied nature of fashion and fashion-oriented promotions highlights the status of both clothing and the series as exercises in memory through which twenty-first-century production engages the history of the 1960s.[4]

MEMORY, HISTORY, AND FASHION

The suggestion that fashion can be a site for the interaction of past and present rather than a static artifact of history draws on Taylor's concept of the archive and the repertoire. It also draws on broader understandings of memory's relationship to history. Pierre Nora makes a distinction between *history*, by which he means authoritative accounts of what happened and when, and *memory*, a manifestation of the past in lived experience. He asserts that memory "is a perpetually actual phenomenon, a bond tying us to the eternal present," whereas "history is a representation of the past" (8). History fixes the past; memory emphasizes the past as a dynamic, flexible, and usable part of everyday life. Yet these two concepts need not be diametrically

opposed. For Marita Sturken, "cultural memory is a field of cultural negotiation through which different stories vie for a place in history" (1). Sturken's
alternative to Nora lies in presenting "cultural memory and history as *entangled* rather than oppositional" (5). The colloquial definition of memory as
rooted in personal experience can be part of this entanglement, yet so are the
pasts constructed by history, collective memory, and nostalgia, as well as the
pasts found in textbooks, museums, public memorials, and popular media.

We can then add Taylor's material archives and performed repertoires to
the already entangled fields of history and memory. For Taylor, the division
of historical sources is not "between the written and spoken word but between the archive of supposedly enduring materials (i.e., texts, documents,
buildings, bones) and the so-called ephemeral repertoire of embodied prac-
tice/knowledge (i.e., spoken language, dance, sports, ritual)" (19). Performance studies thus "allows us to expand what we understand by 'knowledge'" (16). Though *Mad Men*'s narrative of history may be a textual archive,
it is also an embodied repertoire reliant on the performances of actors. Television becomes archival when its performance is recorded, but its performative status allows it to mobilize repertorial aspects as well. Looking at *Mad
Men* though Taylor's archive and repertoire allows us to put alternative histories of gender and resistance in conversation with more vocal and dominant
narratives of the past, constructing a representation of history that is also a
site of memory.

Fashion is pivotal in developing this relationship because, like the show
itself, it is archival as well as repertorial. As artifacts, vintage clothing can act
as "congealed memories of the daily life of times past" (E. Wilson, 1). Yet vintage fashions also establish a performative "dialogue between the present-
day wearers of that clothing and its original wearers" (Silverman, "Fragments," 195).[5] Similarly, retro clothing is not just an object to purchase but
part of an everyday performance of history and gender identity.[6] Through
this dual performance, we can see Kaja Silverman's suggestion that "retro
also provides a means of salvaging the images that have traditionally sustained female subjectivity, images that have been consigned to the waste-
basket not only by fashion but by 'orthodox' feminism" ("Fragments," 195).
Clothing operates as a palimpsest on which social, cultural, and personal histories are written and through which we evoke, embody, and perform those
histories in dialogue with contemporary contexts as part of the repertoire.
Further, as clothing is used to construct gender roles and female identities,
retro fashion becomes a space in which women's histories are in dialogue
with feminist historiographies. Thus, looking at *Mad Men*'s use of embodied

BANANA REPUBLIC IS
MAD ABOUT SKIRTS

Printed Tie Blouse
$69.⁵⁰

C-Buckle Belt
$49.⁵⁰

Flatiron Zip Wallet
(available in August)
$79.⁵⁰

Tassel Bracelet
$39.⁵⁰

Hourglass Pencil Skirt
$79.⁵⁰

Ely Suede Bootie
$160

(Opposite)
Modern Duchess Lattice Ring $39.⁵⁰
Retro Print Scarf $39.⁵⁰
Vintage Pen Necklace (Joan's own)

All items imported.

The Pencil Skirt
Lightweight wool. Day-to-night ease. Sharp and to the point when
paired with a delicate printed blouse. Add a chic belt, bag and heels, and
you're ready to call the shots.

Office Manager

JOAN HOLLOWAY

Joanie always lets 'em know who's boss—and her form-fitting silhouettes and bold accessories complement her in-charge attitude flawlessly.

fashion, we see an archive, but also a repertoire of femininity and feminism, shifting between the past being represented and its present performance; between traditional and alternative ways of understanding these times and places.

AMC's active incitement of viewer performance suggests that *Mad Men* acknowledges both the archival and the dialogic and performative aspects of historical representation. However, the relation between objects and performance in everyday life does not necessarily reproduce what appears on-screen. As a historical drama, *Mad Men* uses fashion as a sign of historical authenticity, "looking *through* clothes," to cite Stella Bruzzi. But the viewer is also given the opportunity to "look *at* clothes," to "create an alternative discourse, and one that usually counters or complicates the ostensible strategy of the overriding narrative" (Bruzzi, 36). I suggest that *Mad Men* encourages an alternative discourse of fashion that performatively links the recreated past to the present, and links the feminisms and femininities of the 1960s to those of the twenty-first century. Watching *Mad Men*, we are encouraged to look *at* clothes and engage actively in a dialogue between the pre–second wave feminism of the characters, the feminism that they will live through in the 1960s and '70s, and more contemporary ideas about feminism, femininity, and gender.

Though the characters I look at here—Betty Draper, Joan Holloway, and Peggy Olson—each negotiate this historical performance in distinct ways and through distinct fashions, their juxtaposition through the television narrative creates an even more dynamic version of women's history, feminist identity, and the pleasures of femininity. While our looking "through" their clothes would place these women squarely in the past, looking "at" their clothes moves the characters back and forth between past and present. The effect highlights not only change over time but also continuities: the progressive aspects of the past as well as the regressive aspects of the present. *Mad Men*'s fashions thus become a site of memory and a field of cultural and historical negotiation rather than a fixed representation of the past.

BETTY DRAPER'S DRESSES

I begin with Betty Draper because she is explicitly connected both to the traditional gender roles of the postwar housewife and to the feminism born out of that era's oppressions.[7] The origins of Betty's New Look fashion and her concomitant role in the family lie in a familiar postwar narrative. During the Second World War, women went to work alongside men and, at least in heavy industry, adopted male fashions: pants, overalls, and caps (Steele, 80–82). After 1945, with soldiers returning from overseas, women were supposed to return to the home, give their jobs back to men, resume their unpaid duties as wives and mothers, and refashion themselves in New Look femininity.

Introduced by Christian Dior on Paris runways in 1947, the New Look highlighted the female form with a structured bodice, fitted waistline, and voluminous skirt that were a break with wartime menswear-inspired, fabric-rationed garments. As Karal Ann Marling argues, the New Look used dress to construct "an artificial, manufactured woman whose anatomical differences were exaggerated to conform to the sexual dimorphism of the 40s and 50s" (12). The 1950s housewife in her New Look dress, high heels, and pearls symbolized a return to normative gender roles and separate spheres.[8] Although Dior claimed that "the collection affirms the natural graces of Woman . . . Woman the stem, Woman the flower" (qtd. in Cawthorne, 119), that "natural," floral shape required "a padded bra . . . along with a boned corset to give the nipped waist, and hip pads" (Cawthorne, 111). Despite its pretenses, the New Look was artificial and impractical, but this, in turn, was strategic and symbolic. The impracticality performed a class function by showing off postwar prosperity, demonstrating that a man's wife need not, "does not and cannot habitually engage in useful work" (Thorstein Veblen qtd. in E. Wilson, 50). The immobility of the New Look and its attendant undergarments thus made the woman into an object, at best "a form of living sculpture," at worst "irrelevant to the dress" and its conspicuous display of consumption, male earning power, and economic status (Marling, 11).

Betty seems to fit this description perfectly. She is constructed as subservient, an archetypal postwar housewife on display. Since she has a maid to help rear her children and clean her house, Betty's functional value is not linked to her labor so much as it is linked to her appearance. We see this, for instance, in "The Benefactor" (2.3) when Don invites Betty to dinner in the city. Upon discovering that this is a business dinner, Betty asks casually, "Is this one where I talk or don't talk?" While agreeing to be "shiny and bright" and to be his "better half," she also tells Don, "I have nothing to wear." This narrative development is further contextualized in the season 2 DVD special feature "An Era of Style."[9] There, fashion historian Valerie Steele explains Betty and her dresses by introducing the designer and author Anne Fogarty's concept of "wife dressing" as the primary principle of 1950s fashion and the New Look. Steele says, "The first principle of wife dressing was complete femininity. A woman should be dressing to please her husband and to help him at his career." She explains how this fashion "was part of the conservative sexual politics of the 1950s and early 1960s . . . the era of the feminine mystique and going back to strict gender roles so women were supposed to dress like women and men were supposed to be like men." Though Steele clearly describes *Mad Men*'s historical context, the show does not only look through Betty's clothes to fix her temporally. It also looks at Betty and her dresses to examine her feminist future as well as our feminist past.

The first time we properly meet Betty is in the second episode of season 1, "Ladies Room"; she is out at dinner with Don, Roger Sterling, and his wife Mona. Betty wears a quintessential New Look dress: white with a blue and pink floral pattern, an excessively full skirt, a curved boat neckline, and a fitted waist with a wide blue satin sash tied in a bow at the back. Betty's sartorially constructed femininity once again serves Don's career at a business dinner. Yet in this episode we also see Betty's anxiety as a recurring hand numbness becomes the physical symptom of a psychological disorder implicitly linked to what Betty Friedan would call "the problem that has no name." As Friedan explained it in 1963, "There was a strange discrepancy between the reality of our lives as women and the image to which we were trying to conform, the image that I came to call the feminine mystique" (7). Or, as Betty puts it on her psychiatrist's couch, her mother "wanted [her] to be beautiful so [she] could find a man. There's nothing wrong with that. But then what? Just sit and smoke and let it go till you're in a box?" ("Shoot," 1.9). Betty's complete femininity is only a fashionable façade, and one that is cracking as it increasingly fails to mask the emptiness and oppression of this limited identity.

Betty's façade is further dismantled by *Mad Men*'s ongoing revelation of gender, fashion, the New Look, and wife dressing as careful constructions. When we see the undergarments, bullet bras, girdles, and corselettes that shape Betty's figure and construct her complete femininity, the natural womanliness of the New Look and dimorphic gender roles is undermined. Further, in the revelation that the female ideal is an artificial manipulation there is an acknowledgment that gender, fashion, and the body are performative and so can be manipulated not only by patriarchal forces but by women themselves. This rewrites the corseted and dressed woman as a subject as well as an object. By acknowledging subjectivity, *Mad Men* opens a space for women to find pleasure in the performance of the ideal image, a space in which they are not just victims of that image.

In "Red in the Face" (1.7), Betty tells Francine that her psychiatrist tried to look down her dress, noting, "As far as I'm concerned, as long as men still look at me that way, I'm earning my keep." This, like the later comments to her psychiatrist in "Shoot," indicates that Betty's social role is dependent on the class and gender cues her appearance provides. Yet it also indicates that Betty, as well as the audience, is aware of the sartorial performance. Not only does she understand that her function is valuable, but she and the series also acknowledge that there is pleasure to be taken in the performance of that function, pleasure that lies outside of her function as an economic asset and as a dressed wife. Indeed, she continues, "Every once in a while I think, no, this is something else. I don't want my husband to see this." To this, Francine replies, "I love to be looked at that way." The male gaze upon these women constructs them as sexual objects, but their self-awareness and self-pleasure complicates that construction and reconstructs them as sexual subjects who manipulate the meaning of their performances of fashion and gender as much as their performances are determined by the desires of the men around them.

In moments like this, *Mad Men* uses Betty to suggest a distinct feminist trajectory that is linked to second wave feminism's rejection of subservience but that also reinterprets the seemingly subservient performances of pre–second wave fashion and femininity. On the one hand this is a process of rereading the past through the lens of the present and through contemporary feminist theory that sees performativity as potentially destabilizing gender essentialism.[10] At the same time, it works historiographically to reject a traditional reading of the past and of the housewife as ignorant, suggesting that the artificiality of the façade was always apparent to the women who constructed it daily. Further, this rewriting of history through Betty suggests that with the knowledge of artifice can come a pleasure in performativity, a pleasure — particularly in feminine excess — that potentially destabilizes traditional gender ideology.

In "A Night to Remember" (2.8), the self-conscious sartorial performance works not only to reclaim the figure of the postwar housewife but also to reinterpret her fashions and reevaluate the symbolism of the New Look in a time beyond the 1950s. In this episode we once again see Betty at a dinner for Don, this time with his bosses and their wives at the Draper home. Betty wears a spaghetti-strap New Look gown in white silk with blue, green, and yellow polka dots. Yet the innocent femininity of the dress and its cheerful color is belied by the fury with which Betty approaches Don after the party, accusing him of embarrassing her and revealing that she knows about his extramarital affair. The next day the dress (which she has slept in) wrinkles and the straps fall off her shoulders as she too comes apart while search-

FIGURE 8.2. Betty and the feminine mystique ("A Night to Remember," 2.8).

ing frantically for proof of Don's infidelity. The dress no longer conveys the façade of idealized femininity but now reflects the anxiety it sought to contain (fig. 8.2). Betty does not have the language to articulate her dissatisfaction, so we see it instead through an appearance that challenges the conventions of her dress's intended construction of gender and a passive female self.

We can see, then, how *Mad Men* encourages the reconstruction of fashion not just as an artifact of history but as a dynamic site of memory. Dress and narrative simultaneously suggest the series' move forward from the 1960s and the contextual move back from the 2000s to explore the past. Beyond the movement between text and context, however, the movement back coincides with contemporary women's explorations of vintage femininity through retro fashion trends. We find this suggestion especially in the promotional encouragement of retro style everywhere from Janie Bryant's *Fashion File* book and the corresponding AMC blog to Banana Republic, from Times Square dress-up parties to vintage boutiques that long predate *Mad Men*. Performativity works to comment not only on the constructedness of gender but also on the negotiation of the past in the present. This allows a renegotiation of the pre–second wave housewife, as well as of second wave feminism. The possibility that dresses and heels and petticoats can suggest feminist values is a rewriting of the popular misconception that fashion and feminism are incompatible. Indeed, in Silverman's words, vintage and retro fashion is a way of "acknowledging that its wearer's identity has been shaped by decades of representational activity" ("Fragments," 195). Though I would argue that these ideas are embedded in every vintage dress worn fifty years later, *Mad Men*'s ability to narrativize this makes these dynamics uniquely explicit. *Mad Men* transforms personal memories and personal histories of individual wearers into cultural memory and public history.

JOAN HOLLOWAY'S HIPS

While Betty is part of a contemporary reevaluation and reclamation of the 1950s housewife, Joan Holloway's relationship to feminist history works by finding continuity between the present and the past in a model of feminism the second wave has generally not accommodated. Like Betty, Joan embraces her femininity through fashion and style in a manner that can become resistant as it foregrounds the constructedness of gender and as she finds pleasure in being a single woman. That this kind of femininity can be feminist has not been easily accepted in the dominant discourses surrounding conventional feminist history. As Jennifer Scanlon argues, "The grand effect of such feminist attempts to deemphasize women's looks was that the movement as a whole most often either avoided the issue of fashion or considered it an element of women's punishment rather than their pleasure, their oppression rather than liberation" (130). Yet because of *Mad Men*'s investment in the history of fashion and feminism, it can pose a question more like Elizabeth Wilson's: "Is fashionable dress part of the oppression of women, or is it a form of adult play? Is it part of the empty consumerism, or is it a site of struggle symbolized in dress codes?" (231). *Mad Men* negotiates these questions by moving between the moments in which each idea dominates. For Betty, the connotations of the New Look collide with the feminine mystique and the contemporary reevaluation of postwar womanhood. In Joan, the potential liberation of the sexy single girl collides with the career limitations of the early 1960s, forcing questions about the politics of appearance, femininity, and sexuality and how they have or have not changed since then.

As Tamar Jeffers argues, and as is made plain through Betty and Joan on *Mad Men*, in the 1950s and early 1960s there were "two predominant outlines for the female costume: the New Look-inspired swing-skirted silhouette, with tight waist and multiple, full stiff petticoats supporting circular skirts, versus more tailored, figure-hugging sheaths" (51). Though both silhouettes highlight the female form with a fitted bodice and cinched waist, the New Look extends the movement from waist to hip while the sheath shows off the legs and rear by following the line of the hip into the knee rather than standing away from it. Jeffers suggests that in contrast to the New Look, "the sheath shape both clung to the body, revealing its curves to the viewer, and simultaneously permitted approach thanks to its more parsimonious occupation of space" (52). She argues that the sheath's connection to the body was a sign of sexual experience, yet at the same time it could emphasize that women like Joan were "in the office to attract men rather than taking their careers seriously" (51). Thus Joan's fashion and body suggest both a traditional expectation for women to find husbands, not careers, and a feminist or proto-feminist embrace of female sexuality on a woman's own terms. Indeed, the show initially emphasizes Joan's highly sexualized position in the workplace but increasingly uses that same style to highlight her personal complexity and professional competence.

While the New Look silhouette constructed one kind of woman in the 1950s, Lee Wright makes a parallel argument about the stiletto heel in the 1960s (fig. 8.3). The physical effect of the heel is to highlight the hourglass silhouette constructed by the sheath dress or the pencil skirt and its attendant undergarments. Socially and politically, however, Wright argues,

> the stiletto was used by some women to represent dissatisfaction with the conventional female image and to replace it with that of a "modern" woman who was more active and economically independent than her predecessors. The paradox is that, in retrospect, it has been labeled a "shackling" instrument which renders women immobile and passive.... I consider it a more important factor that the stiletto did *not* symbolise the housewife. From 1957 the stiletto was associated with glamour, with rebellion: it represented someone ... "modern" and "up to date," and, above all, someone who inhabited a world outside the home. (203)

In other words, fashion and the stiletto heel operate not just as a form of unidirectional containment but also as a site of struggle — and it is clear that many contemporary viewers experience a great deal of pleasure in Joan for precisely the ways in which she seems to struggle against her social roles, her space, even her own clothing. Wright's analysis offers a historical framework for Joan's fashion, femininity, and sexuality as a break with the gender roles and gendered expectations of the New Look and the 1950s housewife. Joan's fashions and the way her sartorial choices publicly highlight her body and her sexuality align her not just with the 1950s sex kitten stereotype but with the sexual revolution, the birth control pill, and a brand of feminism which embraced the possibilities that women might have it all: work and sex, independence and relationships, femininity and feminism. Key to this relationship as embodied in Joan is the possibility that a feminist reading of

FIGURE 8.3. Joan's stiletto heels on disc 1 of
the season 2 DVD box set (Lionsgate, 2009).

the clothed body "no longer rests with the image (whether such a stereo-typed femininity can be perceived as feminist) but with the possession of the image" (Bruzzi, 127). Joan "controls the effect of the image" (Bruzzi, 127) by embracing a 1950s stereotype not because of what it is to men, but because of what it is to women: the opposite of the oppressed and contained housewife.

Joan and her narrative arc also demonstrate the limitations of feminine power rooted in appearance, however. We admire the confidence with which her sexualized body moves around the office, but we also see her feet aching in high heels and the marks her bra straps leave on her shoulder. In "A Night to Remember" Joan fills in as a script reader for the television department at Sterling Cooper. She is uniquely useful in this new position since she offers the perspective of the soap opera's female target audience. Joan also enjoys her new role and responsibility. However, even when her insight is acknowl-edged, it is linked to her appearance. One executive tells Harry Crane, "This is why I didn't want to do this on the phone. I love what she says and I love the way she says it." And once she proves the value of the position, the newly created full-time job is given without discussion to a new male hire. The story line ends with a disappointed Joan, undressing at home, rubbing her shoulder where deep red marks show the physical and emotional cost of her femininity. Despite the power her body exudes and the pleasure it gives her (and the viewer) to wield her curves in the office, despite the insight she brings to the advertisers, her prospects are limited by the very femininity from which she gets those pleasures. She has no ability to leverage her power and insight into anything except an engagement ring. Joan, like Betty, is left looking pretty but questioning the payoff, a move that alerts us to the real need for a coming feminism that will insist on the place of women in the workplace and the possibilities for her outside of the home.

Joan's paradox is not only that the high heel that "has been labeled a 'shackling' instrument" is also a sign of her liberation, but that as much as her emphasis on femininity as power is familiar to and embraced by twenty-first-century feminism, her power nonetheless reads as dated, even tragic, in retrospect. In "The Summer Man" (4.8) Joan chides Peggy for having fired a disrespectful employee who draws an obscene image of Joan: "I'd already handled it. And if I wanted to go further, one dinner with Mr. Cortzer from Sugarberry Ham and Joey would've been off it and out of my hair. . . . No matter how powerful we get around here, they can still just draw a cartoon. So all you've done is prove to them that I'm a meaningless secretary and you're another humorless bitch." Though she does demonstrate the power of femininity and is certainly a powerful woman, in moments like these it is hard not to see as well how the power of Joan's appearance is undermined by that appearance's roots in male ideals designed to keep women in a subordinate position.

Because of her embrace of femininity and sexuality, Joan resonates with women who have grown up after the advances of second wave feminism, women who want to embrace femininity as powerful, not reject it as a sign of patriarchy. However, Joan's limitations may also be a part of this resonance. Joan is a reminder of the difference in context between then and now—women have opportunities today they did not in the early 1960s—but also the similarity, in that women still struggle to be taken seriously in worlds run by men and wrestle with the question of whether power and respect come from appearing more or less feminine or more or less sexual. Fashion continues to be a powerful form of self-expression and an everyday negotiation of femininity and feminism, but it is also still a conditional expression whose meaning can shift depending on who is looking.

Perhaps what *Mad Men* suggests is that just as Joan and Betty are in need of a coming feminism, we too are still in need of that feminism. In our everyday lives, we must continue to find ways to put fashion in conversation with feminism so that they can be productively resistant. One strategy lies in using fashion to evoke women's histories, to evoke previous decades of representational activity. If "cultural memory is produced through objects, images and representations" (Sturken, 9), *Mad Men* produces cultural memory by reinfusing sartorial artifacts and their contemporary counterparts with often ignored social histories, by reinvesting pencil skirts with both sexism and the sexual revolution, by reconnecting swing skirts to both the housewife and the feminine mystique. While Betty and Joan powerfully reposition articles of clothing, the dialogue between feminism and fashion reaches toward its apotheosis in the development of Peggy, her feminism, and her emerging sense of style.

PEGGY OLSON'S PONYTAIL

In *Mad Men*'s pilot episode, "Smoke Gets in Your Eyes," Peggy Olson's first day as a secretary at Sterling Cooper is one of the central story lines. Joan shows her around the office and gives Peggy various pieces of advice, including the need to improve her appearance. While Joan's dress highlights her hourglass silhouette, Peggy's plain figure is made curveless and adolescent by a midlength swing skirt and loose sweater, and she wears her hair in a carefully curled ponytail. Joan tells Peggy, "Go home, take a paper bag and cut some eye holes out of it. Put it over your head, get undressed, and look at yourself in the mirror. Really evaluate where your strengths and weaknesses are. And be honest." Especially in the early seasons, Joan is Peggy's primary model of modern womanhood, and the relationship between Joan and Peggy is shaped by how Peggy often fails to live up to this model.

This plays out clearly in "Maidenform" (2.6). In this episode, the male copywriters come up with an ad campaign idea while out at a bar, without Peggy. Responding to Peggy's frustration, Joan tells her, "You want to be taken seriously? Stop dressing like a little girl." This echoes the advice that Bobbie Barrett gives to Peggy in an earlier episode: "You can't be a man. Don't even try. Be a woman. It's powerful business, when done correctly" ("The New Girl," 2.5). Those around Peggy are telling her she has to be more feminine to be successful, regardless of whether that success is in finding a husband or in her career. At least momentarily, she responds to these pressures and does so sartorially, when at the end of the episode she shows up to the strip club where her male coworkers are celebrating with clients. Peggy is wearing a blue, deep V-neck satin dress, diamond-like jewelry, and bright red lipstick, and her hair is down, no longer in her trademark girlish ponytail (fig. 8.4). Peggy wants to be seen as sexual and attractive here, but her performance of femininity is uncomfortable and uncertain, like the fake diamonds she is wearing. Even in her sexy dress, she fails to be either a Jackie or a Marilyn, a Bobbie Barrett or a Joan Holloway, and her sexuality has little real power. Unlike Joan or Marilyn, Peggy does not possess the image of herself. Peggy dresses simply for the men around her. Yet this is not only reflective of Peggy's inadequacies, it is also reflective of the inadequacies of the ideal. Peggy is not Jackie or Marilyn, but this is not just because she fails at trying. Rather she simply is something else entirely, belying the binary femininity of her era.[11]

While Joan and Bobbie tell Peggy to be a woman, in "Indian Summer" (1.11) Don tells Peggy: "You presented like a man. Now act like one." Similarly, in "The Mountain King" (2.12) after Peggy asks for the office vacated by Freddy Rumsen, Roger Sterling tells her: "You young women are very aggressive. . . . It's cute, there are thirty men out there who didn't have the balls to ask me." Despite the fact that she succeeds at Sterling Cooper because she is a woman and offers a female perspective on products like lipstick and weight-loss belts, as she moves away from her girlishness, there is equal pressure on her to be—and by extension, to appear and to dress— both more feminine and more masculine. After her meager attempt at femininity in "Maidenform," it would seem that her fashion choices, like her

FIGURE 8.4. Peggy dressed up ("Maidenform," 2.6).

career choices, would continue to follow "the second wave's workplace advice, which for decades argued that women had to downplay their femininity in order to fit in to the male worlds they increasingly inhabited" (Scanlon, 133). Yet in seasons 3 and 4, Peggy instead begins to find a middle ground. As Faran Krentcil observes in the AMC *Fashion File* blog posting "The Blues Never Felt So Good," Peggy is consistently clothed in collared shirts and dresses with pussy bows at the neck. Despite her haircut and her evolving silhouette, "she still can't relinquish her necktie." Krentcil goes on to say that in season 3, "it was an attempt at being fashionable," and indeed Joan too sometimes wears a more subtle version of the bow. Yet in season 4, Krentcil suggests "it's gone deeper: Peggy needs to wear a tie because Don, Pete, Roger, and Harry all do. And she'll be damned if she can't be part of that boys' club because of her clothes." Yet I would argue that she combines the feminine bow with the masculine tie not only to move closer to the boys' club but also to define a third path between femininity and feminism.

Though Peggy's moments of imitation in the first three seasons suggest that there are a limited number of identities a woman can take on, as the show moves into its fourth season we see additional possibilities for her. While Betty's and Joan's characters suggest specific and somewhat predictable trajectories, aligned with specific feminist or feminine models, Peggy is increasingly less easily pigeonholed as she both tries on Joan's Manhattan lifestyle and moves toward the counterculture. When she tries the single-girl life in season 3, however, being "out in the city, ready for fun" with her perky new roommate ("The Arrangements," 3.4), she never quite dresses the part and never quite gets the performance right. She more successfully flirts with a wholesale alternative when in "My Old Kentucky Home" (3.3) she proclaims, "I'm Peggy Olson and I wanna smoke some marijuana," and she assertively tells her secretary at the end of the episode, "I'm in a very good place right now. . . . I have a job and an office with my name on the door, and a secretary. . . . Don't worry about me. I am going to get to do everything you want for me." By embracing not only her professional status but also a bohemian version of herself, she begins to invent a middle path between Joan's single-girl sexuality, second wave feminism, and the counterculture. Though this version of Peggy largely disappears from the rest of season 3, it reemerges decisively when season 4 begins in November 1964.

"The Rejected" (4.4) is particularly interesting in this process of sartorial reinvention. Of two particularly notable outfits of Peggy's, the more memorable is the skirt and boots combination she wears with a yellow-and-black-striped mock turtleneck to a party in the Village with her new friend Joyce. More significant, however, is the outfit Peggy wears to the office at the episode's close. Peggy's dress is a bright blue color reminiscent of Joan's bold hues, but it is accented with a geometric, more mod-style collar and has a fuller, pleated skirt that is simultaneously evocative of the evolving New Look and of the plaid pleats of Peggy's earlier schoolgirl dresses. While the first outfit is unexpectedly mod, the blue dress is not wholly one style or another, and neither is Peggy. This Peggy is learning to negotiate Madison Avenue *and* the Village, femininity *and* feminism. It turns out Peggy is the one who can have it all, not Joan. Far from the mousy secretary of season 1, Peggy is now a reminder that models of female identity go far beyond the easy silhouettes of Marilyn, Jackie, and June Cleaver, or Betty Friedan, Helen Gurley Brown, and Gloria Steinem.

Perhaps because it is less distinct and less archetypal, lacking the clear silhouette of Betty's New Look or Joan's hourglass, Peggy's style has not translated as well commercially. Betty and Joan's fashions have appeared as inspirations in contemporary fashion lines such as Michael Kors's and been referenced by companies such as Pinup Couture and Stop Staring! that specialize in vintage reproductions. Peggy's looks, in contrast, are more likely to be found in actual vintage shops and among actual vintage devotees. This may in part result from Peggy's color palette being duller than Betty's and Joan's and thus better matching fifty- and sixty-year-old dresses. Nevertheless, the idea that wearing vintage "involved a change of status and a revaluing of clothing beyond the original time or setting" (DeLong et al., 23) has a particular resonance with the ways in which Peggy constantly revalues her era with her refusal to confine herself to a one-dimensional identity. While Betty's dresses and Joan's skirts are reinvented by twenty-first-century contexts, Peggy more actively works to reinvent her clothes, exactly what twenty-first-century women do when they wear vintage. Once again, the performativity of fashion is pivotal to a character's ability to represent both history and now, reconstructing the dress as a site and technology of memory.

I hope that this chapter, and the general success of Mad Men, can serve as a call for the importance of examining not only the representation of history on television but also television's historical fictions as sites of memory—an aspect that may be easily overlooked amid tenacious discourses of accuracy and authenticity. As Gary Edgerton suggests, in many ways "television is the principal means by which most people learn about history today" ("Television as Historian," 1). Yet this does not simply mean television operates as an audiovisual textbook; objects, images, and representations are, as Sturken notes, "technologies of memory, not vessels of memory in which memory passively resides so much as objects through which memories are shared, produced and given meaning" (9). As a technology of memory, television emerges as a key forum in which personal memories, dominant histories, and alternative narratives interact, facilitating the cultural memory function of a show like Mad Men. Likewise fashion, with its inherent performativity, enables new ways of knowing the past and thus new knowledge about the past. Television, fashion, and television's representation of fashion have unique, if underexamined, places in the construction, representation, and entanglement of history and memory. Mad Men encourages this examination, but the project need not and should not stop there.

NOTES

1. Scott Hornbacher, "Establishing *Mad Men*," *Mad Men: Season 1*, DVD (Lionsgate, 2008).

2. For the eBay bidding war, see the video "Inside Mad Men: Props of the Season Three Premiere" on AMCtv.com (accessed 24 January 2010).

3. Banana Republic's "Mad about Style" promotions have run annually since 2009. Bryant also has a lifestyle website and a book, *The Fashion File*, which, as it says on the cover, "lets you peek into the dressing rooms of *Mad Men* . . . showing you how to find your own leading-lady style." Additionally, Bryant has released a *Mad Men*–inspired clothing line through the home-shopping company QVC, and several cast members have taken part in fashion tie-ins.

4. Though the insistent discourse of accuracy and authenticity has died down somewhat since the first season, it is still pivotal to the popular understanding of the show.

5. I distinguish between vintage clothing (garments actually made in the past) and retro clothing (contemporary reproductions of those styles), both of which are used on *Mad Men*. Ultimately, however, I think vintage and retro work in much the same way (and are often visually indistinguishable) both on *Mad Men* and in everyday life.

6. On gender as performative, see Judith Butler. On fashion as a "technology of self-formation," see Craik, 204.

7. I use the term *postwar* because the early 1960s housewife is still archetypically and semantically associated with the 1950s. The character June Cleaver, for instance, is an archetypal 1950s housewife but appeared on *Leave It to Beaver* from 1957 to 1963.

8. Of course, this historical narrative is predominantly that of white women and white, middle-class families. There is a great deal to be said about fashion among women of color in the 1950s and retro or vintage style among women of color today, though this is beyond the scope of this chapter's focus on *Mad Men*.

9. "An Era of Style," *Mad Men: Season 2*, DVD (Lionsgate, 2009).

10. Again, see Judith Butler, but also work on femininity and the masquerade such as Doane, "Film and Masquerade."

11. See also Lilya Kaganovsky's chapter in this volume.

AGAINST DEPTH

Looking at Surface through the Kodak Carousel

IRENE V. SMALL

The final episode of *Mad Men*'s first season, "The Wheel" (1.13), revolves around what is perhaps the creative director Don Draper's most memorable sales pitch: a plan to brand Kodak's clunky plastic slide projector wheel as "the carousel." Harnessing the associations of the carousel with childhood fantasy and its dreamlike suspension of linear time, Don explains that the wheel should be understood not as a gadget, but a time machine. "It goes backwards, and forwards," he intones as the clients sit transfixed in front of the projector's screen; "It takes us to a place where we ache to go again."

In the tightly orchestrated reflexivity of this incident, the nostalgia Don invokes by way of "the carousel" is doubly operative. Kodak stopped manufacturing slide projectors in 2004, and in all likelihood, *Mad Men*'s adult audience will be the last generation to recall both the slide show's enchantment and the intensely physical aspect of its visual apparatus. Before an image in a darkened room became a vacation snapshot or a masterpiece of art history, such an audience might remember, it was first a material thing: a clackety square of plastic with a frayed label, a thing that might be put in backward, or upside down; a thing that could be lost, traded, or left forgotten in a box.

I call attention to Don's Kodak Carousel pitch both for its double articulation of nostalgia and because the magical transmutation of material thing into dematerialized image seated literally at the heart of the slide projector encapsulates much of what is at stake in *Mad Men*'s imagination of its own relationship to both avant-garde art and the culture industry of the 1960s. Don's brilliance as an ad man and his interest as a character lie in his ability to turn matter into metaphor, objects of consumption into dreams (or here, memories), the vulgar exteriority of the commodity world into the interior realm of the psyche.

Don, in short, turns surface into depth, and this alchemical quality re-curs as both visual cue and narrative trope for his character throughout the show. In the opening credits, for example, Don is blasted into silhouette within a vertiginous sea of skyscrapers glazed with scrims of colossal female bodies. Yet as his jet-black contour doubles in reflection against the build-ings' impenetrable panes of glass, we realize that this image of surface is in fact a diagram of depth. Unlike the flexing bodybuilder of Richard Hamil-ton's famous proto-pop collage *Just What Is It That Makes Today's Homes So Different, So Appealing?* (1956), who gleefully merges into a mediascape of television images and advertising copy, the flatness of Don's silhouette does not facilitate his assimilation into his surroundings. Rather, it throws him into relief. He is a virtual flatness descending through the illusionistic space of the spectacle. But the depth he experiences, the credits sequence would seem to suggest, is real.

Indeed, it is ostensibly Don's depth that is on display in the Kodak Car-ousel scene as he cycles through intimate vignettes of his family's domestic life in order to demonstrate a sales pitch more powerful than the "itch" of the new (fig. 9.1). While the slides evoke the actual etymological roots of nostalgia in *nostos* (homecoming) and *algos* (pain, grief, distress), Don's re-counting of a Greek salesman's definition of the term sounds remarkably like Roland Barthes's description in *Camera Lucida* of the *punctum*—a photo-graphic detail that provokes an emotional shock in its viewer. The punctum, Barthes writes, is "that accident which pricks me (but also bruises me, is poi-gnant to me)" (27). As "a sting, a speck, cut, little hole," the punctum pierces through the surface of the image and lodges itself deep within the viewing subject. It is the sign of Don's emotional authenticity in his slide-show pre-sentation, and it emerges in details such as the child's squinting eye, a mouth half-open in sleep, the glitter of confetti illuminating a forgotten kiss (fig. 9.2). These details touch us, touch Don, and reveal his psychological depth even as he expertly exploits them for the purpose of sales. This is the magic of the ad man who manipulates the mechanism of projection, and it is not for nothing that Don's subordinate Harry Crane, moved to tears by the re-

FIGURE 9.1. Don projects a series of family vignettes ("The Wheel," 1.13).

FIGURE 9.2. Bobby Draper's squinting eye as *punctum* ("The Wheel," 1.13).

verberations of Don's presentation for his own marital woes, is thrown into flat silhouette by the slide projector's stream of light as he leaves the room.

Don has depth. More depth, for example, than the bohemians he meets through his girlfriend, the artist Midge Daniels, who while away their time prancing around her loft and reciting beatnik poetry at Village clubs (fig. 9.3). Don's brief encounters with this bohemian world are *Mad Men*'s only forays into the world of living artists, and they are shown to be cliché in their drug habits, predictable in their political critiques, and most important, bad

FIGURE 9.3. Midge and friends make a conga line ("The Hobo Code," 1.8).

at art. (When a young poet recounts an erotic dream involving Fidel Castro, Nikita Khrushchev, a plucked chicken, and the Waldorf Astoria hotel, Don remarks, "Too much art for me.") Indeed, if Don is attracted to Midge's status as an outsider, the relationship between art and this "outside" remains elusive at best. While Midge's friends endlessly lampoon the shallowness of Don's profession and bourgeois lifestyle, it is ultimately he, rather than they, who approximates the traditional visionary role of the artist—in this case, to reveal hidden truth—when he takes a Polaroid of Midge and her friend Roy at the end of "The Hobo Code" (1.8). Gazing down at the shiny surface of the developed photograph he has just peeled away from its bulky cartridge, Don recognizes in a flash that Midge and Roy are in love (fig. 9.4). And while he knows "what love looks like" from its simulation in advertising, his ability to read and interpret code is linked explicitly to the social marginalization of his youth, for it is precisely during the temporal interim of the Polaroid's development that the narrative flashes back to Don's childhood, when a hobo teaches him the secret marks wanderers and transients leave to communicate among themselves. The bohemian world of artists, the episode suggests, is only a simulation of this outside; all play acting and histrionics, it offers little alternative to the narratives spun by Madison Avenue advertisers uptown.

Perhaps for this reason, the period art that appears most worthy of pause

FIGURE 9.4. The photograph as sign of love ("The Hobo Code," 1.8).

in the narrative arc of *Mad Men* appears not in Midge's downtown loft, but in Bert Cooper's upscale Madison Avenue office. If Don's approximation of an artist in "The Hobo Code" relies on traditional roles of interpretation and revelation, however, this art offers a rather different rubric of signification based not on the romantic notion of the visionary but on a modernist model of pure aesthetic experience. During "The Gold Violin" (2.7), Jane Siegel, Harry Crane, Ken Cosgrove, and Sal Romano break into Cooper's office to inspect his new painting—a Mark Rothko—but are left fumbling as to what it "means" (fig. 9.5). Only Ken, the aspiring writer, appears to "get" the painting. And he puts it this way: "Maybe it doesn't mean anything. Maybe you're just supposed to experience it. Because when you look at it, you feel something." As the camera zooms in on the painting, he continues, "It's like looking into something very deep. You could fall in."

Paradoxically, the operative critical term for abstract expressionist and color-field paintings such as Rothko's was not depth, but flatness, as famously expounded by the American critic Clement Greenberg in essays such as his "Modernist Painting" (1960). Here Greenberg argued that the self-critical tendencies of the modernist ethos dictated that its most advanced practices would explore the limiting conditions of the painterly medium. Hence it would be the ability of a Rothko painting to suspend the pictorial illusion of

FIGURE 9.5. Harry, Jane, Sal, and Ken contemplate Rothko ("The Gold Violin," 2.7).

fictive three-dimensional space in favor of a flattened scheme of color inten-
sities vibrating against, and identical to, the rectangular surface of the picture
plane, that secured its place within the modernist tradition. Yet as the art historian David Joselit has argued, the priority on optical flatness elaborated by
Greenberg was sustained by a simultaneous insistence on emotional depth
that, initially expressed by the figure of the artist, was ultimately understood
to translate into the psychological experience of the viewer (see Joselit). It is
precisely this appeal to authenticity that is mapped out in Cosgrove's comments about "experience" in front of the Rothko. The painting itself is rigor-
ously flat; it is Cosgrove himself, by contrast, who is shown to have depth.

In this episode, the Rothko painting stands in for a modernist art that
requires emotional nuance and the ability to suspend the artifice of "meaning" in favor of an aesthetic experience in which, as Greenberg wrote in his
1952 article, "feeling is all." Yet by 1962, the setting for *Mad Men*'s second season, Rothko was already an outmoded representative of the avant-garde. By
the late 1950s, young artists like Robert Rauschenberg and Jasper Johns had
begun to ironize the abstract expressionist appeal to metaphysical interiority
and subjective expression that provided the rhetorical trappings for modernist paintings like Rothko's. Their deadpan appropriation of American flags,
Coca-Cola bottles, and mechanically produced marks appealed to the conventionality of culture rather than the primal workings of the unconscious.
Rauschenberg and Johns thus made way for the full-blown elaboration of
American pop art in the coming years. If Cosgrove displays emotional depth

FIGURE 9.6. Andy Warhol, *Soup Cans* (1962) © 2011 The Andy Warhol Foundation for the Visual Arts, Inc. / Artists Rights Society (ARS), New York. Photograph: The Andy Warhol Foundation, Inc. / Art Resource, NY.

by way of aesthetic "feeling," after all, "feeling" is also the catchword in the same episode for a pitch to sell Martinson coffee to the young.

In this light, it is useful to consider not simply the period art that cameos within *Mad Men*, but also that which is conspicuously absent from view. For 1962, the year in which *Mad Men*'s Rothko episode is set, was the year that Andy Warhol, who had been trained as a commercial illustrator (we might imagine him as a blonder, more anemic, and diffident version of Sal) had his first show at a fine-art gallery (fig. 9.6). There, at Irving Blum's Ferus Gallery in Los Angeles, Warhol exhibited thirty-two paintings of Campbell's soup cans, one for each of the thirty-two varieties of soup that Campbell's made. Each painting, in turn, was not mounted on the wall, but propped up on a shallow shelf, as if to mimic the display of objects in a grocery store. Unlike Rothko's painting and its presumption of interiority, Warhol's *Soup Cans* proffers an art that is fully aware of its commodity status, that flaunts it, and indeed, that revels in its character as surface and empty value.

This is perhaps what is most interesting about *Mad Men*'s engagement, or rather nonengagement, with the advanced art of its time. Namely, that while the television series utilizes period art to propose a narrative model of psychological depth in antithesis to the flat surfaces of advertising spectacle (a narrative, paradoxically, which ends up endowing the advertisers, rather than the artists, with such depth), the most significant forms of 1960s art analyzed the logic of this spectacle and threw it back to the culture industry *intact*. Thus it was precisely Warhol's willingness to apply a logic of flatness, repetition, and bland surface to soup cans as well as race riots that disclosed the insidiousness of an American culture that could conceive of equivalence only through commodities rather than in the social, economic, and political parity of its citizens. We are accustomed to critiquing advertising's position as the middleman between avant-garde art and the culture industry. Appropriating art's modes and rhetorics, as we see in Sterling Cooper's "feeling" pitch for Martinson coffee, advertising co-opts aesthetics for the purposes of producing commodity desire. Warhol's brilliance was to recognize that art does not escape this commodity circuit. Rather than presuming originality, by contrast, he chose to appropriate advertising's codes for art.

In so doing, Warhol effectively evacuated the psychological depth presumed of the modernist work of art. If his works stand in for subjective experience, they do so only in relation to endlessly repeatable subjects with endlessly replicable desires. Don himself is fully aware of this condition: in "The Color Blue" (3.10) he acknowledges that people don't want to see the world differently; in "A Night to Remember" (2.8) his wife Betty functions as the ideal subject of consumer research; and as he retorts to the bohemians at Midge's apartment in "The Hobo Code," "There is no big lie, there is no system. The world is indifferent." Yet if Don correctly recognizes that the bohemian art world offers no outside, *Mad Men* consistently implies that he does so because he himself constitutes an outside posited in the midst of the encompassing system. This is perhaps why Don does not need to appear in the Rothko episode. Like the modernist painting, he is an image of surface whose effect is to produce depth.

I end these observations by referencing a work by the artist Dan Graham called *Homes for America*, which made its first public appearance as a slide-show installation in an exhibition titled *Projected Art* at the Finch College Museum of Art in 1966 (fig. 9.7).[1] The installation consisted of a slide projector mounted on a pedestal that cycled through a series of deadpan shots of tract housing in New Jersey that Graham had taken with an Instamatic camera over the summer of 1965. In this work, Graham departed from the serial, additive forms of minimalist sculpture that had started to be shown in galleries around this time. In *Homes for America*, he found this repetition ready-made in the landscape around him: the endless sprawl of housing develop-

FIGURE 9.7. Dan Graham, *Homes for America, 1966–67* (20 color 35 mm slides).
Courtesy of the artist and Marian Goodman Gallery, New York/Paris.

ments buttressed at its edges with, as he wrote, "bowling alleys, shopping plazas, car hops, discount houses, lumber yards or factories" (Graham, 22).

As Don does in his Kodak sales pitch, Graham's work lays bare the mechanism of projection and presents the carousel as a material object that produces a sequence of images on a screen. The slide show, in other words, does not simply *convey* the work of art, it is itself the work of art. But in Graham's work, the reflexivity of the mechanism is used to the opposite effect of Don's presentation, where of course the slide show is meant to sell the actual wheel. Unlike the family photos in Don's slide show, the images in Graham's work studiously avoid the punctum. They offer no relief of that pinprick of emotion. Instead, they linger on the blandness and uniformity of the American suburbs, showing not the intimacy of domesticity, but its external container and standardized architectural form. If in Don's slide show the wheel is an instrument of magic, transmuting material things into dematerialized images that wind through time to reveal the hidden recesses of what was once called the soul, Graham's projecting apparatus refuses to escape the deadening metronome of the instrument itself. Each click of the projector announces an image of monotonous architectural surface we have seen a thousand times but cannot remember, and which we will certainly forget once the next slide drops down.

If artists such as Dan Graham and Andy Warhol help us understand Don's Kodak Carousel presentation as an object lesson, it is because their work exposes the historical limits of the depth model on which the episode "The Wheel," and the narrative presumption of *Mad Men* as a whole, relies. As scholars of postmodernism such as Fredric Jameson have persuasively argued, the 1960s marked the beginning of a shift in which traditional modes of cultural interpretation (based on oppositions such as authenticity and inauthenticity, high and low, surface and depth) were rendered obsolete. Within the new configurations of capital and their parallel cultural regime, objects of culture no longer functioned as portals to a larger reality or more truthful experience set apart from commodity culture. Instead, like Warhol's soup cans or Graham's tract housing, they were situated solidly within its bounds, and their critical capacity, if operative at all, functioned not in terms of penetration or revelation, but in terms of equalization, deflation, and the emptying out of value.

Mad Men clearly positions itself in relation to this historical sea change. It is, after all, Don's unforgiving insight that we are all constructed as images that drives the story line of the show. Yet in retaining a dialectic of surface and depth, even as its terms are inverted and displaced in often unexpected ways, *Mad Men* stops short of engaging the radical implications of Warhol's *Soup Cans* and Dan Graham's *Homes for America* at the narrative and structural levels of its plot. Indeed, despite Don's facility with the workings of the new cultural order, it is precisely his shifting of roles as visionary artist, in the romantic mode, and aestheticized work of art, in the modernist mode, that indicates what was at stake to be lost in postmodernism's cultural flattening out.

To we viewers sitting transfixed before computers and flat-screen televisions rather than the slide-projector screens on which Don's Kodak clients fix their gaze, *Mad Men* offers a series of constructed historical punctums that speak to our distance from the past. Such punctums induce both nostalgia and discomfort, and in so doing, they offer complex entry into the 1960s as an object of historical desire. Yet to read *Mad Men*'s historical drama "against depth," as I would argue Warhol and Graham have taught us to do, is to recognize that the series is about an operative, rather than simply represented surface, one that does not remain within the meticulously crafted realism of the series' diegetic world but sprawls out into the historical present of today. Ranging from product placement and sponsorship to licensed Barbie Dolls and *Mad Men*–themed shop windows, from social networking applications and Twitter personas to buy-by-episode iTunes availability and

"*Mad*-vertising" spots, this operative surface weaves diegetic content into a continuous fabric of commercial solicitation in which we, the viewers, rather than the muse of the 1960s, are the ultimate objects of desire.[2] So while Don's Kodak presentation may make us nostalgic for the time when we bought into our current condition, it is useful to remember that the most advanced art of that time reflected this condition back to us, and still does, as pure, unrelenting surface with nothing behind it at all.

NOTES

1. Dan Graham was born in Urbana, Illinois, but grew up largely in New Jersey, from where he drew his inspiration for *Homes for America*. He initially displayed the work as a slide show to friends in his loft. See Graham.

2. On AMC's and Lionsgate's marketing and advertising for *Mad Men*, see Elliot, "A Blitz," "'Mad Men' Dolls," and "What Was Old"; and Lafayette.

10

"IT WILL SHOCK YOU HOW MUCH THIS NEVER HAPPENED"

Antonioni and Mad Men

ROBERT A. RUSHING

There are a number of reasons why the Italian film director Michelangelo Antonioni speaks to the AMC television series *Mad Men*. To begin with, the show has evinced a consistent fascination with things Italian, from the ethnically marked body and desires of Salvatore Romano (the show's gay Italian American artist) to its fascination with Italian style. Betty Draper turns out to speak a fluent if stilted Italian, and showcases her appreciation for Italy by dressing up as an early 1960s Italian film vamp in the episode "Souvenir" (3.8). And Antonioni is explicitly cited in "The New Girl" (2.5), if not by name. When Don's lover Bobbie Barrett discovers he likes movies, she gushes *"Spartacus!"* Then she says, "You seen the foreign ones? So sexy." Don replies with the title of an Antonioni film as his paradigmatic choice for foreign and sexy: *"La notte."*

Mad Men consistently reminds its viewers that Don Draper is a cinephile. Movies, we learn, fill Don's offscreen time: when he's not in his office or another woman's bed, he is catching a matinee. His tastes are catholic, so much so that when it turns out he hasn't seen *Bye Bye Birdie*, his protégée Peggy Olsen is shocked: "But you see everything!" So it's no surprise Don has seen Antonioni. Indeed, Don knows Antonioni better than he realizes.

FIGURE 10.1. Lidia in *La notte* (1961): disconnected and isolated.

Don's familiarity with Antonioni is — as we would expect from the show's obsessively accurate creator, Matthew Weiner — consistent with the era depicted in *Mad Men*. Italian film enjoyed an almost unparalleled period of success and influence from the late 1950s to the early 1970s: directors such as Federico Fellini, Luchino Visconti, Antonioni, and, later, Pier Paolo Pasolini and Bernardo Bertolucci were dominant figures whose fame helps explain Betty Draper's familiarity with the fashion, style, and language of Italy. The same period saw an American love affair with Italy, especially on celluloid: Italy then, as now, was an American fetish, a privileged site of sexual, romantic, melodramatic, and comic fantasies (the films *September Affair* [1950], *Roman Holiday* [1953], *Three Coins in the Fountain* [1954], *Summertime* [1955], *It Started in Naples* [1960], and the comic *Come September* [1961], starring Rock Hudson, Gina Lollobrigida, Sandra Dee, and Bobby Darin, were all set in Italy). By 1963 even Gidget went to Rome (in *Gidget Goes to Rome*) — along with Betty Draper, evidently.

Don Draper, however, seems to prefer the art side of European films. *La notte* (1961), for example, is a typical Antonioni film: it stresses interpersonal, socioeconomic, and existential forms of alienation (figs. 10.1–10.2). Characters stand with their backs to each other. Sequences are long, and often wordless. There is little or no plot, and character actions are not driven

FIGURE 10.2. Giovanni in *La notte*: passive and without direction.

by strong underlying motivations, but are aimless and wandering. Characters are passive or even unresponsive. There is a considerable amount of real time in the film. Characters seek erotic adventures but are left unsatisfied by them—as in *Mad Men*, infidelity is commonplace and yet does not seem to provide any "way out." Antonioni's camera strays away from its human subjects—sometimes while they are speaking—to contemplate the deserted landscape, or architecture uncontaminated by human figures. *Mad Men* has clearly drawn on Antonioni's stylings: the persistent theme of alienation; characters who are dissatisfied or "blank"; infidelity that fails to stem the characters' sense of emptiness; and—by television standards—a surprising willingness to have scenes without dialogue, real-time sequences, and a pacing that is slow, if not Antonioni's glacial pace.

But *Mad Men* shares something deeper with Antonioni, something that goes beyond an early 1960s culture interested in exploring sexual liberation, pervaded by a sense of alienation and a love of midcentury modern style. What *Mad Men* really shares with Antonioni are three fundamental concerns: (1) the impenetrable surface of things, especially other people; (2) the fragility and fluidity of identity, which appears not as a foundational feature of the subject but as an external shell, discarded at will; and (3) a dedication to watching things—especially people—disappear.

In a very significant sense, these three categories—superficiality, identity exchange, and the disappearance of the subject—are all fundamentally linked. Slavoj Žižek has persistently argued that apparently "deep" phenomena (religious belief, identity) are in fact entirely superficial. He is particularly fond of Pascal's motto—Act as if you believe, and you shall believe—but with a twist. For Pascal, the motto suggested that "mere" action, a rote following of banal exterior rituals (genuflecting before the altar, for instance) would later lead to a real interior conviction, a true part of the self. But it also suggests that perhaps the apparently deep, inner conviction of religious belief is nothing more than the habit of mere exterior ritual. Žižek invariably returns to the tag line of the *X-Files*: "The truth is out there." This phrase does not mean that the truth is in some distant and inaccessible place, however—rather, that the truth is "out there," entirely visible, on the surface (Žižek, *Plague of Fantasies*, 3–7).

Indeed, numerous commentators on Antonioni have noted that his "true vision" is not to be found in the "depths" of his characters (who generally appear to have very little interiority in any event), but in the surfaces his camera prefers to film, especially landscapes and architecture.[1] And what these reveal is a preference for flat, closed, and deserted forms. In *L'avventura* (1960), the character Claudia approaches a building in a deserted town that appears to have been designed by the artist Giorgio de Chirico. She presses her face to a shuttered window and gently calls, "C'è nessuno?" (Nobody's there?) Only her own voice replies in an echo. In a Žižekian sense, it contains the "real" her, the rote repetition of her external actions in the form of an echo. Act as if you are Claudia, and you shall be Claudia.

But Claudia herself is not acting as if she is Claudia; how can she, if her "innermost truth" is that she is an empty building, shuttered and inaccessible? "Claudia" means nothing more than a rote repetition of a script. And this brings me to the second category—identity exchange. Antonioni's dissatisfied, restless characters, hoping to find a truth that has depth ("the truth is in here"), often find themselves assuming the role of another. If "Claudia" is just a cipher, a name in scare quotes, perhaps her friend "Anna" has authentic being, depth, and interiority. And so when Anna disappears, Claudia takes her place, and her boyfriend. It is enough, in this vision, to fill the same structural place—Anna's boyfriend now loves Claudia; Claudia now enjoys the same rich hotels and friends as Anna did before. The same exchange takes place in a more radical way in a later Antonioni film, *The Passenger* (1975), in which David Locke (Jack Nicholson) exchanges identities with a recently deceased guest at his hotel, becoming a man named Robertson. Locke does not take on Robertson's mannerisms or personality, or attempt to look like him. Instead, he follows the most superficial and exterior parts of Robertson:

he simply keeps all the appointments in Robertson's appointment book. For the rest of the world, this is enough for Locke to "be" Robertson, to be him in perhaps the most profound way possible: to live and eventually to die as Robertson. Antonioni signals the identity exchange the same way he did for Claudia and Anna: through an exchange of shirts.

For viewers of *Mad Men*, this will sound rather familiar. In the show's backstory (revealed directly in flashback), there is a man named Dick Whitman who is, socioeconomically, a "nobody." He exchanges dog tags, however, with his commanding officer, a certain Don Draper, when the officer is killed. And so Whitman, this whit of a man, both dies (officially, legally) and becomes someone new. It is certainly a symbolic promotion from an everyday Tom, Dick, or Harry—Dick in this case—to a title of minor Spanish nobility, Don (there is of course also an erotic promotion here, from a vulgar term for male genitals to the suggestion of an accomplished seducer: Don Draper is certainly a Don Juan—or he is at least draped in the outfit of a Don Juan). And this transformation brings me to this chapter's title.

After Don's assistant, Peggy, becomes pregnant without realizing and gives birth, she goes a little crazy and spends some time in the hospital. Don eschews conventional ego-bolstering or self-help psychology—he does not tell her to get in touch with her feelings or that she needs to confront what happened. Instead, he urges her to simply forget. Don has already learned from Antonioni that the subject is something like a suit of clothes that may be disposed of at will (he is, after all, quite literally a draper): a shirt or a set of dog tags to be exchanged for something new. He tells her with conviction: "This never happened." Then he pauses, and says as much to himself as to her, "It will *shock* you how much it never happened."

In the ironically titled episode "Souvenir" (3.8), Don's subordinate at the advertising firm, Pete Campbell, goes to a department store with a stained dress. Joan, formerly the head secretary at the agency but now working as a store manager, promises to have the dress replaced as a favor to Pete's wife, Trudy. As they continue speaking, it becomes apparent that each is concealing something, and that the other is aware of it. Joan doesn't want Pete to let anyone know that she has taken a new job (her husband, a doctor, should be providing but cannot), and Pete doesn't want anyone to know about the dress (it doesn't belong to his wife). Without ever openly stating their concerns, they come to an uneasy and familiar truce. "This never happened," Joan assures Pete, a promise that this, too, will disappear from memory. When Pete returns the now unstained dress to its owner, the German au pair next door, and then uses the favor to pressure her into sex, he tries to make the same pact with her. "It never happened," he says, ostensibly about the stain. And indeed, although the girl's employer and then Pete's wife eventually learn that Pete raped or coerced the girl into sex, no one ever says so out loud; everyone appears to forget. A collective, unspoken agreement reigns over the show: this never happened. There is still a dress (even if it has been exchanged), but the stain on it is gone — it becomes a souvenir of what cannot be said or recalled, what never happened. The episode's literal souvenir is a tacky gold charm of the Colosseum that Don gets for Betty from the hotel gift shop in Rome. Betty makes her dissatisfaction clear, saying bitterly that she can look at it when they "talk about the time [they] went to Rome." But what they cannot talk about, cannot recall, is precisely the fleeting Eros so typical of Antonioni: Betty dressing up as an Italian vamp, flirting with Italian men, pretending to meet Don for the first time at a café, sleeping with him on this casual "first date." These fantasies and sex games will have "never happened" back in Betty's domestic, suburban world, and the ruins of the Colosseum are a reminder not of an event, but of the erasure of an event.

This is just one way that, like Antonioni, *Mad Men* is concerned with photographing an absence or a disappearance. It shows things as they are vanishing, and allows us to watch their disappearance so that we too may be shocked by the ease with which the most permanent and foundational categories of our lives are disposed. Within the show, identity (Don), personal history (Peggy, Pete), and desire (virtually all of the characters) disappear, and leave little or no trace of what they were before. The show is often presented as a kind of historical re-creation, but its real investment is in the power of forgetting.[2] Its larger project is tracing the disappearance of a set of economic, sexual, and racial relations that seem unimaginable to many of today's spectators. Don knows that the first thing people want is to forget.

As with Antonioni, the "depth" of *Mad Men* is found in its preoccupation with surfaces and appearances — its obsessive attention to "superficial" exteriors: props, clothes, design, advertisements. This has made the show appear complicit in the superficiality of the advertising culture it sometimes critiques, and many have been happy to celebrate a return to mid-century modern design (from the website Brides.com's advice on how to "*Mad Men* your wedding" to the Banana Republic ad campaign discussed by Mabel Rosenheck in this volume).[3] Here we learn that "to Mad Men" is now a transitive verb in English, and the advertisements reduce binary gender opposition (men and women) to specific items of clothing — suits and skirts. Following Žižek again here I suggest that "the truth is out there," in the sense that it is to be found precisely on those pointless surfaces: these characters *are* what they wear in the most literal sense. "Don Draper" is the person wearing Don Draper's dog tag. The identity "Don Draper" has no other meaning. This is why the counterculture's denigrating epithet for corporate bosses is more accurate than they realized: corporate bosses are literally "suits," not people, something that Don dimly realizes. In Antonioni and in *Mad Men*, to put on a suit makes you a boss.

A few years ago a phenomenon swept the Internet: *"Mad Men* yourself" (the transitive verb, now reflexive). An AMC-sponsored website invited the viewer to construct an avatar or online self-image in early 1960s Saul Bass style, built out of a limited repertoire of hairstyles, corporate outfits, and period-appropriate accessories (fig. 10.3).[4] The site was quite explicit about the nature of this virtual paper doll: "Be sleek, be stylish—be yourself!" If you were not sure how to "be yourself" (an apparently tautological endeavor that strangely requires a great many psychosocial and material props), *Mad Men* could teach you—you do it like Don Draper, by assuming a series of apparently false and superficial signs until a kind of critical ontological mass is achieved. *Voilà!* Overnight, on the popular social networking site Facebook, users' normal photos disappeared and were replaced by these *Mad Men*–ized "suits" and "skirts."[5]

As much as these dress-up games may be consonant with capitalist directives to produce new styles, fashions, and merchandise, I suggest that there is also something potentially *risky* in the exposure of the arbitrary nature of identity. Like Betty with her fantasies of being a "dolce vita" courtesan, we play dress-up at costume parties and online, but such play can be an unspeakable embarrassment—not only because it may not fit with our idea of who we are (mature, restrained, adult, for example) but also because it suggests that the very notion of "who you are" may be arbitrary, something that one day will have "never happened."

To make the model of identity (and its risks) explicit, I turn to Jacques Lacan and his essay "The Mirror Stage as Formative of the *I* Function." In that essay, Lacan argued that the subject assumes an identity early in life by taking an *image* as his or her self, as in a mirror. For Lacan, the key here is that this is a mistake, a misrecognition, akin to confusing things and the words that denote those things. After all, I am *not* my mirror image, not only because it reverses left and right, but more crucially because it represents me as complete, rather than reflecting my psychic disorganization. For the rest of my life I assume a series of specular images, consciously and unconsciously, that I identify as me, images with a coherence and permanence that my own psychic and socioeconomic life lacks.

Here capitalism faces an essential contradiction: on the one hand, it depends on the subject assuming a series of ever-new images as identities in order to sustain its relentless expansion ("Just do it," or "Be all you can be"), but on the other hand, there is an inevitably traumatic dimension in the loss of one's old identity. After all, if my old self—the one before I became a "Gillette man"—was so disposable (like my new razors), why does this new one have such an aura of permanence? Why is *this* the "real me"? The fissure or gap between the trauma of losing who you were and the imperative to become someone new is not a challenge to the dominant ideology; it is the traumatic kernel around which the pearl of ideology grows in the first place. This is the risk at stake in *Mad Men*'s credits, repeatedly fracturing, dropping, and reconstituting the subject; it is the risk in our 1960s costume parties and *Mad Men* Facebook profiles—they encourage us both to consume and to question the value of that consumption (a kind of "psycho-ideology of everyday life"). This is not a naive rhetoric of "resistance": instead, it captures some of how *Mad Men* both attracts us and makes us feel uneasy, how the show makes viewers cognizant of the "ideological work" that advertising does, while simultaneously manipulating viewers with a parade of seamless, seductive images.

In *La notte*, Antonioni's preoccupation with watching people disappear is a constant concern. It is present in the film's opening shots of completely deserted high-rises in Milan. It appears again in the first sequence with dialogue, as the principal characters Giovanni (Marcello Mastroianni) and Lidia (Jeanne Moreau) sit in a hospital room with their dying friend—who afterward disappears from the film, dying offscreen. There are Antonioni's signature tracking shots, in which a camera follows a character—but in Antonioni, when the character moves out of sight, the camera lingers, registering the character's absence. At one point, Lidia stops to watch some boys firing off rockets in a field. Although the spectators crane their necks to see the rocket above, the camera lingers instead on the boys on the ground, watching them slowly vanish in an expanding cloud of smoke, a cloud that expands toward the spectators—and presumably toward us as well (figs. 10.4–10.7). Later Lidia returns to the spot with Giovanni and says, "C'erano lì; adesso sono andati via" (They were over there; now they've gone away), a phrase that could stand for all of Antonioni's work. This gesture is absolutely foundational, as Rohdie remarks: the "fate of characters . . . of objects and images to disappear, to lose form and identity, is a permanent feature of all of Antonioni's films" (4). Elsewhere Rohdie notes Antonioni's preference for "the dissolution of shapes, the disappearance of objects and their reappear-

FIGURE 10.3.
Mad Men Yourself:
the author, dressed in
early 1960s style.

FIGURES 10.4–10.7. A cloud of rocket exhaust grows larger, reaching toward the spectators (*La notte*).

FIGURE 10.8. Sexual desire is stylized, black on white (*La notte*).

ance as other things, still figurative, yet threatened with a loss of identity, a blur of outlines" (15).

Equally, *La notte* films the disappearance of desire. Eros is the only element in Antonioni's films that ever seems to have the potential to drag his characters out of their persistent ennui and alienation. Eros appears unexpectedly, suddenly animating Antonioni's characters—they smile, make eye contact, joke, and play. A nameless female patient asks Giovanni for a match (the heat of desire), only to abruptly blow it out, rather than light her cigarette with it. She pulls Giovanni into her room for an attempted coupling that is as madly passionate as it is stylized and empty (see fig. 10.8, but note how this image is repeated in a darker vein with Valentina [Monica Vitti] at the end of the film [fig. 10.9]). They are interrupted, and Giovanni drifts away. Desire is at war here, as it always is for Antonioni, with the camera's overwhelming interest in photographing empty or nearly empty space, abstract forms, shadows, black and white silhouettes—and so desire turns away from its ultimate aim.

Lidia is the most depressed character in *La notte*, flat and without affect, but she is persistently brought back to life by brief flirtations as she walks about the city—a waiting cabbie, two men passing by, her husband as they are about to go out to a nightclub. In something like the film's climax (if that term can be applied to Antonioni's films), Lidia is caught in a downpour with Roberto (Giorgio Negro), who has pursued her all evening. They are

FIGURE 10.9. Sexual desire is silhouetted, negative space (*La notte*).

filmed largely in silhouette and their speech is inaudible as they drive slowly through the rain. Lidia is luminous, finally happy, beaming, gesticulating, energetic—alive. Until Roberto touches her; then her smile fades, and she returns to the car and asks to be taken home. The disappearance of desire is marked by the return of spoken language—suddenly, the spectator can again hear them speak.

This disappearance of desire is never clearer than in Lidia's brief flirtation with her husband: she emerges in her new dress as the couple prepares to go out to a nightclub. Her husband admires her—there is the "catch" of Eros. He looks at her with desire. She reciprocates and begins to sway her hips, make herself visible for him, and she turns to him with a smile. But Eros fades, and as it fades, so does the person who was animated by it (figs. 10.10–10.11). The eclipse of desire in Antonioni is tantamount to the eclipse of the subject. Lidia turns away, falls back into the shadows, disappears, a gesture repeated elsewhere in the film by other characters.

These two kinds of disappearance are united in *La notte*'s final sequence. Giovanni and Lidia discuss their vanished love. Giovanni desperately embraces her—is this a renewal of their former passion or a grotesque and pathetic "going through the motions"? Antonioni doesn't care. His camera, as it so frequently does, cuts sideways to a deserted, adjacent field. A slow leftward dolly; the sound of their tryst is replaced by the sound of the distant jazz band, oddly close and present. The camera ends by attempting to

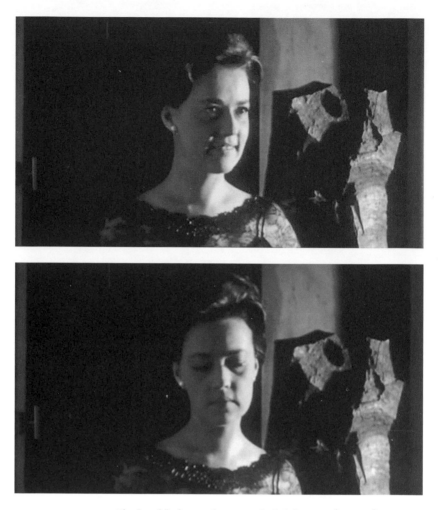

FIGURES 10.10–10.11. The "spark" of erotic desire . . . which fades away (*La notte*).

register an absence. It is hard to convey just how relentlessly Antonioni does this—the filming of absence—but his film *L'eclisse* (*The Eclipse*, 1962) is perhaps the best example. Here another estranged couple makes an appointment to meet and give their relationship another try. Neither shows up—but Antonioni's camera does, for a seven-minute montage of all the places in which they are not. And the closing montage of *L'eclisse* demands to be compared to Antonioni's single most famous shot: the seven-minute circular tracking shot that ends *The Passenger*, one that also photographs the definitive disappearance of the subject, as Locke-cum-Robertson begins the shot alive and asleep on the bed, but ends it dead.

In *Mad Men*, that vanishing is always less definitive — there is always the possibility that Don Draper/Dick Whitman will "get in touch with his true self," or that Betty will "become who she always wanted to be" when she gets away from Don. This is television, after all (and indeed, the fourth season of *Mad Men* flirts with this possibility throughout, as Don attempts to restrain his drinking, get in shape, and crusade against smoking, while the fifth season delights in turning Betty into the person she never wanted to be). But these potential "self-realizations" are constantly put at risk in the show, particularly through the figure of Don. The thrill of Don is the same as the thrill of vertigo — not so much the fear that one might fall as the excitement of giving in to that terrible temptation and jumping. Don shows a remarkable willingness to do this, not only before the show begins when he exchanges "Dick Whitman" for "Don Draper," but also in episodes such as "The Jet Set" (2.11), where he appears perfectly ready to dispose of his old drapery and don a new set of clothes for an endless California vacation. (He does the same in the first season's "Nixon vs. Kennedy" [1.12], where he offers to disappear in Los Angeles with his lover Rachel Menken.) In "Out of Town" (3.1) Don is mistaken for another man by a stewardess. In yet another recall of Antonioni (and Hitchcock, of course), Don has borrowed his brother-in-law's valise, which has "William Hofstadt" engraved on it. He looks baffled when the stewardess addresses him as Mr. Hofstadt, but then he realizes once again the pleasures of the dissolution of identity. "Call me Bill," he says with a smile.

Finally, the credit sequence reminds us in every episode that Draper and the other characters are a collection of flat images (silhouettes, suits), prone to dissolve at any moment (fig. 10.12). (This was the real lesson of AMC's "*Mad Men* Yourself" — learning that you are also an assembly of crude vector graphics, assembled in haste and prone to dissolution, just as in the credit sequence.) Or, as Bert Cooper says when pressuring Don to finally sign with Sterling Cooper: "After all, when it comes down to it, who's really signing this contract?"

Something changes, however, between Antonioni's obsessive photographing of absence and the same interests in *Mad Men*. For Antonioni, the instability of identity is always charged with a sense of inevitability, even doom: in *The Passenger*, Locke can become Robertson, but the itinerary he embarks on when he does so can have only one end. Identity change in Antonioni is always something like suicide (very often it is suicide). *Mad Men*, however, has all the possibilities and limitations of any serial format (although it has not shied away from suicide as a solution to existential dilemmas), as well

FIGURE 10.12. The credit sequence: dissolve, fall, resolve—repeat.

as the particular ones that pertain to television. Draper must go on in some form or another, but "Don Draper" has become a successful brand that cannot be simply dissolved. *Mad Men* watches things disappear, but not always the same way that Antonioni does. At the end of *Blow-Up* (1966), the protagonist simply fades out of existence in a lap dissolve, leaving behind nothing but a field of green grass, while at the end of *Zabriskie Point* (1970) everything literally blows up, a general detonation of the world and film.

But perhaps the most crucial difference between *Mad Men* and Antonioni is in how viewers have responded to the mode of destabilized identity that each makes available. Antonioni was an infamous but not exactly popular director (he called his own films "tremendous commercial failures"), and his lessons about identity and its disappearance were largely seen as avant-garde, radical, and heavy (Chatman, 1). As Peter Bondanella reminds us, "when *Blow-Up* appeared in 1966, the critics and reviewers reacted as if Antonioni had tackled—and resolved—most of the weighty problems of Western metaphysics" (225). But it is quite clear that viewers of *Mad Men* do not conceive of the show, or even of Don Draper's transient and tenuous identity, in this way. The credit sequence reminds us in every episode that Don falls, his world disintegrates, identity is a construction that, when peered at too closely, opens up into a terrifying and vertiginous abyss of nothingness; but at the end, this falling figure is always miraculously reconstituted, apparently seated on a firm foundation, stable. *Fort/da*. Unlike the traumatic dissolution of the subject in Antonioni, *Mad Men*'s "dissolved subject" ap-

FIGURE 10.13. Don Draper, after the world has ended.

pears at ease—the credit sequence begins with Don stiffly upright, shoulders tensed, holding a briefcase, but it ends with him relaxed, an arm casually outstretched, cigarette dangling from his right hand (fig. 10.13). Surely we must imagine a drink in that other, unseen hand.

On some level, the ending of the third season of the show mirrors this movement as a whole; the ad agency of Sterling Cooper becomes progressively more and more entangled in a series of stifling relationships, just as Don's marriage with Betty becomes increasingly untenable. The third season chronicles the disintegration of the old and the reconstitution of the new; its stirring finale ("Shut the Door. Have a Seat," 3.13) features a small band of former Sterling Cooper employees, now ad agency renegades, operating what is effectively a start-up in a hotel room, pretending to be something that they are not (but hope one day to be). They too have changed their name (now Sterling Cooper Draper Pryce). This, of course, is also the story of Don Draper, who re-creates himself as something he is not (an officer, not an enlisted man; a professional Manhattan sophisticate instead of an Illinois bastard doomed to poverty), but something that he will one day be.

In "The Gypsy and the Hobo" (3.11) Don and Betty finally discuss Don's identity change. Twice they address the question of names:

BETTY: Is that you? *Dick*? Is that your name?
DON: People change their names, Betts. You did.
BETTY: I did. I took your name.

DON: Where do you want me to start?

BETTY: What's your name?

DON: [*quietly, but emphatically*] Donald Draper. [*Very long pause*] But, it did used to be Dick Whitman.

Betty's outrage (she uses Don's former name as both a proper name and an insult) is checked somewhat when Don notes, again, the quotidian nature of these identity changes. Don's transformation could be labeled "identity theft," but Don simply claims that everyone changes their name. Elizabeth Hofstadt became Betty Draper, and Don emphasizes this by not using either of those names, calling her instead "Betts" (he also refers to her as "Birdy"). When it comes right down to it, who's really signing her divorce papers, anyway?

NOTES

1. Seymour Chatman writes that "seeking whatever certainties it can find, all [Antonioni's] camera can be sure of is the regularity of plane geometry. In such moments, the screen ceases to be a window looking into deep space and becomes a nearby surface . . . against which the characters are flattened" (119). Chatman also notes that for Antonioni's characters, "no real effort is made to find out what lies under the surface. Perhaps the implication is that there is nothing there, that these people are all surface, that they do not know how they feel" (27). Sam Rohdie's vision of Antonioni's flatness or superficiality is more complex, always linked to dissolution: "a surface, which, though pierced, swallows things up, without a trace, into a nothingness; the loss of figuration, of objects losing shape, and the shimmering between that loss and the figure itself, like a corpse, or an image . . . ; a story, as if appearing from nowhere and just as easily disappearing into a void" (39). Critical attention to the surfaces of Antonioni continues (see Paulicelli, for example).

2. Numerous viewers, including some of the authors in this collection, celebrated the show's third season by dressing up for a *Mad Men*–themed party—and yet it will *shock* you how much *that* never happened.

3. See Cari Wolfert's slide series "10 Ways to *Mad Men* Your Wedding," http://www.brides.com (accessed 7 July 2012).

4. See http://www.amctv.com/originals/madmen/madmenyourself/ (accessed 24 May 2010).

5. If I remember correctly, several of the authors in this volume changed their identities on Facebook in just this way—but perhaps that never happened either.

PART THREE
MADE MEN

11

MEDIA MADNESS

Multiple Identity (Dis)Orders in Mad Men

LYNNE JOYRICH

A HAPPY MEDIUM

In the fall of 2009 the television program *Sesame Street* debuted its own tele-vision network—"EMC, the Emotional Movie Channel"—which proudly presented a stylish period drama. In it, three dapper Muppets meet in a wood-paneled office of a New York advertising firm to pitch ideas for their "Happy Honey Bear" account. They run through various possibilities: an image of raccoons running off with a bear's honey and one of a weeping bear looking at his now empty jar. While the first makes them all "mad, mad men" and the second makes them "sad, sad men," they finally hit on the perfect picture, with the bear as satisfied consumer, dripping with honey as he eats out of the gooey pot, and the ad men themselves are now "happy, happy men." Going from mad to glad, Muppet Draper notes, is quite an "emo-tional roller coaster," but it is one that still yields his praise of "good work, sycophants" for the ad men's ability finally to reach a happy medium—one brought to us literally through the medium of television.

This parody from *Sesame Street* introduces many of *Mad Men*'s notable aspects: the program's emotionality (or lack thereof); the performativity of identity (here literalized by the use of performing puppets); power rela-tions in the image and in the workplace; and change or stasis over time.[1] Yet

I start with this example primarily to raise that question of "medium," happy or otherwise. For fascinating as those issues of affect and identity, style and signification, power and history are (and they are subjects to which I will return), for me the key issue that this skit introduces is that of televisuality itself: the point (so obvious and yet so overlooked) that these are TV shows.

Of course, neither PBS's *Sesame Street* nor AMC's *Mad Men* is a typical television show. Both their evaluative and institutional standings distinguish them from the usual fare: as well-made educational TV for kids and high-production-value drama for adults, they seem to stand out from the rest of the flow—which is further reinforced by their locations not on broadcast commercial TV but on public television and a specialty cable channel. Yet it is precisely what they reveal about TV flow—a term I am using to refer both to television's particular textual/technological form and to the shifting course of that form—that is so telling, indicating something about television's operations as well as its historical changes, with implications for the issues (textual, sexual, technological, ideological, personal, political) treated on *Mad Men*. That is, I am interested in the way in which *Mad Men*'s position as a media product might produce the positions it represents and addresses. Defined by such (re)production and reciprocal flows, *Mad Men* is an ad-supported TV show about advertising, branded by its retro look and airing on a channel that too is branded by a celebration of looks of the past even as it also turns toward the future of new televisualities in digital culture. It is how that media identity *of* the program intersects in complex ways with the identities represented *on* the program (themselves defined by both the enactment and disavowal of past heritages as well as future imaginings) that I explore in this chapter.

FLOWS AND FREE FALLS

To skip to those imaginings, though, is to fast-forward ahead of the argument, risking falling into those futures (much like the figure in *Mad Men*'s opening credits) before surveying the media landscapes and flows from which they emerge (or the media skyscrapers and streams through which the figure falls). So let me go back to the beginning with *Sesame Street*. This is a text, in fact, that I use at the beginning of my TV studies classes—not as my own attempt to lure audiences through nostalgia nor as a coded message about the lessons to expect in my classes. Rather, I use it to introduce exactly that concept of TV flow—which, I would argue, is not only the inaugural concept in television studies but still one of its most important (despite—

maybe even because of—changes in media). First coined as a critical term by Raymond Williams in his book *Television: Technology and Cultural Form*, published in 1974 (though used earlier as an industrial term in broadcasting and, of course, advertising), *television flow* describes how commercial TV is constructed as an ongoing stream of material, with each segment yielding the next, the better to keep viewers tuned in across the lineup and, more importantly, the ads. Yet television flow is equally marked by discontinuity as TV highlights what some critics have called "video bites": separable bits that offer their own small charges of visual, informational, and narrative pleasure (Mullen). In other words, television enacts a curious rhythm of flow and segmentation, protraction and interruption, yielding a paradoxical sense of continuity through discontinuity that forms not only the institutional operations of TV but the televisual experience as a whole.

However odd Williams may have found this experience in 1974, rendering his confusion of promos and ads with a TV program "proper," this flow has since become so naturalized that it not only defines basic U.S. network programming (where, again, it is designed to allow and accentuate TV commercials, which therefore must be defined as TV's "proper texts").[2] It also characterizes the structure even of programs on public and premium channels that do not rely on the implicit contract established between broadcast television and its viewers: the exchange of "free" programming for audiences' willingness to accept commercial "interruptions."[3] *Sesame Street* provides a demonstration of this institutionalization of flow and segmentation even beyond an institutional commercial requirement, as each episode is composed of a succession of bits that is very much like a lineup of ads; indeed, episodes are "sponsored by" letters and numbers. Designed to promote literacy (even emotional literacy, as seen in the *Mad Men* skit) through those building blocks of communication, *Sesame Street* also implicitly teaches "television literacy" through its use of TV flow.

Sesame Street is now hardly alone as a program that is not institutionally dependent on broadcast flow—though most of the others that need not "interrupt" themselves do so not by "public" funding but by "private" sales (subscription channels, pay-per-view, DVDs, and so on). Certainly all of these terms (*public, private, free, pay*) have to be interrogated.[4] In fact, this was Williams's point in detailing how scheduled flow functions as the mechanism of articulation not only between the "technology" and "cultural form" of his title but between television's textuality and its economics, and, beyond that, media formations and social formations more broadly. As the flow of the TV schedule has been ordered by and, in turn, itself ordered the

FIGURE 11.1. Breaking to watch television after the Kennedy assassination ("The Grown-Ups," 3.12).

workday and week, becoming a household timetable and a national calendar, television has produced, in mutual determination, norms of the family and nation. In so doing, it has articulated the "domestic" and the "social," "labor" and "leisure," the "public" and the "private." Bringing outside events into our living rooms even as it gives us access to the living (and board) rooms on our screens, television has served as the means by which the times, spaces, and identities of our lives are both distinguished and connected. As a television program that often includes other television programs, *Mad Men* offers plenty of examples of TV's articulating role: there are scenes of the kids watching Saturday cartoons or "family hour" adventures, while, at other times of the day, the men catch the news, and women, using TV as an extension of their caretaking role, make do with what others have on. When something disrupts these patterns — for instance, when the ambitious account executive Pete Campbell watches a kids' show during the daytime or, more dramatically, everyone breaks for coverage of the Kennedy assassination — it is a sure sign that something is wrong, personally, politically, or both (fig. 11.1).

TIME MACHINES

Some critics say that in our multichannel universe (with specialty channels that compose particular tastes rather than being scheduled to capture the "general audience"), "television flow" is an outmoded concept, applicable to the TV of the 1960s that *Mad Men* references but not to the system to which it owes its own existence. *Mad Men* thus treats historical television like other aspects of history: through a play of sameness and difference, creating a potent mixture of identification and disidentification. There has been much commentary on the program's precise use of period details and the ways in which, through invocation of the past, *Mad Men* reveals how "we" were formed.[5] But those stylized invocations are as likely to produce an exclamation of "not us" as a feeling of recognition, with the program emphasizing precisely those details that are now strange to us (so that we are encouraged to gasp at the smoking and drinking, the careless littering and sexism, as much as to be charmed by the vintage fashions, furniture, and television consoles).

In this way—through our own affective flows—we can move in and out of history and presence, which *Mad Men*, paradoxically, can both engage and disavow: subjecting the past to its aestheticized view, the program raises issues for interrogation yet also allows for their evasion. As this volume demonstrates, many fascinating issues emerge in the program: the rise of corporate culture, the status of women at work and home, perceptions of race and ethnicity, and so on. Yet as easily as *Mad Men* may invite us to ponder these for the present, it also allows us to put them aside, to view them as simply set (as if on an old TV set) in the past. Indeed, as stated on *Mad Men* itself, there is profit in forgetting. That is what Bert Cooper, senior partner at Sterling Cooper Advertising, says when Pete tries to expose the true identity of "Don Draper"; but Don's own words about remembering and forgetting may be even more telling.

I am referring to what is perhaps the program's most famous scene, when Don lyricizes the temporality and emotions operative not in television, but in another media apparatus: the slide projector. Screening the "that-has-been," this is a mediation identified in terms of nostalgia, about which Don says: "It's delicate, but potent. . . . In Greek, 'nostalgia' literally means 'the pain from an old wound.' . . . This device . . . isn't a spaceship, it's a time machine. It goes backwards, and forwards. It takes us to a place where we ache to go again. . . . It lets us travel the way a child travels—around and around and back home again."[6] Television too might be discussed as a kind of time machine that goes forward and backward. Discussions of TV flow emphasize the former, implying that, as it carries us along, television pushes us ever onward. This is its illusion of "liveness": the sense, even in historical programming, that we are continually checking in, being kept up-to-date with ongoing events.[7] The aforementioned Kennedy story provides an excellent example: even long after we, the *Mad Men* viewers, know the outcome, watching the coverage via the characters' ever-present TV sets is still gripping as we too are caught up in television's temporal progression.

Because of this, televisual form has often been seen as impeding historical consciousness. Yet as television theorists such as Mimi White, Gary Edgerton, and Steve Anderson have argued, and programs such as *Mad Men* demonstrate, history is also invoked by television.[8] It is invoked, in fact, in a wide variety of ways: through the genre of "historical drama"; particular strategies of narration like the flashback; familiar actors who play on our memories of prior roles; recasts, remakes, and reruns on TV; shows compiled of clips of previous programming; and even whole channels devoted to "preserving our television heritage."[9] In other words, rather than ahistorical, television might best be described as multiply historical, flowing forward and back, wheels within wheels, letting us travel, not quite like a child, but in a way that only media allow.

STYLE, SENSATION, STRATEGY: THE CINEMATIC AND THE TELEVISUAL

This historicism operates, in *Mad Men*, not just via content but through form, with the same visualization of period details that grant its movement across time yielding what has been characterized as its classic filmic style. From the opening credits to the dolly work, lighting, and low-angle shots, *Mad Men* not only deploys what its cinematographer Phil Abraham describes as a "somewhat mannered, classic visual style . . . influenced more by cinema than TV" (qtd. in Feld et al., 46), but specifically associates it with certain films of the past. Critics have noted precedents in Alfred Hitchcock, Billy Wilder, King Vidor, and others.[10] To those, I would add Douglas Sirk, as *Mad Men*'s attention to costume, color, setting, and décor allows it, as with film melodramas of the 1950s and '60s, to mark meaning and affect through mise-en-scène and style. Imbued in objects, appearing through the placement of people and things, feelings are less voiced by the program's characters than designated by its surface (though, rather than an expression of emotion, this often signals its evacuation, making the show's lessons about the investment of feelings in commodity objects — and *Sesame Street*'s lesson on the basics of affect — even more ironic).

Such emphasis on mediated style does, however, perfectly correspond with *Mad Men*'s placement on AMC (American Movie Classics), given that network's investment — literally — in cinematic form. Yet even that must be seen as a particular TV strategy, linking the "cinematic" and "televisual," as becomes clear when one considers not only those filmic precedents for *Mad Men* but TV precedents too—from anthology series such as *The Twilight Zone* to sitcoms such as *The Dick Van Dyke Show* and from such quotidian fare as soap opera to such "quality" offerings as *The Sopranos* (which is tied to *Mad Men* through not only Matthew Weiner's work but, more generally, that label of distinction).[11] I will return to the question of quality, but it is already clear how the term can serve as a bridge between film and TV, as it is used as code for television that is supposedly "filmlike," and a similar bridge is operative with AMC. Described as "one of the great success stories in the emergence of cable TV in the U.S." (Gomery, 93), AMC marked a shift from the era of TV's "big three" networks (ABC, NBC, and CBS) to a multi-channel era, signifying a television system no longer limited to the "broadcast" but engaged in what has come to be known as "narrowcasting": rather than all networks attempting to reach all viewers by ordering flow, with the TV schedule thus demarcating those "general" viewers as the "family" and "national" audience, each channel might attempt specifically to cater to and constitute the tastes of particular audiences.

For AMC that involved addressing and helping to form cinematic tastes, presented as a specialty appreciation worth paying for: when the network started in 1984, offering uncut movies from the 1930s, '40s, and '50s, it did so as a premium channel. It received rave reviews and impressive subscriber numbers, growing further when it became available on "basic cable" in 1987, quickly doubling its subscriber base.[12] Those subscribers were not only rewarded with the pleasure of viewing films in the comfort of their homes without commercial breaks (as, initially, the network received sufficient revenue from cable providers alone). They were also rewarded with the prestige value of programming marked as "quality"—which must thus be seen as a market category that makes sense only in the context of the television flow from which it tries to be distinct—giving viewers cachet as consumers and the channel a valuable demographic (upscale adults).[13] For, with television, the viewers themselves—not the programs, nor even, exactly, the objects in ads—have always been the true commodities: the industry operates by selling audiences to advertisers, who buy time to reach those target consumers (the more precisely defined, the better). Or, as Don says in one episode, "*you are the product, you feeling something. That's what sells*" ("For Those Who Think Young," 2.1).

While AMC was able to provide its prestige consumer-products with films without commercial interruption for most of its initial eighteen years, it gradually moved to an ad format, inserting them first between, then also within, the movies it showed. Further, in 2002 it shifted its profile from a "classic" film channel to a more general one: younger audiences were sought, and those audiences apparently wanted "younger" movies. According to insiders, ad agencies dictated the move in their demands for programming relevant to their products' consumers and for consumers not yet "set in their ways" whose brand loyalties might be bought (Dempsey).[14] Yet this put AMC in competition with various other stations—for example, TBS, TNT, and USA, all of which also rely on films—and, arguably, suffering in comparison (if not necessarily revenue) to still others, such as Turner Classic Movies, now the go-to site for film classicists, or, more significantly, premium channels such as HBO and Showtime. Indeed, these last have taken over the mantle of the "cinematic" and "quality" labels, whose paradoxes are probably most evident in the tagline "It's not TV, it's HBO," in which the announcement of quality—that this is not like television—is precisely what is used to define it as the television you should watch.

TASTE/TOAST

It was into this nexus that *Mad Men* arrived. Producers had, in fact, tried to sell the program to HBO or Showtime, but they were not interested (Witchel). In the words of its chief operating officer, Ed Carroll, AMC "was looking for distinction in launching its first original series, and we took a bet that quality would win out over formulaic mass appeal" (qtd. in Witchel).[15] Yet in a fascinating inversion, "quality" here meant revisiting TV—returning not to classic films but to televisuality to distinguish itself.[16] Moreover, this was television explicitly *about* television (among other things): a TV program that in exploring the identifications and disidentifications of consumer society also exhibits the growing significance of TV itself. For it is precisely in promoting mass-mediated images that the folks in *Mad Men* pose questions of identity, and the program treats its personal and political issues alongside its treatment of currents of communications, literally thinking *through* the media to think through identity.

In this regard, the show might be linked not just institutionally but ideationally to another—often neglected—AMC program. *Mad Men* tends to be labeled the network's "first original series," yet *Remember WENN* (1996–98), about a fictional radio station in the 1940s, preceded it. While the amnesia around one historical program within the discourses of another might strike us as ironic, the similarities between the two are more symptomatic, pointing again toward the profit not only of remembering but also of forgetting. With both shows narrating the public and private formations of historical identity via media formations (whether radio broadcasting, print advertisement, or the creation and increasing importance of the "television department"), this is a connection that is notable for what it suggests about how, as subjects (*on* or *of* TV), we are constituted through, by, and within media texts and histories.[17]

Yet, as mentioned in regard to HBO's "quality branding," making and marking differences through such media texts and histories is as significant as recalling their connections. *Mad Men* itself provides plenty of examples of this. One of the most instructive occurs in the very first episode, "Smoke Gets in Your Eyes" (1.1), when Don confronts the difficulty of signaling product distinction in a sea of sameness (or, more accurately, a haze of smoke) — a marketing challenge that resonates with the larger social problem, set up in this episode and played out across the series, of finding individuality in the face of conformity. Meeting with Lee Garner Sr. and Lee Garner Jr., the father and son owners of Lucky Strike, the "mad men" of Sterling Cooper (like television promoters trying to commend what has been condemned) are trying to determine how to proceed now that cigarettes have become suspect.[18] Even the usually suave Don is tongue-tied — until the Garners rise to walk out in disgust, with Lee Jr. stating, "At least we know, if we have this problem, everybody has this problem," and inspiration strikes. They must produce a distinction in taste — here, literally. With a flourish, Don suggests the slogan "It's Toasted."

Don expounds: "This is the greatest advertising opportunity since the invention of cereal. We have six identical companies making six identical products. We can say anything we want. . . . Everybody else's tobacco is poisonous. Lucky Strike's is toasted."[19] " 'It's toasted' . . . I get it," Lee Sr. exclaims: one might not notice a special flavor, but the very marking of it yields its own taste. Of course, this is not quite like television, since television texts are not the same in the way that Don describes breakfast cereals or cigarette brands as just "identical products." But whether "toasted" or "quality," this is about making difference from sameness, demarcating segmentation from flow.[20]

TELEVISION PROFILING, DEMOGRAPHIC SETS: THE CASE OF "COLORED TV"

Yet, however telling these textual demarcations may be, ultimately I am less interested in how the program as a media object is marked as "differ-

ent" than in how it reveals the ways in which *our* differences as social subjects are marked by media: in its exploration of the articulation of identity
(which is not merely expressed, but made emergent) within commodified
and mass-mediated flows. One site of this involves *Mad Men*'s treatment of
race, which, though not as elaborated as other subjects the program engages,
is extremely significant. By its very omissions, *Mad Men* presents racial difference not so much as an experienced self or sociality as, from the perspective of corporate culture, a potential market slot — a target demographic to
be distinguished from a so-called general group. While this obviously yields
only a very limited perspective, it calls attention to how identities become,
indeed, delimited — realized, in part, *as* market categories (the ways in which
identities are constituted and reconstituted as they intersect with media formations that, however problematically, give them definition, and vice versa).

As scholars such as Sasha Torres and Kirsten Lentz have noted, this
mutual definition has historically codified terms of both television and
race. The emphasis on the "live" coverage of civil rights protests in the late
1950s and early 1960s, for example, helped to establish both TV's presence
in American culture and a sense of "presence" in race itself (authorizing an
understanding of race as intrinsic to one's very "life being"). This linkage became even further established in the 1970s with the rise of the "realist" and
"relevant" sitcom, in which it was precisely those TV shows that dealt with
race or racism (with what were conceived as "real issues," even if treated
via comedy) that were seen as appropriate to that televisual discourse (see
Lentz; Torres, *Black, White*). In TV's flow and segmentation, race might be
even further defined — with, for instance, as Herman Gray has shown for
African American representation, a division of marked racialized figures into
the pull-oneself-up-by-one's-bootstraps characters foregrounded by the rise
of the so-called black sitcom and the poor, nameless masses in the backdrop of many news reports against whom that individuated character is implicitly positioned (see H. Gray, "Remembering Civil Rights"). *Mad Men*
does not explicitly get into these issues, but in its narration of an early version of "narrowcasting," it does allude to how race starts to become a TV
category — literally, in one example, used for the sale of TV sets.[21]

The idea to deploy race in this way is the brainchild of the account services executive Pete Campbell, whose approach to racial identity might usefully be counterposed to the copywriter Paul Kinsey's. Kinsey is interested
in "beatnik" culture, professes "bohemian" ideas, and, for a time, dates Sheila
White, an African American woman. On a bus trip with her to Mississippi
to register black voters, Paul espouses a utopian notion of an end to racial

difference—even if this is an odd, cynical utopianism, since he sees it as occurring less through the political movement in which he himself is taking part than through the very operations of consumer culture.[22] "Advertising, if anything, helps bring on change. The market, and I am talking in a purely Marxist sense, dictates that we must include everyone. The consumer has no color," he pontificates, as his (almost all African American) bus companions look on with tolerant amusement or ignore him completely ("The Inheritance," 2.10). He brings up Marx again in a later episode in a conversation with Pete about the "catastrophic up and down of the marketplace," leading to a discussion of those aforementioned TV sets ("The Fog," 3.5). Noticing that Admiral television sales are flat in most places but growing in "Atlanta, Oakland, Chicago, Detroit, Newark, D.C., and . . . St. Louis and Kansas City," Pete wonders aloud, "What does that mean?" "Great jazz cities," Paul says, reading this in terms of media and cultural taste. Yet starting to label—or construct—this in terms of identity, Pete's fledgling demographic view is in contrast to Paul's Marxist-democratic vision: "Is it possible that these Admiral sets are being bought by Negroes?" he asks.

For an answer, he turns to one of the few black characters to be seen at Sterling Cooper: Hollis, the elevator operator. Yet Hollis is resistant to Pete's informal brand of demographic profiling, attuned as he is to the risky politics of identity—not just, like Pete, to its commodification and consumer definition. Stating that he has an RCA but not wanting to say more, particularly since Pete starts questioning him in front of some white executives, Hollis tries to be polite but brief (simply shaking his head no to Pete's question about his TV set: "Color?"). Yet Pete persists with his impromptu market testing, pressing against Hollis's resistance: "Look, this is important, and I'd really like to have an honest conversation with you. . . . Do you think I'm a bigot?" When Hollis protests, "I don't even watch the damn thing. . . . We've got bigger problems to worry about than TV, OK?" Pete responds: "You're thinking about this in a very narrow way. The idea is that everyone is going to have a house, a car, a television—the American Dream." Looking incredulous, Hollis starts up the elevator, spurring Pete to justify himself with "It's my job." "Every job has its ups and downs," Hollis replies, cleverly alluding to his own low-wage job—and, by extension, to the distinction in status levels that Pete overlooks in his plug for a (consumerized) American Dream. Yet Pete recognizes in this quip not the sound of Marx's aforementioned catastrophe, but an aphorism as American as mom and apple pie. "You don't watch baseball?" Pete asks with a smile, "I don't believe you," finally earning a grin from Hollis and then a mutual laugh.[23]

The folks at Admiral, however, don't share the sentiments. When Pete suggests advertising their TV sets in publications such as *Ebony, Jet*, and *Amsterdam News*, which "go just to this market," as well as airing an "integrated" TV commercial (to which one executive quips, "I don't think that's legal"), he upsets the Admiral businessmen, who seem unable to accept differences in identity, whether democratically or demographically defined: "Who's to say that Negroes aren't buying Admiral televisions because they think white people want them?" Pete is called in to Bert Cooper's office to be, as they say, "flogged" by the senior partners. "Admiral television has *no* interest in becoming a colored television company," Bert admonishes. Worried about his own job, Pete stands chastened, with *Mad Men* itself seemingly more interested in the quality technical distinction of something like "color TV" than in the social one of "colored TV." Yet Lane Pryce, the new financial officer from Sterling Cooper's British parent company, ultimately concedes: "It *does* seem as though there's money to be made in the Negro market. Obviously, not with Admiral . . . but I don't think it would be wrong of us to pursue it in some way." "Really?" Bert asks. "I just moved here; I'm a stranger in a strange land. But," Lane says, claiming the insight of the outsider (a position like that of the *Mad Men* viewer, also a distanced observer of 1960s America), "I can tell you there's definitely *something* going on."

TARGETING SEX, SCREENING SEXUALITY

Perhaps more so even than with race, something is definitely going on with gender in *Mad Men*. The program explores the enormous significance of sexual politics as they impact men and women, across productive and reproductive spheres, in home and in work life, publicly and privately. Not coincidentally, these are exactly the divisions that TV both partitions and crosses. Publicizing private stories even as it privatizes the public, domesticating the social even as it socializes the family, television sets itself up precisely through the terms by which gender has been ordered—with gender itself becoming "TV-set" (technologized, channeled, and programmed).[24] In reciprocal relation, gender is thus as much constituted by commercial media flows and formations as it is constitutive of them—a point that *Mad Men* makes insistently in its look at sexed identities as both product and process of media and marketing. There are so many examples of this that every viewer can elaborate his or her own favorite cases. One need only think of the campaigns to which the firm's only female copywriter, Peggy Olson, is assigned—Belle Jolie lipstick, Clearasil acne cream, mom-dispensed popsicles, Playtex brassieres, the Relax-A-Cizor vibrating "exercise" machine—to realize how sex roles are targets of and on the show. This is the case not only through target advertisement, but, given the aggression of the sexual politics, literally, as when viewers share Pete's gaze at the secretaries through the barrel of a rifle he gets by exchanging a homey wedding gift ("Red in the Face," 1.7).

As that instance demonstrates, this is a specifically heterosexual aggression. Homosexuality also makes an appearance on *Mad Men*—appears, that is, in its disappearance, in its closeting, and that too is tied to television.[25] This is not to say that, given the history on *Mad Men*, anything like a "gay identity" can be conceptualized as a demographic category the way that a female consumer or the inklings of a commodified African American identity can be—meaning, in the terms of the show (and the society it historicizes), it cannot really be conceptualized at all. But it is notable that homosexual desire often presents (and screens) itself precisely around the presence of TV—for instance, when, at a screening of a program being pitched as a good opportunity for Belle Jolie lipstick, the closeted Sal Romano (Sterling Cooper's art director) nervously reencounters a man whom he had liked but whose proposition he had been too scared to accept ("The Benefactor," 2.3).

That pitched program is actually from the annals of TV history: it is the (in)famous episode of the legal drama *The Defenders* (CBS, 1961–65) in which the defense attorney heroes make a powerful case for sexual choice via the legalization of abortion—so powerful that it led to the program's regular sponsors pulling their support (ironically, given that episode's title of "The Benefactor," after which this *Mad Men* episode too is named).[26] In confirmation of, as well as ironic counterpoint to, that vision of sexual liberation, *Mad Men* claims the scandalous show as must-see TV even as it is also feared as "not wholesome"—a dialectic that still seems to define the presence of queer sexualities on TV (as evidenced by the oh-so-brief, overly polite, yet, for attentive viewers, poignant farewell between Sal and his would-be lover at the end of the meeting).[27]

Sal is later propositioned by another man, Lee Garner Jr. (previously seen during Don's "toasted" pitch), in the episode "Wee Small Hours" (3.9), featuring the filming of a Lucky Strike commercial in which a hunky guy takes a puff from a cigarette and gazes off into the distance with satisfaction. Watching the shoot, Lee suggests instead a direct address to the audience, but he is overruled in his desire for a frontal gaze in an exchange that is full of double entendres. Sal claims, "I want what you want," yet he insists that "it can make people very uncomfortable," to which Lee proposes, "Let's take a risk together, shall we, Sally?" However, Sal is not quite as ready for risk, televisually or sexually—and neither, perhaps, is *Mad Men* itself. Indeed, the Lucky Strike slogan we hear may tout the brand's "honest taste," but textual "tastefulness" and sexual "honesty" seem to be at odds, even as they are bound up together in discourse, as Sal and Lee Jr.'s further conversation reveals. Arriving to see Sal working on the commercial, Lee explains, "I know I'm supposed to stay away . . . but I'm fascinated by this process." Sal asks if he's thinking about switching positions to get into the media business. "Not when my father's alive," Lee replies—though he worries that Sal will expose him for this interest in movies and TV and so asks him to keep this quiet (not to broadcast it, so to speak) before immediately going into a seduction attempt.

Yet Sal refuses Lee's sexual as well as his televisual suggestions. Right after Sal opines that Lee's idea for the TV shot "is going to feel strange," Lee reaches to touch Sal's chest, producing Sal's panicked rejection through references to his marriage and work. "I got it," the rebuffed Lee says—a "getting it" not so unlike his father's earlier "I get it" in understanding the claims of "taste," but, this time, to opposite effect. Far from being pleased, Lee Jr. demands that Sal be fired—and, in fact, this episode is the last in which Sal appears.[28] This simultaneous emergence and erasure of homosexuality in "The Benefactor" and "Wee Small Hours"—both of which are self-reflexive about TV—is telling. For it is between their two televisual lessons—the reminder of the risks (and potential rewards) of controversial programming and yet the refusal of a direct gay gaze—that *Mad Men* reveals the limits of its own treatment of queer sexualities, again enacting and commenting on how identities (sexual, gendered, raced, classed, and so on) are televisually (dis)ordered.

COMMERCIAL CONNECTIONS AND CONTINUATIONS

The aforementioned examples reveal that, in exploring the history and textuality of mass-mediated consumer culture, *Mad Men* also explores the ways in which identities are constituted by and through media formations, and vice versa: the ways in which media constitute themselves by and through identity formations (how our "selves" become embodied in commodity objects, how personal and political identifications appear or disappear along with what media texts envision or erase, how private histories become intertwined with media publicities, how social categories become defined as demographic categories, and how we are articulated as particular subjects through the articulations of media flows and segmentations). More so, *Mad Men* does not just explore these issues; it enacts them in its own flows and segmentations—even in an era that is supposedly "beyond flow" (our so-called postnetwork, narrowcast, niche-marketed, and digitally convergent era).

Of course, AMC is still a network (if a cable network) that supports itself by selling time and space, or, rather, by selling audiences to advertisers. Yet ever since technologies such as the VCR and DVR have made it easy for viewers to speed through ads, networks and advertisers have searched for ways to counter them—or, better, to turn those technologies to their advantage. Some strategies are quite familiar: the use of shorter "video bite" commercials (which operate through attention-grabbing bursts, with little time to evade them), or the insertion of commercial slogans or commodity objects within the framing programs (the old strategies of sponsorship and product placement, retooled for our digital age to ensure that even viewers who evade ads are unable to bypass the brands).

Mad Men uses both of these methods, but, as a program about advertising, it also has other resources with which to make its "interrupting" commercials as compelling as the show: specifically, by making them less like "interruptions" than continuations. This is achieved through the use of bridging "bumpers." At the beginning of a commercial break, AMC displays a *Mad Men*–logoed title card stating some fun fact about a sponsor's product or marketing history against the visual backdrop of the Sterling Cooper building—a gimmick that AMC dubbed "*Mad*-vertising" and Matthew Weiner simply called the use of "TiVo stoppers" (qtd. in Benton).[29] Not only do the informative intertitles resonate with information gleaned from the program, but the commercials that follow are often linked to *Mad Men* through use of some of the same strategies that distinguish the show: an emphasis on retro style, yielding a dialectic of historical identification and disidentification; citations of texts and media events of the past that march ever ahead into our present (so a mix of nostalgia and liveness); the affective personification of objects along with, conversely, the objectification of affect; and, most significant for me, the demarcation of identity through media and marketing forms.

Consider the *Mad*-vertisements that ran during one episode of *Mad Men*, "Souvenir" (3.8). One commercial break, moving across time and space, featured a Bridgestone tire and then a Clorox bleach ad. The first was preceded by a *Mad Men*–logoed title stating (rather obviously), "The Bridgestone commercial featuring rump-shaking astronauts was not filmed on one of

Saturn's moons." In the commercial, titled "Hot Item," hip-hopping astronauts race a lunar vehicle along the surface of (supposedly) Titan, stopping to collect rocks while dancing to the House of Pain song "Jump Around"—only to find, upon returning, their vehicle jacked up on cinder blocks, their desirable tires stolen, and a flying saucer escaping in the distance. Astonishingly, this Bridgestone commercial, which first aired as a hyped Super Bowl ad in 2009, is generally well regarded despite its troubling, universalizing view of race (indeed, asserted as operative across the universe). Evidently, we are supposed to understand that the mere presence of hip-hop music—much as, recalling Paul Kinsey's comments, the earlier presence of jazz—makes any space (even outer space) a black, "urban" area, with this racialization then naturalizing the tire theft, though this occurs in the middle of nowhere and the "gangstas" here are not just alienated but, in fact, extraterrestrial aliens. Thus revealing how media culture continues to be incapable of dealing with race coherently (and nonoffensively)—even as it tries to target race for marketing purposes—the ad demonstrates that, despite the commercial's futurism, things have not changed very much since the awkward beginnings of this targeting narrated in Mad Men.[30]

Keeping with that narrative, the Clorox ad looks backward, not ahead, as suggested by the Mad Men intertitle with the factoid "Prior to 1960, Clorox was sold in amber glass containers." Over the image of a room (prominently featuring some sort of clothes-washing device) that changes over time, remodeled through the decades while people (also remodeled in updated clothes) move through it in fast-motion, a female voiceover states: "Laundry's not new. Your mother, your grandmother, her mother—they all did the laundry, maybe even a man or two. And although a lot has changed—the machines, the detergents, the clothes themselves—one thing has not: the bleach most trusted to keep whites pure white is still Clorox bleach." Here, then, we get another historical gaze in which the attention to period setting and style creates a dialectic of distance and closeness, past and present, nostalgia and irony—indexing gender (not to mention "pure whiteness") through those divisions and so presuming its categories even as it seems to expose gendered identities as particular domestic and work (even if unpaid work) roles. In other words, in its strategies and identity formations, the commercial arguably operates much like Mad Men itself—which may explain why this commercial, after (rightly or wrongly) being shelved because of charges of sexism, reemerged specifically to be used with Mad Men on AMC (see Wallace).[31] (Likewise, Clorox put an ad in the DVD set that created a similar controversy: an image of a man's shirt with lipstick stains on the collar and the slogan "Getting ad guys out of hot water for generations"—again using a kind of historicism as an alibi to dehistoricize gender and sexual hierarchies.)

Keeping with the theme of historical tradition across change, the next commercial break featured an ad for Johnnie Walker Scotch whiskey with a *"Mad Men*–ized" intertitle: "Originally known as Walker's Old Highland Whiskey, Johnnie Walker Black celebrates its 100th anniversary in 2009," the year the episode and ad aired. Over stirring music, we see a wooden door, labeled "John Walker & Sons," bang open as a man rolls out a barrel. Through cuts matched on action to the man's forward-moving stride, the ad transitions to the following shots: men prodding a propeller biplane and the onscreen title "Keep Rising"; a man pushing a steel girder on a skyscraper under construction with the title "Keep Building"; men moving up the side of a mountain with the title "Keep Climbing"; an astronaut floating in space with the title "Keep Exploring"; people climbing atop and then pounding through the Berlin Wall with the title "Keep Uniting"; and a digitized image of a computer-generated figure walking with the title "Keep Innovating," which merges into a shot of a British chap strutting along, becoming, finally, the animated image of the company's "Walking Man" logo with the words "Keep Walking. Johnnie Walker." Apparently documenting key leaps in history through these iconic shots (even sticking to the tasteful sepia-toned or black-and-white imagery now conventionalized in documentary filmmaking), this ad offers an instructive comparison case to the Clorox and Bridgestone commercials in its aestheticized image of white masculinity both remembering its achievements yet striding ever forward to greatness.[32]

Commenting on the aesthetics (if not politics) of advertising, the next *Mad Men* intertitle declares, "Victorian-era pharmaceutical ads were so attractive, they were collected by shop owners," before going into a commercial for the millennial-era cholesterol-lowering medication Lipitor. There are then *Mad*-vertised commercials for, among others, Canada Dry ginger ale (featuring the AMC announcer praising the company's "tradition of creative advertising" over cuts of old print ads and a 1960s-era TV commercial that shows a swinging beach party where "one gulp is for thirst; the other gulps are for kicks") and American Express (featuring stylized shots of everyday objects arranged in the shape of first sad and then happy faces, with the wording "Don't take chances. Take charge."). Such commercials resonate in fascinating, if sometimes frustrating, ways across the program/commercial flow. For example, they encourage us to get our retro "kicks," whether from historical TV texts or a commercial soft drink, yet also warn us, via not simply a pharmaceutical ad but *Mad Men*'s own plots, about the risks such a life of kicks might yield.[33] There is even the way, in the American Express ad, that emotions are invested in—and literally projected onto—objects over which we are told to "take charge," which not only recalls *Mad Men*'s commentary on our investment of emotions in consumer objects but also returns us to *Sesame Street*'s building blocks of feelings. Such resonances will vibrate in different ways with different AMC viewers who see them along the flow.

APPLYING ONESELF: THE LINKS AND LABOR OF NEW MEDIATIONS

Of course, not all *Mad Men* audiences get those vibrations and flows. While these commercial breaks aim to be "TiVo-proof," in today's media universe many viewers access television programs via other technologies (DVDs, computer downloads, and so on). Thus, even other technological and media flows are established for viewer pleasure and commodity profit, which may, but do not necessarily, line up as expected. Indeed, there have been fascinating intermedial connections between *Mad Men* and (so-called) new technologies, by which televisuality—and *Mad Men* identities—get extended and reshaped in digital culture, sometimes with surprising effects. For example, even viewers who do not see AMCtv.com advertised during televised commercial breaks may find it on the Internet through social networks such as Facebook. Such viewers can then also learn how to "get mad" as "a *Mad Men* icon" with *"Mad Men* Yourself"—an application on the AMC site that enables users to transform themselves into graphic avatars, retro-styled to look like possible characters on the show.[34] A hit among *Mad Men* viewers, those avatars spread across social media sites, making fans into their own promoters of the program as they "applied" themselves to its world (or worlds). In fact, the *"Mad Men* Yourself" application was created by a fan (a freelance designer who was then tapped to work on AMC's official site), literally illustrating the ways in which identities—not only from the swanky 1960s, but those of producer and consumer—might be tried on, traded, and transfigured.[35]

An even more intriguing example of fan activity is that of the Twitter community whose members (many of whom happen to work in advertising and marketing, although, significantly, not for *Mad Men*) have taken on the identities of *Mad Men* roles. Some of these roles are established in the series; some are wholly made up by fans, like that of a mailroom clerk or Grandpa Gene's ghost; and some are even nonhuman or inanimate entities, like Duck's dog Chauncey, an ant who escaped from Bert Cooper's ant farm, the Xerox machine, and a bottle of seltzer always watching from the bar (see

Caddell; Isakson; King; Mapes). From posting commentary on the action of the series to making up stories to fill the gaps within and between commercial breaks, episodes, and seasons, these viewers take flow to a whole new level while also finding new forms of affective engagement, media identification, and television publicity. At first, AMC foolishly attempted to stop these fans, forcing Twitter to disable their accounts and threatening to sue over copyright and intellectual property infringement. Quickly, however, they realized that this fan activity was the best advertising for their television show that they could get—that it was, in fact, something that transformed advertising and television.[36] For here viewers offer not only interest in the program but free labor for it. And the audiences are not just the consumers, nor even just the products sold: they become coproducers in their own selling.

REORDERING IDENTITY, RE-VIEWING TV: CHANGING MEDIA STREAMS AND SCREENS

Produced by and in turn productive of both labor and love, these are truly new "applications," with viewers applying themselves technologically and textually, psychically and socially, culturally and commercially.[37] Yet, in noting these developments, I am not trying to suggest that, as television audiences now play all the parts—consumer, commodity, content-producer, advertiser—their identities are fully enclosed in media flows from which there is no escape. To the contrary, activities such as "*Mad Men* Yourself" and Twitter role-playing (and, I would argue, other forms of viewing too, even if their activity is not as noticeably marked) demonstrate how mass-mediated identities can be examined, exercised, appropriated, and (often improperly) assumed as they are literally performed and played. In other words, identities might be articulated through media formations—but those media formations are neither univocal nor fixed. Linked to the past but also open to present and future transformations, they allow for de- and rearticulations as well, for multiple identity orderings and disorderings in our era of multiple mediation.

Thus, while *Mad Men*—both in its plots and in its placement and processes—might show how selves are established in media culture, it also reveals how selves might be revised. That is, it may announce not just commodity fixes but a more fluid culture, demonstrating how viewers invest emotionally as well as economically, how subjectivities are both envisioned and re-viewed, how our multiple identities are formed through television and its related media and consumer technologies, yet how they might potentially be re-formed there as well. Returning to (yet reversing) the *Sesame Street* example with which I began, we might thus see how people are not simply puppets in mass-mediated culture, how happiness is not only an assurance that "we're OK" getting all our honey, how (contrary to *Mad Men*'s credits) we do not just fall into media flows. Rather, we channel those in particular ways, looking forward as well as back, always (re)screening ourselves as we screen TV.

NOTES

Previous versions of this piece were presented at the symposium "Mad World: Sex, Politics, Style and the 1960s," sponsored by the Unit for Criticism and Interpretive Theory, University of Illinois at Urbana-Champaign, and for the 2010 Gender and Sexuality Studies Lecture at Brown University; I'd like to thank the organizers and participants of both of those events for their work and for their valuable and thought-provoking comments and questions. Thanks also to my television studies students (especially students-into-colleagues Hunter Hargraves and Julie Levin Russo) and to Melissa Getreu for their help and always stimulating conversations.

  1. The latter is marked by the history of *Sesame Street* itself, as this bit was created for its fortieth anniversary season, which authorizes the skit's cross-generational address: wide-eyed kids can learn the lessons of emotions while adults can indulge their own emotions of nostalgia for a TV show with which they grew up.

  2. For those not familiar with this description of his own unfamiliarity with U.S. television, Williams writes:

> One night in Miami, still dazed from a week on an Atlantic liner, I began watching a film [on TV] and at first had some difficulty adjusting to a much greater frequency of commercial "breaks." Yet this was a minor problem compared to what eventually happened. Two other films, which were due to be shown on the same channel on other nights, began to be inserted as trailers. A crime in San Francisco (the subject of the original film) began to operate in an extraordinary counterpoint not only with the deodorant and cereal commercials but with a romance in Paris and the eruption of a prehistoric monster who laid waste New York. Moreover, this was sequence in a new sense . . . since the transitions from film to commercial and from film A to films B and C were in effect unmarked. There is in any case enough similarity between certain kinds of films, and between several kinds of film and the "situation" commercials which often consciously imitate them, to make a sequence of this kind a very difficult experience to interpret. I can still not be sure what I

took from that whole flow. I believe I registered some incidents as happening in the wrong film, and some characters in the commercials as involved in the film episodes, in what came to seem — for all the occasional bizarre disparities — a single irresponsible flow of images and feelings. (*Television*, 91–92)

3. Indeed, today almost every television program — including those that air on channels without commercial breaks — is "prestructured," with the goal of eventual syndication, to fit into the flow of a commercial channel. Here too, however, flow is actually a mixture of continuity and disruption, since older programs were designed for fewer commercial interruptions even while today's programs are discovering new ways of advertising within the flow (as suggested by the "*Mad*-vertising" discussed later in the chapter).

4. For what *is* the distinction between public TV's corporate sponsorship, as it communicates prestige value, and corporations advertising on commercial networks? What costs more: "free TV," for which we all pay through the higher prices of goods that advertise on television, or the various "pay" viewing services?

5. Or, more accurately, it shows the multiple "we"s that have been articulated across that history and the ways in which those identities and histories have been formed, in great part, by consumer dynamics, commodified relations, and commercial media industries.

6. As Roland Barthes writes, "The name of Photography's *noeme* will therefore be: 'That-has-been'" (77). Irene V. Small in this volume references Don's Carousel pitch as an example of *Mad Men*'s engagement with "both avant-garde art and the culture industry of the 1960s."

7. Many television scholars have written on "liveness," but for an inaugural theorization of this, see especially Feuer, "Concept." Other important pieces on television "liveness" include Auslander; Dayan and Katz; Dienst; Doane, "Information"; Gripsrud; Heath and Skirrow; McPherson; Morse; and M. White, "Television Liveness."

8. For scholarly discussions of television's construction of history, see especially S. Anderson; Edgerton and Rollins; and M. White, "Television: A Narrative." Also interesting for considering issues of television's construction of history and memory are O'Connor; Spigel, "From the Dark"; and Wales.

9. "Preserving our television heritage" was used (both seriously and ironically, I would argue) as the slogan for Nick at Nite's "TV Land" block (and, later, station, when TV Land spun off to its own channel).

10. Gary Edgerton, writing in *In Media Res*, describes *Mad Men*'s title sequences as a "pastiche of Saul Bass's title work from *Vertigo* (the optical disorientation), *North by Northwest* (the iconography of the Manhattan skyline), and *Psycho* (the foreboding strings à la Bernard Herrmann)," noting that "the use of a protagonist in black silhouette even suggests the 1955–1965 television series, *Alfred Hitchcock Presents*, where the producer-director steps right into a black silhouetted profile of himself

during the opening credits of that show" ("Falling Man"). Jeremy Butler, also writing and curating for *In Media Res*'s "Mad Men Theme Week" (20–24 April 2009), compares *Mad Men*'s low-angle shooting to Billy Wilder's work.

11. See, for instance, Waldman, "*Mad Men–Twilight Zone.*" The series creator Matthew Weiner specifically names *The Twilight Zone* (along with other anthology series) and *The Dick Van Dyke Show* as precedents for *Mad Men*. See Waldman, "Matt Weiner."

12. According to Douglas Gomery, "AMC began in October of 1984 as a pay service, but switched onto cable's 'basic tier' in 1987 when it had grown to seven million subscribers in one thousand systems across the U.S. This growth curve continued and by the end of 1989 AMC had doubled its subscriber base. Two years later it could count 39 million subscribers" (94).

13. In other words, this is a television system in which the multiplication of channels is less about reaching all kinds of viewers in a democracy of media pleasures than about commodifying those viewers in a demography of media consumers. For discussions of the connection or disconnect between "democracy" and "demography" in and for television, see Ang; and Marc.

14. See the quotes by Tom Karsch, executive vice-president and general manager of Turner Classic Movies, and Kate McEnroe, AMC president, in John Dempsey's *Variety* article. See also Battaglio.

15. Ed Carroll heads Rainbow Entertainment Services, owner of AMC.

16. In fact, by 2003 AMC had started going almost solely by these initials, downplaying the original wording of "American Movie Classics" in the light of their not-solely-cinematic rebranding.

17. For another comparison of these programs, see Fredericks.

18. Or, as the senior partner Roger Sterling says, "Through manipulation of the mass media, the public is under the impression that your cigarettes are linked to . . . [*awkward pause*] certain fatal diseases." "Manipulation of the media?" scoffs the senior Mr. Garner; "Hell, that's what I pay you for!"

19. "It's Toasted" was indeed the actual slogan for Lucky Strike cigarettes, though it was introduced in 1917 (not, as in *Mad Men*'s story, 1960). For historical discussions of this slogan, see two articles from *Time*: "Advertising: It's Toasted" (1938) and "Advertising: Toasted" (1951).

20. *Mad Men* stages its own debate about the possibility of such demarcation on and in the light of TV. In an episode about the future of Sterling Cooper (in fact, the very future of the planet, given that the episode is set amid the looming Cuban missile crisis), rivals Don Draper and Herman "Duck" Phillips have their own showdown ("Meditations in an Emergency," 2.13). According to Duck, advertising need not be tied to "creative's fantasies of persuasion" (like the "toasted" label); rather, it is simply about "buying time and space, and right now that means television" — a medium that Duck sees as merely a filler, taking up all capacity and consciousness as opposed to particularizing specific goods (let alone good texts). Yet Don, again

staking a claim for distinction, declares, "I sell products, not advertising," and the episode demonstrates how this particularization applies to television as much as anything else. Indeed, this exchange occurs in an episode filled with scenes of characters watching very particular things: most notably, Kennedy's addresses about the build-up of arms or, in pointed contrast to those "significant" media moments, the "harmless" TV shows that Betty and Don have the kids watch instead (*Leave It to Beaver* and *Wagon Train*). In this way, in its performances, even if not in what (some) characters profess, *Mad Men* acknowledges the differences within televisual flow—a lesson that the program itself, in its own distinction and "taste," certainly teaches.

21. Important work analyzing the construction of race as a category for television includes, among others, H. Gray, *Watching Race*; Hunt; Jhally and Lewis; J. Mac-Donald; and Torres, *Living Color*.

22. Paul actually seems to try to evade this trip by trying instead to take a business trip to an aerospace convention in California—a minor detail, but one that strikes me as telling not only for how it marks Paul's preference for expansive fantasy over rough work on the ground, but for how it alludes to television's own expansive fantasies of space. I am referring to the discourses and imagery of "universal" (supposedly "postracial") humanism that tend to accompany U.S. TV's treatment of space—as seen, for example, in the classic case of the program *Star Trek* (NBC, 1966–69), which stands as the prototypical "progressive" version of this, but also in some of the TV commercials discussed later in which the futurism of space imagery authorizes both a deployment and a disavowal of present constructions of race and, indeed, of these ads' own racism. For further discussion of such "universal" fantasies, see Joyrich, "Feminist Enterprise?"; and, particularly helpful for contextualizing this in terms of the decade on which *Mad Men* focuses, Spigel and Curtin, especially the essays by Jeffery Sconce, Lynn Spigel, and Thomas Streeter.

23. For alternative discussions of this scene, see the chapters by Clarence Lang and Kent Ono in this volume.

24. Many television scholars have written on the mutual construction of gender and television. For just some work on this topic, see Baehr and Dyer; Bruns-don, D'Acci, and Spigel; D'Acci, *Defining Women*, and "Television"; Haralovich and Rabinovitz; Joyrich, *Re-viewing Reception*; E. A. Kaplan, "Feminist Criticism"; Morley; L. Mumford; and Spigel, *Make Room*.

25. I explore the connections between TV and the closet (and the ways in which sexuality is both announced and erased) in more detail in my essay "Epistemology of the Console." For other interesting (and very diverse) work in queer television studies, see (among others) Becker; S. Chambers; G. Davis and Needham; Doty; Gamson; Gross; S. Jones; McCarthy, "Must See"; and Torres, "Television/Feminism."

26. For information about the *Defenders* episode, see Alvey. See also Leslie J. Reagan's chapter in this volume.

27. Of course, in its scandal about sexual and reproductive choices, the *Defenders*

episode poignantly resonates not only with Sal's story but, more obviously even, with Peggy, who, in season 1, becomes pregnant in a casual sexual encounter with Pete, has a nervous breakdown and denies the pregnancy and birth, gives the child up for adoption, and (until she eventually tells Pete in season 2) keeps all of this secret from those at work (and, arguably, from even herself). For each story, though, we see both the risks and the rewards of television "controversy." Though not about either *The Defenders* or *Mad Men*, interesting analyses of the construction and operation of TV "scandal" can be found in Lull and Hinerman.

28. For further discussion of this scene in the context of *Mad Men*'s treatment of sexuality, see Alexander Doty's essay in this volume.

29. Joshua Benton also cites one blogger who writes: "They do this neat, 'tivo-proof' type of commercial billboard before most commercials. . . . I bite. Originally, I paused because I think that maybe the show is coming back—a la traditional billboard/bumper. Now I am conditioned to stop, because I am getting some value in exchange—I get ad history/trivia, facts, music/artists in spots, etc. . . . All good. I watch more, stay through commercial breaks, AND I have a high recall of the ads." See also Flaherty.

30. The commercial's use of music from the 1992 hit "Jump Around" by the hip-hop group House of Pain both contributes to and complicates the racialization discussed here (an insight for which I am indebted to Melissa Getreu). Because House of Pain is well known as a white, Irish American hip-hop group, it is the presence of the theft, not just the music, that creates the racializing effect—one that, on a secondary level, is even remarked on in the ad by the way that this appropriation of hip-hop is itself overtaken by the eruption of the "ghetto" into this (literally) "universalized" scene. In the light of my reading of the commercial's racism, some of the comments posted about the video on the YouTube website are instructive (if irritating, or worse). For instance, they include the following: "Figures . . . tryin to party on the moon and the darkies are already raising the crime rate and lowering the property value"; "just like in Detroit!"; "Even in space u have black ppl stealing rims"; and "Are ghetto aliens covered by insurance?" See http://www.youtube.com/comment_servlet?all_comments&v=lBk878H3ZzY&fromurl=/watch%3Fv%3DlBk878H3ZzY and http://www.youtube.com/comment_servlet?all_comments&v=HblFjj_HM84&fromurl=/watch%3Fv%3DHblFjj_HM84%26feature%3Drelated (accessed 11 October 2010).

31. In noting in this chapter both these charges and the ties between the Clorox ad and *Mad Men*'s own strategies of representation, I do not mean to imply that *Mad Men* can simply be dismissed as "sexist" (nor, for that matter, would I dismiss the commercial so simply). Rather, I would suggest that through its deployment of style and sensation, history and memory, address and (dis)identification, flow and segmentation, *Mad Men* manages to explore gender relations (often in very complex and compelling ways) even as it also manages to disavow its own reiteration of certain conventional constructions of gender. In this way, much as I discuss in more

detail about sexuality here, *Mad Men* paradoxically both interrogates and reproduces gender hierarchies, making any one pronouncement about its "sexism" (or, conversely, its "feminism") too blunt-edged and univocal adequately to characterize the program's multifaceted gender and sexual politics.

32. Interestingly, the version of this commercial posted on Johnnie Walker's own website also includes civil rights marchers, both male and female, thus diversifying the imagery (delimited by race and gender, even if presented as expansively world historical) of the ad that played on AMC. See "Strides" in the Video Gallery at http://www.johnniewalker.com/en-us/VideoGallery/ (accessed 11 October 2010).

33. I'm thinking specifically here of the story of Roger Sterling's heart attack (after his countless "gulps . . . for kicks," with no help from cholesterol-lowering medications). But of course, *Mad Men* explores the many risks of a life of "kicks" — health-related and otherwise — across the series.

34. See http://www.amctv.com/madmenyourself/ (accessed 18 February 2010).

35. The designer of the application goes by the name Dyna Moe. For an interview with her, see Oei. See also Meghan Keane; Molitor; and Van Grove.

36. There has been a great deal of discussion and debate about the ways in which fan activity operates to reinforce and transform television. For some key work in this area, see Bacon-Smith; Bury; J. Gray et al.; C. Harris and Alexander; Hellekson and Busse; Hills; Jenkins, *Fans, Bloggers, Convergence Culture*, and *Textual Poachers*; L. Lewis; and Pearson and Gwenllian-Jones. For ongoing analyses of fandom, see also the online journal *Transformative Works and Cultures*, and Henry Jenkins's blog, *Confessions of an Aca-Fan*.

37. For a fascinating discussion of the relation between television and "new media" formations and of fan activity as both labor and love, see Russo.

12

"MAIDENFORM"

Masculinity as Masquerade

LILYA KAGANOVSKY

In his book *Ways of Seeing* (1972), John Berger observed: "In the average European oil painting of the nude, the principal protagonist is never painted. He is the spectator in front of the picture and he is presumed to be a man. Everything is addressed to him. Everything must appear to be the result of his being there. It is for him that the figures have assumed their nudity. But he, by definition, is a stranger with his clothes still on" (54). Addressing the gendered nature of spectatorship, this passage anticipates by a few years Laura Mulvey's pronouncement in 1975 on the male gaze in classic Hollywood cinema ("Visual Pleasure"). The structure of the "invisible" male spectator for whom the female nude obligingly exhibits herself has haunted the discourse of representation, opening up questions concerning the construction of gender, the limits of identification, and the uses of pleasure (whether voyeuristic, scopophilic, fetishistic, or other).

For Mulvey, the position of the cinematic spectator was gendered male in relation to the "feminized" visual image. The woman herself, when she appeared on the screen, displayed the quality of what Mulvey called "to-be-looked-at-ness": she was made up, dressed, and photographed in such a way as to put herself on visual display, to exhibit herself to our gaze. Indeed, cinema itself has often been referred to as the meeting of the "voyeur" and the "exhibitionist." No matter what their gender, the spectators' pleasure comes from sneaking a peak into the "private world" of the characters, while everything about the moviegoing experience is meant to heighten the feeling of the spectator–as–Peeping Tom. We look, but we cannot be seen; we are "outside" in the dark, while they are inside with all the lights turned on.

More vitally, as Berger and Mulvey both argued, the gaze of the ideal spectator was firmly aligned with the male subject. In other words, the classic cinematic apparatus seemed to produce a "hegemonic, masculine, Oedipal bourgeois spectator, who gained illusory power and coherence in his alignment with the camera eye on the one hand, and the male protagonist on the other" (L. Williams, "Introduction," 2). The male look was conflated with the "gaze," and power seemed to be entirely on the side of the one doing all the looking. Looking at women, it seemed, was fairly "straightforward."[1]

I have started with Berger and Mulvey because I am interested in our spectatorial relationship to the character/image of Don Draper (played by the very handsome Jon Hamm), offered by the show as an ideal male subject: autonomous, daring, masterful—but in free fall. Many of the show's scenes are framed lower than eye line to incorporate the ceilings into the composition of the frame. This composition reflects the photography, graphic design, and architecture of the 1960s, but it also speaks to a certain placement of the spectator vis-à-vis the visual image. We are always looking up at the characters on the screen, always looking up at Don, and watching him is one of the show's strongest "visual pleasures." Yet in trying to see how Don is constructed by our gaze (and here I am including actual spectators of the show, the ideal spectator imagined *by* the show, and the eye of the camera), we can see the ways in which this construct is troubled by the show's own awareness of itself as fiction. In its depiction of the American 1960s as a moment of the disintegration of white male privilege and dominance, *Mad Men* produces a rather complex staging of gender relations and gender construction, troubling our normative identification not only with its male lead, but with the masculine gaze.

"Maidenform" (2.6) is an episode that begins with men looking at women and ends with women looking at men. Structured exactly like Mulvey's version of a classic Hollywood film, the episode opens with a montage of our three main female protagonists in their undergarments, and closes (with about five minutes left to spare) with a striptease at the Tom Tom Club. The central story line concerns a Playtex bra campaign. About ten minutes in, we see girls modeling bikinis during the annual Memorial Day "ribs and fashion show" at the Country Club. And even Peggy's office–cum–copy room has a prominent ad on the wall of two women wearing corsets. Practically quoting Berger's formulation a decade later, Paul Kinsey says: "Bras are for men. Women want to see themselves the way men see them." ("Men look at women," wrote Berger; "Women watch themselves being looked at" [47].) "You want to be ogled?" Don asks Betty when she suggests going to the pool in her new bikini. "Has your wife seen that yet?" asks Roger Sterling admiring Don's new secretary, the very sunburned Jane Siegel. "If we were to take you to see some girls in their underwear, would you feel like you're at work?" Freddy Rumsen asks the Playtex clients, underscoring once again the episode's focus on the male gaze. Indeed, every element of the episode suggests that if Don and the ad men have not yet read Berger and Mulvey, Matthew Weiner certainly has. As though to epitomize the gaze Mulvey describes, Don explains halfway through the episode: "Jacqueline Kennedy, Marilyn Monroe—women have feelings about these women because men do. Because *we* want both, they want to *be* both. It's about how they want to be seen, by *us*—their husbands, their boyfriends, their friends' husbands." He adds, "It's a very flattering mirror."

The episode opens to the tune of the Decemberists' "The Infanta," as we watch Betty, Joan, and Peggy get ready for their day (figs. 12.1–12.3). Probably one of the first things to note about this sequence (besides the music, which goes against the show's usual fetish for period accuracy) is its attention to clothing as costume.[2] Betty and Joan both dress in front of the mirror, focusing our attention not only on their double enframing but also on their relationship to the specular image. Each in her own way, Betty and Joan perform ideal femininity for the gaze of the other, and their relationship to their image is mediated through the mirror, in which, like Jacques Lacan's *infans* (or *Infanta*), they see an ideal *I* reflected back at them. (Notice the smile on Betty's lips and Joanie's pout. One blogger remarked, "I like how Joan does that fake-pouty Marilyn mouth thing even when she's alone" [Robertson].)

This ideal image is shaped, on the one hand, by the undergarments that the women put on, and on the other, by the forces of style, fashion, beauty, race, class, and gender that create the subject (whether onscreen or off-screen). In fashion, a "foundation garment," also known as "shapewear" or "shaping underwear," is an undergarment designed to temporarily alter the wearer's body shape to achieve a more fashionable figure. The function of a foundation garment is not to enhance a bodily feature (as would, for example, a padded bra) but to smooth or control the display of one. Corsets, brassieres, girdles, and corselettes—all these are designed primarily to alter the shape of the body, to give it a form that, although it might exaggerate certain natural features, is far from "natural." A corset is a garment worn to mold

FIGURES 12.1–12.3. Betty, Joan, and Peggy get ready for their day ("Maidenform," 2.6).

and shape the torso into a desired shape for aesthetic or medical purposes (either for the duration of wearing it, or with a more lasting effect), while the corselet was originally a piece of armor, covering the torso (the origin of the English word comes from *cors*, an Old French word meaning "bodice"). In other words, the foundation garment temporarily does for the body what the "mirror stage" permanently does for the ego: it provides an "armor" that, as Lacan tells us, "will mark [the subject's] entire mental development with its rigid structure" (78).

It is worthwhile to recall Lacan's famous discussion of the baby in front of the mirror here in some detail, to see the ways in which "Maidenform" plays with the by now familiar text of the "mirror stage." Lacan writes: "It suffices to understand the mirror stage in this context *as an identification*, in the full sense that analysis gives to the term: namely, the transformation that takes place in the subject when he assumes an image—an image that is seemingly predestined to have an effect at this phase, as witnessed by the use in analytic theory of antiquity's term, 'imago'" (76). For the subject "caught up in the lure of spatial identification," the mirror stage turns out fantasies that proceed "from a fragmented image of the body" to an "orthopedic" form of its totality—and finally, to the "donned armor of an alienating identity that will mark his entire mental development with its rigid structure" (78). Caught up in the "lure of spatial identification," Betty and Joan collect themselves, putting on the foundation garments that will shape the body even as they assume the imago that will shape their subjectivity. "Maidenform" seems determined to teach us this basic Lacanian lesson, to insist on revealing the ways in which we are shaped, ordered, and framed by our identifications. But it is also interested in destroying those identifications, in undermining the "spatial captation," both for the characters and for the viewers.

Betty and Joan's superior *adult* femininity is contrasted to Peggy's awkward and childish gestures, as she jumps up and down, pulling up her pantyhose.[3] As Joan insists to her later in the episode, "You want to be taken seriously? Stop dressing like a little girl." The concern of the episode seems to be precisely with the notion of woman and masquerade; with the underclothes that *shape* the woman. The choice is given as one between Playtex and Maidenform, with Playtex, a company known for making solid and comfortable bras for women, hoping to branch out into the decidedly sexier Maidenform territory.

As we see from several close-ups of the ads, in contrast to Maidenform's "dreams," "fantasies," and "reveries," Playtex advertises itself as a "living" bra. One Playtex ad, for example, is a medium shot of a woman, half-turned, her

FIGURE 12.4. Jackie, Marilyn, Jackie, Marilyn . . . ("Maidenform," 2.6).

face entirely obscured by her arm holding a camera. The ad emphasizes the possibility of an active lifestyle and one not necessarily aimed at the gaze of the *other*, unlike the Maidenform copy that reads "I dreamed I stopped them in *their* tracks in my Maidenform bra" and "I dreamed I was WANTED in my Maidenform bra." Hearing that Playtex is jealous of a ten-year-old Maidenform campaign, Don is dismissive: "Maidenform is a dream," he says; "Playtex is a bra."[4]

The ad campaign for Playtex turns on the moment of revelation. Every woman, Paul Kinsey tells Don, is either a Marilyn or a Jackie: "We went out the other night, after the meeting, y'know, a little extra hours after hours. And, I looked around the bar. [Ken affirms: "We all did."] Women right now already have a fantasy, and it's not going up the Nile, it's right here in America: Jackie Kennedy and Marilyn Monroe. Every single woman is one of them."[5] (Speaking about JFK, Jimmy Barrett tells Betty a few episodes earlier, "You're not Jackie, but you're his type, I know" ["The Benefactor," 2.3].) When Peggy seems dubious about this observation, the men do a quick sweep of the steno pool, identifying every woman as one or the other (fig. 12.4). "Well, Marilyn's really a Joan, not the other way around," Paul notes, admiringly. "You're a Jackie or a Marilyn; a line or a curve; nothing goes better together," explains Sal. Yet, while Paul's observation is that every woman is *either* a Marilyn or a Jackie, Don's point is that every woman is actually both: "Two sides of one woman—Jackie by day, Marilyn by night." Thus the final ad campaign pictures the same model twice, once in black, once in white (fig. 12.5).

As I have suggested, however, this episode is not *merely* about men looking at women. After all, the Maidenform/Playtex story line is distanced from us. We watch the men looking at the women and are thereby denied that same

FIGURE 12.5. "Nothing fits both sides of a woman, better than Playtex" ("Maidenform," 2.6).

kind of relationship of pure, uncontaminated voyeurism on which the episode is premised. *We* have read Laura Mulvey, even if they have not. Moreover, the Playtex campaign is complicated from the start by the presence of Peggy, who fails to fit into either of the two feminine positions allowed by the pitch (and occupied by Betty and Joan in the opening sequence). When she complains to Joan that "there's business going on after hours" and she "is not invited," she is told, "You're in their country, learn to speak the language." ("You're just the man for the job," Freddy tells her.) Asked by Ken which bra she wears, Peggy hedges her bets by saying that she chooses Playtex because she agrees with the ninety-five women they surveyed about how it fits (we know that Joan too is asked about her bra, but we never learn the answer). Neither a Marilyn nor a Jackie, Peggy is told that she is Gertrude Stein—a comment immediately softened by Don, who suggests Irene Dunne.

Indeed, at the end of the episode, Peggy tries to negotiate her uncharted position by attempting to fill the place of the male spectator, as she joins the men at the Tom Tom Club to watch the striptease. The position is clearly uncomfortable; perched on the lap of the Playtex client, watched disapprovingly by Pete, Peggy occupies precisely that in between position she has been assigned throughout the episode (figs. 12.6–12.8). She is neither Marilyn nor Jackie. Neither adult woman nor little girl. Neither spectator nor exhibit.

Yet this episode (and indeed the series as a whole) has more at stake than an analysis of the look and the gaze that reaffirms, even via the distance of

FIGURES 12.6–12.8. "Men look at women. Women watch themselves being looked at" (Berger) ("Maidenform," 2.6).

superior knowledge, the structures of heteronormative patriarchy. What it does, in fact, is put the entire operation of looking (and with it, spectatorship and identification) under investigation. Having opened with the three female protagonists dressing in front of the mirror, "Maidenform" ends with a completely different mirror scene: Don Draper alone, the split reflection of his face caught by the tri-part bathroom mirror. As the AMC episode guide succinctly states, "At the Draper house the next morning, daughter Sally watches Don shave until he suddenly asks her to leave. Sitting on the toilet and staring blankly, he slowly wipes the shaving cream off his face. He didn't like something he saw in the mirror" (figs. 12.9–12.12).[6]

An episode that opens with three women getting ready for their day ends with Don doing the same, and indeed the last shots recall the framing and doubling techniques that were used in the beginning for Betty and Joan. Like the Marilyn/Jackie campaign, this double image speaks to the performativity of gender identity, but now of *masculinity* as masquerade, of a put-on show that requires certain basic foundation garments, though these maybe more symbolic than actual. (Jimmy Barrett recognizes both Don and Betty as "types" as soon as he meets them, quipping, "Are you two sold separately?"; he later calls Don "the man in the gray flannel suit," and tells him he loved him in *Gentleman's Agreement*. "I'm sorry, nobody wants to think they're a type," Dr. Faye Miller tells Don two seasons later, after suggesting he'll be remarried at the end of the year.)

Masculinity may not be propped up by obvious foundation garments (though a quick look at men's underwear in a Paris department store will tell you otherwise), but like femininity, it is altered and shaped to fit the cultural mold. Don's crisis in front of the bathroom mirror has to do with moving from a position of the one who looks to one being looked at—finding himself, by the end of the episode, in what Mary Ann Doane refers to as the "feminine position":

> While the male is locked into sexual identity, the female can at least pretend that she is other—in fact, sexual mobility would seem to be a distinguishing feature of femininity in its cultural construction. . . . The idea seems to be this: it is understandable that women would want to be men, for everyone wants to be elsewhere than in the feminine position. What is not understandable within the given terms is why a woman might flaunt her femininity, produce herself as an excess of femininity, in other words, foreground the masquerade. Masquerade is not as recuperable as transvestism precisely because it constitutes an acknowl-

edgement that it is femininity itself which is constructed as a mask—as the decorative layer which conceals a non-identity. ("Film and Masquerade," 81)

Like Peggy, Don occupies a distanced position vis-à-vis his assigned or assumed gender role, choosing to stay away from the strip clubs, uncomfortable (for good reason) with his status as "war hero," refusing for the most part to prop up his masculinity with misogynous humor or male camaraderie. He tells Duck Phillips, who tries to win him over with a story of his army days, "Who am I in this story? What do you want me to say? That we're on the same team? That I love being in your unit? Sarge, I'm scared?" ("Maidenform"). We come to believe that Don is more secure in his masculinity precisely *because* he is able to recognize it as a construction and a prop. As Don knows full well he is not the man he claims to be, his masculine identity is nothing but a series of performances meant to create an illusion of the ideal male subject. "Look at that man!" Betty's neighbor Francine says, watching Don in the backyard. "I know!" Betty replies ("Marriage of Figaro," 1.3).

Though he may not be interested in joining the junior executives for "a little extra hours after hours," Don nonetheless has his own extracurricular activities, which in "Maidenform" involve a somewhat risqué hotel tryst with Bobbie Barrett, who just won't stop talking. Shocked to discover that he has a "reputation," and "fans," and that women have been talking about him behind his back, Don abandons Bobbie Barrett tied to the bedpost in her hotel room, but not before she gets in the final word: "Oh stop, this is nobody's maiden voyage." Bobbie offers to have herself blindfolded, but it's already too late, she has already seen and understood something about Don that he did not want (us) to see. The choice of "maiden" voyage is of course not accidental here and brings us back to the central conceit (and title) of the episode: the foundation garments by which femininity and masculinity are organized and kept in "shape." A form of the subject that can only be called, recalling Lacan, "orthopedic."

An episode that begins with us looking at women ends with us looking at men—or one man, our ideally constructed male subject. Don's crisis in the closing sequence seems to be precipitated by his daughter's look of pure admiration. And in fact, we have seen this look before, from both Betty and Sally during the Memorial Day "ribs and fashion show" at the Country Club (figs. 12.13–12.14). Responding to the call, "Please, heroes, on your feet!" Don stands up to be applauded for his military service, only to be made increasingly uncomfortable by the look on Sally's face. Again, noting the position of

FIGURES 12.9–12.12. A different mirror scene: Sally and Don ("Maidenform," 2.6).

FIGURES 12.13–12.14. Betty and Sally looking up at Don ("Maidenform," 2.6).

the camera eye, Don is shot from bottom up, while Sally is framed from bottom left corner to upper right corner, looking up at him with eyes full of love.

In the final sequence, as if continuing the earlier scene with Bobbie Barrett, Sally promises to keep quiet while watching Don shave. "I'm not going to talk," she says; "I don't want you to cut yourself." Sally is a good and true fan, happy to occupy her place as spectator. But her seemingly passive spectatorship nevertheless produces Don as spectacle, as object rather than subject of the gaze. Certainly, he is an object for Bobbie Barrett and for all those "fans" in the fictional world of the show, and—naked, clad only in a towel—he is surely also an object for the show's fans, who promise, along with Sally, "not to talk" but simply to watch. Sally's concern is that if she talks, Don might cut himself, and we understand that this scene is about symbolic castration: the coming apart of the subject, and the production of the fragmented body in place of the image of its totality.[7]

While the male may be "locked into sexual identity," masculinity too is a decorative layer that conceals a nonidentity, and this truth is signaled to us by the multiple mirror reflections that split the image of Don into fragments. We already know that Don Draper is not Don Draper, just as we know that he is neither the war hero, nor the good father, nor the good husband that the world takes him to be. But we also know that no matter how much Adam Whitman might want it to be the case, Don Draper is also not Dick Whitman. "What kind of a man are you?" asks Rachel Menken when Don proposes they drop everything and run away together. "I think I am only now beginning to see you clearly for the first time" ("Nixon vs. Kennedy," 1.12).

Mad Men is not the only contemporary TV series to foreground masculinity as performance. The episode "Hello, Dexter Morgan" (4.11) of *Dexter* (Showtime, 2006–) shows us Dexter standing in front of a four-pane mirror, his reflection quadrupled. "You're juggling too many people," his ghostly father tells him. When Dexter misunderstands, he specifies: "I mean Dexter Morgan, blood tech, husband, father, serial killer . . . Which one are you?"—a question that echoes *Mad Men*'s often repeated "Who is Don Draper?" Like Don, Dexter has a secret identity, a "dark passenger" whose true nature he cannot reveal to friends or family. Dexter, as he repeatedly tells us, wears a "mask" in order to hide his real self. Yet what the series so clearly shows us is that the alienating armor of identity produced through identifications and misrecognitions is all the identity we have. "Which one are you?" asks the father. "All of them," says Dexter.

For Doane, the masquerade, in flaunting femininity, holds it at a distance. "Womanliness is a mask which can be worn or removed," she writes, a "decorative layer" that conceals a nonidentity ("Film and Masquerade," 81). Similarly, *Mad Men* returns us again and again to this problem of nonidentity: there is no Don Draper and there is no Dick Whitman. Pete has nothing on Don because Don himself is nothing—this is the frightening lack that Rachel sees in a flash, while it takes Betty a long time to face up to the fact that the image she has believed in is a construct that she herself helped to form. Betty is caught up in the lure of spatial identification (as Lacan would put it), and her worries are always cosmetic. "You're painting a masterpiece," she says, quoting her mother; "make sure to hide the brush strokes." Betty's disenchantment with Don has less to do with his marital infidelities, or even with the revelation of his "true" identity, than with the fact that in turning out to be different from what she believed, he spoils the perfect picture of suburban marital bliss. "I want to scream at you for ruining all this!" she tells him ("The Grown-Ups," 3.12).

Throughout "Maidenform," men have been imagining themselves in control of the "gaze"—an unquestioned phallic mastery over the spectacle of woman. Yet the distinction between the gaze and the "eye" (look) is similar to the distinction between the phallus and the penis. The gaze, in other words, is the transcendental ideal—omniscient, omnipotent—that the look can never achieve but to which it ceaselessly aspires. "The best the look can hope for," writes Carol Clover, "is to pose and pass itself off as the gaze." Clover goes on to suggest that (in horror films in particular, but for others as well), "*whenever* a man imagines himself as the controlling voyeur—imagines, in Lacanian terms, that his 'look' constitutes a 'gaze'—some sort of humiliation is soon to follow, typically in the form of his being overwhelmed, in one form or another, by the sexuality of the very female he meant to master" ("Eye of Horror," 206–7; see also Clover, *Men*).

"Maidenform" suggests precisely such a loss of control. Something in the way Sally looks at him—and what she sees—forces Don to confront his image in the mirror not through the lens of *méconnaissance* (and its accompanying "illusion of autonomy" [Lacan, 80]) but as a naked truth. The end of the mirror stage for Lacan "decisively tips the whole of human knowledge into being mediated by the other's desire . . . and turns the *I* into an apparatus to which every instinctual pressure constitutes a danger, even if it corresponds to a natural maturation process" (79). The end of "Maidenform" produces a similar kind of maturation for Don, showing the ways in which his subjectivity is mediated through the desire of the other (whether that be Betty's bourgeois dream of the perfect home, the predatory sexual appetites of Bobbie Barrett, or Sally's strongly Oedipal admiration).[8] As the camera slowly pulls back, we see Don, with one pink towel wrapped around him and another in his hands, seated with his head down. As usual, he is too big for the space he occupies inside Betty's house—the pink towels, frilly curtains, and fuzzy bathroom rugs making no sense with his masculine frame (figs. 12.15–12.16).

Doane writes that "films play out scenarios of looking in order to outline the terms of their own understanding. And given the divergence between masculine and feminine scenarios, those terms would seem to be explicitly negotiated as markers of sexual difference" ("Film as Masquerade," 87). Although *Mad Men* in general and "Maidenform" in particular may seem at first glance to be participating in a "classical" production of sexual difference, the episode actually erases the divergence between masculine and feminine scenarios, placing the hypermasculine Don Draper in the "feminine position" in order to demonstrate the convergence of the forms of masquerade. As Richard Dyer and others have shown, heteronormative structures of representation dictate the ways in which the male body can and cannot be shown, producing complicated negotiations between where and how a man must look while being looked at. The male pin-up, the hard body, the boxer (Clint Eastwood, Arnold Schwarzenegger, Robert De Niro in *Raging Bull* [1980]), and so on—the representation of all of these figures must chart the difficult path between action and passivity, between the quality of "to-be-looked-at-ness" and the power/pleasure of looking:

> The idea of looking (staring) as power and being looked at as powerlessness overlaps with ideas of activity/passivity. Thus to look is thought of as active; whereas to be looked at is passive. In reality, this is not true. The model prepares her- or himself to be looked at, the artist or photographer constructs the image to be looked at; and, on the other hand, the image that the viewer looks at is not summoned up by his or her act of looking but in collaboration with those who have put the image there. Most of us probably experience looking and being looked at, in life as in art, somewhere among these shifting relations of activity and passivity. Yet it remains the case that images of men must disavow this element of passivity if they are to be kept in line with dominant ideas of masculinity-as-activity. (Dyer, "Don't Look Now," 66)[9]

Television, because of its serial nature and ongoing "flow," must constantly offer us new spectacle, new forms of masculinity-as-activity. As a result it risks turning its male characters into "spectacle," their actions never quite leading to closure. As Lynne Joyrich puts it, speaking specifically about television melodrama (to which *Mad Men* certainly belongs) and its weekly

FIGURES 12.15–12.16. The body, in bits and pieces ("Maidenform," 2.6).

repetition of "male masquerade": "the reiteration—the exhibition and production of masculinity through constant refiguration—exacerbates the very 'gender trouble' that television tries so hard to avoid. Caught in a bind in which only repeated evidence of performance can suffice, television's construction of masculinity becomes dependent on its 'look,' making it recall the same feminine connotations of spectacle and image that it wishes to combat" (Re-viewing Reception, 84).

One of the visual pleasures of Mad Men is looking at Don. This pleasure is explicitly problematized in "Maidenform," an episode dedicated to understanding the power of the look/gaze. Our pleasure in looking comes at a price: we are repeatedly asked to admire and identify with a character who is, as Pete Campbell puts it, "a liar and a cheat and possibly worse" ("Nixon vs. Kennedy"). Mad Men, in fact, offers us three paths for identification in relation to its male star. The first comes at the credit sequence that shows us first, Don Draper falling out of a high-rise building, and then, with a sudden switch in perspective, ourselves falling. The second is identification through love: like Sally, we look up at Don with eyes full of love. He is, after all, the center of the spectatorial gaze, *the* fetish object of the show. But the third is the image we find at the end of "Maidenform": the image of Don in bits in pieces, with the camera slowly pulling away.

NOTES

1. It obviously was not, and many studies have followed Berger's and Mulvey's seminal works, including Mulvey's own "Some Afterthoughts on 'Visual Pleasure and Narrative Cinema.'" See most recently L. Williams, Viewing Positions. Moreover, cinematic spectatorship is different from the televisual, where the proximity of the viewer to the screen, television's location inside the home, and its status as "popular culture" together gender the television viewer as female rather than male. See Ellis. For feminist television theory, see Brunsdon, D'Acci, and Spigel; Johnson; Joyrich, Reviewing Reception.

2. The selection of "The Infanta," a track from the Decemberists' album Picaresque, released in 2005, and the most controversial musical choice to date for the show, was made by Weiner himself, as he told Alexandra Patsavas, the music supervisor for Mad Men, in an interview on The Sound of Young America (PRI, 30 November 2009).

3. The choice of pantyhose rather than stockings makes Peggy less "sexual" but also more modern: the introduction of pantyhose in 1959 provided a convenient alternative to stockings, and the use of stockings declined dramatically. For details, see Gant.

4. Interestingly, the Mad Men season 2 DVD "extras" suggest that the Maidenform

campaign was perceived at the time as both "revolutionary" and "feminist," while the Playtex ads in contrast were perceived as conservative and traditional. See "Maidenform," disc 2, *Mad Men: Season 2*, DVD (Lionsgate, 2009).

5. A Maidenform ad in *Life* magazine of 23 November 1962 showed a woman dressed as Cleopatra, with golden hair, headpiece, and long blue skirt. The copy read "I dreamed I barged down the Nile in my Maidenform Bra."

6. See http://www.amctv.com/shows/mad-men/episodes/season-2/maidenform (accessed 28 June 2012).

7. There is another unbearable "look" in this episode: Chauncey-the-dog's devoted look at Duck, his master, a look that duplicates Sally's expression of pure adoration.

8. In season 4, Don's accountant remarks, "Now please tell me you're *shtupping* that girl" — after which Don seemingly notices his secretary Megan for the first time.

9. See also Cook. For masculinity and the cinema, see Cohan and Hark; Easthope; Penley and Willis; Silverman, *Male Subjectivities*.

HISTORY GETS IN YOUR EYES

Mad Men, *Misrecognition, and the Masculine Mystique*

JEREMY VARON

Accompanying the meteoric rise in the popularity of *Mad Men* have been proliferating attempts to account for that affection. The explanations root the show's appeal in everything from its impeccable period stylings; to the exquisite entanglements of its gorgeous male and female leads; to postfeminist lust for a cad and vicarious pleasure in "casual vice"; to, in weightier fashion, its meticulous reconstruction and artful evocation of an era tantalizingly just beyond the reach of its target audience.[1] Viewers in their late twenties through forties learn, with varying focus on their parents' moment, about the agonies of the feminine mystique, the evolution of the consumer culture, and the national mood circa the Kennedy assassination. So enthralling has this quasi-documentary quality been that each installment sends pundits and fans scrambling to unpack the historical inspiration for particular plotlines and characters while scrutinizing each detail for its "truthiness." But perhaps the most interesting appraisal of *Mad Men*, enunciated by early critics, takes a dramatically contrary tack: to accuse the show of a lack of realism where it most counts, rendering it an exercise in generational sanctimony. By extension, the show becomes grist for a new round of history wars. These allegedly pit the virtuous, politically correct present against the sinful, benighted past and, summoning a tired *Kulturkampf*, the emancipated 1960s against the stolid 1950s.[2]

I propose to think about the show's relationship to history in a different way, defying its admirers and detractors both. Above all, I question that *Mad Man* adopts a fundamental stance of distance from the past such that it essentially offers either a skillful explication or facile put-down (or glamorization) of the epoch it depicts. Indeed, in my view the show is more plausibly the staging of a fantasy than the rendering of history.

Congenitally male and heterosexual, and offering ultimately futile escape from the burdens of conventional expectation, the fantasy remains painfully resonant and has present-day echoes, including in film and television. Ostensibly trained on the power of historical change, *Mad Men* actually testifies instead to the chronic quality of a postwar unhappiness that is little changed by being put in different settings. And far from presenting the 1960s as deliverance from the discontents of the 1950s, *Mad Men* implies that the 1960s failed before the 1960s even "happen." The show may therefore remain captive to the condition it diagnoses, equipping neither its characters nor—as yet—its viewers with the internal resources or genuine historical inspiration to find a way out. In this way, *Mad Men*'s phantasmic "history" functions as a broad-ranging, deeply pessimistic social critique. The show, I argue, does not entirely escape the question of history, but misses an opportunity to engage it more deeply.

When the curtain rises on *Mad Men*, we are treated to the sleek elegance of Madison Avenue in 1960, as well as an onslaught of vice. So inured may we become to the show's accretion of sins, which pile up like cigarettes in an ad man's ashtray, that it is worth recounting them to recoup the initial shock. In the inaugural episode ("Smoke Gets in Your Eyes," 1.1), our hero Don Draper puzzles over how best to shill for a tobacco industry whose product is becoming scientifically linked to mortal illness. For distraction or inspiration, he does an overnight with his beatnik mistress Midge, pulling from his desk the following morning a crisp shirt from a stack assembled to mask such evenings. Liquor, we learn, may be enjoyed after, during, or before a client meeting.

Pete Campbell, the punky junior executive, verbally undresses "the new girl," Peggy. The only reprimand from Don is that if he remains that obnoxious (not sexist), "no one will like" him, condemning him to stagnation on the company ladder. Campbell then decamps to a strip club for his bachelor party, where he deals a vile come-on to otherwise game single girls. Peggy's initiation as Don's secretary is handled by the office women, who instruct that she tart up her look. So advised, Peggy engages in a clumsy seduction of Don, rebuffed by his merciful recognition that she is not that kind of girl. Yet later that evening, she quickly succumbs, sans protection, to the desire of a drunk Campbell desperately mopping up his waning bachelordom.

Though Don is more refined, he nonetheless upbraids a demanding Jewish female client by insisting, "I'm not going to let a woman talk to me like this!" (This, after he has joked with his boss about employment discrimination against Jews.) She, even so, seems already to want to sleep with him and consents to a flirt-and-make-up rendezvous that holds the door open for business mixed with pleasure. Don then returns to his beautiful wife, his sleeping children, and his suburban home having completely obliterated, all in two days' "work," whatever sanctity they nominally represent.

To all this turpitude — which subsequent episodes largely expound — some critics cried foul, noting a curious dissonance: that a show so attentive to historical detail so overplays the "WASP men behaving badly" aspect of the epoch it depicts. Advertising may well have been an especially bawdy corporate culture (as the vintage ad exec and *Mad Men* consultant Jerry Della Femina loudly boasts, but other veterans dispute).[3] And the 1950s and early 1960s were never as chaste as the dominant morality expressed in the iconic depiction of middle-class American life, *Father Knows Best* (1954–60): they always included an admixture of Christian homeliness and chauvinistic prurience. Even so, the show so skews the balance as to exceed credulity. An oft-quoted quip in *Mad Men* commentary declares that the show "explains why the '60s," defined by the imperatives of feminism and civil rights, "had to happen."[4] But it also leads us to wonder whether the 1960s — in their equally defining hedonism — would ever have happened if the 1950s had been so licentious.

As Mark Greif's oft-cited opening volley in the assault of the literati contends, *Mad Men* positions present-day viewers to "watch and know better with respect to male chauvinism, homophobia, anti-semitism, workplace harassment, housewives' depression, nutrition and smoking," thus proffering "an unearned pride in our supposed superiority." An essay in *Commentary* titled "The Television Show That Says You're Better Than Your Parents" similarly asserted that "*Mad Men* invites us to congratulate ourselves for having found solutions to every failure of the [past]" (Schulman, 46). For Benjamin Schwarz, the literary editor of the *Atlantic Monthly*, *Mad Men* "encourages the condescension of posterity."[5] But this elite take on the show has its own curiosities. It presumes to know, without asking viewers, precisely why they are so devoted. It thereby leaves itself near powerless to refute precisely the opposite claim: that the show's popularity lies in the titillating glimpse it offers into lives of dissolute danger, given the comparative safety and productivity of our own. As speculation, moreover, the generational self-congratulation thesis is not terribly persuasive. One may indeed also covet, and not simply condemn, the "sinful" behavior of the Mad World. This identification potentially collapses the sense of historical distance in the audience that must underwrite generational conceit. I suspect, moreover, that the notion that the show plays up the smoking, drinking, and straying merely to denounce them could come only from someone who has never had a pack-a-day cigarette habit, too great a love of booze, or a professionally dangerous liaison.[6]

Watching *Mad Men*'s grand entrance, I had the sensation of being introduced to the inner workings of a well-oiled system of licensed transgression—a floating world of white, middle-class male desire in which vice is carefully built into the rituals of the workplace and broader grammar of its inhabitants' lives. Secretaries dutifully protect their bosses from the intrusions of home. The office women themselves charge up the sexual currents. "Sorry honey, I have to work late tonight" somehow holds up as routine cover for affairs. And a clipped charm masks how crude so much of it is. As an added kick, the Mad Men are in a creative line of work, which eschews button-down rules and rewards a maverick nature.

If the setting is novel, the basic presentation is not. It has ample precedent in the Mob film. The characteristic gesture of this beloved American genre is to school the viewer in the mechanics of a subculture that dispenses with both the most sacred rules and the quotidian norms of "straight" society while imposing its own. Martin Scorsese's *Goodfellas* (1990)—set in the same era as *Mad Men* and also meticulous in its period detail—provides a signal example. Like a didactic ethnographer, the narrator Henry Hill explains the varieties of theft, the many occasions for violence, the system of tribute, and the protocol for maintaining both wives and mistresses. Amid piles of cash and later cocaine, he extols the goodfellas' contemptuous disregard of the "goody-two-shoes" existence of middle-class sops who play by the rules that crush them. Though tackier than the stylish Mad Men, wiseguys do a similar end run around the repressive 1950s.

The point of the Mob movie is not, of course, simply to snigger at how depraved the mobsters are. Rather, it is to induce both repulsion and attraction, summoning a disturbing insight. The ostensibly alien world of seeming sociopaths becomes a mirror to our own, such that "official" capitalism may also appear a system of ruthless predation, the police just another gang, and politics another syndicate. (The tobacco that the Mad Men are paid to push legally remains greatly more lethal than Mob violence or illicit drugs.) And the mobsters' desire for money, power, and sex becomes an intensification of our own desires, which sustain the consumer culture. This dynamic suggests a way of reading *Mad Men* by which the construction of the Mad World and the Mob World, as realms of sanctioned indulgence at the boundary of prevailing norms, is essentially the same.

A last germane aspect of the Mob genre is the obsession with family and religion, evident in mobsters' perverse desire to see themselves as good husbands, fathers, and Catholics despite being cheats and murderers. This contradiction points to the dual nature of the fantasy, which seeks both the fulfillment of sociocultural norms and their violation. Hence the archetypal male version of "having it all" demands professional success, the sumptuous home, and the family, but also the netherworld of illicit pleasure.

The most recent icon of this triumph is, of course, Tony Soprano of *The Sopranos* (HBO, 1999–2007), perhaps the best-known New Jersey suburbanite of our day. Tony's life is thick with the stuff of macho dreams, from the office in a strip club, to the luxury SUV, the mandate for violence, and a sex appeal undiminished by an expanding waistline. (For some viewers the Soprano crew's racism and misogyny may be added bonuses.) But Tony also wants his wife to be content, his children well-adjusted Ivy Leaguers, and their futures taken care of. This is what "all of us" want, making his struggles resonant and the incongruity of his life acute. Swapping seduction for violence, Don Draper from Ossining, New York, presents a comparable embodiment of this duality. By this likeness, *Mad Men* would be the conceptual twin of the *Sopranos* even if *Mad Men*'s creator, Matthew Weiner, had not been an award-winning writer for the Mob drama.

But there is, alas, a flaw in this picture, no matter the version. Things don't end well for the goodfellas. They cannot contain their need for money and power and so violate their own code, whether by killing a "made man" or ratting out their friends. (Landing in the witness protection program, Henry Hill becomes precisely the "shnook" he once disdained.)[7] Tony Soprano has anxiety attacks and need of a therapist. And Don Draper, along with most everybody in the Mad World, is miserable.

Early on, *Mad Men* gives us important clues as to the quality of Don's misery and its hold on the show. In some of the most arresting dialogue in the entire saga, Don in "Smoke Gets in Your Eyes" says to his client Rachel Menken, "You're born alone, you die alone, and this world just drops a bunch of rules on top of you to make you forget those facts, but I never forget. I'm living like there is no tomorrow. Because there isn't one." Don combines nuclear-age nihilism with an oddly stoic "Be Here Now" spiritualism of the coming 1960s. They are as close to a personal philosophy as he utters, referencing his rebel nature, the resignation at its core, and the tyranny of the "rules" he so resists.

Equally suggestive is Rachel's reply: "I don't think I realized it until this moment. But it must be hard to be a man, too. . . . I don't know what it is you really believe, but I do know what it feels like to be out of place, to be disconnected, to see the whole world laid out in front of you the way other people live it. Something tells me you know it too." By virtue of her insider/outsider status as a businessperson, a woman, and a Jew, she is able to appreciate his own outsiderness (though without knowing its source). Chiefly, she intuits that Don has both the gift and the curse of reflexivity. This capacity to see the grooves of desire and habit in others makes him the kind of ad man who can perfectly match the right product to the right emotions. But it also leads him to believe that everything, including love and happiness, is artifice. Although season 2 finds him declaring that the essence of advertising is to make people "feel," he himself can scarcely feel at all ("For Those Who Think Young," 2.1). In a final irony, he is acutely perceptive about the inner life of others but has almost no insight into his own. The question that most troubles him recurs again and again: "Who is Don Draper?" ("Public Relations," 4.1).[8]

Rachel's lines about the burdens of manhood telegraph what will be a dominant theme across many episodes. The story lines concerning the women's struggles are certainly better structured, more historically compelling, and more obviously gendered than those of the men. With admirable pathos, we are given portraits of the afflictions of suburban womanhood (Betty), the struggles of a professional pioneer (Peggy), and the ambivalence of a savvy "single girl" caught between competing ambitions (Joan).[9] And yet the male angst—a masculine mystique our culture never tires of pondering—proves the stronger term. If there is any structural sexism to the show's otherwise enlightened treatment of gender, it is that it demands we devote so much attention to—and feel protracted sympathy for—the trials of men blessed with nearly every form of privilege and success. All the while the women (if often privileged themselves) are *really* suffering.

With this focus, *Mad Men* joins a pageant of iconic representations of white masculinity in crisis and, specifically, the hazards of upper-middle-class mediocrity and ennui as experienced by men. This lineage includes Sinclair Lewis's *Babbitt* (1922); the fiction of John Cheever, on which the show explicitly draws; the films *The Graduate* (1967, based on a novel from 1963), *American Beauty* (1999); and of course *The Sopranos*.[10] The scenario of *Mad*

Men, however, also differs from most of these archetypes in making the spectacle of masculinity in crisis at once so elegant, alluring, and instructive.

George Babbitt trades bland conformity for adventure and excess, only to be disillusioned with them. *The Graduate*'s Benjamin Braddock seeks deliverance, instigated by the appearance of Mrs. Robinson's exquisite leg, from the descending cage of a career in plastics. But his is at best an ambivalent escape, as he scarcely loves his unexceptional bride and seems too unhinged to be happy. The bloodhounds of discontent will likely find his scent, trailing from his getaway bus and whatever life he builds. *American Beauty*'s Lester Burnham, an advertising executive, gives us a version of Ben had he succumbed to plastics. For the forty-three-year-old Lester, the rebellion comes too late. Covetous of his teenage daughter's hot friend, he plunges into adolescent regression ending with him slumped over his kitchen table in a puddle of blood.

A Mad Man like Don has it much better. Don does not have to choose between the domestic ideal and his suave debauchery—at least during the first three seasons. Up until his divorce in season 4, he gets to have both at the same time: the family life and the floating world, along with every age and variety of woman, including a stunning wife. Talented and charismatic, he is hardly some drab everyman. It is as though *Mad Men*'s creators have, as a thought experiment, stacked the deck in favor of male fulfillment. (Cut of the same cloth, HBO's *Big Love* [2006–11] imagines a man wed to three wives—each smart, attractive, pious, and lusty—to see how he copes.) The stakes are likewise raised: if the men cannot make a good go of it under *these* circumstances, then the flaws in what likely remains the dominant, aspirational ideal of American life—one essentially designed for (white) men—must run distressingly deep.

In this way, the show suggests ample grounds for worry. *Mad Men* repeatedly stages the twin implosion of the domestic ideal and its hedonistic alternative. Ideally, the latter should make the former bearable, while the former should give life substance and meaning to balance the indulgence. But the Mad Men continually experience disappointment with both the angel and the devil they struggle to separate. Even the fulfilled wish fails to satisfy. Chronicling that frustration, *Mad Men* is at its best.

An early episode, "Marriage of Figaro" (1.3), uses the device of the "ritual gone wrong," applied to the birthday party of Don and Betty's daughter, Sally, to savage the calm surface of postwar suburbia. Going back at least to Gustave Flaubert's *Madame Bovary*, and running through sitcom treatments of weddings, funerals, and dinner parties, this device enables potent satires of social conventions and the vanity often at their core.[11] As with most things *Mad Men*, however, the work-up of the party is decidedly dark, and it ultimately indicts Don's life and character.

The evening prior to the birthday, Don's seduction of Rachel Menken temporarily aborts when she learns he is married. The following morning, he must play suburban patriarch and assemble as his daughter's gift a life-size playhouse in the backyard. He must, that is, erect a replica of a fake, insofar as the real Draper house is hardly the happy home it appears. With Rachel still in his thoughts, he stomachs the task only by getting quietly bombed on beer. The mingling at the party is likewise repellant to him. The men tell crass jokes, softly leer at the women, and congratulate each other on their success. "We got it all, Don," one neighbor boasts. "Yup, this is it," Don replies. A pretty divorcée deflects the obvious advance of a married man preying on her supposed vulnerability with the offer to throw a ball around with her son. When making a home movie of the party, Don catches a glimpse of a kiss between cheating neighbors. And, alerted by her girlfriend Francine, Betty runs interference when Don and the divorcée begin to chat, dispatching him to the bakery to fetch the cake.

Don's filming of the scene, with the TV viewer looking through the camera's lens, typifies his detached perception. What he observes — the totality of the party and the kiss especially, given his own perfidy — stirs in him both disgust and shame. More visceral than self-aware, his reaction suggests that he feels himself at once too good for, and not worthy of, his storybook life. Doubly unable to face the ceremony of the birthday cake, he drives in his car for hours, even stopping at a railroad crossing, the show faintly suggests, to contemplate suicide.[12] He returns home with the gift to Sally of a dog. Betty, who had been quietly seething, is left stupefied.

In the same season, Pete Campbell, installed in a Manhattan apartment with his new, wealthy bride, offers a portrait of male panic before the full pressures of family have even set in. Shortly after his wedding, he returns to the department store bridal registry a hideous, duplicate chip-and-dip — an emblem of the banality of postwar domesticity ("Red in the Face," 1.7). Made insecure by a chance encounter with a dashing acquaintance, he hits on the department store girl. Rebuffed, he exchanges the chip-and-dip for a .22-caliber rifle. Back at the office, he scopes the office women through the gun sight in a fantasy of sexual possession and annihilation — an explicit linking of sex and violence, and a wish that the women disappear. Later at home, his wife curses his "stupid toy," clearly a salve for his beleaguered manhood.

Pete later confesses to Peggy, with whom he has had sex earlier in the day, a bizarre fantasy of hunting and skinning a deer. In the fantasy, his "woman," reduced to some frontier concubine in a secluded cabin, cooks and serves it to him. This profoundly regressive desire, which seeks escape from gendered modernity altogether, conveys postwar manhood gone haywire (though Peggy herself finds the imagery powerfully erotic, if also disturbing). The needle on its compass does not even know where to point.

What *Mad Men* repeatedly shows is its characters' maladaptation to prescribed roles. Even when those roles are altered by the bending or breaking of rules, the disaffection persists, and weariness sets in. The questions of what they need multiply: Different roles? Rules more rigid or flexible? Better selves? Then too, for all its attention to social roles and cultural forms, *Mad Men*'s sharpest focus is on the particularities of character. And though the characters may be archetypes, they are never merely so.[13] The show's biggest meanings derive from how the characters handle their special predicaments and pathologies.

The central predicament is, of course, Don's life, which is not sustainable as he lives it. It has the quality of a spiral pushed downward by mounting threats: the appearance of his brother and questions about his past; his increasingly brazen affairs, which push beyond even the allowances of the floating world; and Betty's growing awareness of her unhappiness and distrust of him. In the third season he tries and fails to please a major client, the hotel mogul Conrad "Connie" Hilton. He is, in short, not just a cheat on the verge of being definitively found out but also a man with profound afflictions on the verge of cracking up. The question of whether and how he can save himself provides both the show's signal tension and, in a roundabout way, its most important means of addressing culture and history.

As a psychological study, Don is fairly transparent and certainly tragic. He is haunted, we learn, by an intuition of the memory of his own birth. His prostitute mother had warned a john that if she got into "trouble" she would "cut [his] dick off and boil it in hog fat" ("Out of Town," 3.1). (Don's "memory" is triggered by the boiling over of milk he prepares for the pregnant Betty, as he tries to mend ways with her.) "Trouble" comes in the form of an unwanted pregnancy and a fatal childbirth. As she dies, she repeats the foul curse. The confused nursemaids name the child Dick to honor her apparent wish. Don is thus born under the sign of castration, his phallic power swallowed up in the grave of his ignominious mother. This lack is compounded by his biological father's early death and his stepfather's disapproval and physical abuse of him.

Reinvented during the Korean War, Dick takes the name of his dead commanding officer and becomes Don, suggestive of Don Juan—the great seducer of cross-cultural legend. He first uses his new name in civilian life to answer the seductive query of a bombshell broad on a train, eager to comfort a handsome, returning soldier ("Nixon vs. Kennedy," 1.12). Thereafter, Don wields his "dick" as power in serial compensation for his phallic loss and chronic unhappiness. Even to his wife, his lovemaking has the aura of conquest—a ritual they literally stage when in Rome ("Souvenir," 3.8). Midge asks Don to "savage me and leave me for dead" ("5G," 1.5). Tied up to the bed frame, Bobbie Barrett craves "the full Don Draper treatment" ("Maidenform," 2.6). Sex for Don plainly tends toward violence. Wrapping up a conversation about business rather than sex, Don tells his junior colleagues, "You'll realize in your private life that at a certain point seduction is over and force is being requested" ("The Hobo Code," 1.8). Applied directly to sex, this is a potent line. Ostensibly empowering, sex for Don can be merely the fulfillment of a demand by others that he perform his masculinity, sometimes aggressively so. Even in business, he meets a version of this in the punishing expectations of Connie Hilton, clearly a father figure, whom he also disappoints.

The more insistent demand, however, is internal. Shattered by childhood neglect and abuse, his adult esteem structure calls on sex for repair. But with the underlying trauma left unaddressed, this psychic mechanism surely fails. His affairs, and their often joyless sex, are partly based on a repetition compulsion, giving an edge of despair to his suave maneuverings and bedroom prowess, and they culminate in the even tawdrier one-night stands depicted in season 4 and his impulsive proposal of marriage to his secretary Megan.[14]

It is Don, and not Betty, who most needs the therapist's couch, chiefly for treatment of what we would today diagnose as a "sex addiction." (Don is thus an ideal figure for the age of Tiger Woods, in whom the willingness to risk it all while "having it all" reached absurd proportions.)[15] Not by accident does Midge confess pleasure at being Don's "medicine" ("5G"). But such therapy is neither a clinical nor a cultural option for the men of his time. It is likewise incongruous with Don's lack of introspection and "strong, silent type" persona—the very persona, famously possessed by the film star Gary Cooper, to which the emotionally sloppy Tony Soprano vainly aspires. And no one quite wants a prudish Don, chastened by psychoanalysis. Emotionally isolated and bereft of a therapeutic language, Don must make his way alone.[16] *Mad Men* wisely transcends narrow considerations of psychology, freighting Don's journey instead with existential and even ethical significance. The quest for "wellness" is necessarily a quest for "meaning."

The elemental question of Don's journey is whether he is capable of genuine transformation. We have reason to doubt it, with big implications for how we see the show. Whenever he is cornered, Don's instinct is to scoop up the woman du jour and escape, which is something far different from change. When Pete outs his past as Dick Whitman, a distraught Don rushes to Rachel Menken with the plea that they run away and "start over, like Adam and Eve." She wisely asks what will become of his children and calls him a "coward," ending their affair ("Nixon vs. Kennedy").

The discovery of a subsequent affair with Bobbie Barrett in season 2 causes Betty's anger, which has simmered through years of suspicion, to boil over. She bounces Don from his house. A trip Don then takes to California brings the prospect of renewal. After a cathartic reunion with the wife of the original Don Draper, complete with his drawing a "resurrection" tarot card, Don drifts into the ocean waves. The scene initially appears to depict an image of existential man at infinity's edge — an organic complement to his artful free fall through skyscrapers in the opening credits. Yet it soon seems a baptism, coded by the "old time religion" track that wades in during the credits ("The Mountain King," 2.12).[17] He returns east with the promise of having been cleansed, reborn. Essentially confessing his indiscretions, he begs his way back into his home.

Yet Don's inaugural act of the following season is a one-night stand with a dippy stewardess ("Out of Town"). (The metaphor of the ocean tide as repetition wins out.) When his daughter finds the stewardess's airline pin, which Don accidentally brought home, he passes it off as a memento for her from his trip. Sleazy even by his low standards, this gesture exacerbates his daughter's episodes-long freak-out. She becomes pure symptom, unselfconsciously registering the corruption that has made her father and the Draper household toxic.[18] Further buds of possible regeneration are quickly cut down. Watching the springtime rite of a maypole dance at his daughter's school, Don mainly covets the nubile teacher, who leads the feeble recital like a wood nymph ("Love among the Ruins," 3.2). "Renewal" for Don is merely the sexual possession of youth. He later shrugs off an offer of grace. While in the maternity ward awaiting his third child, Don meets an anxious, first-time father-to-be. The man, as if seeking redemption for unnamed sins, pledges to Don, "This is a fresh start. . . . I'm gonna be better. I'm gonna be a better man!" ("The Fog," 3.5). Finding neither lesson nor inspiration for his own life, Don eventually beds the teacher.

When Betty at last discovers the lie of Don's identity, dissolving their marriage, it only tops off a long legacy of deceit, humiliation, and outright cruelty. Betty, perhaps, would have tolerated Don's failure to be truthful about his past had he only been faithful to her.[19] And with the home wrecked, the floating world—always conjoined to the domestic ideal as its constitutive outside—dissipates too. Don is left the ungainly bachelor we find at the beginning of season 4.

Through the show's arc, Don's greatest need is for moral redemption; the question "who is Don Draper?" remains grounded in the question of whether Don Draper—whoever he is—is a good man. He in fact has periodic flashes of concern with his moral state. The most powerful comes via a childhood memory of a charismatic wayfarer visiting his home during the Depression. Cheated out of pay by Don's stepfather, the man marks the house with the hobo code signifying that "a dishonest man lives here" ("The Hobo Code"). From the stranger, who had willfully abandoned the comforts of job and family for the "freedom" of itinerant poverty, the young Dick gets an early image of escape. But he also witnesses a damning judgment that will one day apply to his own home. Freedom hits its self-extinguishing limit in the illusory quality of his escape from repetition: for all his efforts to renounce his stepfather and overcome his origins as a "whore child," he too is a dishonest man. Intuiting this, he nonetheless lacks the insight, courage, and tools to do anything about it. Just before his "baptism," he insists, "People don't change" ("The Mountain King"). Indeed.

There is a sense, pegged perfectly to the times, in which the psychological imperative of self-awareness and the moral imperative of self-reckoning combine. This links the two sides of the Don Draper puzzle and again elevates the show above a mere character study. After the war, the great Protestant theologian Paul Tillich labored in his adoptive American home to make Christianity relevant for the "Age of Anxiety," in which concern for the self was displacing concern for the soul. So resonant was Tillich's blend of theology, existentialism, and depth psychology that *Time* put him on a cover in 1959 (fig. 13.1). Tillich sought to recast and update the meaning of core Christian concepts (while being, we would later learn from his wife, a hopeless cheat).[20] Among them was sin, which Tillich defined by its etymological root as separation or estrangement: separation from God but also, crucially, from self in both its glory and its torments.[21] The cover image itself is evocative of Tillich's provocative "theology." Tillich presents salvation as the acceptance—and not casting out—of all that is unholy in oneself. The portrait is in mottled pastel, appearing less an image of the man than a double of him, peering as if from, or into, a mirror. Behind Tillich's head shoots a cross in shadows, which also rises behind a small skeleton, or death's head,

FIGURE 13.1. Paul Tillich on the cover of *Time* (1959).

atop a shelf. Here we see represented not the dichotomous nature of "man" as "saint and sinner" but rather the struggle to come to terms with the death drive, which may take introjected pleasure to self-annihilating extremes. Literally doubled via his assumed identity, and ever fearful of having his tenuous rebirth shattered, Don can get right with the world only by confronting his estrangement from himself. The personal, at the very least, is the spiritual.

Mad Men takes on an impressive, if also bewildering, variety of identities. It is a male fantasy; a Don Juan tale; a possible redemption narrative; a sprawling history lesson; a feminist polemic; and a meditation on the masculine mystique billowing to a broader reflection on modern discontent. The analytic challenge is to see both this variety and how it may constellate into a legible pattern of meanings, situated in the proper galaxy of cultural reference points.

Such vision has proved elusive. History, fetishized by both the show and its audience, seems to have gotten in our eyes, yielding distorted views of *Mad Men* as being fundamentally about the past—about history and our relationship to it. This misrecognition holds whether the show is thought to covet past glamour or to condemn past recklessness. Retracing the hazy refractions of both views helps to highlight the statement I think the show makes and, ultimately, the failure it risks by not taking history seriously enough.

Katie Roiphe, extrapolating far too much from the racy milieu of her literary mother, reads *Mad Men* as a virtual documentary of the Way We Lived, and the Fun We Had, in which boardroom, barroom, and bedroom were scarcely distinguishable. For her, the show bids us to welcome "some vividness, some wild pleasure" and "just a little of the madness" into our own lives ("On 'Mad Men'"). While right about the seduction of appearances, such a view seems blind to the ruin that accompanies the "fun," as the show amply depicts, and both the cultural function and Faustian quality of the floating world. (Don, after all, is likened to Oscar Wilde's Dorian Gray in the premiere of season 4.) It projects, perhaps on the basis of a personal wistfulness for a lost youth, a collective longing for some golden, historical age of allegedly guiltless pleasure. In a society in which alcoholism, drug addiction (including to nicotine), infidelity, divorce, and depression still run rampant, why assume that the typical viewer of *Mad Men* is guilty only of tepid transgressions, and yearns for vicarious snatches of ill-health and chaos?

The opposite view of the show as an incitement to self-congratulation traffics in the same premise that *Mad Men* constructs our world and the Mad World as essentially different. On this basis, it dubiously asserts that both *Mad Men* and its audience presume that we have overcome the past and "found solutions" to each of its failures. But perhaps above all, *Mad Men* screams that we have not found a solution to the happiness problem (at least among an influential slice of American life), no matter the advent of the 1960s and their enlightening sensitivities. If we had, why would our culture continually stage the saga of upper-middle-class discontent, with *Mad*

Men itself emerging as the latest, captivating edition? The 1960s, put otherwise, did not make Lester Burnham or Tony Soprano or even Don Draper— whether in fact or in the imagination—impossible or obsolete.

Far from being an object of distant scorn or longing, the show may well offer a despairing portrait of postwar American life in a permanent twilight, with happiness eluding even those who embody a ubiquitous, social ideal. Don's personal resistance to change, by extension, mirrors that of the broader culture. Despite its very conscious construction as a brand and frequent celebration of the "art" of advertising, the show may ultimately force speculation that the very consumer culture its characters so skillfully guide is somehow responsible for the condition of misery it dissects.

It is, of course, too early to say what the show's final message will be, or whether it will even have one. The fate of Tony Soprano, as Don Draper's unlikely double, is instructive with respect to both *Mad Men*'s possible trajectory and its likely limitations. Even more so than Don, Tony is on a quest, in which he seeks a code or system of meaning by which to live. He looks to his family, Catholicism, his Mob family, his profession (such as it is), its pleasures, and even to psychotherapy. But his wife and children demand too much of him. He is far too sinful for religion. His Mob family will betray him in a heartbeat, proving the lie of the Mafia code. Power, money, and sex do not ultimately satisfy him. His therapist, finally, comes to suspect that he is a true sociopath, incorrigibly resistant to any cure.

The controversial final episode punctuates Tony's failure. Leaving us with the image of a jittery Soprano family having a public dinner, the *Sopranos* creator David Chase was excoriated for denying both narrative closure and satisfying drama. A massive constituency wished for Tony to be whacked. Yet Chase, by my reading, realized that the far greater, and more appropriate, punishment for Tony was to live on *essentially unchanged*, his family reattached to him like parasites to a host.

Those attachments begin to fill in the grim picture. Tony's high-achieving daughter, once on a do-gooder path, is now poised to become consigliere to the Soprano crime family. His layabout son had had a fit of conscience, growing troubled by such things as the "war on terror." That spell quickly passed, and he is handed a nightclub by his father. Tony's wife, Carmela, worried for her troubled marriage, at one point sought a therapist's counsel. The analyst, an elderly Jewish man, was more concerned with her troubled soul. He instructed her to rid herself of her murderous husband and every penny of his blood money. But Carmela, as Tony knows, is hardly satisfied with a Hyundai and a keepsake locket. Refusing her moment of grace, she sticks with Tony. The picture is complete with Tony left to stew in his depravity, unresolved Oedipal conflicts, and anger issues, forever fearful of being killed by friends and rivals alike. By this conclusion, the entire show appears an indictment of greed and small-mindedness, the hollowness and even constitutive corruption of the American Dream.

The stakes are much lower for Don and the Mad Men. A cheating heart is not a loaded gun, and even tobacco wealth is not quite what we think of as blood money (though one could make the case, as Don himself nearly does in season 4). Should the Mad Men remain substantially unchanged, a hell both gentler and more stylish awaits them; the corresponding "statement" made by the show would largely affirm that of Chase's masterpiece. But the Soprano parable is perhaps most valuable to the Mad Men as a lesson in how to avoid such a fate.

The suffering of the Soprano clan is rooted, at bottom, in the failure of the moral imagination and of empathetic engagement—in their obsessive self-focus, vanity, materialism, and ambition. The characters each face a potentially liberating call to conscience that would take them beyond themselves and their wants, but turn away. This myopia, I would argue, is the core affliction of Don and the others. As a group, they are painfully bereft of political curiosity, and scarcely have a conversation of genuine intellectual or moral substance (however much they philosophize at client pitches). Their reaction to the Kennedy assassination is wholly visceral, and the entire event mostly intensifies their personal sense of struggle. The narrowness extends to their private lives. Don cannot properly ask what it means to be a good man, and remains captive to his trauma. Betty, once circling the idea that her malaise has something to do with gender norms, appears ready simply to replace a fallen provider (Don) with a more upstanding one (Henry Francis). Pete is too self-involved and internally conflicted to muster any genuine sympathy for his infertile wife, with her imperiled dream of a family. And Peggy, for all her proto-feminist determination, can scarcely face the reality that she has had a baby. Indeed, the Mad World is almost entirely devoid of ethical conduct, defined by altruism and moral awareness. Instead, the characters mostly serve as accomplices to each other's deceptions.[22] Even if they grow likeable, they are never admirable.

The great irony and provocation is that the show occurs at the outset of the 1960s, an epoch defined by the massive incitement of the moral imagination. To great effect, individuals and groups sought to dismantle structures of oppression; newly saw their "unhappiness" as a consequence of power-laden norms; and sought "authenticity" and personal fulfillment through commitment to causes and destinies greater than themselves. The show is widely praised for its brilliance in depicting a world quivering at the threshold of this great change. But it may also be, I think, faulted for overplaying its characters' stubborn resistance to change already under way, and remaining trapped in the Mad World it creates.

Conventional wisdom holds that everything "un-1960s" about the show—especially the characters' attitudes toward gender and race—is an implicit argument in favor of the 1960s, as defined by its iconic struggles and storied transformations. This wisdom comes too quickly. Writing in the conservative *National Review*, Natasha Simons takes a refreshingly different stance. She divines a political divide in the show's audience, with liberals naturally welcoming the approach of the iconic 1960s and conservatives lamenting it.[23] But to her, the 1960s connote primarily the intensification of narrow self-seeking and hedonistic pleasure fully compatible with an increasingly gluttonous consumer culture. This view suggests that the indiscretions of the Mad World are an anticipation of further cultural degeneration, not something the 1960s will undo. Without condemning the decade so broadly, we can nonetheless imagine the compulsive adultery of Don Draper et al. morphing some years later into wife swapping and key parties, with whatever added damage to the children. A similar continuum could link the Mad Men's drinking and the worst of the drug culture. Rather than stumping for the 1960s, the show may cleverly sound a note of caution.

My concern is with what the show says about the 1960s through its more direct representations of the era's famous archetypes and signal causes. Though few seem to have noticed, *Mad Men*'s depiction of this "familiar" 1960s is ham-fisted and largely negative. Don mostly wins his verbal jousts with the insufferably earnest beatniks. In an entirely implausible scenario, Paul Kinsey, the office's faux-bohemian, goes south on something approximating a Freedom Ride mostly to impress his African American girlfriend. (Far from shallow and self-aggrandizing, the first actual Freedom Riders faced firebombs and near-lethal beatings.) Badly mangling the real history, the show matches its characters' insensitivity to the civil rights struggle with its own.[24] The young hitchhiker Don picks up is no principled draft resister but instead a thrill-seeking thug, who clubs and robs him ("Guy Walks into an Advertising Agency," 3.6).[25]

In her drug-induced "twilight sleep" just before giving birth, Betty has a vision of her deceased father as an orderly mopping blood ("The Fog"). In a questionable coupling, his image evokes that of Chief Broom—the gentle Native American giant crushed by the asylum and larger forces of the Combine in Ken Kesey's counterculture classic *One Flew Over the Cuckoo's Nest* (1962). In the same sequence, Betty's mother tends to a bloody Medgar Evers (recently killed in the chronology of the show) while explaining to Betty, "You see what happens to people who speak up? Be happy with what you have." Associating the stifling self-censorship of overbred WASPs in suburban comfort with the silencing of Evers by murder, *Mad Men* strikes a troubling note.

Finally, we see Don, while scheming to bed the sexy teacher, reacting indifferently to a radio report—replete with excerpts of Dr. King's oration—on the famous March on Washington a day earlier. Worse, he interprets her interest in the story as a sign that she is some otherworldly idealist—as if literate, northern whites like Don could by late 1963 have no clue about or rooting interest in the civil rights movement.[26]

Mad Men has been accused of being too favorable to the 1960s as a way of congratulating the present and the post-1960s generations. But the problem may be just the opposite: that, fearful of indulging 1960s sanctimony, the show makes its leading characters' detachment and cynicism its own. Far from being congratulated, younger viewers are given an oddly dispiriting history lesson.

Part of the innovation of *Mad Men* is that it portrays a milieu in the early part of the 1960s that departs from the familiar representations of rebellion commonly associated with the latter part of the decade. As the show moves forward in time, no one wants to see Pete Campbell become an antiwar leader, condemning the weapons industry for which he once shilled; or Joan Holloway as a women's libber, reconnected with the lesbian admirer who briefly appeared in the show's first season; or Don as a Werner Erhard–esque guru of self-actualization.[27] To remain a success, the show must remain true to its characters, whom the changing times may just as well pass by as sweep up.

But it would be nice, for our sake, if not theirs, if they would sometimes question their circumstances, assumptions, and habits. The ad executives could at least reflect on how even creative work, done in maverick fashion, can fuel the engines of war, the profits of disease merchants, and a pervasive discontent born partly of consumer striving. The office women might quell their compulsive advice about how to make it in a "man's world" long enough to realize that, aided by an incipient sisterhood, they can make the world too. And Don might revisit his core beliefs, such as that "love" is merely a mirage "invented by guys like [him] to sell nylons" ("Smoke Gets in Your Eyes"). The whole of the 1960s, understood a certain way, sought to disprove that jaded view. There remained the romantic love still enjoyed by its many true believers, but also the spiritual, world-changing kind proclaimed by Martin Luther King Jr. and sung by a whole generation. Above all, Don might come off the arch-conviction at the bottom of his nihilism that "people don't change." They of course do, along with whole cultures and societies.

But to change is harder than to stay the same. And change does not occur once, fixing everything for all time, but must constantly be renewed. The 1960s are important in this context less for their specific struggles and accomplishments than for their moral imagination and impulse for change, shared by young people especially. (Indeed, less than a year after *Mad Men*'s fourth season ended, the youth-driven Occupy Wall Street movement erupted; its idealism may appear a rebuke of the cynical ethos of the show, exposing how out of joint it is with at least the longings of the present.) Ingeniously set in a world of change, *Mad Men* might also do well to educate us with examples, useful for addressing our own times in both their regressions and their unique failures, of that impulse.

Failing such inspiration, whatever its source, we risk shrinking from the challenges of our time and staying the same, such that Don Draper, after all, is us.

NOTES

1. Many of these are skillfully articulated in Goodlad, "Why We Love." The focus on "casual vice" comes from Roiphe, "On 'Mad Men.'" Perhaps the most inventive of the many historical appreciations is *The Footnotes of Mad Men*, first presented by Natasha Vargas-Cooper in a blog on *The Awl* (http://www.theawl.com/tag /footnotes-of-mad-men). Vargas-Cooper does an impressive work-up of each episode, unpacking the historical references and contexts while inviting her readers to embellish and extend her own insights — as well as check the show's "accuracy." In so doing, she re-expands a context that the show compresses, introducing a new network of associations and paratexts. The blog served as the inspiration for her book *Mad Men Unbuttoned*, which reprises to some extent Jesse McLean's prior effort in *Kings of Madison Avenue*. As the introduction to the present volume also notes, the *New York Times* has printed several stories highlighting *Mad Men*'s engagement of history and illuminating its backstories (e.g., Egner; Maynard; *New York Times*, "Mad Men City"). The high praise this historical drama has received for these references is itself conspicuous, likely reflecting poor historical literacy and consciousness in contemporary America.

2. For the *National Review*'s conservative take on the show, see Simons.

3. Femina's testimony, dripping with braggadocio and possibly embellishment, is recorded in Dean; Roiphe, "Real Mad Man"; *USA Today*. An ad man confirms the extent of the smoking, but denies that of the drinking (in his firm at least), in *New York Times*, "Plenty of Smoke."

4. Originally appearing in the *New York Times*, the quote is repeated in Simons.

5. Testifying to its influence, one columnist called Schwarz's essay "the best piece yet written on *Mad Men*" (Schiffren).

6. Greif at least acknowledges that the show mixes "Now We Know Better" with dollops of "Doesn't That Look Good." But this, for him, dooms it to a mixed message and bad faith. I would argue that the very tension between official censure and illicit desire propels many of the show's richer meanings, which little concern a supposed hierarchy of eras and go way beyond vicarious thrills.

7. As an added twist, the closing credits reveal that Henry Hill, in real life, was convicted of narcotics distribution while in the witness protection program.

8. Don's estranged brother asks the question in "5G" (1.5), and it also opens season 4.

9. For this *Mad Men* focus, I cannot help but feel grateful on behalf of my late mother. Like so many women of her time, she was limited by convention. Equipped with a titanic intelligence and, by 1960, an Ivy League postgraduate degree, she first worked to support her husband and then shelved any effort at a career for two decades to tend to family and home. She later became a political activist and part of local government.

10. I am careful to stress here the class quality of this genre. There are, of course, other narratives, many less bleak, of American family life. One popular for decades on TV chronicles the lower-middle-/upper-working-class family drawing on pluck, love, and a basic optimism to get by: for example, *The Honeymooners*, *All in the Family*, *Roseanne*, *Married with Children*, *The King of Queens*, and even *The Simpsons*. Such shows suggest that the relative absence of wealth, ubiquitously coveted in our society, increases the chance of genuine happiness. Other programs, such as *Six Feet Under*, depict families outside of heteronormative boundaries or, like *Friends*, recast the family so as to include coworkers and friends.

11. On representations of the "ritual gone wrong" and their carnivalesque qualities, see LaCapra, *Madame Bovary*, 203–5.

12. In this subtle scene Don's suicidal thoughts are telegraphed through his anguished expression as the train approaches and then passes. The prior episode sets up the moment: when Paul Kinsey explains his tardiness with "Act of God, sorry, someone threw themselves in front of a train," Don responds, "Ah, suicide" ("Ladies Room," 1.2).

13. Rather unfairly, Greif reads the show as little more than an assemblage of stock characters, such as the "Old Mentor," "Stifled Wife," "Assertive Woman," and "Bohemian Artist." Alessandra Stanley, by contrast, argues that the characters possess an "elusive weirdness" that saves them from this fate.

14. This broadly Freudian work-up of Don draws on LaCapra's understanding of trauma, presented, among other places, in *Writing History, Writing Trauma* and *History and Memory after Auschwitz*. Key to trauma theory is the idea that mourning entails a working through of loss through which loss is acknowledged and incorporated into one's subjectivity. In a revealing line, Don tells Betty, who still thinks about her late mother, that "mourning is just extended self-pity" ("Babylon," 1.6). This macho attitude reinforces the sense that Don has never confronted his psychic pain and its source, and is thus trapped in a condition akin to melancholy, defined by the repetition compulsion.

15. The revelations of Woods's womanizing came in 2009, long after *Mad Men*'s debut. Dwarfing Don in fame and fortune, Woods nonetheless shares with Don the squandered treasure of the beautiful, Nordic wife and two children.

16. Don's season 4 relationship with Faye Miller opens the possibility for a more self-knowing Don; but true to the character's fundamental isolation, he does not make it last.

17. The song begins, "I say Christian pilgrim / soul redeemed from sin / called out of darkness / a new life to begin."

18. Sally's conspicuous upset at the death of her grandfather likely reflects her displaced awareness that her own father is already lost to the family—if he was ever quite there.

19. This speculation about Betty has, I think, ample support. At one point she says outright to her therapist, "I can't help but think that I'd be happy if my husband was faithful to me" ("The Wheel," 1.13). With the passionate lines "I want you so badly," she confesses in an earlier episode an intense craving for Don ("Babylon"). That craving, I would argue, is sexual but also seeks a more total possession of him. I think she appreciates, moreover, his specialness, and even considers his mysteriousness—to a point—part of his allure. When he comes fully clean with her, she does seem to disdain his lowly social origin. But here I think she reverts to the biases of her elevated class partly as a defense mechanism against her feelings of hurt.

20. Hannah Tillich recounts Paul's infidelities and her eventual peace with them in *From Time to Time*.

21. Tillich develops the idea in many places, among them, "You Are Accepted" and *Systematic Theology*, 44–47.

22. Don does help Peggy while she is in a sanatorium after giving birth, essentially telling her to forget the entire episode. But with this advice, which aids her in moving on, he instructs her in the powers of a denial that has caused him great damage. And pledging to support his mistress's troubled brother, he mostly seeks to make up for his abandonment of his own brother. Such acts of virtue, in sum, are either compromised or self-serving.

23. While plausibly defining an ideal-typical liberal and conservative *position*, Simons in no sense demonstrates an actual split in audience reaction.

24. Schwarz points out that the show seems to confuse the Freedom Rides of 1961,

which sought enforcement of the integration of interstate business, with the voter registration work in Mississippi of some years later. Given the show's fanatical attention to detail, this blurring is inexcusable.

25. It is, moreover, extremely unlikely that such a man in the summer of 1963 — long before large-scale troop deployments to Vietnam and even before the conflict had attracted much media attention — would have had the foresight to avoid the draft so as not to go to Vietnam. I thank Michael S. Foley, an expert on the Vietnam-era draft, for pointing out this problem in the depiction of the character.

26. Interestingly, the most positive embodiment of the 1960s on the show is the young guitar-playing priest, who represents a twist on a traditional source of morality. Seemingly set to hit on Peggy, his true concern is for her conscience and her child. Without judgment, he encourages Peggy to address that part of her life and her own self-estrangement.

27. Werner Erhard was the founder of EST, a form of group therapy popular in the early 1970s. Born John Rosenberg, he reinvented himself as Erhard after the demise of his first marriage in the early 1960s.

THE HOMOSEXUAL
AND THE SINGLE GIRL

ALEXANDER DOTY

The title of this essay is taken from two essential popular texts of the 1960s: the CBS *Reports* documentary "The Homosexuals" (1967), and Helen Gurley Brown's best-selling self-help book *Sex and the Single Girl* (1962), which became a lifestyle bible for millions of white, middle-class, white-collar working women.[1] These two texts are crucial Zeitgeist artifacts, offering more-complex-than-you-might-expect overviews of the changing psychic and social landscape for homosexuals and "career girls" in the United States in the 1960s. Already famous for its creators' and writers' omnivorous use of all things 1960s, *Mad Men* simultaneously borrows from and critiques the representation of the homosexual and the single career woman in these iconic texts, while also juxtaposing these figures in evocative and provocative ways.[2] The series' carefully calibrated palimpsest of the 2000s and 2010s over the 1960s allows it to be accurate and engaging in presenting the temper (and look) of the earlier period with regard to homosexuals and career girls, while also offering a complex contemporary (re)vision of these figures.

"The Homosexuals" is framed by interviews with men who represent "the happy homosexual" and "the closeted married man." The first is a fully visible, good-looking, young blond identified as Lars Larson, who tells reporter Mike Wallace that while he initially felt that homosexuality was "furtive" and "ugly," an encounter with a serviceman in New Orleans "was just a grand, grand experience. It was the first moment in my life where I was open, where I didn't have to hide. . . . I had all the freedom in the world to be Lars Larson." Earlier in the interview, Larson says that he had the choice to "be a nice little robot and go through the motions of life for some sixty, seventy, eighty years. . . . But it wouldn't be right, not for me. And I couldn't sit back and take that." At the end of the documentary, however, we are shown someone who has decided to "sit back and take that," in the person of a homosexual man, shown in silhouette, who has a wife and two children, and who suggests that he married a woman because "the gay crowd is so narcissistic that they can't establish a love relationship with another male."

Considering what the documentary has to say about mainstream U.S. attitudes about homosexuals in the 1960s, the life choice of this shadowed homosexual husband and father is understandable — if not his comments on gay narcissism. Directly after the opening interview with Larson, Wallace explains that Larson is a member of "the most despised minority in America," and that a CBS poll found that "Americans consider homosexuality more harmful to society than adultery, abortion, or prostitution. . . . Two out of three Americans look upon homosexuals with 'disgust, discomfort, or fear.' One in ten says 'hatred.' A vast majority believes that homosexuality is an illness; only ten percent say it is a crime." Yet, paradoxically, the CBS poll found that "the majority of Americans favor legal punishment" even for private homosexual acts between consenting adults.

This is the cultural history against which *Mad Men*'s Sal Romano and Kurt — or, the closeted, married homosexual and the happy homosexual of "The Homosexuals" — are situated. Sal and Kurt come to represent the alpha and the omega of 1960s homosexuality for the series' first four seasons, just as the opening and closing interviewees might have for viewers watching "The Homosexuals" in the 60s. Importantly, however, *Mad Men* reverses the trajectory of "The Homosexuals" from the cautiously out (Larson) to the closeted (final married interviewee) by introducing Kurt into the series after Sal. Like Larson, Kurt is a young, blond, "out" homosexual. And while Lars does not have an accent like Kurt's, his name conjures a European openness toward sexuality — think *La dolce vita* (1960), Swedish films such as *Through a Glass Darkly* (1962) and *Loving Couples* (1964), and films of the French New Wave.

In "The Jet Set" (2.11), Kurt invites Peggy Olson to a Bob Dylan concert while several coworkers look on. When Harry Crane remarks, "Peggy and Kurt in the Village, oh my!" he little realizes that conjuring Greenwich Village and *The Wizard of Oz* in a single sentence will result in Kurt's casually announcing that he is "a homosexual" to make it clear that Peggy is not his "date." Ken Cosgrove nervously assumes — perhaps hopes? — that Kurt, being foreign, does not understand what he is saying. While Kurt's friend Smitty tries to stop him from saying more, Kurt insists that he "make[s] love with" men. Once Kurt leaves, Smitty explains by telling everyone that Kurt is "from Europe, it's different there." Ken, still a bit rattled, offers a line that could have come from that CBS poll: "I knew queers existed, I just don't want to work with them." Smitty snaps, "What, he's the first homo you've met in advertising?" This is all it takes for Ken and the rest of the young executives left behind to practice a little McCarthy-era guilt by association. "You think Smitty's in love?" Ken asks. "Which bathroom does he use?" Harry jokes, resorting to the gender inversion model of homosexuality still prevalent in the 1960s that understood feminine men and masculine women as queer.

Tellingly, off to the side or offscreen for most of Kurt's coming out scene is *Mad Men*'s other recurring homosexual character, the closeted Sal, who, unsurprisingly, looks upset but has nothing to say, even about his choice of donuts from the variety on offer in the break room. The series thus far seems to construct its closeted homosexual character largely through the deployment of some of the tropes that 1960s mainstream America associated with homosexuals: Sal is connected to foreignness (he is Italian American), sartorial stylishness that is generally a touch or two more "colorful" than a straightforward Brooks Brothers look, and closeness to his mother (in one scene the office telephone operators talk about how devoted Sal is to his mother). In the first episode ("Smoke Gets in Your Eyes," 1.1) Sal uses his being Italian as an excuse for not having a girlfriend — which, of course, might be understood as indicating a hyperheterosexual libido, but, with our knowledge of Sal, can also be understood as indicating his homosexuality through the sign of foreignness. To complicate the representation of sexuality in another way, the series also makes Don Draper and Roger Sterling stylishly "metrosexual" *avant la lettre*. By contrast, the young, out Kurt evidently does not have to try as hard as Sal, Don, or Roger, and favors a more casual style of dress. Finally, then, the series suggests that both middle-aged heterosexual and middle-aged closeted homosexual men are slaves to appearance in ways that the up-and-coming (gay and straight) youth culture of the 1960s, which Kurt seems to anticipate, will not be.

Cleverly, if potentially problematically, the series also associates Sal with Bruno Antony (Robert Walker), the psychopathic queer killer in Alfred Hitchcock's *Strangers on a Train* (1951), a film that some critics have condemned as homophobic and others have praised as a critique of phallic masculinity. Like Bruno, Sal has a snappy wardrobe and is very close to his mother. Like Bruno, Sal has a crush on another man who is straight—or ostensibly so in the Hitchcock film. And like Bruno, Sal admires his crush's talent: in *Mad Men* for writing fiction; in the Hitchcock film for playing tennis. Sal and his crush, Ken Cosgrove, bond over literature and Ken's ability to explain a Rothko painting. The show suggests that, with his artistic skills and interests—which we later find out extend to opera—Ken may be a latent queer guy, and that Sal has some reason to hope. To the degree that we feel for Sal's circumstances, we are asked to hopefully take on the 1960s cultural cliché of an interest in art and literature as the sign of a queer man, only to have this hope dashed during an at-home dinner to which Sal invites Ken ("The Gold Violin," 2.7).

During dinner, the now married Sal tells his wife, Kitty, about Ken's short story, "The Gold Violin." In a moment of painful irony, Sal tells Kitty that the gold violin "was perfect in every way, except it couldn't make music." Now while it is clear that Sal would like to "make beautiful music" with Ken, the melodramatic construction of Sal's narrative segments in *Mad Men* are invested in keeping him a secondary, silent, and tormented figure of pathos, by and large. In terms of melodrama, irony, pathos, and victimhood, it is no accident that the object of Sal's affections is the person who, four episodes after the dinner party, displays the most homophobic response to Kurt's coming out, and who fails to notice a silent, chastened, anxious Sal standing nearby. There is further melodramatic irony in the fact that young, thin, blond Ken is the straight double of young, thin, blond, but openly homosexual Kurt.

The coda to the dinner-party scene takes us back to *Strangers on a Train*. After dinner, Ken leaves his lighter behind. Just as crazy queer Bruno takes the lighter Guy (Farley Granger) leaves behind after their meal together, so Sal keeps Ken's lighter as a fetishistic token marking a potentially obsessive desire—after all, Bruno tries to use the lighter to frame Guy for murder when Guy won't do his bidding. Viewers of the Hitchcock film may find that the final shot of Sal in the bedroom, in the eerie glow of a television set, lighting his cigarette with Ken's lighter, while, in the background, his clueless wife does needlepoint sitting in bed, makes them wonder whether Sal could be thinking dark thoughts, and if he might be capable of dark deeds in order to express thwarted homosexual desires. After all, Bruno seems like a charming, affable guy at first too.

Another fascinating aspect of Sal's character development is his relationship with his "straight-but-not-narrow" boss Don. *Mad Men*'s first episode, "Smoke Gets in Your Eyes," establishes a subtle connection between the two men through Don's involvement with Midge, a free-spirited, independent female artist who lives in countercultural Greenwich Village—*the queer space* in New York City in the 1950s and 1960s. After establishing Don's sexual liaison with the artist, the episode has art director Sal enter Don's office to find him exercising with a chest-building isometric device. "Look at you, Gidget, trying to fit into that bikini!" Sal campily quips to Don. Because Don takes in this outrageous quip with such equanimity, one might wonder whether he is not deploying some very dry version of camp humor as a retort to the Gidget remark when he looks over Sal's Lucky Strike ad, which features a handsome, muscular man in a swimsuit, and says that the image would probably be "better off with some sex appeal"—so could Sal put a woman in a bathing suit next to the man? Sal is more than happy to comply as it provides him with the opportunity to act the part of "one of the boys" with Don. But whether or not we understand Don as being aware of making a joke, the narrative is constructed to have his comment about a "girl" in a swimsuit campily play off of Sal's opening remark in order to position Don-as-Gidget next to the muscular man on the beach. This is but one example of how *Mad Men* develops Sal's relationship with Don in ways that, layering the present over the 1960s, slyly challenge and complicate gender and sexuality binaries.

Why would Sal feel comfortable enough to direct an over-the-top camp comment at his boss, who not only lets it pass, but perhaps, consciously or subconsciously, takes up the banter? Considered within a broad psychosocial context, it makes sense that someone like Don who is desperate to hide his own outsider identity (the illegitimate son of a prostitute, raised as "poor, white trash," an army deserter and identity thief) would connect at some unspoken level with the closeted Italian American Sal and might feel a little less guarded around him. On its most manifest narrative level, *Mad Men* has Don and Sal making suggestive comments about women to each other, but the series also appears to be intent on building up a suggestive queerness under and around their relationship—a queerness that is implicitly supported for certain viewers by things we find out about Don, such as his Greenwich Village artist mistress, his love of European art films, and his move into a Greenwich Village apartment of his own at the end of season 3.

The next and—considering the permanent departure of Sal from the cast by the end of season 3—perhaps the final time the series allows for this kind of playful free and easy interaction between the two men occurs during their joint business trip to Baltimore ("Out of Town," 3.1). The queer suggestiveness begins on the plane when Don points out a magazine ad to Sal. Set

FIGURE 14.1. Fleischmann's "big bottle" ("Out of Town," 3.1).

in the French Quarter of New Orleans, the illustration has a business man carrying an outsized bottle of Fleischmann's whiskey while a smiling, well-dressed young woman looks on (fig. 14.1). "Can you believe this?" Don asks Sal; "What's this world coming to?" "That *is* a big bottle," Sal replies. "That's not a bottle, that's his date," Don remarks. Perhaps inspired by the French Quarter ad setting, as well as the pre–take off drinks in which they are indulging, Sal and Don improvise a dialogue. As the ad fills the frame, Sal speaks for the woman: "My, oh my, what a big bottle you have!" Don continues as the man (also in voiceover): "I'm sorry honey, but I'm taken. I just pawned my typewriter so we could be together for the weekend."

What is being suggested here is complex, but finally points to queer possibilities for and in Don whom, as we know, is struggling to remain faithful to his pregnant wife, Betty, after an affair in season 2 nearly ended their marriage. Don is willing to play along with Sal's campy, cross-sex opening, but in turning down Sal-as-the-woman's come-on, Don would appear to be saying "no" to queerness by reasserting his straight masculinity. When Shelly, a flight attendant, mistakes him for William Hofstadt—Don's brother-in-law who has left his name tag on the suitcase—Don goes along with it and pulls Sal into what turns out to be an ongoing game of fluid identities in this episode. Don introduces Sal as "my associate, Mr. Fleischmann"—the brand of whiskey in the magazine ad. In a classic illustration of the functioning of the unconscious, Don "just happens" to name Sal after the "date" (the big bottle of Fleischmann's whiskey) for which Don's ad double has rejected the woman (or Sal-as-the-woman). Here Don Draper/Dick Whitman (or his unconscious mind)/his ad double/William Hofstadt fends off a date with a woman (or a man-playing-a-woman) for another man (Sal/the big bottle/ Mr. Fleischmann). He almost does this again with Shelly when she proposes they all meet for dinner with a friend of hers, but she is insistent while Don is strangely passive.

Adding to the queer suggestiveness in the scene on the plane is Don's final line for the man in the ad—"I just pawned my typewriter so we could be together for the weekend"—which is a reference to the novel *The Lost Weekend* (1944) by Charles Jackson, and the film based on it (1945), whose alcoholic protagonist shares a first name with Don, and whose "problem" in the original novel is repressed homosexuality. On some level, this episode entertains the possibility that this "out-of-town" business trip might end with Don ditching the woman he usually finds to sleep with for the "big bottle" of Fleischmann's sitting next to him on the plane.

If so, the manifest narrative challenges, if not fully represses, this latent queer possibility by introducing Shelly, who insists that Don and Sal go to dinner with her and her coworker. Don does not seem particularly interested in this available, attractive woman—perhaps because she is coming on so strong. At dinner, he seems far less intent on seducing Shelly (indeed, she will later have to put the moves on him as the woman in the ad does) than in having Sal go along with his story that the two of them are accountants, possibly working for the government on the Jimmy Hoffa case. Interestingly, the dinner sequence is initially constructed largely from two-shots of Don and Sal in business suits alternating with two-shots of the flight attendants still in their uniforms, reinforcing same-sex pairing (figs. 14.2–14.3). It is only with the unexpected appearance, in a medium long shot, of a pilot (also still in uniform but wearing a lobster bib) sitting across from Sal that the shots become more varied, including classic "sexual difference" shot–reverse shot close-ups of Don and Shelly (fig. 14.4).

But if, in one way, the pilot's appearance disrupts certain queer undercurrents at the table, it also activates others. After all, we know that while Don may eventually be coupled with one of the flight attendants, Sal will not be. A man in uniform across the table has been abruptly introduced into the mise-en-scène as a possible match for Sal. Could this be another time, as with Shelly's emphatic appearance, when the text suddenly introduces an additional figure to diffuse the possibility of a Don-Sal pairing? As it turns out, this episode will provide Sal with a man, just not the pilot (or Don, for that matter). However, it is interesting to discover that while the

FIGURES 14.2–14.4. A series of shots of same-sex pairs is interrupted by a medium long shot ("Out of Town," 3.1).

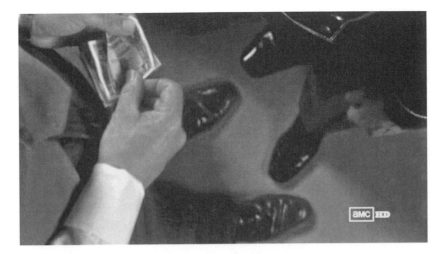

FIGURE 14.5. The money shot ("Out of Town," 3.1).

writers originally planned for Sal and the pilot to have a one-nighter to parallel Don and Shelly's, they finally decided to pair him with another man in a
uniform: the bellboy who comes to check on Sal's air conditioner.[3] Although
he is not given a name, his looks, and the name of the actor who plays him,
Orestes Arcuni, suggest the bellboy is Latino. This bellboy initiates sex with
Sal, established by a shot from Sal's point of view as he takes out his money
clip. While Sal is ostensibly going through his bills to find a tip for the bellboy, the appearance of the bellboy's shoes in this shot also suggests a sex-for-
pay arrangement (fig. 14.5). The move by the series' writers from a tall, fair,
WASP pilot to a short, dark, bellboy-cum-hustler for Sal's first homosexual
experience deploys certain white, middle- and upper-class cultural tropes
that eroticize race, ethnicity, and the working class. While Don is upstairs
with a tall, blonde, WASPy flight attendant, Sal is downstairs with a Latino
bellboy/hustler.

Both Don's and Sal's liaisons end in coitus interruptus, which frustrates
audiences who have been waiting for a very long time to see Sal act on his
sexual desires. But the fire alarm that melodramatically conspires to thwart
Don's liaison with Shelly and Sal's with the bellboy also functions to bring
Don face-to-face with Sal's homosexuality—and, perhaps, with his own
latent queer desires. Granting its problematic dominant cultural erotic politics, the scene between Sal and the bellboy is constructed to encourage
viewer empathy for Sal, and, even more, to encourage viewers to be as excited as Sal is by the bellboy's actions—there is even a (risky for basic cable)

FIGURE 14.6. Sal and the bellboy as Don looks on ("Out of Town," 3.1).

shot of the bellboy's hand going down Sal's boxers. Once that fire alarm goes off, however, the sequence quickly shifts to record Don's progress out of his room and down the fire escape. As he stops by Sal's window to watch him put on his clothes, we are momentarily placed in the classic male erotic voyeur position, except here it is a man watching another man. Don raps on the window, which triggers a shot of an anxious Sal, followed by his view of Don on the fire escape. "Come on!" Don yells at Sal. A shot over Don's shoulder reveals the bellboy in his T-shirt entering the room and coming over to Sal (fig. 14.6). In an episode that repeatedly foregrounds Don's gaze, a final medium close-up shows Don staring into the window at Sal and the bellboy, looking less appalled than dumbfounded and pained, at which point a female leg enters the frame to remind Don of his own "illicit" liaison (fig. 14.7).

Once on the street in front of the hotel, we return to Don's point of view as Sal and the bellboy emerge from the crowd. Sal looks at Don and briefly casts his eyes downward as the bellboy leaves the frame. In Sal's point-of-view reverse shot of Don, the flight attendant has also left the frame. For a moment Don and Sal are (re)constructed as a couple, and we are given a shot of Don's blurred profile as he looks over at Sal, who is looking up (and who is in the center-frame "power" position). When the flight attendant (and heterosexuality) pops back into the frame, Sal's image is thrown out of focus, but we notice Don is now following Sal's upward gaze with the same grave and enigmatic look that he had earlier at the window. Of course, one way to read what has happened here is that Don is unpleasantly surprised

FIGURE 14.7. Don's reaction ("Out of Town," 3.1).

at the sight of Sal with the bellboy because he wonders what Sal's homosexuality might mean in terms of their maintaining a comfortable working relationship. But considered within the queerness rippling through this episode—beginning with the double-entendre play with the ad (or perhaps even earlier in the episode with Don's imagining his illegitimate birth)—this sequence also suggests that the flight attendant may have been a narrative diversion from the expression of Don's (and the series') more inchoate, unconscious queer desires. In this context, Don's enigmatic looks just might contain some measure of a confused and troubling awareness of his interest in things queer (even if we understand this interest as being limited to playacting and looking). On the street in front of the hotel, Don follows Sal's gaze back up to the scene of homosexual or queer possibility where he stood transfixed at the sight of Sal with the bellboy.

This possibility is suggested by events later in the episode. On the plane back to New York, instead of the stern lecture Sal expects, Don pitches a London Fog ad that features a woman wearing nothing but a London Fog raincoat flashing a man on the subway. Clearly meant to be a friendly warning to Sal, Don suggests "Limit your exposure" as the ad's tagline. If the tagline is cautioning Sal about his sexual expression, however, the sight of Sal with the bellboy has inspired Don to create a new, more boldly (hetero) sexual, campaign for London Fog. Back in the office, Sal shows his sketch for the ad to Paul Kinsey and Harry Crane. Wondering who to cast as the man in the ad, Kinsey asks Sal, "What does he look like?" "I don't know . . .

a little excited, a little shocked," Sal suggests, perhaps thinking of Don's face as he looked in from the fire escape and his own face when he caught sight of Don. "No," Kinsey retorts, "What's he *look* like?" Snapping out of his reverie, Sal is also probably thinking about Don on that fire escape when he says, "Oh, oh—handsome." Tellingly, if somewhat stereotypically, Sal is cast as the flashing woman and Don as the man on the subway who is both "excited" and "shocked" at what he is seeing. But in doing this, the episode also provocatively, and homosexually, recasts the scene in which Don insists that Shelly undress first while he looks at her.

With this ad campaign, Sal is once again the "picture" to Don's "words" (something the owner of London Fog says makes them a great team), and Don (protectively? possessively?) wants Sal to "limit his exposure" to one man—to Don as the man on the subway. It is fitting that Don comes up with this tagline/advice since he has been trying to limit his own exposure during the series by taking on an elaborate "imitation of life" as Don Draper to hide his identity as Dick Whitman. Ironically, Don's next plum assignment for Sal actually encourages Sal to "come out" a bit more ("The Arrangements," 3.4). Don asks Sal to take over as the director of a Patio (read: Pepsi) diet cola commercial based on the opening of the musical film *Bye Bye Birdie* (1963)—in spite of Peggy's assertion that the Ann-Margret/*Bye Bye Birdie* concept won't appeal to young women. Perhaps she realizes that this concept is calculated to appeal only to men, whether they are straight (the sexy Ann-Margret look-alike) or homosexual (the musical and camp elements). In his enthusiasm to show his wife what the TV ad will look like, Sal forgets Don's advice and, far from limiting his "exposure," plays the Ann-Margret part for all it's worth as he performs for his increasingly confused and uncomfortable wife. While the clients admit the commercial was a "meticulous" recreation of the number in the film, they don't like it: "There's something not right about it. I can't put my finger on it . . . but it's just not right." After the clients leave, Kinsey agrees with them: "It looks right, it sounds right, it smells right, but it's not right." While Sal's wife, the straight-laced clients, and the junior executive Kinsey do not appreciate the commercial, a more queerly positioned Don certainly does, and tells Sal, "You're a commercial director," which is "the only good thing to come of all this."

But Don's protectiveness toward his new protégé—another sign of the implicit queer charge between them—is short-lived. Their final major scene together happens some time after Sal has fended off the advances of a Lucky Strike executive in the editing room where they are working on a commercial ("Wee Small Hours," 3.9). When the executive asks that Sal be fired as the director, Sal tries to explain to Don that the client was drunk and cornered him, but that he resisted. Sarcastically and incredulously, Don asks Sal, "But nothing happened, because nothing could happen, because you're married?" Perhaps recalling that confusing and painful moment on the hotel fire escape, Don spits out, "Who do you think you're talking to?" "I guess I was just supposed to do whatever he wanted? What if it was some girl?" Sal asks Don. "That would depend upon what kind of girl it was and what I knew about her," Don says. A stern look crosses his face as he mutters, "You people . . ." shortly before firing Sal. In a poignant moment, we see Sal packing up his office, placing on top of the pile that Lucky Strike ad he and Don worked on during the series' first episode. In a striking move, this episode ends not with a clear-cut image of Sal as a melodramatic victim, but with a shot of him in a public phone booth calling his wife, telling her not to wait up for him. As he makes the call, we see that he is in a public park cruising area replete with leathermen. But the scene fades out before we see what happens next. So we are left with a more homosexually proactive Sal, but within a mise-en-scène and narrative context that might be connected with promiscuity and self-destructiveness for certain viewers.

One of Don's final lines to Sal also suggests how, when push comes to shove, homosexual men and single women can be lumped together under the sign of a despised sexuality that should, however, be at the disposal of patriarchal capitalism and the powerful men within it. Revealing that he might consider asking one of the women who work at the agency to sleep with a client, Don quickly moves from calling these sexual women "it" to conflating sexually active single women with homosexual men (which has a long tradition in Western culture): "That would depend upon what kind of girl it was, and what I knew about her. You people." This is placing homosexual men in the women's room in another form. Don might have been willing and able to stand by his man (or to stand by one of the women in the office) in the face of a client like Patio, but, as he tells Sal, Sterling Cooper can't afford to lose the Lucky Strike account. In firing Sal, Don—and possibly the series as a whole—has finally made (or has been culturally "forced" to make) the choice, painful as it may be, to put aside queer possibilities, queer playfulness, and queer desire in the service of patriarchal capitalism.

By the end of season 3, Don has become more attached to his other protégé, Peggy Olson, who shares with Sal a need to keep her sexual desires a secret, as well as a complicated mentor relationship with fellow secret-keeper Don. Torn between being a good Catholic girl and a modern career woman, Peggy seeks out and enjoys sex, but not without some residual

Catholic guilt. Initially, Joan is set up as the show's *Sex and the Single Girl* model for Peggy, dispensing advice like "Don't overdo the perfume," "Know where the booze is for the boss," "Men don't really want a secretary, most of the time they want something between a mother and a waitress—and the other times, well . . ." In the first episode she also advises Peggy, "Go home, take a paper bag and cut some eye holes out of it. Put it over your head, get undressed, and look at yourself in the mirror. Really evaluate where your strengths and weaknesses are. And be honest." While what she says to Peggy is all very much in line with what Helen Gurley Brown advocates for young career women, Joan, unlike Brown, does not encourage her girls to aspire much beyond the secretarial pool and marriage, telling Peggy that if she makes the right moves she'll be in the city like the rest of them, or, even better, "married and in the country." On the other hand, *Sex and the Single Girl* states quite emphatically at the end of its first chapter that it "is not a study of how to get married but how to stay single—in superlative style" (11). The tips about meeting and forming relationships with men in Brown's book are largely concerned with satisfying a single girl's libido and advancing her career.

Indeed, Brown's story could be the model for Peggy's narrative arc in *Mad Men*. Brown admits that she was not pretty but developed a style that got her noticed, while also presenting herself as eager to take on extra work and new challenges. At one point Brown was a secretary to an advertising agency head, who "was responsible for [her] getting a chance to write advertising copy" (16). But while Don offers the ambitious Peggy the chance to write ad copy, her professional relationship with Sal helps to establish her as a successful advertising "man." During the first three seasons, Sal and Peggy—the homosexual and the single career girl—become a very successful "go-to" pair for those ad campaigns featuring feminine products: lipstick, bras, and vibrating weight-loss devices. As a team, Peggy and Sal are able to move out of this gender ghetto only when they are forced to present a campaign for Samsonite after the executive in charge, Freddy Rumsen, becomes incapacitated at the last minute ("Six Month Leave," 2.9). With a "show must go on" attitude, understudies Peggy and Sal take over and do an excellent job—or so we are told, since we do not see their presentation. In not showing us this presentation, the narrative deemphasizes Sal's contribution to Peggy's rise, while also throwing more weight onto scenes before and after the presentation that emphasize Freddy's importance to Peggy as a professional mentor—a role that Don also plays. All this recognizes what Helen Gurley Brown knew: ambitious single girls need to cultivate (straight) male mentors if they want to climb up the career ladder. But *Mad Men* takes things a step further, and darker, by suggesting that career girls might also gain professionally from the decline and fall of their male mentors. Although Peggy feels conflicted about this situation, she does finally take Freddy's office.

Once *Mad Men* has used closeted Sal to assist the talented and intelligent Peggy in establishing herself professionally, the series begins to associate her with a homosexual who can help her on the personal front, and fulfill *Sex and the Single Girl*'s exhortation that all single career girls develop an eye-catching, feminine style that is at once sexy and ladylike. Enter the chic, modern, and, let us not forget, European Kurt. While Sal is stylish in his own way, it is too much of the suit, ascot, and vest school to be of much help to Peggy—and his being closeted would prevent him from offering any sartorial advice to his female coworker in any case. Helen Gurley Brown betrays her conventional attitudes by labeling homosexual men "girls," even if they look like "men," but she does find that they make wonderful friends and confidants for a single woman (28). And, she adds, "they have the most exquisite taste," a tired trope *Mad Men* seems only too happy to reinforce with a more contemporary, but equally tired, trope: the gay makeover (31). Arriving at Peggy's apartment before the Dylan concert, Kurt is almost immediately placed in the role of confidant and adviser when Peggy laments, "I don't know why I pick the wrong boys. . . . What's wrong with me?" "You're wrong style," Kurt replies in his charmingly broken English, as he touches Peggy's bangs ("The Jet Set"). Replacing Joan as Peggy's *Sex and the Single Girl* mentor, Kurt goes on to say that her look "is not modern office working woman." He immediately offers to "fix" her, thus fulfilling his narrative duty as a good homosexual, which is, first and foremost, to help heterosexual people in distress—here played out as a kind of *Queer Eye for the Straight Woman*. At this point in the series, we know nothing about (let alone see anything of) Kurt's private life. Thus far, we have seen as much of Sal's private life as we have, I suspect, because much of Sal's personal life as a closeted, married man is rendered in melodramatic terms that cast Sal as pathetic victim.

The show's happy, out homosexual, Kurt, begins his makeover by placing Peggy on a chair, telling her he's "very good," and proceeding to chop off her girlish ponytail (fig. 14.8). The next day, Peggy has been transformed into a *Sex and the Single Girl*–style career woman, complete with flip hairdo. "You look different," Pete remarks on seeing her. "It's my hair," Peggy replies. Then Ken pops up to tell Pete, "Kurt's a homo," little realizing that the look they now admire on Peggy and on other women in the office is often the result of collaborations between "homos" and single career women. But if the charac-

FIGURE 14.8. Kurt gives Peggy a gay makeover ("The Jet Set, 2.11").

ters are unaware, the series itself seems fully aware of the irony that it takes a homosexual man to conjure up the single-girl style that turns on heterosexual men.

But what happens when the single career girl is herself homosexual? "The Homosexuals" cuts out women except for brief footage of them participating in a protest outside Independence Hall, thus suggesting that the only homosexuality to be concerned about is male—perhaps because male homosexuality seems to pose a greater threat to straight men, or because straight men don't really consider women as sexual beings of any sort. Helen Gurley Brown's treatment of lesbians and lesbianism is even briefer than what she accords homosexual men, but it is, on the whole, more empathetic. Interestingly enough, "Suppose You Like Girls" is one of the subheadings in a *Sex and the Single Girl* chapter titled "The Affair." In this section Brown admits that she can "contribute no helpful advice" to women who love women, because she knows nothing about lesbian "pleasures" (234). But she seems sympathetic to a 1960s lesbian's lot in life, saying, "I'm sure your problems are many. . . . At any rate, it's *your* business and I think it's a shame you have to be so surreptitious about your choice of a way of life" (234). What I find most fascinating about this liberal outburst is that, rhetorically, it addresses lesbians directly, and assumes that they might buy a book titled *Sex and the*

Single Girl in the hopes of . . . what? Finding lesbian sex tips? Finding a way to pass as heterosexual career girls?

Mad Men has a little femme passing and a little mannish lesbian coding in the first season, and a soft butch "career girl" in the fourth season. In this, it joins most U.S. television programming, including "The Homosexuals," in not being particularly interested in lesbians on the job or in the bedroom. *Mad Men*'s first potential lesbian appears in the pilot in the form of a tailored, middle-aged woman named Greta Guttman—possibly to evoke Sapphic associations with Greta Garbo or more general homosexual associations with the character of Kasper Gutman (Sydney Greenstreet) in *The Maltese Falcon* (1941). Before we see Greta, Don tells Sal that the head of the research department is coming in to deliver their findings about marketing cigarettes. "Great," Sal remarks snidely, "now I get to hear from our man in research." Instead of a man, the mannish Greta enters. Sal's joke is on Greta, whose severe style, Germanic accent, and Freudian doctrines are not likely to win over the audience. If there is one thing men—both straight and queer—can bond over, apparently, it is being lesbophobic. Pitching her report into the trash can, Don tells Greta, "I find your approach perverse." We might understand Don's negative response here as not only triggered by his reading of Greta's sexuality (coded by his use of the term *perverse*) but also by her being an intellectual European woman who advocates scientific/psychoanalytic explanations for human behavior and motivations, something Don and his advertising peers seem to distrust but feel they need to use in a postwar, pop Freud world.

More benign, if just a hair's breadth away from *The Children's Hour* (1961), is the series' treatment of Joan's roommate, Carol. When Carol gets fired for covering for her boss, Joan decides to have a "girls' night out" during which they will exact their revenge on men by looking for bachelors and emptying their wallets ("Long Weekend," 1.10). As they prepare to go out, Carol looks admiringly at Joan, who is fixing herself up in a mirror. "You never say die, do you?" Carol asks Joan, going on to tell her how happy she has been sharing an apartment and a life with her. Of course, Joan (willfully?) misunderstands Carol's confession of love, but Carol presses on, telling Joan that she saw her their first week in college, fell in love, and followed her to New York so she could be near Joan as co–career girl and roommate. Coming closer, Carol asks "Joanie" to think of her "as a boy." Joan, struck silent for a moment, says, "You've had a hard day. Let's go out and try to forget about it." This leads to a scene in which they are in their apartment with two men. Joan quickly takes one of them into her bedroom, leaving a sad and humiliated Carol on the sofa telling the other man that she will do "whatever [he] want[s]." While this is not a suicide as in *Children's Hour*, it is presented as a ritual debasement filled with sexual jealously and self-loathing—and we never see Carol again, so as far as the series is concerned, she *is* dead.

But the spirit of Carol lives on in many of the websites devoted to the series. It seems that pairing the Erotic Earth Mother Joan with a lesbian roommate even for part of one episode has encouraged more than one self-identified straight woman in online fan forums to admit to a "girl crush" on Joan, or the actor Christina Hendricks, who plays her. "Pegster," for example, says, "My sister and I are totally straight, but we can't take our eyes off your fabulous body," to which "SCfan" adds, "We are all going to have to 'go gay'" for Joan/Hendricks.[4] The comments on this board are typical of fan remarks about the show as they reveal how each of the major characters has provoked a range of complex—and often complexly erotic—reactions among fans.

But I began to yearn for some *Mad Men* lesbian or gay slash literature by the end of season 3, when Don sets up a new renegade ad agency that includes Peggy and Joan but that seems to have no place for Sal or Kurt ("Shut the Door. Have a Seat," 3.13). While I remained intrigued by the show's representation of the sexual desires and careers of single straight women, by the end of the third season I was starting to get that old "seduced and abandoned" feeling about *Mad Men* and homosexuality. As far as I could tell, it looked as if we homosexuals had once again done our cultural and narrative duty serving, supporting, styling, and titillating straight Mad Men and the career girls who love them, and now we needed to move on and find a new roommate, cruise Central Park, or go back to Europe.

Then Joyce Ramsay appeared in season 4 ("The Rejected," 4.4). Because I have been burned in the past, however, I was cautiously optimistic about Joyce developing into an important recurring secondary character whose narrative life extends beyond the ways she can serve or develop one of the main characters—in this case, Peggy. Peggy first meets Joyce, an assistant photo editor at *Life* magazine, in an elevator where she notices Joyce holding a file with the word "Rejected" stamped on it. Inside the file are photos of nude women taken by Joyce's (male) friend. Peggy says she would be "shocked" to see them in *Life*, but finds one of them "beautiful" and reaches out to touch it as Joyce playfully snaps shut the portfolio. Soon after this, Joyce comes to Peggy's workplace to invite her to a party. The scene begins with Peggy walking into an arresting butch-femme tableau: Joyce clad in a gray tailored jacket leaning over a desk toward a voluptuous receptionist in a bright red dress.

Peggy arrives at the party in the Village looking like a chic beatnik in her black-striped green pullover. This outfit elicits an admiring "You look swelle-gant" from Joyce, who has been speaking with Sharon, a black women who is one of her friends' nude models. When Peggy asks for a beer, Joyce says she is already "high" and offers Peggy a hit from her joint, which Peggy accepts. But when Joyce moves in to kiss or rub against her cheek (it's unclear which), Peggy pulls back a little with a good-humored "Hey! I have a boyfriend." "He doesn't own your vagina," Joyce snaps back, to which Peggy replies, "No, but he's renting it," after which they both laugh.

Thus far, Joyce is set up as someone who encourages Peggy's queer (if not specifically lesbian) expressiveness, as well as someone with the potential to become Peggy's best friend or new romantic partner. However, Joyce's queer bohemian world and Peggy's queer expressiveness in it are ceded to Peggy's heterosexual romance with Abe, Joyce's friend. When Peggy's office mate snidely calls Joyce Peggy's "boyfriend," Joyce licks a smiling Peggy's cheek. Later at a bar, however, Abe barges in and stands between Peggy and Joyce until Joyce makes a weak excuse and leaves.

The show quickly resolves a potentially provocative romantic/sexual tri-angle between Peggy, Joyce, and Abe in favor of the man, with Joyce put in the heterosexualized role of the gallant would-be lover who steps aside for his/her friend. During her next visit to Peggy's office, Joyce lets slip that her past sexual experiences with men have been bad, which unfortunately gestures toward a cliché about why women become lesbians. In spite of her own bad luck with men, Joyce suggests that she "helped Abe out" because he seems a worthwhile candidate for a relationship with Peggy ("The Beau-tiful Girls," 4.9). Is Joyce being reduced into another of *Mad Men*'s "helper homosexuals" who are then kicked off the show for their pains? The final mo-ments of this episode suggest as much, capturing Joyce in a shadowy long shot getting in an elevator while a medium shot places Peggy, Joan, and Faye Miller in a brightly lit one.

The same melodramatic pathos evoked for Joyce recurs in the opening scene of "Chinese Wall" (4.11). Joyce and Peggy have spent the day at Jones Beach, but all we see is the end: Joyce in the driver's seat of her car, with Peggy on Abe's lap to accommodate the crowd of friends. Cut to Peggy and Abe entering her bedroom and immediately falling into bed. The next morn-ing, Peggy gets Abe back into bed as he is about to leave. "You're incred-ible," Abe tells her, to which she replies, "I'm usually not like this." After her (hetero)sexcapades with Abe, subsequent scenes show Peggy becoming more assured and inspired in thinking up and pitching ad copy. Should we

FIGURE 14.9. Helper homosexual? Joyce with her companion ("Tomorrowland," 4.13).

conclude that Peggy's (homo)eroticized friendship with Joyce—and her entry into Joyce's queer bohemian world—allows Peggy to become a more free, open, and sensuous woman? That this, in turn, leads to an exciting (hetero)sexual relationship with Abe, while feeding her creativity so she can develop better (heterocentric) ad campaigns and more persuasively charm her (male) clients into using them?

If this was where season 4 left Joyce, I would have been prepared to write off the series at this point in terms of its uses (and abuses) of homosexuality, though still somewhat fascinated by the straight queerness of Don and Peggy. But Joyce made an appearance in the final episode ("Tomorrowland," 4.13), which offered a small ray of hope that the show's next season would not limit her to melodramatic "helper homosexual." Entering in another gray tailored jacket with a glamorous woman in tow, Joyce introduces her companion to Peggy as Carolyn Jones, a model. Carolyn has just been fired from her last job and Joyce wants to know whether Peggy's agency might have any work for her. As they sit together on a small sofa, Joyce places her arm comfortably behind Carolyn (fig. 14.9). This time it is Harry who intrudes, sitting on the arm of the sofa next to Carolyn and trying to insinuate himself by promising to see about getting a job for her. Irritated by Harry's behavior—and perhaps recalling what happened with Abe and Peggy—Joyce stands up, saying to Carolyn, "We should be going, honey," which makes it clear even to the most obtuse viewer (if not to Harry) that Joyce at least would like to think of herself and Carolyn as a couple.

This is where *Mad Men*'s fourth season leaves Joyce. She has moved on from her position as Peggy's abject, character-developing "helper homosexual" to once again show signs of having a life (including a relationship) of her own apart from one of the major characters. There are many ways *Mad Men* might develop Joyce's life and her relationship with Carolyn. Unfortunately, given the show's track record, the most likely scenario may be splitting up our potential butch-femme couple, this time courtesy of Harry's interest in Carolyn—in other words, by adhering to long-standing narrative conventions that have femmes go off with men, leaving butches out of the picture to fend for themselves (remember *Personal Best* [1982]?). Will Joyce be the latest victim of *Mad Men*'s love-'em-and-leave-'em relationship with homosexual men and women, or will she be allowed to live on and tell her tale of being a lesbian "career girl" in the 1960s, balancing a job at *Life*, a relationship with another woman, and exciting times with her bohemian friends? I, for one, will tune in to season 5 expecting the worst, but with my fingers crossed.

POST–SEASON 5 POSTSCRIPT: Since I wrote this essay, season 5 has come and gone, and with it Carolyn, Joyce, and any chance *Mad Men* had of keeping me around for a sixth season. Carolyn never shows up again, and Joyce makes one appearance early in the fourth episode, "Mystery Date," in which she rather callously flashes around some graphic photos of the nurses murdered by Richard Speck. This sets up a narrative thread in which many characters— but not Joyce—get to have character-illuminating responses to the crime. It is bitterly ironic, at least to me, that Joyce's only appearance during the season (and most likely her final appearance in the series) is as the bearer of images of murdered women. RIP, Joyce, I'll miss you—but *Mad Men*, not so much.

NOTES

1. "The Homosexuals," narrated by Mike Wallace and produced by William Peters, aired on 7 March 1967.

2. For the creator Matthew Weiner describing Brown's influence on Joan's dialogue, see Zimmer.

3. Bryan Batt, "Commentary," "Out of Town" (writ. Matthew Weiner), *Mad Men: Season 3*, DVD (Lionsgate, 2010).

4. Comments in response to the interview with Hendricks posted by Clayton Neuman on AMCtv.com.

MAD MEN'S POSTRACIAL
FIGURATION OF A RACIAL PAST

KENT ONO

Teddy told me that in Greek, "nostalgia" literally means
"the pain from an old wound." — Don Draper ("The Wheel," 1.13)

To think of *Mad Men* as nostalgic, as desirous of the past, might strike faithful viewers of the show as counterintuitive, because the show's embrace of
the past is not merely a loving but also an uncomfortable one. As such, *Mad
Men*'s nostalgia is both like and not like Hollywood films such as *Pleasantville*
(1998). Like *Pleasantville* it has a largely white cast and its narrative functions
by way of whiteness. Yet unlike *Pleasantville*, *Mad Men* does not promise
audiences secure, white, suburban domestic spaces, or loving white families
with rebuilt home lives (Dickinson). Even as *Mad Men* is more dystopic in
its imagining of the suburbs, it does not reject suburbia entirely. The show
draws a dichotomy between city life, where one can encounter people of
color and pot smokers, and the less daring suburbs, where one can always
return, where people of color are subservient domestics, and where alcohol and cigarette consumption top the list of quotidian vices. In short, *Mad
Men*'s vision renders the lives of its characters "more meaningful through
nostalgic invocations of the past and more tantalizing with just the slightest
hint of racialized or sexualized danger, or both" (Dickinson, 218).

To conceive of nostalgia as psychological as well as romantic — as "the
pain from an old wound," in Don Draper's turn of phrase — helps to explain
the show's representation of the racial past. *Mad Men*'s account of the past

uses *demographic realism*: in other words, the show documents the actions of characters through the lens of white society, from a vantage point resonant with contemporary logics of whiteness. The focus of this chapter, therefore, is not past but present-day racism — especially *Mad Men*'s racist representational strategies, which are made possible through its construction of past racism.

To understand *Mad Men*'s representation, it is necessary to elucidate racial politics' distinct rhetorical strategy in contemporary postracial culture. Less often discussed than postfeminism, postracism's analogous cultural condition is premised on the assumption that race and racism are of little importance in modern life (if they ever were significant) and are therefore passé. For Ralina Joseph, postracism assumes "that the civil rights movement effectively eradicated racism to the extent that not only does racism no longer exist but race itself no longer matters" (239). In his discussion of whether Barack Obama's presidency signifies the end of racism in the United States, Thomas F. Pettigrew describes postracism as a "national hunger for racial optimism" and a moment when "race has substantially lost its special significance" (279). Postracism is characterized by a discomfort with, and related desire to forget, race and racism, which enables them to operate beyond ordinary thresholds of popular consciousness through deferral, repression, and forgetting. Popular culture tends either to absent racism altogether, or to demonstrate progress by staging overt racism that is magically cured by good white people.[1] Typically, narrative representations of race indirectly (and perhaps inadvertently) juxtapose a mature and modern postracial present against the no longer relevant — and backward and archaic — racial past.

Mad Men is self-conscious about race and racism, as it is about gender and sexual politics, history, and, thus, its production values. Because of its self-reflective mode of representation, *Mad Men* may appear to operate outside of traditional racial logics. It may seem *extra*racial or *trans*racial, or even (from a perspective of reflective white people) *antiracist*—which, of course, fits the definition of *post*racial. Furthermore, the show's lack of major characters of color and lack of complex perspectives of characters of color — including point-of-view shots, narrative development, and home or family settings — construct a white racial perspective. The series also displays long-standing racially exclusionary practices in televisual and popular culture.[2]

Because actors of color play such a minor role on the show, making *Mad Men* a typical "white show," studying its representation of race may appear to be an obvious exercise. There are certainly things about *Mad Men* that are typical of the representations of race on U.S. television. Nevertheless, in what has been hailed as a "postracial" era, when the appearance of race in media is rarely straightforward, identifying racial dimensions alone is not sufficient for understanding the representational politics of *Mad Men*. The task requires careful attention to inferentiality, absence, and alternative representational possibilities.

The rhetorics of postracism function to insist that racism is elsewhere but not here, in this time or place, thus bracketing or altogether ignoring present-day racism. Yet, even as they defer racism in the here and now, postracial rhetorics cannot escape history. As William Faulkner wrote in *Requiem for a Nun*, "The past is never dead. It's not even past" (92). Thus *Mad Men*'s representations of race are often self-reflective in relation to the representation of African Americans, but less so in relation to Asians and Asian Americans. *Mad Men*'s postracial rhetoric, then, operates both by way of self-reflectivity and by reproducing historical representations of race well ensconced within U.S. television culture. A study of the series has much to tell us about the way race functions in today's popular culture and in U.S. society more broadly.

While this is not an audience study per se, part of the complexity of the representation of race in *Mad Men* is evident in the largely paradoxical response of reviewers. Many articles and blogs celebrate the show's smart production values, visual elegance, and attention to historical detail. The *San Francisco Chronicle*, for instance, finds the show "a stylized, visually arresting piece of work" and "wonderfully evocative of time and place" (Goodman). For many, the mise-en-scène—mnemonically equipped with mementos of an earlier era—is evidence of the show's at times sublime engagement with the historical.[3] The *Boston Globe* noted that *Mad Men* "is a gorgeously fashioned period piece, from its IBM typewriters and rotary phones to the constant fog of cigarette smoke hanging over every scene" (M. Gilbert). The show effects a nostalgic mood through the striking placement of referents from the early 1960s, whether the quotidian consumption of alcohol and cigarettes, the performance of feigned deference, or the panoply of period clothing. *Mad Men*'s fastidious attention to detail and handling of the script, direction, tempo, dialogue, cinematography, editing, and particularly mise-en-scène (including props, fashion, architecture, and so on) affirm the show's ability to "get things right," which for critics often includes getting race "right." Media articles commonly mention that race is a regular theme on the show (as are gender, sexuality, class, and ability). Reviewers thus praise *Mad Men* for, as Alex Williams puts it, "its unflinching portrayal of Eisenhower/Kennedy-era sexism, racism, anti-Semitism and Scotch before 5 p.m."

Yet some articles, while praising *Mad Men*'s care for production, challenge the problematics of racial representation. For example, Latoya Peterson, writing in *Slate*, suggests that despite its inventiveness, *Mad Men* fails to recognize the material reality of racism ("Afraid"; see also Schwarz). She comments on the lack of affective black characters and the thinness of black culture and contexts. For instance, she notes the lack of tears shed by the show's characters when they hear of "the little girls killed at the 16th Street Baptist Church." Melissa Witkowski describes *Mad Men* as "an attractive fantasy that creates an illusion of distance between our past and our present." The histories of "women and people of color," she believes, are trivialized through "the erasure of [their] real accomplishments," and the "downplaying" of "institutional and systemic oppression in favour of presenting easier (and more salacious) targets such as sexual harassment and racist banter . . . in the workplace."[4] Hence commentators who reflect on the role race plays in people's lives existentially criticize *Mad Men* for the disjuncture between its racialization of characters and the history of race and racism in the 1960s (see also Little).

Given reviewers' bifurcated responses, how do we make sense of this smartly dressed television show's politics of racial representation? The answer is to look further at *Mad Men*'s self-conscious representational style, which pairs awareness of how far U.S. race relations have come with recognition of just how awful they were in the early 1960s. The show thus comments intelligently and knowingly on how race functioned just before the civil rights successes of the 1960s and '70s. Some might suggest that by representing the racial past, the show indirectly comments on contemporary race relations. Is it possible that *Mad Men*'s awareness of the distance between "us now" and "them then" simultaneously implies that the distance is not as great as one might think?

Herman Gray's work on the television of the 1980s and '90s provides an important schema for addressing this question. In *Watching Race*, Gray emphasizes not only racial demography but also the degree to which cultural sensibility is televisually encoded, developing three different categories for specifically racial analysis. *Assimilationist* shows, he explains, may include characters of color while treating race as largely irrelevant. As on *L.A. Law* (NBC, 1986–94), characters of color are included primarily for diversity's sake (85). By contrast, *pluralist* shows may be made up primarily of African American characters, yet the story lines are not dissimilar from story lines for shows with predominantly white characters, with specific experiential and institutional differences between racial groups downplayed; for instance, *Fresh Prince of Bel-Air* (NBC, 1990–96) (85). Gray calls shows with the greatest awareness of ethnicity and race *multicultural*. These shows—for example, *Frank's Place* (CBS, 1987–88)—emphasize cultural and racial identities and experiences and, unlike assimilationist and pluralist programs, are not determined by an overarching logic of whiteness. However, Gray notes that few shows are truly multicultural: even when shows foreground racial identity and experiences, they mostly fail to be progressive since they do not challenge political institutions and are rarely socially critical in a general way (91).

What Gray's scheme does not anticipate are shows like *Mad Men* that are both limited in numbers of characters (and therefore actors) of color, like assimilationist shows before them, but that are nevertheless self-conscious about race. Indeed, *Mad Men* seems to require a fourth category of racial representation that we might label *self-reflective*. Although these shows do not generate narratives from the perspective of characters of color, they nevertheless contain a thoughtful and thought-provoking representation of racial politics. In a sense, what Gray does not anticipate, but which his schema can help us understand, is the *postracial* context that affords *Mad Men* the capacity both to maintain historical demographic segregation for the most part and to bypass the cultural sensibility argument Gray makes, while simultaneously projecting itself, at least to some viewers, as aware, knowledgeable, and progressive about racial representation.

Mad Men emerges out of a contemporary postracial context when straightforward racial representation is no longer (if it ever was) the principal means of representing race—the very terms of racial representation on which *Mad Men* draws have changed significantly since Gray's book. As the sociologist Eduardo Bonilla-Silva suggests, we now live in an era saturated by "color-blind racism." More than a decade ago, the scholar George Lipsitz noted the historical emergence of a race-neutral and race-conscious racism, both of which figure in Bonilla-Silva's conception of "color-blindness." Lipsitz argued that racism was "created anew" over the fifty years that saw "the putatively race-neutral, liberal, social democratic reforms of the New Deal Era" along with "the more overtly race-conscious neoconservative reactions against liberalism since the Nixon years" (5). Thus, postracial representation grows out of a putatively race-neutral standpoint, in an attempt to avoid negative forms of racial presentation. Moreover, an entirely new racial signifying system has emerged—one that operates primarily through relatively subtle processes of deferral, indirection, and self-reflectivity. Postracial representational politics are typically not straightforward: race is more commonly represented indirectly and inferentially; thus what is being said about race requires careful analysis of rhetoric that obfuscates more direct ways of understanding racial politics and racial experience (see, e.g., Ono).

Under Gray's schema, *Mad Men* is assimilationist insofar as it lacks major characters of color or focus on diverse cultures. Yet because it in fact takes race seriously, even as characters of color and themes and content related to them are sparse, it cannot be understood through the representational logics of the Gray-era studies. That said, the series cannot simply be championed for acknowledging the history of racism and offering nuanced depictions of whiteness since these achievements depend on the marginalization of characters of color, issues relating to race, and racial consciousness of the other. To put this another way, just because we recognize that *Mad Men* operates in a self-conscious mode does not mean that its representation of race is beyond critique; nor does it mean that the show moves beyond race. Hence, though *Mad Men*'s televisual production qualities and representational practices may be exceptional, its politics of racial representation are familiar.[5]

When characters of color do appear on the show—notably Carla (the Drapers' maid), Sheila (Paul's girlfriend), and Hollis (an elevator attendant)[6]—they are frequently the subject of racism, as when Betty Draper's father Eugene seems to imply that Carla has stolen his missing five dollars ("My Old Kentucky Home," 3.3). Although racism is often the main point of the scenes in which these characters appear, the show circumscribes their roles, creating an aching and overpowering sense of the absence of their agency and home life. Carla's world as she privately sees it, along with her house, friends, family, and acquaintances, is never visible. We learn about her only through her relation to the white characters. As the lives of the white characters unfold in front of our eyes, Carla stays in the background: a crucial, yet supplemental, element.[7] For example, noting the Drapers' marital difficulties, Carla tries to get Betty to open up to her, saying, "I've been married almost twenty years, you know" ("Six Month Leave," 2.9). Although we see that Carla observes and has consciousness, the show merely gestures toward that consciousness in a way that centers on her efforts to support Betty rather than on Carla herself. Carla thus signifies *Mad Men*'s self-conscious awareness of the fact that racism existed in the 1960s. By not showing her before and after work, or during private and intimate moments, the show has two effects: first, it produces a historically realist representation of the irrelevance of her personal life to white people in the 1960s; second, it unnecessarily and objectionably produces the irrelevance of her personal life to television viewers now.

Mad Men's historical realism and the implicit claim that the show is true to the historical record enables persuasive commentary on race relations. This mode of addressing race distinguishes it within television's history of racial representation, marking it as distinctly postracial. As Robin Givhan of the *Washington Post* writes, "You don't get the feeling that the show, in its willingness to relegate black characters to elevator operators and lunch cart attendants, is attempting to self-consciously ridicule this historic truth but merely to represent it accurately." If we were to follow Givhan's logic to the extreme, we would need to assume that every presence or absence of race was planned: the invisibility of black characters' homes, the lack of Latinos, the number of lines each speaks, and even the choice not to give actors of color much work on the series. On this view, all are self-conscious choices necessary to demonstrating awareness of the reality of racism in the 1960s. But does awareness mean we should overlook Gray's representational schema and ignore the material impact on actors of color? In the service of realism, are we to overlook the fact that the show does not represent black life and culture separately from white culture, nor anywhere as fully? Are we to overlook the particular racializations the show offers when people of color do appear onscreen?

The center of the show is, of course, Don, a privileged white man though not a positive or even especially likeable hero. Indeed, the show addresses a complex notion of racial identity through Don, who is so identified with marginalization that Michael Szalay (in this volume) likens him to a "white negro." As Don strives to come to self-knowledge through a plethora of identity struggles, his narrative is an unfulfilled bildungsroman. That Don is not what he appears to be supports the view of him as a white character signifying a stereotypical and highly problematic notion of what blackness could be conceived to be. A deserter, an identity thief, and the illegitimate child of a prostitute, he keeps secrets to maintain his upper-middle-class status.

Moreover, Don is often associated with (publicly) marginalized characters. For example, in the opening scene of the pilot ("Smoke Gets in Your Eyes," 1.1), the first face we see is that of a black waiter in a busy bar where Don is working. The scene sets up Don's character and the premise of the show. The camera breaks away from the black waiter to give us a view of the back of Don's head and his hat and coat. We see that Don is sitting alone

FIGURE 15.1. A moment of intimacy ("Smoke Gets in Your Eyes," 1.1).

writing on a napkin by candlelight. There are no recognizable words, only pen scrawls, some with letters crossed out or made illegible by copious ink. A second black waiter, this one middle-aged, approaches Don, who needs a light. His hand moves closer to Don to offer the light. Their hands even touch gently in the process, producing a moment of intimacy, at least from Don's perspective. Don looks at him and asks, "Old Gold man, huh? Lucky Strike here" (fig. 15.1). The waiter looks at him, possibly surprised or even frightened by the implications of conversing with a white customer. Don says, "Can I ask you a question? Why do you smoke Old Gold?" A middle-aged white man, taller than the waiter, comes to the table and asks, "I'm sorry, sir. Is Sam here bothering you?" and casts a stern look at Sam.[8] "He can be a little chatty," he says to Don, and glances at Sam from the side again. Don replies, "No, we're actually just having a conversation. Is that OK?" Don orders a drink from the white man and proceeds to ask Sam what, if anything, would make him change from Old Gold to Lucky Strike. Sam reveals that he loves to smoke; Don responds by writing, "I Love Smoking." The waiter tells Don his wife reads *Reader's Digest*, which has reported that smoking is bad for you. "Ladies love their magazines," he adds. They both laugh, engaging in a moment of heterosexual male bonding at the expense of women.

One reason the scene is so interesting is that it shows Don defending his right to have a desegregated conversation with a black server. This defense requires a post–civil rights understanding of how one responds to racism, hence an awareness lacking in the period the show wants to portray.[9] Don is not merely defending his right to information but also making a point about race. The tension produced by their interracial talking overdetermines the situation in such a way as to ensure that Don's challenge of the white waiter constitutes a racial confrontation. Yet it also illustrates Don's willingness to put the black waiter's job at risk. An extradiegetic possibility is that Sam loses his job, is chided for having broken unspoken rules, or experiences some other (possibly harsher) racial violence, antagonism, or retribution for having crossed the color barrier or for embarrassing the white boss.

By taking a public stand against segregation, Don is also positioning Sam as a laborer waiting tables *and* as a laborer unknowingly helping him with his ad campaign. In essence, Don enlists Sam's intellectual labor, from which his own career will benefit. His capitalist goal is to co-opt the black man's idea for Lucky Strike; indeed, he is a cog in the wheel of the cigarette industry's efforts to persuade blacks to consume Lucky Strike cigarettes.[10] The scene also demonstrates Don's ability to wield power, which in this instance renders the white waiter subservient. He asks Sam's ostensible supervisor to refill his glass, enabling his own access to Sam while putting the white supervisor in his place (the way black subordinates were typically treated). In aligning himself with black people against the white establishment for a career-serving end, while nevertheless acting from a position of white, classed authority within that establishment, Don figures as a postracial man.

Each instance of his identification with marginality—falling in love with a Jewish woman, helping Peggy move out of the secretarial pool, keeping Sal's homosexuality secret, and smoking dope—marks him as what Ralina Joseph labels a "post-" ("race-, gender-, and sexuality-based discrimination") figure (238). Yet the show does not position Don as unidimensionally pro–civil rights and progressive. Indeed, one could read all of these examples primarily in terms of Don's career interests, suggesting his indifference to politics so long as he succeeds in his job; hence his work for the conservative Nixon campaign, his quashing Betty's modeling career when he chooses not to work for McCann, and his willingness (despite misgivings) to sacrifice Mohawk Airlines in order to try for American Airlines. And while supporting Peggy professionally at notable points (including keeping her childbirth a secret), he later scolds her for striving too much.

Don's complex character, both heroic and nonheroic illuminates the profound nature of the show's white identity. His nuanced multiple roles (e.g., father and son, lover and foe, boss and subordinate, conservative and liberal) all insist on a more intricate (even sublime) reading. He is an everyman, so multifaceted as to be all-encompassing, so white and dark as to encompass the ubiquity of racial and class identity in a figure of white masculinity. This highly developed and even overprivileged role stands in stark contrast to the characters of color, who primarily represent their race and exist to enhance Don's meaning and that of other white characters. Indeed, Don's stunning complexity relies on his ability to instrumentalize (and in some instances love and befriend) marginal characters such as Sam, Midge, and Rachel. In this way the show *includes* characters of color to get enough credit to be able *to tell the story* of white characters. As Peterson suggests, we never see any person of color outside a white-dominated environment.

I have already suggested Carla's particular importance in constituting the character of the Drapers. Don's character depends on Carla, who functions in an asymmetrical dialectic with him. If Carla has alone-time with the camera it is brief, isolated, contemplative, and passive; the purpose is to enable the spectator's rumination and to mark the show's self-consciousness, not to allow Carla action or interaction.

Yet Carla is the most developed character of color on the show thus far. If her role is limited during the show's first season, she begins to be more central beginning in the first episode of the second season. Although she never has many lines, Carla is positioned as a knowing agent within Don's family context. For instance, toward the end of "For Those Who Think Young" (2.1), Don returns home from work, kisses his son, and pours himself a drink. As he is pouring, he asks Carla if she wants a ride home. We get a shot from her point of view of him pouring the alcohol, before she courteously declines, saying that she enjoys the fresh air. Her view of Don as someone whose drinking makes him an unsafe driver is brought home through minimalist cinematography and editing. Despite the fact that "drinking and driving" as we know it today did not have the same meaning in the early 1960s, the overlay of contemporary knowledge that informs the show's historical realism recurs (as in Don's post–civil rights challenge of segregation in the pilot).

Instances like these gesture toward an awareness of Carla's deep understanding of the Drapers and perhaps of the white society beyond their domain. Carla is clearly aware of her social position, understanding not only her role as maid and nanny but also her role as black, female subordinate.[11] Yet, while these moments enable us to see Carla more clearly, our knowledge of her is never satisfying. The moments are teasers, flirtations with the spectator's desire for more—more knowledge about Carla's life and her perspectives, more consequences for the Drapers' behaviors, more connection to the material constraints of minority characters. Instead we get a fascinating story about Don and an exploration of the power dynamics of his white-

FIGURE 15.2. Carla smiling at Francine about having to do more work ("Souvenir," 3.8).

ness, without it being named as such.[12] Carla's observation of Don's drinking aids our understanding of his character, while we learn little of hers. She is not even the Sacagawea of the narrative, being neither a main character nor someone with a history. Because of Carla's work as Betty's domestic part- ner/laborer, Don is able to have regular affairs without dramatically upset- ting his home life. Thus in season 2 Carla takes care of the house and kids so that Betty is able to sleep on the couch while she copes with the knowledge of Don's affair with Bobbie Barrett. In season 3 she makes it possible for the couple to vacation in Rome. Rather than seeing her story we are left know- ing only that, like other characters of color, she understands the racism and white domination she faces.

There are lapses in the text's treatment of Carla. One example is a missed opportunity for a reaction shot by Carla during a particularly useful moment. In "Souvenir" (3.8), while Betty and Don are in Rome and Carla is caring for their three children, Francine drops by the house to deliver her son Ernie so she can attend a board meeting. Carla greets her, smiling. After Francine leaves, there is a moment when a reaction shot is possible. In response to having to take care of yet another child, the gentle smile seems insufficient. Yet the show forgoes the chance to show a different aspect of Carla (fig. 15.2).[13] The scene thus raises the question: Is the show representing a critical view of 1960s race relations or is it, rather, locked into a 1960s view of race relations? The authenticity of this scene would not have been compromised by this glimpse of Carla, unseen by any white person.

FIGURE 15.3. An Asian family in Pete's office ("Marriage of Figaro," 1.3).

Then too, *Mad Men*'s self-consciousness about African American racism does not extend to other racialized groups. The show's inconsistent representational politics show it to be locked into a black/white/Jewish notion of race. This uneven self-reflectiveness is part of the show's postracial rhetoric, which on the one hand defers racism and on the other falls back into racist patterns of minority representation. As opposed to the problematic yet self-reflective representation of African American characters, the show unreflectively features Asians and Asian Americans for comedic effect or as sexualized oriental figures—a representation that merely continues the derogations of the past.

For example, in "Marriage of Figaro" (1.3), Pete returns to the office after his honeymoon. In the elevator, Paul, Ken, and Harry tease him about what happened *after* the wedding. On the way to his office Pete is greeted by a phalanx of secretaries who welcome him back. No sooner does Pete comment on this unusual friendliness than he opens his office door to the sound of a clucking chicken. From Pete's point of view, the camera reveals an Asian man with chopsticks eating out of a bowl, sitting atop Pete's desk (fig. 15.3). Facing Pete is an Asian woman with chopsticks, smiling and speaking quietly, ostensibly in an Asian language. To the right in the distance is an elderly Asian woman also eating with chopsticks. A chicken stands atop the desk. The Asian man says, "Close the door"; the chicken clucks, and the man exclaims more emphatically, "Close the door!" followed by some nonsensical word like "*Banha!*" Closing his office door, Pete smiles and asks his fellow office workers, "Who put the Chinamen in my office?" The assembled company bursts out laughing. "Welcome back," says Harry, and they begin clapping. Peggy later tells Don, "They paid an Oriental family to be in Mr. Campbell's office," to which Don responds, "Someone will finally be working in there."

The scene sets up Asians, who rarely appear on the show, as comic relief. Because they are out of place, their startling appearance augments the humorous effect for Pete, his office mates, and the audience, which, through a singular composition of point of view, is encouraged to take the perspective of the white workers, not the Asian family. They are backward and primitive, with chickens clucking—the irony and humor is in their incongruity, their out-of-time and out-of-place-ness. In a modern midcentury office suite, in a story focused on the dramas of white people, the sight of Asian people eating rice with chopsticks, sitting on Pete's desk, disrupts modern normative relations—physical, temporal, spatial, and material—and thus creates humor.

In fact, the appearance of Asians in this scene would be merely humorous were it not for the powerful ways that Asians in Western media since the nineteenth century have been figured so dependably as other. As noncitizen foreigners, culturally deviant, primitive, and hostile, Asians threaten to invade Western, white space—especially the space of capitalism. The ironic and startling appearance of Asians in *Mad Men*, which simultaneously constructs them as irrelevant, is reminiscent of Mr. Yunioshi's incongruous appearance in *Breakfast at Tiffany's* (1961), a story about a social climber (Audrey Hepburn) who depends on men but nevertheless reads as an ingénue trying to find herself, and a budding young writer (George Peppard) dependent on women who first befriends and then falls in love with her. While the stories are nothing alike and *Mad Men* does not explicitly cite the film, the parallel way in which humor is evoked through the appearance of Asians or Asian Americans who seem out of place is suggestive. Like Yunioshi, the Asian family's purpose in *Mad Men* is to titillate; the roles in both cases are insignificant for the central story. The Asian family is backward, hostile, and invasive, whereas Yunioshi is bumbling, clumsy, loud, obnoxious, and sexually perverse (for example, exhibiting public excitement at the thought of taking "pictures" of Holly), offering audiences comic relief in part through a xenophobic projection of Asians and Asian Americans as peculiar and out of place within white worlds.

Two further representations of Asians and Asian Americans in *Mad Men* are decidedly orientalist, projecting the historical construction of Asian and Asian American women as erotic, sexually wanton, and available to white

FIGURE 15.4. *The Dream of the Fisherman's Wife* (c. 1820) in Cooper's office: "I picked it for its sensuality" ("Out of Town," 3.1).

male suitors. In a scene in "Out of Town" (3.1), besides making those entering his office take off their shoes, Bert Cooper has a rice-paper divider standing in front of his office window, an oriental room divider, bamboo trees, oriental lamp stands, and an Asian-themed painting of a flute player.[14] The show's expert on all things Asian, Bert is an Asiaphile as well as an art collector.[15] In this scene the focus is on an erotic painting of a Japanese woman (fig. 15.4). Dating from around 1820, the work, by Hokusai, is called *The Dream of the Fisherman's Wife* and is often cited as the origin of Japanese "tentacle porn." Displaying a woman in a sexual embrace with two octopi, the image is popular on the Internet. The *Mad Men* scene begins with a contemplative shot of the picture, concealing its whereabouts until the camera cuts to an admiring Lane Pryce. Cooper, drinking tea in the background, says, "I picked it for its sensuality but it also in some way reminds me of . . . our business." The camera cuts to a closer shot of the woman's upper body, as Cooper asks, "Who is the man who imagined her ecstasy?" followed by a shot of Pryce replying, "Who, indeed?" At that moment, the viewer hears the sound of a doorknob turning. In comes Don through Cooper's door, and Cooper says, "We were just talking about you."

Asian women thus function as the object of white men's orientalist gaze and desire. They help produce the complexity of the white male characters while lacking complexity of their own. The second orientalist representation occurs in "Flight 1," when Don meets a client representing Mohawk Airlines in a Japanese restaurant to tell him that Sterling Cooper is dropping the account. The unhappy client says he is glad Don picked this place, because it reminds him of Pearl Harbor. Later, a guilty Don sits alone while we hear "Ue o muite arukō," retitled "Sukiyaki" in the United States, a song from 1961 by the Japanese crooner Kyu Sakamoto.[16] The camera tracks around the side of Don's face while he drinks, showing wooden slats in the foreground and background. Suddenly, Don looks up and the camera cuts to an Asian woman (Elizabeth Tsing) in a body-hugging Asian dress, with a rice-paper lantern above and behind her. She is heavily made up with mascara, red lipstick, and darkened eyebrows, as well as shiny base, and has linear cut bangs, with both sides of her hair cutting sharply into her jaw line. She comes up to him slowly and asks if she can help him. He seems stunned, as if transfixed and unable to hear her. She says in unaccented English, "Can I get you a menu?" He looks down and then up and replies, "I don't think so." She says, "I have to drop this off, but I can swing back by on my way out." His expression gradually changes into a smile. "Not tonight," he says. She smiles and leaves, and he watches her go. In an unusual moment, Don decides against sexual escapism as a response to his guilty conscience.

The credit simply calls her "Asian waitress," despite the fact that in the early 1960s she would likely be Asian American, since Asian immigration to the United States between 1924 and 1965 was severely curtailed. She is constructed as sexually available—in fact, sexually forward and assertive. The payment Don leaves, perhaps a tip (we see shots of him choosing a bill from his wad of cash), gives emphasis to the act of financial compensation (especially since she tells Don his waiter has already left). In a throwback to early twentieth-century Hollywood films about Suzy Wong, Mad Men's "Asian waitress" is constructed as sexually available to white men. With so few and noncomplex representations of Asians on the show, her stereotypical role here has the further effect of being iconic, of linking "Asian women" to prostitution, being available for sexual favors—available, that is, if Don were willing.[17]

Despite an overall ethos of sophistication about race relations—evident, for instance, in the show's representation of Rachel Menken, a wealthy client and businesswoman who understands her racial positioning as a Jewish woman vis-à-vis white Anglo men—the show employs a postracial stance with regard to race. Within today's postracial context, representational strategies for addressing race vary from indirection, implicitness, and refocusing on whites, to rendering charges and critiques of racism anachronistic, intrusive, or no longer relevant.

I maintain that *Mad Men* implies the necessity of seeing race and racism as part of the historical past in the United States. Temporally, the show depicts race as a product of the past. The past thus functions as a container for racism, making racism's *present* disappear. Nevertheless, as I argue here, race itself is not simply a cliché or a relic on the show. It is a means by which *Mad Men* stakes a claim on what race and racism really were like in the past, seemingly unaware of the postracial effects of such a move in the present. Focusing on race and racism in the early 1960s draws attention to that era's encounter with them; while it is possible then to reflect on race and racism in the present, that kind of reflection is made more difficult by the show's explicit and insistent concern with the past. In fact, I would suggest it produces the past as an object of discourse and understanding, indirectly, perhaps inadvertently, drawing attention away from the present and thereby rendering an understanding of how race works in the postracial present and beyond (through the past on this show) much more difficult.

This sense of a postracial beyondness is produced by the text and potentially taken up by the audience. As Lipsitz writes about the relation to music, "Audiences and critics want to 'own' the pleasures and powers of popular music without embracing the commercial and industrial matrices in which they are embedded; they want to imagine that art that they have discovered through commercial cultures is somehow better than commercial culture itself, that their investment in music grants them an immunity from the embarrassing manipulation, pandering, and trivialization of culture intrinsic to a market society" (123). I think Lipsitz here provides a way to understand how *Mad Men* works as a postracial product.

Through a discourse self-conscious about cultural representation and production—positioned on a "marginal" yet also "quality" cable channel, AMC—*Mad Men* assures its audience that they have discovered something special. In this context, *Mad Men* comments on the past and is itself praised for its conception of that past. But as I have shown, *Mad Men* reports the past from the perspective of white people, as well as through the lens and bodies of white people through whom we view unfolding events. In this chapter I suggest that the show's strategies of whiteness, which invariably center white perspectives, also structure overall attitudes about race, including the way people of color are understood.[18] The whiteness of the text accounts for the negated voice and lives of African Americans, the hypersexual or comic representation of Asians or Asian Americans, and the general lack of emphasis on characters of color—all of whose presence exists in order to authenticate the show's rhetoric of historical verisimilitude. The story is told from the position of its dominant white characters, including their awareness and understanding of the lives and histories of people of color. People of color occupy roles that expand our understanding of the white characters. They are figments of the white imagination. Unlike Shylock, they do not cry and bleed like people of color, but rather are made immune to such embodiment, as they are ciphers of white history's memory of them. This is how the show sacrifices meaningful narratives about people of color in favor of subordinated characters playing roles that enhance, if not define, those of the central white figures.

Mad Men flexes its media production muscle by highlighting its power to represent people of color, using its structural advantage vis-à-vis people of color who themselves lack the power of self-representation. The series does not account for the structural disadvantages faced by people of color or the unequal distribution of social resources, wealth, and power. *Mad Men*'s post-racial figuration of race dramatizes, emphasizes, and yet plays fast and loose with race and racism. As such, the show is both an effect of the structure of whiteness and also a contributor to the larger structuring system of race of which it is a part. Even during moments when the show could be said to offer a critique of problematic race relations, the consistent focus on white characters compromises its position. That is, its opposition can be understood as a strategic use of the representation of freedom, offering up the potential for freedom from problematic race relations in the process of negating freedom through its own structural position of racial advantage, a position people of color in comparative racial terms cannot and do not occupy.

Despite its few representations of Asians and Asian Americans and its representation of Latinos in "The Jet Set" (2.11), as well as its mention of a Native American–themed airline, the show largely operates by way of a black/white/Jewish ternary racial project.[19] Thus despite the particular way in which people of color appear, they are irrelevant within the context of the show, not important in and of themselves for commentary; indeed, the few representations we do get demonstrate their ultimate irrelevance to both narrative and characters.

Paradoxically, *Mad Men* negotiates its power to represent and its lack of interest in race and racism's then and there, even if interested in its own white-centric terms and usefulness in understanding contemporary representation of race and here and now, by foregrounding the fact that race and racism did occur during the time it covers. Part of what the show suggests is that racism in the early 1960s is an incontrovertible fact. Whether it is the white restaurant waiter keeping the black help in line or the construction of Jewish alterity within an Anglo-Saxon masculine world of business, racial difference did exist. It *did* matter. So if the show gets it right, represents things accurately, and tells a good story, it will include these facts, and is therefore trustworthy, can be imagined to operate rationally and counted on to represent race ethically, even as it invents that racial history. Moreover, while many of the show's critics and commentators give *Mad Men* credit for being historically accurate, true to the time, hence generating for some viewers myriad happy, nostalgic comments and feelings about the past in the present, the show's reputation as historically accurate about architecture, fashion, and personal relations also invests it with the creative license to represent race authoritatively. This is an authority we would do well to question.

NOTES

1. One particular subgenre of this kind of narrative shows the progress from false accusation of a crime based on race to eventual acquittal, through the efforts primarily of hardworking, moral, white men. Examples include the historical *To Kill a Mockingbird* (1962), *A Time to Kill* (1996), and *Snow Falling on Cedars* (1999).

2. Notably, the show includes documentaries as DVD "extras" that address some of the series' missing histories. Most are directed by Cicely Gilkey, an African American documentary filmmaker; for example, season 3's DVD set (Lionsgate, 2010) includes "Medgar Evers: The Patriarch. The Activist. The Hero," and "We Shall Overcome: The March on Washington."

3. Bernie Heidkamp praises the show's ambitious representation of the "allegorical past," commenting on the appealing realism of the show: "You feel like you are peeking under someone's bed, into their medicine cabinets and their closets . . . and through their dirty laundry."

4. For a critique of the use of history and the representation of race in *Mad Men*, see also Little.

5. Gray also explores labor issues in Hollywood, a material reality that mirrors the representational one. Even in 1999, several years after Gray's book first appeared, the *Los Angeles Times* reported on the lack of people of color on television in a story called "A White, White World on TV's Fall Schedule" (G. Braxton). "Of the 26 new

comedies and dramas premiering on the major broadcast networks," the story noted, "not one feature[d] a minority in a leading role" and even secondary characters of color were sparse. "Quality" cable shows such as *Mad Men* and *The Sopranos* (HBO, 1999–2007) conspicuously lack lead characters of color. On the labor front, actors of color have either no jobs or bit parts. *Mad Men*'s marginalization of characters of color also slots the actors of color who portray them in the lowest pay scale.

6. African American men largely appear as service workers: visible bodies with little or no dialogue. Black women appear as maids, service workers, and girlfriends of white men.

7. Hence, while Carla is significant in the first two episodes of season 2, she disappears for several episodes afterward. Viewers of season 2 may be led to believe the show will address race more fully only to find their enhanced interest in Carla disappointed. For such viewers, Carla's absence from several episodes is felt more powerfully than the comparable absence of a white character such as Joan.

8. Sam, of course, is the name of the most famous black servant in Hollywood cinematic history: "play it again" Sam from *Casablanca* (1942).

9. Compare to season 4's "The Chrysanthemum and the Sword" (4.5) in which Roger, a veteran of the Second World War, is hostile toward Japanese clients; his colleagues, lacking Roger's direct connection, reflect an acceptance more typical of a civil rights consciousness, seeming to regard Roger's emotional response as out of place, even archaic.

10. Compare to Pete's attempt to extract information from Hollis, halting the elevator until Hollis answers in "The Fog" (3.5); as well as the use of office secretaries for market research on lipstick in "Babylon" (1.6). The degree to which Don plans to focus on black consumers is debatable. But in "The Fog," Pete suggests targeting the "Negro market" to executives of Admiral, who reject the idea for fear of being labeled a Negro brand.

11. In "The Chrysanthemum and the Sword" Carla takes Don's daughter, Sally, to the psychiatrist's office, demonstrating her intimate relation to the family and, hence, the complexity of her character; the scene is noteworthy because of Carla's lack of dialogue, which renders it profound, yet still marginal.

12. Of course, Don is not the only white character in this position. In "Flight 1" (2.2), Joan displays racist behavior toward Paul's girlfriend Sheila, telling her that she is surprised about their relationship since when *she* dated Paul he was racist; the scene tells us more about Joan than about Sheila. Similarly, on a Freedom Ride, Paul holds forth with a vision of race neutrality as Sheila listens quietly ("The Inheritance," 2.10).

13. The upshot of this is that Sally and Francine's son have a fight. Carla tells the Drapers about it when they return from their trip. Betty is annoyed both at Carla for being the bearer of bad news and Don, who again avoids uncomfortable parenting.

14. For a discussion of this Orientalia, primarily japonisme (although the scene mixes Orientalia indiscriminately), see two postings on the popular website Mad

Men Unbuttoned: http://madmenunbuttoned.com/post/184102355/those-cream-ceramic-lamps-in-berts-office-are/ (9 September 2009) and http://madmenun buttoned.com/post/195617564/this-guy-has-been-lurking-around-berts-office/ (24 September 2009).

15. Yet in "The Chrysanthemum and the Sword," when the agency's success ostensibly depends on knowing Japanese culture, his position is minimized.

16. The song has been recorded by artists such as Blue Diamonds (1963), the Fabulous Echoes (1965), Taste of Honey (1981), and Selena (1990).

17. Given Don's postracial identity as sympathizer of the marginalized and given his many sexual exploits, why he does not buck antimiscegenation like his colleague Paul is unclear. Despite Don's being the show's exemplary bridge between racial consciousness then and now, antimiscegenation in his character is preserved. Even with the added eroticism of orientalism, he denies himself and averts miscegenation, not made legal federally in the United States until *Loving v. Virginia* in 1967.

18. See Richard Dyer on "the invisibility of whiteness as a racial position in which white (which is to say dominant) discourse is of a piece with its ubiquity" (*White*, 3).

19. The show does not say whether Mohawk is a Native American–owned airline or if, like a Native American sports mascot, Mohawk has simply appropriated Native American identity. Very likely it is the latter, which thus suggests the commonplace way the show simultaneously appropriates and defers race.

THE *MAD MEN* IN THE ATTIC

Seriality and Identity in the Modern Babylon

LAUREN M. E. GOODLAD

"He had no father or mother, no uncle, aunt, brother or sister, no cousin even whom he could mention in a cursory way to his dearest friend. . . . The fact remained that though a great many men and not a few women knew [him] very well, none of them knew whence he had come, or what was his family." "He was certainly a handsome man, — his beauty being of a sort which men are apt to deny and women to admit lavishly."

This and much more greet the reader in the opening pages of *The Prime Minister*, the fifth in Anthony Trollope's six-part series of Palliser novels, which appeared in eight monthly parts between November 1875 and June 1876 and then in a three-volume edition.[1] The subject of this description is Ferdinand Lopez, one of Victorian literature's most famous frauds. As the narrator goes on to say, though few "believed that Ferdinand Lopez was well born," he was, nevertheless, "a gentleman" (11). If this sounds like a simple statement of fact, appearances can deceive. For Lopez is not only *not* a gentleman but is "one of the author's most obviously blatant cads."[2]

There are at least two reasons to look at *The Prime Minister* in a volume on *Mad Men*. The first is to do with Trollope's mastery of a mode of realist narrative that, like today's "quality" television, won its first and most devoted audience in serial form. In the mid-Victorian decades during which Britain transitioned into a formal empire and male democracy, realism and seriality were linked in classic works by Charles Dickens, George Eliot, and Trollope, among others, all of which appeared in weekly or monthly installments before being published as multivolume novels that could be purchased or borrowed from circulating libraries. An interesting parallel finds the most acclaimed television dramas of our own day—including *The Sopranos* (HBO, 1999–2007), *The Wire* (HBO, 2002–8), *Deadwood* (HBO, 2004–6), and *Mad Men* (AMC, 2007–)—broadcast serially and then packaged in DVD box sets that can be purchased, rented, or downloaded in digital form.

Of course, Lopez is also suspected of being a Jew: "a swarthy son of Judah" in the words of the English "man of ancestry" who reluctantly becomes his father-in-law (35, 10). That is the second reason that *The Prime Minister* illuminates *Mad Men*. Both texts represent a long line of realist narratives in which figures of the outsider within—always parvenus, and often Jews or probable Jews—help to assimilate the myriad impacts of capitalist globalization. These "strangers in a strange land" are vilified others. But in a more complicated way, these figurative Jews represent a condition of exile that resonates for insiders and outsiders alike. Expressive at once of capitalism's *longue durée* and the recurring power of serialized realism, these often racialized aliens inhabit modern lifeworlds, from Trollope's mid-Victorian City of London to *Mad Men*'s early-1960s Madison Avenue. In this chapter I identify the realist aesthetic peculiar to serialized "narratives of capitalist globalization" in the nineteenth century and today. If one recurrent feature of this genre is the Jewish or Judaized subject, another, I suggest, is the trope of Babylon: a space of modernity haunted by an existential condition, "singing the Lord's song in a strange land."

SERIALITY, QUALITY TELEVISION, AND REALISM

Scholars such as Jason Mittell, Sean O'Sullivan, and Robyn Warhol have compared today's serial media to Victorian precursors, describing the kind of intensely felt serial habitus cultivated through narrative installments spread over time. Yet none of these critics argues that realism, the dominant form of the nineteenth-century canon, is central to seriality. In *The Victorian Serial* (1991), Linda K. Hughes and Michael Lund argue that serial fiction's interruptive temporality encouraged authors to adopt realist form: "Reading one installment, then pausing in that story, the Victorian audience turned to their own world with much the same set of critical faculties they had used to understand the literature" (11). But subsequent work on noncanonical genres such as the "penny dreadful" shows that Victorian seriality was diverse and often nonrealist (see Law). One might make comparable observations about today's quality television. The game-changing aesthetic prestige of *The Sopranos* rests partly on the vivid character development often associated with realist narrative. But *The Sopranos* is actually a postmodern hybrid that tends toward narrative dispersion, logical discontinuity, and formal experimentation. Serial television since *The Sopranos* has taken a variety of nonrealist forms including *Deadwood*, a kind of national romance; *Dexter* (Showtime, 2006–), a cross between black comedy and crime drama; *The Tudors* (Showtime, 2007–10), a mix of biopic and blue movie; and *Damages* (FX, 2007–10), a blend of courtroom drama and postmodern thriller.

Still, it is no surprise that two of the most critically acclaimed serial dramas stand out for their resonance with nineteenth-century realism. The first is *The Wire*, a show so self-consciously engaged with Victorian social forms that one of its season 5 episodes is titled "The Dickensian Aspect." The second is *Mad Men*, the Victorianesque quality of which is captured in its famously measured pace. The Victorians "valued slow, steady development in installments over time," in contrast to the "fast-forward" temporality that dominates more recent literature and thought (Hughes and Lund, 275). *Mad Men*'s distinctive style works partly by rejecting this hypermodern tempo: the show is "glacially slow" — a "masterpiece" precisely because "almost nothing happens in any single episode."[3] Contrary to appearances, *Mad Men*'s distinct aesthetic is not the effect merely of its focus on the early 1960s, but also of its reinvention of a realist aesthetic like that of Gustave Flaubert or Anthony Trollope.

Television's invention of neorealist forms coincides with a reconsideration of Victorian realism that is long overdue (see Shaw). For decades a poststructuralist critique of realism has found it guilty of naive referentiality, while a Marxist critique, spearheaded by Georg Lukács, has tasked fiction to apprehend totality in a revolutionary way that realist novels allegedly abandoned after the failed European upheavals of 1848. Whereas Lukács famously argues that novels such as *Madame Bovary* (1856) symptomatize bourgeois stasis (*Historical Novel*), Fredric Jameson contends that realist fiction reproduces a nation-bound frame ("Cognitive Mapping," 349). This tendency to dismiss realism as a depoliticized and moribund form, disarticulated from global process and historical consciousness, extends beyond nineteenth-century examples. When Terry Eagleton wrote in 1976 that Trollope's works are bathed "in a self-consistent blandly undifferentiated ideological space" (191), he anticipated the kind of critique some critics today level against *Mad Men*. Thus for Mark Greif the show exemplifies a smug historical pastiche that arises when realist depiction "of the past is used to congratulate the present."

At its best, nineteenth-century realism is characterized by dense social description, the skillful interlacing of political and domestic plots, and—as a result—the vivid capture of world-historical processes of capitalist globalization. Lukács and Jameson regard literary form as a sensitive index of such change but maintain that realism's capacity to perform this function declined in the mid-nineteenth century, when Flaubert innovated the literary techniques that Emile Zola later codified as "naturalism." Novels such as *Madame Bovary* and *The Prime Minister* subject principal characters to devastating modern forces while maintaining cool narrative distance from the wreckage. For Lukács, fiction of this sort marks the acceptance of "human values" overcome by "the commodity structure of capitalism" (*Studies*, 63). The resulting crisis in bourgeois aesthetics isolates characters, fetishizes detail, reduces the author to "a mere spectator and chronicler of public life," and divorces art from "the real, dramatic and epic movement of social happening" (89, 143).

In our own day, the contrast between a realism that connects human experience to "social happening" and one that dramatizes atomization, deracination, and the quashing of *Bildung* recurs in *The Wire* and *Mad Men*. Like the Dickensian fiction it explicitly invokes, *The Wire*'s multiplot structure, spread over five seasons and sixty episodes, "privileges the social network over the representative character" (C. Levine, "Historicism"; compare Polan, "Invisible City"). Nevertheless, just as Esther's narration in *Bleak House* (1852–53) tempers and subjectivizes the world of Chesney Wold and Tom-all-Alone's, so characters such as the heroized Omar and the honorable Cedric Daniels inject human purpose into *The Wire*'s urban Baltimore.

Yet another aspect of *The Wire*'s Dickensian slant is its autoethnographic structure. For all the multiple webs (drug dealing, law enforcement, labor unions, and so on), the show's implicit scope is consistently Baltimore: an archetype of the U.S. city. While metonymizing urban America as a patchwork of competing matrices of state, federal, and multinational power, "Baltimore" remains a sustainable imagined community (compare Buzard). *The Wire*'s centripetal setting thus stands in marked contrast to *Mad Men*'s early-1960s New York City, which is less an urban infrastructure ("New York" is depicted through a small number of sets) than a hub for the marketing of global commodities. In all of these ways, *Mad Men*'s story world is, in Lukács's terms, more Flaubertian than that of *The Wire*; the "mad" experience it portrays is that of captured human values. Although such fictions are often called naturalistic, they can also be described as *narratives of capitalist globalization* in which conventional modes of bourgeois sovereignty are breached by conspicuous outsiders including speculators, parvenus, people of color, and—most especially—Jews.

Of course, *Mad Men* is also historical fiction, the genre Lukács singles out in *The Historical Novel*. For Lukács, such genres offer the best possible expression of the "life sentiments that [grow] out of concrete, social, historical situations" ("Hegel's *Aesthetics*," 106). And in Europe after the French Revolution that situation is the experience of history itself. This transformation of consciousness became the crucible for works such as Walter Scott's *Ivanhoe* (1819), which figure ongoing class struggle through the typical character. Precisely because he is an "average" man, Ivanhoe embodies contemporary struggles rather than individual greatness—rendering epic history in popular form (Lukács, *Historical Novel*, 33).

Lukács's analysis might seem to bode ill for *Mad Men*, a show celebrated for gorgeous surfaces, meticulous attention to period details, and a male protagonist whose potential to transcend average manhood is at times almost Nietzschean. Yet, for a number of reasons, that appearance is misleading. For example, Lukács holds that forms such as the historical novel are destined to rise, fall, and, potentially, rise again. As genres respond to the *Weltzustand* (state of the world), their shape is determined by "their capacity to bring to expression" the signal features of their sociohistorical moment ("Hegel's *Aesthetics*," 98–99). Hence, as Jameson notes, Lukács's book "calls for a revitalization of the historical novel in radically new social and political configurations": for Lukács, the postrevolutionary Stalinist era, and "for us," "a new moment of multinational capitalism" ("Introduction," 4). This is a noteworthy claim from a critic who tends to treat realism as a passé aesthetic. When Jameson looks for dialectically engaged genres, he generally seeks them in modernism, postmodern film, or science fiction.

That said, Jameson's *The Geopolitical Aesthetic: Cinema and Space in the World System* (1995) describes a conspiratorial genre that is primarily realist. American films such as Alan J. Pakula's *All the President's Men* (1976) and Oliver Stone's *Salvador* (1986) illustrate a vital geopolitical aesthetic at work, bending realist form in the effort "to grasp . . . the social totality as a whole" (36). In such films, rebellious characters become the instigators of crises situated among "the anachronistic traces . . . of a recent historical past"— "the waning of the 1960s" (77). In thus marking the 1960s as the subversive backstory that haunts the postmodern moment, Jameson references what Terry Anderson calls a decade of "social activism and cultural change" (v);

what Todd Gitlin names as "years of hope, days of rage"; and what the editors of a journal on the topic describe as an era of "transformative longing" for, and belief in, "the possibility of dramatic change and the mobilization of this hope" (Varon et al., 2).

Needless to say, this is not the 1960s depicted in the first three seasons of *Mad Men*. By taking the years between March 1960 and December 1963 for its mise-en-scène, the show's first three seasons foreground the opening years of a decade that has been remembered for its dynamic close. Indeed, the show's "glacial" pace and serial form elongate those years indefinitely. To watch *Mad Men* is thus to sublimate and defer that "transformative longing": to wait endlessly (and communally) for the radical 1960s whose "waning" signifies the fallen condition of the present. If *Mad Men* invites its audience to believe in anything, it is not social movements, but isolated feats of self-invention. Protean self-fashioning — a mode of self-advertisement — enables Don to maintain his limited mastery over office politics, geopolitics, and domestic and sexual politics. That is the secret to his having nine lives.

In fact, *Mad Men*'s objective situation is not the 1960s at all, but today's neoliberal condition: a *Weltzustand* in which the radical 1960s are not so much "waning" as mythologized, derided, and repressed — if never quite forgotten. The show might even seem to be nostalgic pastiche — a form "beyond history" in representing a "pathological" inability to deal with time (Jameson, "Postmodernism," 117) — but for its likeness to the nineteenth century's serial novels. Distinct from nonserial media like movies, as well as postmodern serial television like *The Sopranos*, *Mad Men*'s nonpastiche aesthetic recreates the tempo of mid-Victorian serial fiction in making the lived experiences of its characters stretch slowly *over* time and, thus, *in* it. A serialized successor to the conspiratorial films of the 1980s and '90s, *Mad Men* embeds its aberrant protagonist in a "process of historical obsolescence" (Jameson, *Geopolitical Aesthetic*, 77): a world of broadsheet newspapers, electric typewriters, middle-class prosperity, glamorous air travel, and overt sexism and racism, which defamiliarizes present-day experience while remaining palpable to it. Aiding *Mad Men* in evoking this realist geopolitical aesthetic are a set of formal structures that work through the motifs of Judaized otherness and virtualized Jewishness.

VIRTUALIZED JEWISHNESS AS GEOPOLITICAL AESTHETIC

In a vivid account of mid-Victorian London, Lynda Nead cites an article from 1862 that declares: "In forming our idea of the great capital of the British Empire and of the nineteenth century . . . we naturally . . . call her 'the Modern Babylon'" (3). This image of London as Victorian Babylon—"the centre of a global commerce that was subjugating the rest of the world"—was double edged. For then as now, Babylon conjured destructive "worship of the commodity" as well as the awe of modern progress (Nead, 3). Of course, Babylon is also the setting for the haunting Psalm 137, "By the waters/river of Babylon," which, along with comparable passages from the Book of Exodus, figures the experience of exile, captivity, and estrangement. Ordered by their Babylonian captors to "sing us one of the songs of Zion," the exiled Jews of Psalm 137 ask, "How shall we sing the Lord's song in a strange land?"

The mid-Victorian era was a period of rising anti-Semitism as Benjamin Disraeli's political ascent saw the biblical narrative of Moses in Egypt used to "underscore the idea of the secret Jew who subverts and eventually destroys the dominant culture in which he lives" (Ragussis, 236). As the gas-lit emporium became an ambivalent sign of modern commerce, firms such as Moses and Son, a well-known outfitter of men's ready-to-wear clothing, became the "butt of mid-Victorian anti-Semitism," singled out for its "ostentatious" display (Nead, 89). If the best-known literary example of Victorian Mosaism is Eliot's philo-Semitic *Daniel Deronda*, whose story of emergent Jewish nationalism began to appear in February 1876, Trollope's Lopez was already providing a less sympathetic instance of the "secret Jew." Lopez explicitly identifies himself with Moses, describing his father-in-law as "an Egyptian" whom he "will despoil" just as "the Israelites despoiled the Egyptians" (456; see Exodus 3:22). Lopez's secret status is ambiguous: his Jewish descent is alleged but never confirmed. Trollope's narrative thus indicts ambiguity as much as Jewishness itself; as Ragussis writes, "Jewish ancestry" becomes almost synonymous with "unknown ancestry" (249).

Mad Men's Don Draper is another self-made man with mysterious origins. Don's hidden identity is the show's central motif: "He could be Batman," says Harry Crane ("Marriage of Figaro," 1.3). "Who's in there?" Betty whispers to her sleeping husband at the end of the second episode ("Ladies Room," 1.2). For while she knows that Don "doesn't like to talk about himself," she also suspects that the husband whose family she has never met has more than infidelity to hide. As her father reminds her, "He's got no people. You can't trust a man like that" ("The Color Blue," 3.10). When Roger Sterling prods Don about his childhood, Don replies: "Think of me as Moses. I was a baby in a basket" (1.2).

It may, nonetheless, seem perverse to compare Trollope's largely pejorative depiction of the secret Jew to *Mad Men*—a turn-of-the-millennium narrative about America's postwar past in which the figure of the Jew often stands for the assimilative pressures of the so-called American Century. Yet as Aamir Mufti argues, Europe's nineteenth-century "Jewish Question" provides an illuminating paradigm for minority subjects in our postcolonial moment. Then too, Trollope's anti-Semitism is not straightforward. If Lopez expresses Trollope's perception "that the traditional British enclosure of gentleman and ladies was being invaded by golddiggers, speculators, and Jews" (Kendrick, 136–37), it is also true that this arch-figure of the stranger is as clearly the victim of prejudice as the embodiment of Judaized depredation. The most consistent feature of the Jewishness depicted in British writing, according to Bryan Cheyette, is its "protean instability" (8). Nineteenth-century literature does not "draw on eternal myths of 'the Jew'" so much as illustrate the dialectic between constructions of Jewishness and of Britain's own national, ethnic, and—I would add—global identities (268).

What is true for British literature is true also for *Mad Men*, which depicts American experience through the prism of Madison Avenue's golden age, in dialogue with Jewishness in various forms. Indeed, *Mad Men* indulges in an unapologetic Jewish exceptionalism. Peppered with Jewish referents, the show includes few African Americans and other minorities. By contrast, *Mad Men* makes anti-Semitism endemic to a postwar New York City in which Jews are both ubiquitous and excluded. "Have we ever hired any Jews?" asks Roger in the pilot, hoping to impress a Jewish client. "Not on my watch," Don replies ("Smoke Gets in Your Eyes," 1.1).

Such remarks would not surprise Rachel Menken, the Jewish department store heiress and client with whom Don has a passionate affair. Rachel is the first of several Judaized love interests for Don in a pattern that finds him married to the Nordic-Teutonic Betty—a Bryn Mawr graduate and "Main Line brat" ("Shut the Door. Have a Seat," 3.13)—while having affairs with women whose social situation and unconventional femininity more closely resemble his own invented persona.[4] More interesting than this split in male desire are the subject positions of secret and virtual Jewishness it enacts. While Rachel figures explicit Jewish identity, *Mad Men* features many characters who in various ways appear to be Jewish. Indeed, the showrunner Matthew Weiner has said that he "hope[s] people can tell," or "know at some level," that certain assimilated characters are Jews (qtd. in Itzkoff). Jimmy Barrett and his wife Bobbie (with whom Don has an affair in season 2) are, according to Weiner, "transparently Jewish," while Faye Miller (Don's lover throughout much of season 4) is someone whom Weiner hopes people can tell is Jewish (qtd. in Itzkoff).

Hopes people can tell. If so, why not give Faye an unmistakably Jewish name, or a father named Yankel or Solly? And if Bobbie is "transparently" Jewish, why not have her use Yiddish words, as does Don's accountant, or the Hebrew phrase *l'chaim* for a toast, as does Roy, the young playwright who eventually comes between Don and his beatnik mistress Midge? Why, in other words, does Weiner confirm the Jewish identity of certain characters in interviews, while *Mad Men* itself stops at suggesting the possibility that these and many other characters *might* be Jewish?[5]

The answer, I believe, is to cast these figures as secret Jews: the kind whose ultimate referent, like Lopez's, is not Jewishness per se, but ambiguous identity. That *Mad Men* is thick with characters who may be Jews means that Weiner's "story about . . . assimilation" demonstrates neither the erasure of Jewish difference nor a tolerant multiculturalism in which self-proclaimed Jews claim the same respect as social insiders such as Betty or Pete Campbell (qtd. in Itzkoff). Rather, *Mad Men* depicts Jewishness as at once legible (inviting viewers to detect Jewish signs) and ambiguous (denying the certainty granted to Rachel). Historically, "secret Jew" was one of the names given to Spanish or Portuguese Jews who, though forced to convert during the Inquisition, maintained stealthy allegiance to Jewish faith. This early-modern notion of subterranean Jewry was exacerbated by the later nineteenth century's tendency to racialize ethnic difference—suggesting the impossibility of authentic Jewish conversion. The upshot in Trollope's imaginary is to make unconverted Jews more sympathetic than self-proclaimed Christians like Lopez and the real-life Disraeli. Rather than egregious prejudice, Trollope's ambivalence shows how anti-Semitism thrives within modernity's universalistic premise. Victorian Britain instances the nation-state's tendency to suppress "alternative collectivities, local and diasporic loyalties" in the effort to modernize and unify a diverse population (Cheyette and Valman, 2). Jewish immutability is thus as central to Eliot's philo-Semitic imaginary as to Trollope's Lopez: both novels adopt an Exodus narrative in which departure for the Promised Land—through Zionism or death—is the only escape from troubled identity.

An exemplary narrative of capitalist globalization, *The Prime Minister* portrays Victorian Babylon as the disenchanted site of breached sovereignty and substanceless exchange (see Goodlad, "Trollopian 'Foreign Policy'"). *Mad Men*'s neoliberal variation secularizes the motif of the secret Jew, shifting the stakes of ethnic immutability from nineteenth-century *conversion* to twentieth-century *assimilation*. Rachel aside, the show figures metropolitan

Jewishness as the paradoxical state of both revealing and hiding one's "true" identity. In doing so, *Mad Men* instances the kind of double bind that Eve Sedgwick called the regime of the "open secret" (67). Yet *Mad Men* goes further still in universalizing the condition of secret Jewry. Whereas *The Prime Minister* and *Daniel Deronda* are famous for narrative splitting—the Lopez plot versus the Palliser plot, and the "Jewish" Deronda plot versus the "English" Gwendolen plot—*Mad Men* articulates today's metropolitan imaginary by making Don a "virtual Jew" in whom the minority subject's aberrant particularity and the majority subject's universalist status collide. If this is a demonstrably late-capitalist phenomenon, enabled by the ever more contingent and hybrid content of "identity" under neoliberalism, it is also a message that has been legible in Exodus and Psalm 137 for centuries.

Don's virtual Jewishness is the heart of *Mad Men*'s geopolitical aesthetic, enabling the show's reinvention of a mid-Victorian motif: precarious identity amplified through the form of serialized realism. But crucial to this premise is the viewer's awareness that Don is not, in actuality, a secret Jew—or, for that matter, a closeted gay or passing black man. Rather, as viewers learn in the first season, Don is actually Dick Whitman—a Midwestern farm boy who, like a latter-day Jay Gatsby, took the fog of war as the opportunity to re-create himself. An enlisted soldier who deserts after stealing the identity of his dead commanding officer, Don, or rather Dick, was born dirt poor. He is the bastard son of a crusty farmer's illicit union with a prostitute. These fragments emerge through flashbacks spread across multiple episodes, inflecting Don's efforts to maintain his invented persona and conceal his past. *Mad Men* thus makes sustaining Don's unknowability the core of its story line: its open secret.[6]

While this narrative is potentially melodramatic and sensational, the slow pace (thirty-six episodes for a wife to look inside her husband's desk drawer!), the emphasis on character, and the structure of synchronic episodes in a diachronic story line endow the first three seasons of *Mad Men* with the novelistic cast of naturalist aesthetics. Through the serial form's gradual unfolding, these multiplot but thematically unified episodes can stand alone artistically, even while contributing to an overarching trajectory. Richest of all, and indicative of *Mad Men*'s neo-Lukácsian form, is the careful emplotment of Don's story in early-1960s history. Season 1 aligns the troubled Draper marriage with Kennedy's win over Nixon, auguring change; season 2 pairs Betty's pregnancy and the couple's reconciliation with the Cuban missile crisis; and season 3 finds Betty leaving Don for the staid

Henry amid the turmoil of the Kennedy assassination. Don's virtual Jewishness is thus a slow-burning realist effect, meditated and discussed by viewers from episode to episode, season to season.

THE MODERN BABYLON

While *Mad Men*'s play with Jewishness recurs throughout the series, one particular episode — "Babylon" (1.6) — encapsulates the show's distinct geopolitical aesthetic. Laden with biblical references, the episode begins with Genesis as Don, falling on the stairs, flashes back to a "fall" after the birth of his half brother, Adam. "Babylon" then moves to Exodus courtesy of a visit from the Israeli Ministry of Tourism who, encouraged by the popularity of Leon Uris's 1958 novel, seeks the help of Madison Avenue. While reading *Exodus*, Don learns that Betty's first kiss was from a Jewish boy named Rosenberg at a dance organized to help "those poor skinny people in the boats" — that is, refugees from the Holocaust like those on the real-life SS *Exodus*, the inspiration for Uris's novel and the movie of 1960 to come.[7]

"Babylon" combines Psalm 137's meditations on exile and captivity with the Old Testament's most powerful deliverance story. As George Bornstein writes, "For centuries the narrative of Moses leading the enslaved children of Israel out of bondage in Egypt into freedom in Canaan has represented liberation of the spirit from things of this world" (374). Exodus has been invoked by English Puritans, African Americans, Irish republicans, Rastafarians, and Mormons, among others. Psalm 137, with its haunting rendering of "Babylon" as chronotope, also resonates across time and space.[8] Frederick Douglass made the psalm a centerpiece of his speech "The Meaning of July Fourth for the Negro" (1852), and Benjamin Zephaniah gave it a dub spin in his poem "City River Blues" (1996). The psalm has inspired musical arrangements from Lord Byron's collaboration with Isaac Nathan in 1814 to "Babylon," a track on Don McLean's album *American Pie* (1971) — the arrangement used in *Mad Men*.

Of course, Exodus is also a focal point for Middle East politics. Exodus motifs were central to England's colonial imaginary, supplying a vision of Anglo-Saxon settlement as Promised Land that became a founding myth of the United States. But, according to Jonathan Boyarin, it was not until the 1940s — the period of Betty's refugees — that Exodus was harnessed to a project of Jewish nationhood. The travails of ships like the SS *Exodus*, which carried Jewish refugees to Palestine in the face of British hostility, fostered pro-Zionist analogies between liberation from Egypt and the founding of

FIGURE 16.1. Paul Newman as Ari Ben Canaan and George Maharis as Yoav (*Exodus*, 1960).

a Jewish homeland. The use of "Exodus" to denote a continuum of Jewish experience—in Egypt, in Europe under the Nazis, in transit to Palestine, and, finally, in Israel fighting for nationhood—was "popularized immensely" through Uris's novel and Otto Preminger's film (Boyarin, 59). In this way, *Exodus* helped to affirm a "special relationship" between Israel and the United States at around the same time that the term *Holocaust* came to signify the Nazis' genocidal assault on Europe's Jews.

Central both to novel and film was the construction of the "new Jew" as product of postdiasporic nationhood. Critics have noted the remarkable casting of the fair-haired, blue-eyed Paul Newman (of Jewish descent on his father's side) in the role of Ari Ben Canaan—literally "Lion, child of Canaan"—alongside actors such as the Italian American Sal Mineo and the Greek American George Maharis (the latter a sex symbol after his starring role in the macho television series *Route 66*).[9] These Hollywood stars portrayed Jewish manhood as handsome, action oriented, and aggressive, thus overturning anti-Semitic caricature and the status of victimhood (fig. 16.1). Yet another noteworthy choice was the casting of the British Jill Haworth to play Karen, a blonde Holocaust survivor befriended by Kitty Fremont, an American Christian portrayed by Eva Marie Saint. Over the course of the narrative Kitty transits from American spectator to Karen's substitute mother and Ari's lover. As Ella Shohat writes, "the same Waspish-looking woman" who confides to a British officer that she "feel[s] strange among" Jews "becomes an enthusiastic supporter of Zionism" (66). *Exodus*'s cultural work included translating Zionism into U.S.-friendly form, neutralizing Arabs (through Ari's Palestinian "brother"), and burying the Shoah (through Karen's death). In all of these ways, the text depicts a post-Holocaust Jewry redeemed through nationhood and a "new Israeli identity free of the burden of Jewish diaspora" (Loshitzky, 125).

Mad Men's engagement of this terrain hardly illuminates the Palestinian plight, but neither does it hew to *Exodus*'s Zionist narrative. Perusing photographs of Holocaust victims and a boat like the *Exodus*, Don opines, "I can see why they want the guns." But during most of the episode he is less moved by Jewish suffering or stirred by Jewish heroism than stumped by the task of making Israel a tourist destination. "So," he quips, "we have a quasi-communist state where women have guns. And it's filled with Jews. Well, not completely filled; let's not forget there are also Arabs."

As we have seen, *Exodus*'s "new Jew" squares the circle of liberal universalism, elevating Jews from diaspora into the family of nations; Newman's Westernized, masculine Ari stably occupies the double position of idealized sabra and universal paragon, just as Israel stands for Jewish homeland as well as Promised Land. By contrast, *Mad Men*—to borrow a line from the Paul Simon song that closes one of season 4's episodes—depicts a "long road to Canaan" with no end in sight.[10] Whereas *Exodus* proffers Israeli identity "free from the burden of the Jewish diaspora," *Mad Men* makes diaspora the archetypal condition of global modernity and makes New York City the new Modern Babylon (Loshitzky, 128).[11]

This revision of *Exodus* is announced by the hyper-Judaized form of Lily Meyer and Yoram Ben Shulhai, the visiting Israelis. In contrast to Rachel, an icon of diasporic glamour, or to assimilated secret Jews like the Barretts, Lily's heavy accent, wrinkled mien, and dowdy dress mark her as an "old Jew" and probable Holocaust survivor. If her name recalls Golda Meir, the future Iron Lady of Israeli politics, Lily's demeanor evokes Frau Blücher, the dour housekeeper of Mel Brooks's *Young Frankenstein* (1974), played for laughs by Cloris Leachman. Her younger male colleague, Yoram (mispronounced as "Urine" by a clueless Roger), is a swarthy sabra in contrast to the dashing Hollywood alternatives portrayed by Newman and Maharis. The same patriotism that heroizes the *Exodus* characters makes Lily and Yoram look out of place—their earnestness alien to a world in which hedonism and stylish self-fashioning are the ethos of the day. "This is America," says Bobbie in a line that defines her as secret Jew as well as neoliberal subject; "Pick a job and then become the person that does it" ("For Those Who Think Young," 2.1). Such protean self-fashioning is precisely the aspect of a commodity culture that the Israelis seek for the economic well-being of their fledgling nation, but which they—saturated with Jewish history—cannot perform. Their exchange with Don is ironic as *Mad Men*'s viewers, trained to applaud self-invention, confront a robust identity, morally superior to Madison Avenue, but stripped of the glamour of the new Modern Babylon.

Still, Don is visibly discomfited by the Israelis, whose embodied Jewishness troubles his cool Manhattan façade. Though their wish to parlay the popularity of *Exodus* into tourism is straightforward, Don protests too much—repeatedly reminding them they are outsiders. As Roger explains, the task at hand is to portray Israel as "a land of exotic luxury," positioning Haifa as the Rome of the Middle East. "Of course," Don objects, "Rome has the Colosseum." "And Tel Aviv is about to have a Hilton," returns Roger. His remark anticipates season 3, in which the eccentric Conrad Hilton takes a shine to Don, whom he imagines as a self-made maverick like himself. In a crucial line that he attributes to Don, Hilton captures the hubris of global hegemony: "America is wherever we look, wherever we're going to be" ("Wee Small Hours," 3.9).

The Israeli plan to partner with Olympic Cruise Lines indexes an epoch in capitalism's history when success in the global market meant seducing America's consumers. Don's Hilton campaign plays to American hubris. "How do you say 'fresh towels' in Farsi?" his tagline reads, prompting the answer, "Hilton" (3.9). The "Babylon" episode thus finds Don resisting his own game, reluctant to accept Israel as a global commodity Americans will buy. Brandishing *Exodus*, Lily insists, "This book has been on the best-seller list for two years in the States. . . . America has a love affair with Israel." But Don's answer is a nod to religion: "You saved me some leg work. All *I* have is the Bible." "Let's stay away from *that*," Yoram answers. The scene closes with Don asking the Israelis to describe their "ideal tourist." He asks, "What's their yearly salary?" Lily replies, "Whatever *you* make."

In season 3 Don and Betty travel to Rome ("Souvenir," 3.8), rekindling their romance in a setting that invites comparison to the courtship of Kitty and Ari in *Exodus* (figs. 16.2–16.3). The analogy explains Don's reluctance to pursue America's "love affair with Israel." Whereas the *Exodus* scenario aligns him with the American Kitty, Don, of course, is what passes for *Mad Men*'s hero. A closeted outsider and virtual Jew, he can no more incarnate Kitty's Midwestern wonder than Ari's devotion to the Promised Land.

When Sal holds up the image of a dark-haired Jewess to suggest a selling point for Israel—"The people are good looking"—Don recalls his passion for Rachel, who warily agrees to meet him for lunch. Rachel's importance is established in the show's opening episodes: her stable diasporic Jewishness stands for a feminized power that, for all its glamour, is more substance than show. When Pete suggests that "there are a dozen agencies better suited to

FIGURE 16.2. Ari and Kitty in the "Rome of the Middle East" (*Exodus*, 1960).

FIGURE 16.3. Don and Betty in Rome ("Souvenir," 3.8).

[Rachel's] needs," she retorts that if she wanted an ad man "from the same village as [her] father," she would not be meeting with Sterling Cooper (1.1). Rachel thus defines herself as one who does not hide Jewish identity, but will not be defined by it either. Her family business is a luxury department store adjacent to Tiffany's, not a *Jewish* department store. Frustrated by her resistance, Don asks her the same question he later puts to Lily and Yoram: "So what kind of people do you want?" "I want *your* kind of people, Mr. Draper," she replies, identifying Don (just as the Israelis do) as the American ideal.

Don's anxieties in the pilot ostensibly stem from his having nothing to pitch to Lucky Strike, the firm's biggest account. The entire episode is framed by a marketing problem: how does one advertise an addictive and lethal product when bogus health claims are no longer permissible? Soon after the encounter with Rachel, Don meets with market researcher Greta Guttman, another heavily accented and austere middle-aged woman who, like Lily, appears to be an "old Jew" and possible Holocaust survivor. "Before the war, when I studied with Adler in Vienna," she says apropos of Lucky Strike, "we postulated that what Freud called 'the Death Wish' is as powerful a drive as those for sexual reproduction and physical sustenance." Don's aversion is palpable: "Dr. Guttman, psychology is terrific at a cocktail party," but "people were buying cigarettes before Freud was born."[12] When he tosses her report into the trash, viewers know that her findings are partly correct: she offers "conclusive proof" that neither low-tar nor filtered cigarettes reduce the incidence of lung cancer. Still, Don is also correct: the issue for advertisers is not *"why* should people smoke?" but "why should people smoke *Lucky Strike?"*

Though he does not realize it, Don's sparring with this probable Jew inspires the insight that later wows the Lucky Strike executives: while "everybody else's tobacco is poisonous," he tells them, "Lucky Strike's is toasted." Don's strategy extracts a desirable particular from a universal negation. Advertising, he explains, is "freedom from fear. It's a billboard on the side of the road that screams with reassurance that whatever you're doing is OK." Ironically, the fear that prompts this winning insight is not Don's fear of death, but the fear of unmasking that Greta's ambiguous identity provokes.

In "Babylon," when Don meets Rachel he tells her that the Israelis ("those people") were "definitely Zionists." "Zion just means Israel," she answers; "It's a very old name." "I'm American," she says, "I'm really not very Jewish"—though she is Jewish enough to point out the significance of Adolf Eichmann's recent arrest. A "country for 'those people,' as you call us," she says (with her use of "us" linking her with the Israelis), "seems very important." "My life is here," she goes on; "I'll visit but I don't need to live there. It just has to *be*." Rachel thus voices a common Jewish American standpoint: both identified and nonidentified with Israel, she professes to balance Jewish and American identities as though they were seamless. She endorses Jewish nationhood but neither regards herself as an Israeli nor acknowledges Zionism as a political construction. Still less does she consider the Palestinian people. Like the popularity of *Exodus*, such reflexive pro-Zionism among Jewish Americans who regard themselves as "not very Jewish" has been integral to forging the "special relationship" between Israel and the United States.

But in *Mad Men*'s symbolic imaginary, Rachel's support for a Jewish homeland is less salient than the "Babylon" she helps to evoke. Neither wholly assimilated like a secret Jew nor affixed to Israel like a committed Zionist, she is the only character to exemplify diaspora as a kind of rooted cosmopolitanism. As such, Rachel sees beneath Don's façade: "I know what it feels like to be out of place," she tells him, "and there is something about you that tells me you know it too" (1.1). If these words announce her as the one woman who can help Don face up to his secrets, the moment is fleeting. A married man, he cannot pledge himself to this diasporic goddess, or find Canaan in her embrace.

Mad Men thus reads Psalm 137 against a redemptive narrative of return. In *Exodus*, Kitty tells Ari that there "are no differences" between Jews and Christians, cementing the love affair between Israel and America. But in "Babylon," when Don asks Rachel to explain "the difference," she points to the condition of exiles singing for their captors. "Look," she says, "Jews have lived in exile for a long time. First in Babylon. Then all over the world . . . and we've managed to make a go of it. It might have something to do with the fact that we thrive at doing business with people who hate us." Whereas Kitty's comment universalizes the Promised Land, Rachel's anticipates Babylon as global condition, and the exilic Jew as its paradigmatic subject.

Later in the season, Don shows up at Rachel's door. Consummating his long-simmering desire, he tells her he is the bastard son of a drunk and a prostitute ("Long Weekend," 1.10). But though Rachel has anticipated this mélange of passion and confession, she knows their coupling has "no future" (1.6). When Pete discovers Don's fraudulent identity, Don asks Rachel to start a new life in California. "What kind of man *are* you?" she asks, stunned by his readiness to uproot their lives. "This was a dalliance, a cheap affair. You don't want to run away with me; you just want to run away" ("Nixon vs. Kennedy," 1.12). This finale is foreshadowed in "Babylon" through the allusion to utopia, which, as Rachel tells Don, etymologically combines "good place" and "no place." In a coded exchange as much about their romance as about Zionism, Rachel intimates that the Promised Land is "the place that cannot be." "Babylon" thus concludes with Don's visit to Midge, his Greenwich Village mistress, where their tryst is interrupted by a visit from the jealous Roy. The episode ends with the three assembled at a nightclub to hear the live performance of a friend, the male rivalry shut down by a musical version of Psalm 137.

SINGING THE LORD'S SONG IN A STRANGE LAND

"By the rivers of Babylon, there we sat down, yeah, we wept, when
    we remembered Zion. . . .
For there they that carried us away captive required of us a song;
    and they that wasted us
required of us mirth, saying, Sing us one of the songs of Zion.
How shall we sing the LORD's song in a strange land?"
(Psalm 137, ll. 1, 3–4)

The sixth of thirteen episodes, "Babylon" is the center of season 1's arc, proffering a rich illustration of how *Mad Men*'s "chapters" reinvent the synchronicity of serialized realism. As a virtual story line in a multiplot web, Don's narrative intersects with the stories of four female characters (Rachel, Joan, Betty, and Peggy), each of whom exerts her own center of gravity while refracting his. Whereas Victorian multiplot fictions use free indirect style to enmesh secret Jews in the lives of others, *Mad Men* uses televisual forms such as music and montage to articulate synchronous experience. Thus, "Babylon" discloses Joan's affair with Roger, who has bought her a caged bird—an age-old symbol of female captivity (fig. 16.4). Likewise, "Babylon" highlights a new dimension of Betty's dependence. Frequently likened to a child, she is also sexually hungry, thinking about her husband "all day." "It's all in a kind of fog because . . . I want you so badly," she tells Don, intensifying the "secret" of his infidelity. Finally, with the introduction of Belle Jolie's lipstick account, "Babylon" features Peggy Olson's chance remark about a "basket of kisses," revealing to her male superiors that Don's young secretary is a creative force (it's "like watching a dog play piano," says Freddy Rumsen).

    The montage that accompanies the performance of Psalm 137 synchronizes Don's response with the contemporaneous experiences of the show's "mad women." As a trio of musicians begins literally to sing the Lord's song,

FIGURE 16.4. Joan looks at a caged bird ("Babylon," 1.6).

the camera closes in on Don's expression. The scene then fades to a wistful Rachel, arranging men's ties; and then to Betty playing dress-up with Sally, teaching her how to apply lipstick. The latter image not only figures Betty's own dress-up—the dependent marriage that infantilizes her—but also Peggy's earlier moment during the Belle Jolie focus group in which, while the other "chickens" play compliantly with lipsticks, Peggy refuses to be "one of a hundred colors in a box." When the camera fades back to Don, he is immersed in mournful reflection (fig. 16.5). The scene then cuts to Roger and Joan departing from their tryst, the caged bird in Joan's hands. Finally, as the music reaches an end, Joan and Roger stand on opposite sides of the hotel entrance, pretending to be strangers.

The white, middle-class patriarchy of *Mad Men* divides wives from husbands and deforms the ambitions of working women. Yet Don's emotional world is also dominated by the "images of enclosure and escape," "maddened doubles," and "metaphors of physical discomfort" familiar to nineteenth-century women's writing (S. Gilbert and Gubar, xi), as the image used to publicize season 3 (fig. 16.6) perfectly demonstrates. That Don is himself a "Mad Man in the attic" is occasionally literalized, as in season 4's allusion to Dorian Gray.[13] But at a figurative level, Don's virtuality opens him to a range of alienated identifications whose common threads are exile, captivity, and the necessity of singing. From this perspective Don is not only a closeted male like Lopez or Dorian, but also a madwoman in his own right, like Flaubert's Emma Bovary.

I have suggested that *Mad Men* and *The Prime Minister* are serialized nar-

FIGURE 16.5. Don, fading in, listens to "Babylon" as Sally and Betty, playing dress-up, fade out ("Babylon," 1.6).

ratives of capitalist globalization that exemplify a rich naturalist engagement of global forces. While Trollope's secret Jew anticipates *Mad Men*'s troping on neoliberal identity, the show is famous for a conscious aestheticism that Trollope, by and large, eschews. In this respect, Flaubert is *Mad Men*'s most salient precursor. For while Flaubert's Modern Babylon abjures the racial animus that would Judaize a figure like his Monsieur Lheureux in a Trollope novel, *Madame Bovary* anticipates *Mad Men*'s stake in the stylized surfaces and sensuous textures that punctuate the life lived through commodities.

"This is all there is," Don insists as he embraces Rachel, persuading her for a time that adulterous passion is better than no passion at all (1.10). *Mad Men*'s narrative arc has something of *Madame Bovary*'s finitude: although Don does not end his life at the close of season 3 (with Sterling Cooper's reboot signaling new beginnings), there is a sense in which *Mad Men* is to this point a three-decker novel whose denouement is Betty's discovery of Don's "Jewishness" and the subsequent collapse of their marriage. Formally, *Mad Men* cultivates Bovaryesque pace, a Flaubertian eye for detail, and what Caroline Levine, writing in this volume, calls "the shock of the banal." While *Madame Bovary* is not a multiplot novel, it produces careful synchronies, as when the blind beggar's song shatters Emma's fantasy of a magical "Babylon" (207). Like Don's hearing Psalm 137 in the company of his mistress, the beggar's voice pierces Emma's escapist pleasure, revealing a well of melancholy. As Don might say, she lived her life "like there's no tomorrow" (1.1).

Yet while Emma and Don are both ardent hedonists, neither is wholly

FIGURE 16.6.
Metaphors of
physical discomfort
(season 3 publicity).

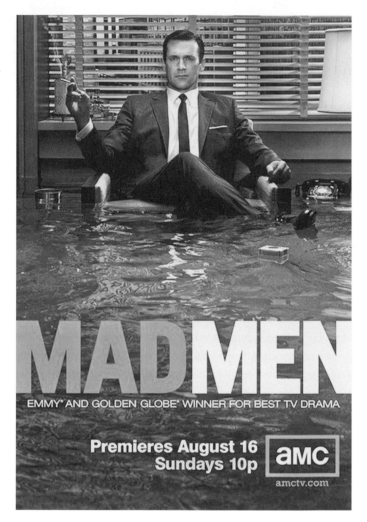

cynical; each believes in illusions at least some of the time. Both, to borrow
Henry James's line about Emma, remain "absorbed in romantic intention
and vision while fairly rolling in the dust" (80). Their intense yearning for
the realization of what is only imaginary paradoxically humanizes as well as
corrupts them. If Don fares better it is because his male privilege includes
the modern vocation Flaubert's novel foreshadows. While both live their
lives as "one long tissue of lies" (Flaubert, 213), Don alone is a paid story-
teller — saved, though never redeemed, by his work in advertising. Emma, by
contrast, is an ad man *avant la lettre*. Though highly skilled in "readaptations"
of life (Ferguson, 11) — her every move intended to "scream with reassurance that whatever she's doing is OK" — Emma must invent herself through

buying. This is how she sings for her captors, personified by the insidious Lheureux.[14]

The point of *Mad Men*'s aestheticism, like that of Flaubert, is hardly to express complacency. As Michael Schudson has shown, advertising's mode is *capitalist realism*—a form antithetical to historical engagement (209–33). In contrast to Lukács's call for a realism of concrete social situations, advertising offers dematerialized abstractions. Advertising's trick is its appeal to the emotions: as Don tells Peggy, "*You* are the product, you feeling something. That's what sells" (2.1). Advertising produces this phantasmatic effect in the effort to fill the gap between human needs and the consumer habits that leave them unsated. As Raymond Williams writes, "the system of organised magic which is modern advertising" is first and foremost a means of obscuring political alternatives ("Advertising"). In such a world, adultery is to needy modern subjects what advertising is to capitalism; for, as Schudson puts it, "advertising is capitalism's way of saying I love you to itself" (232). When Don tells Rachel that "guys like me" invented love to sell nylons (1.1), he explains why he gives his best hours to the task of mystifying commodities. Along with the latest romantic seduction, creating new ways for capitalism to say "I love you to itself" is the only channel he knows for poiesis and self-love alike.

Were *Mad Men*'s achievement merely to ironize the advertising world it aestheticizes, the show might risk the kind of naturalist impasse that Lukács calls "mirroring . . . the humdrum reality of capitalism" (*Studies*, 93). But in various ways, its reinvention of serialized realism does considerably more. By cultivating the viewer's belief that the show's virtual subject is better than the world that made him—as when it synchronizes Don's experience with that of compelling female characters—*Mad Men* intensifies the habits of watching his (and their) stories unfold over time, inducing private reflection, communal discussion, and waiting (waiting for the next season, waiting for the 1960s to come at last, waiting for what Frank Kermode called "the sense of an ending").

Studies of advertising and literature that have not considered the impact of seriality thus neglect a feature of realist narrative worth considering.[15] In *Advertising Fictions: Literature, Advertisement, and Social Reading* (1988), Jennifer Wicke writes that advertising is, for the foreseeable future, "interminable . . . because there will be a plethora of stories to tell" (175). Likewise, Bill Brown argues that advertising is interesting to Henry James because it intuits how artistic forms assert the imaginative "subject over the object" (20). To consider advertising from this aesthetic perspective is to confront the fact that all forms of realism, like all forms of art, rely on imaginative subjectivities of some kind.

Yet when James writes on *Madame Bovary*, he sets aside *l'art pour l'art* to emphasize a moment in time. He writes:

> The author of these remarks remembers . . . that when a very young person in Paris he took up from the parental table the latest number of the periodical in which Flaubert's then duly unrecognized masterpiece was in course of publication. The moment is not historic, but it was to become in the light of history . . . so unforgettable that every small feature of it yet again lives for him: it rests there like the backward end of the span. The cover of the old *Revue de Paris* was yellow . . . and *Madame Bovary: Moeurs de Province* . . . was already . . . as a title, mysteriously arresting, inscrutably charged. I was ignorant of what had preceded and was not to know till much later what followed; but present to me still is the act of standing there before the fire . . . and taking in what I might of that installment, taking it in with so surprised an interest, and perhaps as well such a stir of faint foreknowledge, that the sunny little salon, the autumn day, the window ajar and the cheerful outside clatter of the Rue Montaigne are all now for me more or less in the story and the story more or less in them. (77–78)

As James makes clear, his adequate appreciation of *Madame Bovary* requires him to consider Flaubert's story as an experience in seriality that takes place in time. That experience, moreover, inhabits James's memory indistinguishably from certain histories that only later become accessible to his cognition: Emma's full narrative arc, *Madame Bovary*'s evolution from scandalous text to literary masterpiece, and James's own development from "very young person" into the "author of these remarks." Finally, James's experience — what Don might call "*James* feeling something" — is no less an experience of seriality for its entering in medias res, temporarily isolated from the beginnings and endings that structure realist form. So far from decadent detail, James's *Madame Bovary* lives in its rescue of an otherwise fragmentary moment, its vivid affects (the "surprised" interest and "stir" of foreknowledge) now woven inseparably into Emma's history, the history of *Madame Bovary*, and the (then) ongoing history of Henry James. James's account of *Madame Bovary* is thus different from any imaginable account of a particular advertising text, no matter how charged, surprised, or stirring. For while advertising artfully produces feeling in medias res, its fragments are absolute; not histories but abstractions of histories that cannot "rest there like the backward end of the span."

It is therefore crucial to recognize that *Mad Men*, however playfully coy, knows the difference between advertising and its own serial realism. Indeed, in one of its most famous scenes, Don pitches the Kodak "Carousel" by way of illustrating this very point. "Nostalgia," as he explains, "literally means 'the pain from an old wound.' It's a twinge in your heart far more powerful than memory alone." Using Kodak's new device to screen happy scenes from a marriage that he is inexorably destroying, Don tells us (and his clients) that we are looking at a "time machine." "It goes backwards, and forwards," taking us "to a place where we ache to go again. . . . It lets us travel the way a child travels—around and around and back home again" ("The Wheel," 1.13).

Don's winning pitch is precisely the form Schudson identifies as capitalist realism: isolating a series of attractive moments, it disarticulates them from concrete histories, and elevates the sentimentality to an abstract ideal—eliciting desire for the sentiment and, presumably, for the product. By the end of season 1, *Mad Men*'s savvy viewers can see that Don has exploited his own reservoir of despair to produce this affective "story" for advertising. But "The Wheel" is not advertising, but the concluding episode in a long season arc at the heart of which is the lingering aperçu of Don in Babylon, singing for his captors. Thus Don's description of the "time machine," its backward and forward motion taking us "around and around and back home again," is a metaphor for the experience of serial viewers. His painful wound, aching for any number of objects he has lost while spinning a long tissue of lies in the first volume of *Mad Men*'s three-decker novel, is not (or not only) a brilliant pitch. It is also a structure of feeling that lives for the viewer of serialized realism, resting there like the backward span of time.

NOTES

1. The quotes are from Trollope, 10, 11.

2. See the introduction by Asa Briggs for the Trollope Society's edition of *The Prime Minister*: http://www.trollopesociety.org/palliser.php#thepm (accessed November 2011).

3. See Lucy Mangan's comments on the show in Tim Lusher's blog posting for the UK newspaper *The Guardian*, which in 2010 voted *Mad Men* fourth in a list of the fifty best television dramas of all time.

4. Season 4's surprise ending confirms Don's unwillingness to marry the sort of Judaized professional woman who persistently attracts him.

5. Faye uses the Yiddish word *punim* (face) in "Chinese Wall" (4.11); but Harry Crane, who does not appear to be Jewish, uses *gonifs* (thieves) in "The Rejected" (4.4). Use of Yiddish thus ambiguously stands either for Jewish identity or simply for the currency of Yiddish in a city with a large Jewish population. Season 5 includes the first explicitly Jewish character since Rachel, the copywriter Michael Ginsberg.

6. When Jimmy tells Don "I loved you in *Gentleman's Agreement*," he links Don to a movie from 1947 about a character who impersonates a Jew to explore Jewish positionality. This virtual Jewishness predicts Don's ability to inhabit other virtual positions (see, e.g., Doty, this volume).

7. Compare to Sal's description of a lipstick shade as "Ethel Rosenberg Pink," a joking reference to the 1953 execution.

8. The "return to Zion" anticipated in Psalm 137 "was an indisputable historical event (unlike the Exodus from Egypt)" (Yaacov Shavit, qtd. in Boyarin, 60). By contrast, the Babylon evoked in *Mad Men* signals alienation, not redemptive return.

9. On Uris's "new Jew," see Boyarin; Loshitzky; Shohat; Weissbrod. On Uris's attraction to Israel's "fighting" Jews, see A. Kaplan.

10. The song is "Bleecker Street"; the episode is "The Suitcase" (4.7).

11. In the season 5 episode "Far Away Places" (5.6), Ginsberg's intimation that his origins are uncertain aligns him with the same Exodus motif. Indeed, the cryptic remark that he is "from Mars" may be a reference to the protagonist of a period book that also cites Exodus — Robert A. Heinlein's *Stranger in a Strange Land* (1961) — who was raised on Mars.

12. Don is mistaken: the invention of the cigarette machine in 1881 came more than twenty years after Freud's birth in 1856. Initially considered unmanly, cigarettes did not overtake male pipe and cigar smoking until the 1920s (Schudson, 178–208).

13. For allusions to Oscar Wilde, see Hansen, this volume.

14. Frances Ferguson calls Emma a "social engineer," convinced, like many *Mad Men* characters, that "there is nothing genuinely bad or sad" in life, only actions calling out "for a different context" (110–11). Unlike Emma, Don is seldom seen purchasing anything, his fabulous male wardrobe notwithstanding. An interesting exception occurs in "The Gold Violin" (2.7), when Don buys a Cadillac in which Betty, learning of his affair with Bobbie, vomits.

15. My understanding of seriality does not presume a loss of the communal effect when viewers choose DVDs over original broadcasts. "What should I watch?," a question often put to friends by DVD watchers, is not only a request for information but also an invitation to a future conversation. This fluidity was doubtless true for nineteenth-century readers of novels.

A CHANGE IS GONNA COME, SAME AS IT EVER WAS

MICHAEL BÉRUBÉ

YOU'RE NOT THERE

The single most annoying criticism of *Mad Men* is the complaint that the series is, in the words of Mark Greif, "an unpleasant little entry in the genre of Now We Know Better." Annoying, because it expresses the kind of partial truth that doesn't know how partial it is; I think of it as the kind of thing uttered by people to whom my sister-in-law refers as "Know-Some-of-It-Alls." There's no point trying to deny it: when you watch the Draper children scamper around in dry-cleaning bags and tumble in seatbeltless cars; when you gasp at the casual-but-intense sexism, racism, anti-Semitism, and homophobia in the office; when you snicker at Francine worrying that the arrival of a divorced woman will drive down the local property values in Ossining; or when you shudder at Betty Draper shaking the picnic blanket and leaving the Drapers' trash on the ground—there's no way *not* to reflect on the differences in social mores between then and now. Much of the *Mad Men* commentary across the length and breadth of the infinite Internets consists of such reflection. When a self-described "product of early 80s schooling where littering will land you in, or around, the lowest depths of the netherworld" showed up at Ask Metafilter and questioned whether people really acted that way, dozens of respondents replied—by reminding everyone what the archaic word *litterbug* meant and why a national campaign was mounted against littering, by suggesting that it was common to throw soda cans and sandwiches out of car windows but not to trash a picnic site, or to take some version of Benjamin Schwarz's line that "*nice* people—the educated and affluent—didn't hit other people's kids, and they didn't, especially in front of their children, walk away from a pile of trash they had created."[1] Because, you know, only trash did that.

Schwarz, like Greif, claims that "*Mad Men* directs its audience to indulge in a most unlovely—because wholly unearned—smugness"; interestingly, this line of argument can be and has been pressed into the service of an even more elaborate smugness, as evidenced by Melissa Witkowski's *Guardian* essay in which *Mad Men* is castigated not only for its unpleasant, unearned smugness ("the expected, self-congratulatory response is: 'Look how far we've come!'") but also for making the early 1960s look *worse* than they really were. Witkowski thus concludes that the times, they have been a-stayin' pretty much the same: "By ignoring the successes and struggles of women and people of colour in advertising in the 1960s, *Mad Men* obscures the fact that we are not much further along than we were then. The advertising world is still largely controlled by white men (with white women making greater strides in increased presence than black men and women), and the exceptions are still ultimately outliers, if somewhat greater in number." The show's overemphasis on institutional racism and sexism thus underemphasizes institutional racism and sexism—and, having read Witkowski's essay, Now We Know Better. Similarly, Greif knows perfectly well what the series wants us to think, what it directs its audience to feel:

> It does at least expose what's most pompous and self-regarding in our own time: namely, an unearned pride in our supposed superiority when it comes to health and restraint, the condition of women, and the toleration of (some) difference in ethnicity and sexuality. *Mad Men* flatters us where we deserve to be scourged. As I see it, the whole spectacle has the bad faith of, say, an 18th-century American slaveholding society happily ridiculing a 17th-century Puritan society—"Look, they used to burn their witches!"—while secretly envying the ease of a time when you could still tie uppity women to the stake.

Beginning with the editors' introduction, several of the contributors to this volume have refreshingly bracing responses to this school of thought. Caroline Levine points out that "the shock of the banal would not work in a representation that merely distanced us from the world represented: it must offer us the play of familiarity in strangeness"; thus, she writes, "from episode to episode, *Mad Men* actually gives us very little reason to leap to the conclusion that we are now postrace and postgender, but it does give us a strong incentive to entertain the serious and radical political questions: Is change possible? And if so, how does it happen?" Similarly, Jeremy Varon suggests that "the very tension between official censure and illicit desire propels many of the show's richer meanings, which little concern a supposed hierarchy of eras and go way beyond vicarious thrills," and concludes, "*Mad Men* screams that we have not found a solution to the happiness problem (at least among an influential slice of American life), no matter the advent of the 1960s and their enlightening sensitivities. If we had, why would our culture continually stage the saga of upper-middle-class discontent, with *Mad Men* itself emerging as the latest, captivating edition?" It is good to be reminded by essays like these that viewers' responses to the series don't have to be simple and monochromatic, and that people don't always do what television supposedly "directs" them to do. And it is particularly satisfying to see that Varon makes better sense of Greif's Now We Know Better / Doesn't That Look Good dichotomy than Greif himself does. But can I point out something even more obvious? *Mad Men*, as Kent Ono has it, is both like and unlike *Pleasantville* (1998), but I think Ono misses the most important structural difference between the two: in *Pleasantville*, you yourself (in the persons of Tobey Maguire and Reese Witherspoon) go back to the black-and-white world of *Leave It to Beaver* and teach the benighted inhabitants of Pleasantville about sex, segregation, and modern art. In *Mad Men*, you're not there. Accordingly, your response to the world of *Mad Men* is far less "directed" than it is in *Pleasantville*, because your contemporary, TV-watching self has no representative on the set inducing the principals to acknowledge Joan's talent, to listen to Carla when she says she's been married for twenty years, to quit smoking and cut back on the drinking, and (not least) to clean up after their picnic lest they make a wizened Native American cry.

In other words, you can try to capture the American scene just prior to the social transformations of the 1960s by transporting a couple of us directly back to the period—"back to the future," say, where Michael J. Fox can introduce black folk to the possibilities of rhythm-and-blues guitar, or where Witherspoon can introduce Joan Allen to the joys of masturbation. Or, more complexly, you could cast six people as Bob Dylan, including a British woman and a thirteen-year-old African American boy, thereby recreating the early 1960s with as much attention to period detail and style as *Mad Men* while winking at us in every frame, constantly reminding us that these are the early 1960s filtered through the present. (Your mileage may vary, but I found Todd Haynes's *I'm Not There* [2007] unwatchable for that very reason. Dylan may be elusive, but Haynes is ubiquitous.) *Mad Men* does neither. It therefore allows for far more latitude in audience response than an alternation between condemning and secretly envying witch burning. You may, if you desire, shudder at the picnic scene and congratulate yourself on your enlightened shudder; or, conversely, you might stop to reflect that although our parks and highways are cleaner now than they were fifty years ago, we've pumped a great deal of carbon into the atmosphere and have produced and consumed approximately one quadrillion plastic containers of bottled water. You may, if you desire, tsk-tsk about the marginalization of persons of color on the show; or, conversely, you might be moved to reflect on how white the advertising industry remains today.

As Varon writes, following Natasha Simons's "refreshingly different stance" on the show in the *National Review*, "without condemning the decade so broadly [as Simons does], we can nonetheless imagine the compulsive adultery of Don Draper et al. morphing some years later into wife swapping and key parties. . . . A similar continuum could link the Mad Men's drinking and the worst of the drug culture. Rather than stumping for the 1960s, the show may cleverly sound a note of caution." The note of caution sounded here is only slightly off-key; while the Mad Men descend to alcoholism and Don, Roger, and Duck take turns retching onscreen, the road to the worst of the drug culture begins elsewhere, in Greenwich Village—as we see in the stunning reappearance of Midge Daniels in season 4 ("Blowing Smoke," 4.12). "A victim of her bohemian indiscretions," wrote Ginia Bellafante in the *New York Times* the next day, "Midge emerges as a full-blown heroin addict whose husband is eager to pimp her out for drug money" ("'Mad Men' Watch"). There's at least one note of caution, and it is sounded loud and clear. But how you fill in the gap between *Mad Men* and now—on gender, on race, on sexuality, on abortion, on littering, on household and automobile safety, on beating your brain with the liquor and drugs—is entirely up to you.

THE UNBEARABLE WHITENESS OF MAD WORLD;
OR, WHY YOU SHOULDN'T WANT TO FOLLOW CARLA HOME

Though Varon deftly counters the claim that *Mad Men* is all about our own self-satisfaction (partly because we still can't get no), he ends his chapter with a problematic wish: "Ingeniously set in a world of change, *Mad Men* might also do well to educate us with examples, useful for addressing our

own times in both their regressions and their unique failures, of that impulse." I call this problematic for two reasons. For one, it is not clear that
the ad execs have *not* reflected on the profits of disease merchants (wasn't
that the point of Don's full-page *New York Times* ad in Season 4's "Blowing
Smoke"? Or was Don merely blowing smoke?) or that the office women
have not begun to discover that they can make the world too (isn't that what
everyone hopes for Peggy and Joan, beginning with their conversation after
Don announces his plans to marry Megan?). These developments, at the
very end of season 4, remind us — as does Dana Polan in this volume — that
it is dangerous to talk about what a series has not done when the series is
still in the process of unfolding. (Or, to follow Lauren Goodlad's savvy parallel to the Victorian triple-decker in this volume, one wonders what it would
have been like for Dickens, Eliot, and Trollope to work amid the chatter of
the blogosphere and the twitterverse.) But the second, and more important,
reason is that it is not clear that *Mad Men* would be enhanced if it provided
us with "examples useful for addressing our own times." I suspect that such
characters would inevitably lead us on the road back to *Pleasantville*, providing us with acceptable avatars of the people we might like to think of as the
people we eventually turned out to be. Though Varon is right to suggest that
Mad Men may be legitimately "faulted for overplaying its characters' stubborn resistance to change already under way, and remaining trapped in the
Mad World it creates," I wonder whether the available alternatives might not
be even worse.

Everyone watching the show now knows that much of our social world
has changed in the past fifty years, and, as Levine says, we are surely invited
to think about how and why those changes happened. But I for one would
not want the series to gesture more emphatically at, or make itself more
useful for addressing, the present. I don't even want to see more characters
who agree, in their own time, that what is most important in their world is
what we will have decided, fifty years later, was most important about their
world. I don't want Don to develop a deep appreciation for the Beatles as
innovators, just as I don't mind that the literate Cosgrove isn't following
Dylan's career more closely. I would wince if Betty showed up with a copy
of *The Feminine Mystique* or if we saw Peggy reading *Sex and the Single Girl*.
It would be downright weird if Don or Kinsey fell into a conversation about
Michael Harrington's *The Other America* (though it would have some purchase for Don). And speaking of Kinsey: about the civil rights movement . . .

No aspect of *Mad Men* has been as controversial or as disappointing (for
some viewers) as its representation of race. The Latoya Peterson essay refer-

enced in several chapters (published under different titles at *Slate* and *The Root*) was written in August 2009 at the outset of season 3, and kicked off a series of fascinating exchanges about the show's treatment of civil rights (distant, in various senses of the term) and, relatedly, its extremely limited roles for African American characters. (Ono is right to suggest in his chapter that its treatment of Asian American characters is even more severe.) I think this is critical not only for the obvious reason — how can a series praised for its mimetic accuracy be so obtuse about the most important world-historical events of its time? — but also because it has everything to do with who "you" are in my "you're not there" formulation. If you're white like me, you're not there in the sense that your contemporary sensibility (whatever that may be), or the early-1960s emergence of what would eventually become your contemporary sensibility (whatever *that* may be), is not represented on the show. And if you're not white, well, you're simply not there.

So what are "we" (whoever we may be) to make of this? In September 2010, in the midst of season 4, Ta-Nehisi Coates summed up his take on the previous year's discussion:

> There is some sentiment that Weiner isn't addressing race powerfully enough, or that he isn't including enough black people on the show. I've said before that I think the absence, or rather the peripheral awareness of race among the characters, is a powerful statement about the class of people Weiner is presenting. As much as I'd like to see some black actors and actresses (of whom there are many greats) get some work, I really hope Weiner sticks to whatever plan is in his head — whether that includes black people or not.
>
> That aside, I think I must be one of the few people who's actually enjoying watching a show about the '60s that isn't actually about race. *Mad Men* is a story, to my mind, about how a gender revolution is playing out among a particular group of people. Perhaps this is personal, but thinking about gender, in that context, is a welcome relief from the constant heaviness of my thinking around race. In terms of the '60s, race is the air. I don't know that we need Matt Weiner's take on it. There have been so many.

Though I think *Mad Men* is more than a story about a gender revolution — I sometimes say that it is a stylish visualization of the social dynamics catalogued in Erving Goffman's *Stigma* (1963), right down to the epileptic kid who's being institutionalized for his condition ("The Color Blue," 3.10) — I think Coates is right to insist on what this representation of race says about "the class of people Weiner is representing." Another writer (an anonymous student writing for the *Ivy Horsemen*, a blog created by "Ivy League students/alums & men of color") makes a similar point about the Mad World then and now:

> It is safe to say that the majority of Madison Avenue executives probably didn't wrestle that hard with the injustices that were going on just a few hundred [actually, a few dozen] blocks north of them in Harlem at the time. I'm confident in saying this because I can very easily go unnoticed to the ad executives on Madison Avenue today. They created a world in which the struggles of the Black experience didn't have to exist for them because they treated the busboy or the housekeeper well and lived in neighborhoods where there by and large was never a black v. white question, but a question of whether to let the Jew in.

Once we recognize just how segregated the Mad World was (Witkowski adduces Clarence Holte, hired by BBDO in 1952, and Georg Olden, BBDO art director from 1960–63, as if they were not the exceptions who proved the rule), the question of how to represent race in this milieu becomes much trickier than it first appears, and this trickiness has unsettling implications for some of the essays in this volume.

Let me start by dispensing with the worst-case scenario. The website Stuff White People Like is (a) often very funny and (b) right on target, as Ono suggests, when it says "Mad Men is a TV show on cable with low ratings, multiple awards, critical praise, and full seasons available on DVD. It's no surprise white people love it" (Lander). Touché. But do you know what else white people love? We love stories about American history in which the drama of race is vividly front and center *and features some good white people.* Elsewhere, I've called this the Huckleberry Finn Fantasy—"the seductive notion that if *we* were alive back then, even if we were poor backwoods kids whose only formal education included lessons about how abolitionism was immoral and 'lowdown,' we would somehow, all by our lonesomes, come to the conclusion that we should save Jim and go to Hell" (144). That desire to imagine our contemporary white selves as Good White People produces films like *Mississippi Burning* (1988) and *The Long Walk Home* (1990), in which sympathetic white people turn out to be the real heroes of the civil rights movement. Suffice it to say that *Mad Men* does well to smack down that desire ASAP, by giving the structural role of the Good White Person to the cringe-inducing Paul Kinsey in season 1.

No one in this collection is asking for Good White People, of course.

Rather, Ono and Leslie Reagan offer the more nuanced proposal that the series could, at some point, have followed Carla home, rather than letting Betty's rebuff (and eventual firing) of Carla stand as the final word on her role in the Draper household—namely, that of the patient, reliable, long-suffering servant. Ono, writing of a "spectator's desire for more—more knowledge about Carla's life and her perspectives," underscores Varon's point about the show's perspectival limitations: "By not showing her before and after work, or during private and intimate moments, the show has two effects: first, it produces a historically realist representation of the irrelevance of her personal life to white people in the 1960s; second, it unnecessarily and objectionably produces the irrelevance of her personal life to television viewers now." Similarly, Reagan points out that greater representation of women of color would not only usefully complicate the show's treatment of sex and abortion, rendering a more accurate version of the era as a whole; it would also afford us another satisfaction: "By moving away from the perspective of the Drapers, the series could give viewers the pleasure of knowing more than the Drapers do about Carla."

Here we see why the question of race is so intimately tied to the question of whether the series really tells us that We Know Better Now. For if Ono is right (and he is) that Carla's personal life is relevant to television viewers now, and Reagan is right (and she is) that it would be a pleasure to transcend the Drapercentric worldview, then, in effect, they are asking for the series to accommodate more of What We Know Now by letting us see what the white inhabitants of Mad World neither knew nor cared about. Twenty-first-century white viewers may not be able to rest content with the stories of good white people who were on the right side of history and the arc of the moral universe, because Kinsey is such a pompous buffoon; but at least, thank goodness, we know enough now to know that we *should* want to know more about the lived experiences of Carla and Hollis. Fortunately, thanks to the miracle product History Regenerator ("you'll love the way it makes you feel"), we can be privy to some of that knowledge to which we would not have had access in the early 1960s *unless* we were in Carla's or Hollis's immediate circle of family and friends. That is, unless we were black.

"The show seems to reveal some self-consciousness about its failure to explore race," Peterson wrote in her initial critique. Indeed it does, and I tend to agree with Coates that the absence of black characters' interiority in *Mad Men* is itself a statement about the advertising industry. Clarence Lang's essay in this volume thus strikes me as entirely justified in one way, for of course *Mad Men* has nothing useful or interesting to say about northern black resistance. But in another way Lang is asking for another series entirely. A TV show about the early-1960s advertising industry that also managed to be about Adam Clayton Powell Jr., Amiri Baraka, and the potential appeal of Malcolm X and the NOI for a working man like Hollis would be something like a TV show about the early-1960s Professional Golfers Association tour that also managed to offer fresh insights into the work of John Coltrane and Eric Dolphy. It would undoubtedly be a more accurate look at what was actually going on in the United States at the time, far beyond the unbearably white world of Arnie vs. Jack. But it would not be a show about the PGA tour. As Polan has it, *Mad Men* "is not a total or totalized picture of the times as they were but a deliberately partial and incomplete picture of how some people lived some parts of those times and, in some cases, groped toward other ways of living them." Though this representational strategy clearly courts the objection that it is perpetuating that partiality and incompleteness in the present, I've looked at *Mad Men* from both sides now, from black and white, and still somehow, I think it's better than the corrective alternatives suggested so far.

ADVERTISEMENTS FOR MYSELF

If I could ask for anything from this already formidable collection, it would be more discussion of some of Don's major advertising pitches and campaigns. The introduction to this volume nicely situates Sterling Cooper's place in an industry that is about to be transformed by the creatives at Doyle Dane Bernbach—a story that, according to the editors, *Mad Men* both does and does not seek to tell. The editors give us Thomas Frank and Michael Schudson on the history of advertising along with a take on the self-referential Patio ad in season 3. Lilya Kaganovsky does a great reading of season 2's "Jackie/ Marilyn" campaign for Maidenform. Dianne Harris and Mabel Rosenheck are wonderful on matters of style and substance; and Irene Small offers a terrific reading of the "Carousel" scene. Lynne Joyrich notes that the series is inseparable from its multimedia marketing of itself, and that the ads on *Mad Men* are inevitably part of the representational apparatus of the show, some even paying homage to the look and feel of the series. Goodlad is interested in how a prospective client—the Israeli Tourist Board—provides the occasion for deeper narrative attention to historical changes in the global economy. But for the most part, the discussions of Don turn away from the content of his day job in favor of the other rich possibilities provided by this handsome cipher who, like Gatsby, is somehow black and Jewish—if actually a "virtual Jew" (as in Goodlad's reading) and black-by-way-of-PWT (Michael Szalay, though his actual words are "symbolically black, he is . . . possessed of an outsider's purchase on the fantasies of white Americans"). For Jim Hansen Don is a version of the dandy, and if, for Alexander Doty, Don is not quite a closeted gay man, he certainly enables a richly queer reading of the multilayered banter he shares with Sal in "Out of Town." But aside from the Carousel scene, which is universally acknowledged as the best sales pitch ever dramatized on TV, why should we care about the quality of Don's work? Does it matter that *Mad Men* is about advertising, as opposed to, say, the publishing industry?

Perhaps this avoidance of the show's ostensible subject matter stems from our broader skepticism about the advertising business. For decades, Madison Avenue has been understood to be not merely the vehicle but the very symbol of commercial culture, and advertising has been portrayed as the emptiest and most superficial of endeavors in a deeply superficial society. But let's not forget that there really is such a thing as good advertising. It's rare, but it happens. Sometimes, as in Don's pitch for the "Eat Life by the bowlful" campaign, it's a question of getting people together in a market — and Life, just for the record, is one of the better cereals on the market by any measure; it certainly deserved a better campaign than it had in 1965, when its sixty-second spot featured egg-shaped "useful proteins" wearing what appear to be preacher's hats, bouncing back and forth on the screen, and proclaiming their status as "the most useful protein ever in a ready-to-eat cereal." Don's proposed campaign for Life, like his proposed campaign for Hilton Hotels, is *a really good idea*. The idea, in the Life campaign, is to try to appeal to kids' desires to eat a big bowl of crunchy, tasty (yet nutritious!) Life cereal without being put off by the name, while appealing to mothers' desires to see their children as tiny and vulnerable even as they worry about . . . life; in the Hilton campaign, as Goodlad notes, the idea is to present capitalist globalization with comfort and style, assuring Americans that even in strange lands where people speak Italian, Farsi, or Japanese they will also speak Hilton — that is, American. (Regardless of whether you like the idea of capitalist globalization being presented with comfort and style, or the idea that Hilton is a universal language that supersedes all national, regional, and cultural difference, the point remains that Don's pitch is a very good pitch.) But the representatives from Quaker Oats complain that the Life campaign is "kinda smart for regular folks — the irony," and the eccentric Conrad Hilton unfathomably rejects the "how do you say . . ." campaign because it does not include the still-not-yet-built Hilton hotel on the moon.

It's worth noting that the only famous Life ad, "Mikey likes it," developed by Doyle Dane Bernbach in 1972, followed Don's formula to the letter: forget the health angle, make it *fun*, give it to little kids. The result was one of the most recognizable and successful campaigns in the history of advertising. We are thus invited to see Don's "bowlful" pitch as the proto-Mikey campaign that would have changed Life's image and business seven years earlier.

A good deal of the show depends on Don's remarkable mixture of assertiveness and elusiveness; he is the subject supposed to know about whom no one is supposed to know. And yet nothing about Don's allure would work, for me — nor would dandy Don, virtual-Jewish Don, or black-by-proxy Don — if *Mad Men* offered a stale, stereotypical, one-dimensional view of the advertising industry. For *Mad Men* to work as a show about ad men, Don's ad campaigns have to be attractive and engaging, not snake-oil salesmanship or the cynical, world-weary hawking of shiny surfaces. And the show has to have some substantial investment in the very idea of "attractive" and "engaging" ad campaigns — campaigns that require creativity and serious mental labor. If this were simply a show about the vapidity of the industry, what would be the point?

If you agree that the principal characters can be deeply unpleasant people — and they can: think of the composite Cosgrove rendered here by Doty and Small, whereby the savvy Rothko-appreciating, confident-yet-modest writer is also the firm's most emphatic homophobe, frustrating every enlightened, right-minded contemporary viewer's desire that an appreciation of modern art go hand in hand with an appreciation of modern sexuality (as it does in *Pleasantville*) — then why should you spend a moment's thought on these often-unpleasant people if you believe that their profession is bullshit? (And it's not as if Don isn't haunted by the thought that his hillbilly father would use precisely that word.) But anyone who sticks around for season 2 will come upon the discussion of the Mohawk Airlines campaign, in which Peggy says, "Sex sells" and Don replies sharply, "Says who? Just so you know, the people who talk that way think that monkeys can do this. . . . *You* are the product, you feeling something. That's what sells. Not them. Not sex. They can't do what we do, and they hate us for it" ("For Those Who Think Young," 2.1). And anyone who makes it all the way to season 4 will hear Peggy and Don, in "The Suitcase" (4.7), agonizing about the Samsonite ad. "I can't tell the difference any more between something that's good and something that's awful," Peggy confesses in the Greek diner to which they have repaired for a late dinner. "Well, they're very close," Don replies (anticipating Spinal Tap's classic formulation, "There's a fine line between stupid and clever"). "But the best idea always wins, and you know it when you see it." Yes, well. The problem is that the best idea *doesn't* always win. "Most ad men believe that clients are the thing that gets in the way of good work," an exasperated Don says when it becomes clear to him that Connie Hilton literally wanted the moon ("Wee Small Hours," 3.9). "I've never experienced that." But he will—first with Hilton, and then in season 4 with Jantzen (who are upset at the idea of sexual suggestiveness in their bikini ads, because it's not "wholesome") and Life (who respond enthusiastically to Don's desperate borrowing of the incompetent Danny's idea, "the cure for the common breakfast," by spouting clichés like "a home run" and "that dog will hunt" ["Waldorf Stories," 4.6]).

I suspect that *Mad Men* has struck such a chord among (most) critics and (many) academics for precisely this reason: it depicts a nebulous and oft-derided form of intellectual labor in which good, creative, compelling ideas are shot down by crazy old coots and uncomprehending stick-in-the-muds or adopted but put to no socially useful function. Don Draper, *mon semblable, mon frère*! And yet I have great sympathy with the blogger Jason Mittell's complaint that too much academic criticism of popular culture, and *Mad Men* in particular, adopts the role of Henry Jenkins's "acafans," in which one is obliged to profess one's deep and sympathetic immersion in the object before one proceeds to write about it ("On Disliking"). So maybe, I think, just maybe my concentration on *Mad Men*'s representation of advertising is just my own version of acafandom. I am, I will admit, especially drawn to these depictions of the daily work of Mad World. Three decades ago I had planned to go into the advertising industry, until that moment during my senior year in college when I decided that I should apply to graduate school in English instead. I didn't have much experience—I had worked for a variety of small firms during the summers—but I knew I was a good copywriter, and took some pride in the fact that my attempt to sell my tiny dorm-room refrigerator as an exclusive European "designer refrigerator" (an Avanti, really just a garden-variety appliance line) not only sold the thing within the hour (not a difficult thing on a college campus, though the asking price of $50 was a bit steep) but also got me an invitation to write copy for WKCR-FM (which I declined, because I needed a better-paying job). My father tried to shame me away from advertising, asking me if I wanted to go down in history as the guy who wrote "you deserve a break today"; I replied that "you deserve a break today" was a very good tagline, as evidenced by the fact that he was taking it as a shorthand reference to advertising in general, but that I found more inspiration in the work of Julian Koenig, whose famous "lemon" VW ad so befuddles the Sterling Cooper crew in season 1.

I knew that my decision to abandon advertising for graduate school amounted to agreeing to spend my twenties and thirties in the lower reaches of the tax code, but I didn't give in to the temptation to think of it as choosing a meaningful over a meaningless field of endeavor. On the contrary, I worried that I had turned my back on a career in which one tries to communicate with millions for a career in which one tries to please the four members of one's dissertation committee. And sure enough, in 1989, just as I was finishing my dissertation, I came upon a TV ad for Rolling Rock beer. It looked like an outtake from the long opening scene of *The Deer Hunter* (1978), except that it had that late-1980s handheld shaky-cam; it consisted of an "interview" with a crusty old man who tells us that he danced with his wife in this very bar—indeed, that he danced with all his wives here. The tagline: "same as it ever was." I knew at once that a more cynical version of myself had managed to capitalize on Rolling Rock's surprising popularity among yuppies by associating it simultaneously with old-school hardscrabble western Pennsylvania and the most accessible song ("Once in a Lifetime") from the Talking Heads' album *Remain in Light*, thereby staking claim to Rolling Rock's prewar, working-class authenticity while winking knowingly at the very idea of "prewar, working-class authenticity" by routing it through a Talking Heads lyric. And I thought to myself: *you opportunistic bastard, you could have written that campaign. And you would hate yourself in the morning, though you would have spent the night sleeping on a bed made of money.*

Monkeys can't do that. And bad advertising can kill a product, as when the creatives at Leo Burnett killed Schlitz beer in the late 1970s, taking the then number two brand in America (just behind Budweiser) and consigning it to oblivion. Good advertising, like the (fictional) Hilton campaign or the (real) Rolling Rock campaign, is, as Don says to Connie, "modern, witty, eye-catching." The Bridgestone ad critiqued by Joyrich in this volume is a case in point: it can be said to offer a "troubling, universalizing view of race" only if one assumes that the tire-swiping aliens have some identifiable "racial" characteristics even though we never see them, and that House of Pain, or the astronauts listening to "Jump Around," are black. Otherwise, the joke is clear: the astronauts are not the clipped, nerdy Apollo bunch but a madcap, fun-loving pair hippity-hopping their way across a lunar landscape, and Bridgestone tires are so famous that even extraterrestrial species will want to steal them. But still, the best idea doesn't always win: the Richards

Group, the same agency that gave Bridgestone the moon—and the very successful spots involving an orca ("Whale of a Tale") and an email faux pas ("Reply All")—also gave you the straight-up sexist fantasy of a nagging Mrs. Potato Head losing her mouth, much to Mr. Potato Head's relief and delight.

Such is the nature of my acafandom. I watch the show not so much for its soap-opera aspects or for its sense of period style (both of which I enjoy in moderation) but for its willingness to take advertising seriously *while* offering a critique of the social milieu of the profession. It speaks to me the way the Rolling Rock ad did, leaving me feeling a mixture of admiration and aversion (I am the product, me feeling something), and reminding me that the line between art and commerce, like the line between stupid and clever, is very fine indeed. As *Spin* magazine put it in October 1989, "The new Rolling Rock slogan—'same as it ever was'—is less conclusive proof that the avant-garde has slid into the marketplace than evidence that David Byrne is a really great advertising copywriter." This is very much in the spirit of Irene Small's analysis of Andy Warhol in her chapter, in which she writes: "We are accustomed to critiquing advertising's position as the middleman between avant-garde art and the culture industry. Appropriating art's modes and rhetorics, as we see in Sterling Cooper's 'feeling' pitch for Martinson coffee, advertising co-opts aesthetics for the purposes of producing commodity desire. Warhol's brilliance was to recognize that art does not escape this commodity circuit. Rather than presuming originality, by contrast, he chose to appropriate advertising's codes for art." The curious thing about Don Draper, in this respect, is not that he shuttles between beatniks and tobacco execs, reading *Meditations in an Emergency* while Roger reads David Ogilvy's *Confessions of an Ad Man*. Rather, as Polan points out in this volume, it's that Draper's judgment is so often "on the wrong side of history." Polan mentions Nixon, Ali, the Beatles, the vw campaign, and the demolition of Penn Station; I might add Joe Namath, whom Don dislikes for much the same reason he bets against Ali. "*Mad Men* needs from us this recognition of the characters' fallibility in history," writes Polan, "because it is key to the way we watch the show from our historical present and reflect back on fraught lives such as Don's." *Mad Men* thus asks that we watch the show in a kind of ambivalent parallax view with regard to Don's brilliance as an ad man and his obtuseness as to the fact that a change is gonna come, oh yes it is—though in order to accept that invitation, we first have to accept the premise that there is such a thing as brilliance as an ad man.

Robert Rushing's chapter sums up one crucial consequence of that ambivalence: "This is the risk at stake in *Mad Men*'s credits, repeatedly fracturing, dropping, and reconstituting the subject; it is the risk in our 1960s costume parties and *Mad Men* Facebook profiles—they encourage us both to consume and to question the value of that consumption (a kind of 'psycho-ideology of everyday life'). This is not a naive rhetoric of 'resistance': instead, it captures some of how *Mad Men* both attracts us and makes us feel uneasy, how the show makes viewers cognizant of the 'ideological work' that advertising does, while simultaneously manipulating viewers with a parade of seamless, seductive images." I think this is exactly right—not only about *Mad Men* and its marketing, but about good advertising in general. "Sex sells" is too reductive, as are the various theories of hidden persuaders and media manipulators. I know people are tired of hearing cultural studies theorists insist that people aren't simply duped, but you know what? People aren't simply duped, just as they aren't simply congratulating themselves for being better than their early-1960s counterparts just because a TV show allegedly "directs" them to do so. Think of the difference, say, between your average tedious sexist mind-numbing Bud Lite or Miller Lite commercial and the "Most Interesting Man in the World" campaign for Dos Equis. Does anyone really buy Dos Equis in the hopes of becoming more like the most interesting man in the world? Or do we appreciate the campaign's sly mockery of the "be like me/us" genre of endorsements? Aren't we being encouraged to consume and to question the value of that consumption, with a nod and a wink and an injunction to stay thirsty? That's the kind of structural irony that makes *Mad Men* work: it is a good series about good advertising that advertises itself well while calling advertising into question. Structural irony, *Mad Men* style. You'll love, and at the same time you won't love, the way it makes you feel.

NOTE

1. See the posting "Don Draper Is a Litterbug" by snwod (16 November 2008), and the responses, on the Ask Metafilter website (accessed 15 May 2011).

A CONVERSATION WITH PHIL ABRAHAM, DIRECTOR AND CINEMATOGRAPHER

LAUREN M. E. GOODLAD AND JEREMY VARON

EDITED BY LAUREN M. E. GOODLAD AND CARL LEHNEN

Mad Men is famously the brainchild of Matthew Weiner, whose pilot screenplay for a show about advertising in the early 1960s landed him a job as a screenwriter for *The Sopranos*. Roughly ten years later, the screenplay became an award-winning pilot, "Smoke Gets in Your Eyes," which launched *Mad Men* as a series. But like all serial television, *Mad Men* is a collaborative effort: no matter how visionary the show's creator, "quality" television involves synthesizing the creative talents of writers, story editors, directors, cinematographers, and designers of various kinds.

Among those collaborators is Phil Abraham, who has worked extensively in film (he was a camera operator on films from *The Witches of Eastwick* [1987] to *Primary Colors* [1998]), as well as television. He is well known for his work on *The Sopranos*, where he was a camera operator before becoming an Emmy-nominated cinematographer and then director of several episodes. He continued his collaboration with Matt Weiner on *Mad Men*, doing the cinematography for five of the series' first six episodes, including "Smoke Gets in Your Eyes," for which he won an Emmy for Outstanding Cinematography. He later directed nine episodes of *Mad Men*, including "The Hobo Code" (1.8), "Maidenform" (2.6), and "The Jet Set" (2.11)—for the latter of which he was nominated for an Emmy for Outstanding Directing. In the third and fourth seasons Abraham directed "Out of Town" (3.1), "The Fog (3.5), "Souvenir" (3.8), "Public Relations" (4.1), "The Summer Man" (4.8), and "Chinese Wall" (4.11), and his director credits for season 5 include the controversial eleventh episode, "The Other Woman." He works widely in television including shows such as *Crash, Mercy,*

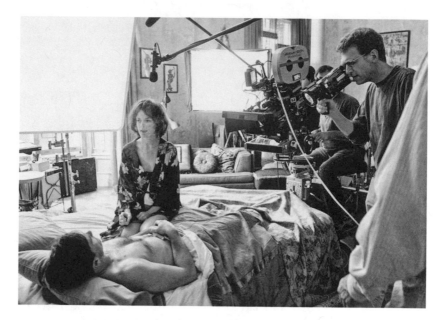

FIGURE APP.1. Phil Abraham (right) filming the *Mad Men* pilot, "Smoke Gets in Your Eyes" (1.1).

Sons of Anarchy, Breaking Bad, The Good Wife, Breakout Kings, and *The Killing,* among others.

The following interview with Abraham took place on May 5, 2011, in New York City, with Lauren Goodlad and Jeremy Varon.

LAUREN GOODLAD:

Tell us how you started working in television.

PHIL ABRAHAM:

TV was really just an offspring of my work in the camera department in movies. There was nothing really particular about it in terms of learning a craft. *The Sopranos* was the very first TV show I ever worked on; I was a camera operator on the pilot, and they called to see if I was interested in doing the series. My wife was expecting a child, and I was offered a movie at the same time, but *The Sopranos* were willing to give me a break. They said take off whenever you want—have a baby, take an episode off, come back. I could never do that on a movie. So it worked out well. And then the DP [director of photography] left, and I moved up, and there you have it.

LG: *Were you surprised when you began working on* The Sopranos *that this is what television was doing, as opposed to what you had been used to as a viewer?*

PA: I knew it was a different show for sure. It was quirky and the characters were great, but it didn't seem like . . . you know, it was cable, HBO, which I didn't really have a sense of as a source for original programming. I think we were a season after *Sex and the City*. I knew it was different, but I didn't necessarily know it was really amazing.

LG: *And with* Mad Men?

PA: *Mad Men* was sort of a special offshoot of *The Sopranos* in that Matt Weiner was one of the writers on *The Sopranos*. So he had this pilot, and in between our last two seasons, which was essentially one extended season with a three-month break in between, I had a pilot already lined up to shoot for ABC called *Six Degrees*, and they wanted me to do *Mad Men* right after that. So my *Sopranos* crew came and did both of those pilots with me.

JEREMY VARON:
When you started on The Sopranos *you didn't yet know it was amazing, and then at some point it dawned on you that you're really on to something with this show. With* Mad Men *was there a similar moment of awakening when you understood this was something special?*

PA: No, I think with *Mad Men* it was clearer from the get go, and maybe that's a function of my just being more attuned to it having spent seven years on the set of *The Sopranos*, or just being older. But the script, and once those actors came on, and we saw what was going on, it was clear to me that this is fantastic. I didn't know if anyone would watch it, I could never speak to that. I mean, we all thought that no one would watch *The Sopranos* either. And I wasn't saying, this is going to be a big hit. We were hopeful that it would be picked up, but we knew we were doing great work.

JV: *And then it does become a huge hit. I suppose it doesn't surprise you, but the investment—*

PA: It does surprise me.

JV: *Part of its hit status is the extraordinary investment that the audience has in it. No sooner does an episode end than bloggers are picking through every detail and trying to figure out what it meant. How conscious is the production team and Matt Weiner about how it's playing among the fans, what people are writing about, saying about it. Does that distract or does it help?*

PA: I don't read any of it so I don't know about it. I know Matt does. He stays very tuned in to what is being written about the show. I know that he really invests himself in that. Does that then influence his decisions going forward? I don't know. I think it probably stirs him up. I've heard him rant, "How could they think this, how could they think that?"

LG: *Such as?*

PA: A lot of it was people's reaction to Betty Draper, which took him by surprise. So is he going to shift the character to appease those people? No. That's what it is. There are always going to be people out there who think not at all what you had intended them to think.

LG: *Can you explain what directing an individual episode of a television series is like?*

PA: Basically, when you're doing an episode of television, especially serialized television, it's much more important for the director to really understand where the story's going, what the story is. I think in a normal more procedural episode of television, you get a sense of the characters and work with that, but each episode is more stand-alone. In a show like *Mad Men*, though, what happens in each episode follows from what came before and has an impact on what comes after. But I still look at my episode as a thing unto itself, despite those ramifications. When I do multiple shows on something like *Mad Men*, I'm aware of where the story's going. It's different for actors, who don't really want to know what the last episode's going to be when they're doing the first episode, because they don't want to play the result, and neither do I. If there's a moment that will resonate later, I should probably be aware of it, but I don't necessarily want to hit it over the head.

LG: *I wonder if you could give an example. "Maidenform" maybe? That seems to have a lot going on in terms of the arc of the plot of the second season.*

PA: It does in terms of the character of Don, and his perception of his own truths, and who he is: the mystery of Don Draper. There are moments in "Maidenform" that stand out because you know of his past; like when they're at the country club and the emcee says, "Heroes, please stand up and take a well-deserved round of applause." And he does, and we know that that is a lie, that he's living that double truth. That's a moment that's important, and brought out more so by Sally's looking up at him. I think that's what makes him feel, in that moment, like a fraud, if I would even say that he feels *that*. I think he's feeling something that he can't quite wrap his head around.

LG: *What does he see at the end of the episode when he looks in the mirror?*

PA: It's exactly the same thing. He's starting to become more aware of the falsehoods of his life when confronted with his daughter who, once again, is looking up to him. . . . In that episode it was all about one's perception of oneself and others' perceptions of you. So as a motif I liked the idea of using mirrors just because you get to see what others, in theory, are seeing, and yet not. It's a nice, interesting way to formally bring out that part of the script. When he's looking at the mirror and shaving, it's just an ordinary routine thing, but with Sally looking at him it becomes something else.

LG: *In between there's the moment with Bobbie Barrett. Does that connect as well?*

PA: Well, it does connect, because it's about that perception, his reputation out there. He doesn't perceive himself as *having* any reputation. He doesn't like the idea that other people would even be talking about him, let alone his girl-friend getting the full "Don Draper treatment" and saying it's every bit as good as they said it was. That makes him completely snap. But also with Bobbie, at the beginning of that scene we see them in the mirror, so that's also part of that visual motif. But I think the Bobbie Barrett scene does influence the later moment because he starts to look at himself: "How *do* people see me? Who *is* Don Draper?" There is always that question that goes throughout the whole series, and it runs through his mind too, I'm sure.

JV: *Now a process question: How much discretion do you have in terms of dramatizing what's in the script? You said that you like to use mirrors. Is that you, or is that in the way the scenes are already constructed?*

PA: I suppose that's me in that it's not specifically written into the script—but it is the script that triggers the thought. For instance, I was on the set thinking about the bathroom scene, and I discovered the idea for the closing image of Don in the mirror. Just like any show, you have a passageway to the bathroom on the set, and there's a place for the bathroom on the plan, but they're not going to build it until we're in it because it costs money, so the minute they script it we get to build it. So because we're now building it from scratch I can go over it with Dan Bishop, the production designer, and I can say, "This is what I have in mind," and, "No, I really want the camera here, and I want people to be able to see Don looking in the mirror. Is there any way we can put the sink more here?" And he says, "Sure, you can do anything you want." So we could work that out, because I had the luxury of being the first person to shoot in the bathroom. I mean, it's not like I deviated, there's nothing weird about how the bathroom is laid out, but I had the opportunity of at least being able to custom-ize some of it.

JV: *Can you think of other examples where you had an "a-ha!" moment in thinking about how to visualize themes?*

PA: For instance, I put the mirror on the back of the hallway door because I thought there might be a fun moment at the end for the camera to pull back and to see his reflection [fig. 12.16]. It wasn't like something that if it didn't work I would say, "What the hell am I going to do?" It was really just a thought, but it paid off really nicely.

LG: *It's really nice, though, the way it amplified what I imagine was in the script, because what the dialogue emphasizes is not talking. He's angry at Bobbie for talking, and Sally says, "I won't talk," but what you added was looking.*

PA: Yeah, I think that was all there, it was all on the page, but the job of the director is to visually bring that to bear.

LG: *How about what Alexander Doty calls "the money shot" [fig. 14.5] in "Out of Town"?*
PA: It's funny that you —

LG: *Do you mind it being called that?*
PA: No, no, because that's an example of an absolutely one hundred percent scripted shot. It's in the script, or it's possible that Matt explained to me what he wanted. So in the script the bellman comes over and Sal is taking money out of his pocket and you see the bellman's feet — I think it's written that way. So that was something that Matt absolutely had in his head. In fact, I shot it, and he said, "Oh, no, no, no, that's not the way I envisioned it." And so we did it again. And this happens a lot with Matt, truthfully. It's like he'll have an idea in his head, and he tries to articulate it to you either in the script, or if it can't really be articulated on the page he'll then pull you over and say, "OK, I wrote the scene, but really what I want to do is have the camera here and do this." And then of course invariably you do it and it's not what he imagined. It was funny because I think I was on another episode already, and he ended up shooting that shot. It was literally an insert. Because I had done something that moved and came around on it, and he just really wanted down the leg with the money. And then, as he was shooting it, he said, "Well, maybe yours was better, I don't know." It's like, you always have an idea, but as you're executing it it's not syncing up all the time with that imaginary idea that you had in your head. In a way that's the fun part of directing, because you can visualize things and yet when you're there putting it together it's not the way your brain visualized it for whatever reason. And sometimes it's just a little thing, and then it clicks into place and then you decide how important it is, whatever it is. It's that disconnect between intellectually thinking about a visual thing and actually executing it.

JV: *One last question on this train: what are some things that you execute that you're especially proud of that a person in the audience might not appreciate?*
PA: Truthfully, I'm not sure why I do this, but I think my inclination normally is to be as efficient visually as possible, and to avoid a kind of mundane cutting pattern. Like, if there are three of us in the room right now, how do I cover the scene and make it interesting? Well, you could have shots on the two of you and then turn around and have a shot on me, but is there anything else you can do? And you take your cues from the dialogue and the way it's structured as a scene and the way it's written. For instance, in "The Jet Set," that shot of Don by the pool. In the script, it'll say: "Don waits by the pool, Pete comes up, and then they have their conversation." So I can have a shot of Don from the other side of the pool and that would make Don and Pete very small, and Pete would

come up and the pool would sort of be in the foreground and Don and Pete would be in the background, and then you just end up cutting in. So I thought, well, why don't we just have him wait, this figure waiting by the pool, and I can just push in and around and as I hook around it Pete's coming up and I land in a two shot and it's one take, and I've told the story. To me, if I can tell the story in a visual way in one shot, especially for a scene that's a page or less in the script, that's what I want to do.

LG: *I have other questions about "The Jet Set," but I really wanted to hear you talk about the periodness of* Mad Men. *Cinematographically, my coeditor Lilya Kaganovsky has compared* Mad Men *to a Douglas Sirk movie because it's doing something with color that reminds her of that.*

PA: Perhaps. I don't think of *Mad Men* as being as Technicolor as Sirk's movies were, but there is an aspect of that, chiefly as production design and costumes. I don't think with the camera I'm doing anything that's necessarily period. At least I'm not thinking, "OK, this is 1960, we're going to shoot it this way." I don't do that. In the very early stages of *Mad Men* when we talked about the pilot and when we were prepping the pilot, we were consciously saying we don't want to make this show look like *The Apartment* [1960] or anything like that, but we want to be influenced in the way the people who made *The Apartment* were influenced. So certain things bear out of that. Initially we said, as a rule, let's not use any Steadicam, because they didn't have any Steadicam in 1960, or because, with that piece of equipment, you were creating a look that takes you out of the conceit of what might have been possible then. If you look at early 1960s movies, a lot of times you can have tracking shots that were in front of people. We accomplish these shots on the dolly where most productions might ordinarily employ a Steadicam. Great care and expense goes into making our floors in the office as "dolly friendly" as possible so we snake around that place in the more traditional way with the dolly. We do those shots all the time — and where we can't because the floor isn't smooth, we find another way.

LG: *Can you tell us more about your sense of* Mad Men *as a show about the 1960s?*

PA: It's definitely a show about the 1960s, but I guess the reason it captured some sort of zeitgeist that's going on today, in a sense, is that it reflects on who we are today. I think that's the ingenious part of the writing, setting the show in a time period and then to reflect on what we're doing today.

JV: *What are some of those aspects of what we're doing today that are reflected in the show?*

PA: That's a good question. I think it's really just the humanity of it, honestly. There's something that happens when you take a group of fictional characters and put them in a historical setting, as historically accurate as one can be, and certainly the show is as historically accurate as it can be. There's nothing casual about any decision that's made in terms of a newspaper headline or anything. When Don is at home and he turns on the TV, a date has been set in the writer's mind — "Oh, that's a Sunday and we're in this week on the calendar" — and they'll have a choice of what was on, to the day. They're very concerned about that. But how does it reflect on who we are as a culture today? I don't know if I can speak to that specifically. It's just a great piece of drama. There's a mystery of this man and how he weaves in and out of these lives. There's also a sense of nostalgia when we look back on this. It separates it from being too instantly relatable — it resonates a bit more because of that separation in time, as opposed to seeing a contemporary show where it feels like "yes, this speaks to me" or "no, it doesn't." There's something about that separation, and you might look back on it in a nostalgic way, but it resonates in a more meaningful way today.

JV: *The show does take on some big historical events and iconic moments like the assassination of Kennedy, which I didn't live through, and which I assume you didn't live through. It's just a distant memory. What was it like putting that episode ["The Grown-Ups," 3.12] together?*

PA: Well, Barbet Schroeder directed that episode. But I think it's a big deal. I have to say it's a big moment in the script and it's a big historical moment for any director.

LG: *People knew it was coming all along because of the date of the wedding —*

PA: People were waiting for it, yeah, because you saw that invitation for the wedding — it's like, oh boy — and that was quite a few episodes earlier. So in a way the scene was planted. But I have to say that I don't really treat those things in any way formally special other than that it's an event occurring at that time and these people are reacting to it. It resonates for us because it's a big event in our collective historical memory.

JV: Mad Men *is a show about the 1960s, but it's not a show about the 1960s we're familiar with. It's not about civil rights protests, Vietnam protests, even the counterculture. It's this drab suburbia, it's this floating world of Madison Avenue that seems very boozy, very indulgent, and very libidinal — in many ways a profoundly sinful environment, like the curtain's been pulled. What's it like opening us up onto that world, and how did that fit into your understanding of what the 1960s were?*

PA: I don't think it fit into what my understanding of what the 1960s were at all . . . and while Matt might maintain that all this stuff is really true, you know it may or may not be, there's a lot of use of dramatic license in terms of what these people are doing, they are fictional characters. However, all the smoking and all the drinking, that was definitely part of what that culture was. People smoked like crazy. And we don't do it on the show to say, "Oh, hey, look at us, we're smoking all the time." I mean, we try not to. I'm actually more conscious of that. I always feel like, if they're smoking *all* the time, is it going to be just distracting from what's going on? That's my 2010 mentality imposing itself on what those characters may or may not do. Matt is always saying, "They're smoking, they smoked two, three packs a day and the ashtrays are bulging over with stubs. And the place was dirty. You go outside, there was trash on the ground." The idea being that there's a tendency in television, and it comes from the collective craftspeople being inculcated into that notion that everything has to be a little bit sanitized for its display on television. And that's part of the culture of Hollywood or the culture of television or the culture of the fact that you're spending all this money and you're getting all these professional people to paint this picture, and then you see some stray piece of crap, and people say, "Oh, get that out of there." You don't even think about doing it, and yet then you look at it and it's all so sanitized. In a way, I feel like *Boardwalk Empire* is just too clean. It's funny because it's a great show, and we'll all talk about it, but amongst the *Mad Men*-ites, well, it's just too clean.

JV: *Some people have attributed the popularity of the show in part to the way it gives us a vicarious experience of vice. It's a world that's repulsive and seductive at the same time. How conscious of that tension are you, and do you consciously play to stimulating desire?*

PA: Yeah, I think you said it exactly. It is both enticing and off-putting at the same time, but you've put your finger on what makes drama. When you're appealing to someone's inner yearnings and yet you're making a character like Tony Soprano, that very notion is dramatic. I mean, the audience completely allied themselves with him, and yet we're repulsed at the notion that they were doing that with this man. That was for me the brilliance of that show, where you can take this monster and make him likable, and they did that really well. It's creating a tension with your audience and it puts them on unsure footing a little bit, which is really a great dramatic thing.

LG: *Do you think* Mad Men *ups the ante just a little bit? Some people really dislike the show in a way that I don't think was ever true of* The Sopranos. *They feel it's bad; they feel it's smug; they feel it asks us to congratulate ourselves for not being them. They are disturbed by this jarring blend of naturalism and glamor.*

PA: That's interesting. I know Betty Draper has been getting a lot of bad press—you know, the worst mother in the world kind of thing. It's funny, I don't relate to her that way at all, as a viewer or as a fan of the show. In a way, I relate—not because my mother was like Betty, but because things were not so protected and were much more natural, as you were saying. But I do think that the Tony Soprano character *was* glamorous in a way, and was a very unusual kind of sex symbol, and had that relationship with the audience. He was very charismatic.

So while he may have been ugly, there was something very approachable about that guy, whereas someone like Jon Hamm who is so movie star and statuesque has a much harder façade that is harder to crack. Where with Tony you can feel his pain, with Don it's much more mannered, truthfully. It feels, not necessarily like a dramatic device but . . . You asked me [earlier] about whether *Mad Men* is like a novel—I actually think of the show *as* a novel. It plays out like a novel. I've talked to Matt about this and he's thought about it too, and a lot of that has to do with observing these characters in moments when they are unobserved. There are moments in life—like when I'm having this conversation with you and I turn to go down the hall there might be some countenance shift that might signal what I felt about what was happening or what it meant to me. And those are very important moments in *Mad Men*, and they're kind of unscripted, but they speak volumes in trying to make sense dramatically of these internal moments. I don't mean to say there is a subtle use of facial expressions that the actors are mastering to lay commentary on the scene—what I am saying is that when you end a scene on a shot on someone's face, it can serve as a commentary like punctuation can—just allowing the screen time for the processing to occur in one's mind is in many ways a hallmark of the show. A lot of people say, what moves it? It's a lot about the internal relationships of the characters.

LG: *You were the cinematographer for "Babylon" [1.6] Can you tell me about the concluding montage in that episode?*

PA: Those montages are written in the script. Andrew Bernstein was the director of that episode, and when you have a montage written, the thing you think about as a director is how you get in and out of those shots and what brings you into one, out of another, because you know they're going to be cut together that way. And as opposed to just cutting, I personally like to move the camera a lot, and I think it helps bridge those things.

LG: *Who decided when to fade and when to cut? Because it's very interesting in that montage that it fades from Don to Rachel and back, from to Sally and Betty and back, and then cuts to Joan and Roger.*

PA: Right. The Joan and Roger aspect of it is not Don's side of the story. I think Andrew and I may have talked about that. I don't remember. Maybe Andrew did that in the cutting room. It makes total sense to do that, but that choice, while formally meaningful, wasn't part of what we were shooting, because you could've either faded or cut to it with any of them. But the camera move—for instance, I know in that montage scene with Joan and Roger, we had designed this spectacular single shot, which Matt then cut up. Because you have to give options sometimes too. And that very wide shot, that tableau that the show goes out on, with Joan and Roger outside. That was always a shot that we wanted to get. But there was a shot, which was sort of technically difficult to achieve, where we started down the street, dollying toward the entrance of the Waldorf Astoria, from which Joan exits, then she goes out of frame, and we continue dollying, and then pick up Roger coming through the lobby. He comes out, and then we continue dollying, and he comes up to the curb, and then it lands with him in a big profile close up lighting a cigarette. And then we see Joan all the way down the block waiting for a cab, and then we were going to cut wide. But I guess it must've gone too long for Matt, or he just lost interest, so he cut that shot up, which happens all the time. It still resonates tremendously. It's a great montage, but there's an example of an aspect that wasn't pre-planned in exactly the way it landed on the screen. And Matt does that a lot. Directors have ideas that are not Matt's ideas — not to say that it has to be his idea, but he just sort of saw it differently, and then he tries to construct it more. . . . Unless he gravitates to what he saw and says, "Wow." Which is what he's always telling me: "I want you to come up with ideas that I haven't thought of that I love every bit as much as my own." But you're not always successful.

LG: *"The Summer Man" seems like an episode that had a lot of weight put on it because up until that point Don is in a relentless downward spiral, and something has to show that he'll be able to turn things around.*

PA: Right. That's exactly right. He goes on his alcohol-free diet, and starts to crawl out of the hole. I think the idea of writing in the journal was all part of that. And the swimming is all that renewal, that's all that it represented. There's also an aspect of — there's a scene when he's first doing the swimming, where he's coughing his lungs out, and some young guy says, "Hey, you need a hand, old man?" And there's a sense that he is getting older. And when you get older it happens very insidiously, where all of a sudden all these things start to happen. . . . And that was part of the thinking behind that scene. We had Don in the locker room and the guy puts the transistor down and you hear "Satisfaction" [by the Rolling Stones]. This is the revolution to come, and Don isn't part of it yet. That music that is coming: he hears it but he doesn't really understand it.

LG: *The show's use of music is so interesting. There have been some surprising choices here and there. Can you tell me about the process?*

PA: I can tell you I'm not really involved in it. Dave Carbonara writes all the original music and breaks the script down for music. Matt is very hands on with the music and all of those things. So "Satisfaction" was scripted. It's just expensive. You can't always have what you want.

LG: *Do you know if that was the reason why there was an instrumental version of the Beatles' "Do You Want to Know a Secret?" [at the end of "Hands and Knees" (4.10)]?*

PA: The Beatles turned us down. We couldn't get Beatles music.

LG: *Simultaneity is another one of those novelistic qualities that* Mad Men *develops in an interesting way: for example, when a scene cuts to another scene in a different location but taking place in the same stream of time. In "Chinese Wall," when Don ends up having what we think will be a temporary fling with Megan, the camera cuts to Roger's wife Jane alone in what looks to be a cavernous, empty Sterling home. Was that sequence scripted? That is, since it ends up being the case that Don emulates Roger by marrying his secretary, was that one of those moments where something was going to happen that you wanted to emphasize?*

PA: No. In a word, no. That juxtaposition was there in the script. I'm aware of what it does, and I knew how the story would develop, but was there something that I did directorially to make that scene play to that thought? I don't think so.

LG: *The apartment is so cold looking.*

PA: We had a lot of discussion about what would Roger's apartment be. We ended up shooting it on location. We wanted to build it. There was a thought about having old prewar bones with more modern furniture, so these are design tweaks that go through the production process. But we only saw one view on his living room. I couldn't turn around because there was nothing there. Many times, truthfully, the way you shoot things is born out of the limitations that are present on set. I liked the idea of Jane as this kept Siamese cat in her lair and Roger coming in all beat up for having done what he did with Lucky Strike. And his knife stab is to see Jane so excited about his book. I thought that was a great moment for him to be confronted with *Sterling's Gold*. But did I do anything to say Roger and Jane, Don and Megan, there they are, that's what's going to happen? No.

LG: *While we are on the topic of location: it's so interesting to me that you're a New Yorker and* Mad Men *is set in New York, but has a frame of it ever been shot in New York?*

PA: The pilot was shot in New York . . . but then, subsequently, not a single frame. I've on occasion had the idea to introduce more shots of New York. I think it was in "The Summer Man" when Don was in a cab with Bethany and he says good-bye and then later on he's in a cab with Faye, and there's all these cabs. The way it was scripted, the way it was written, you're in cab, cab, cab, cab, and we have to do all these cab shots on a dark stage with crappy light effects. So, how the hell do I bring life to that? And I really wanted post-production to dig into a 1960s cab drive by on the streets, some piece of stock footage. Every time I mentioned it, Scott Hornbacher, our producer, and Blake McCormick, our post-producer, would look at me like, "Oh, we've never done that before." Yeah, but how great would it be if you found something—even from a movie, and you license the clip? But the show doesn't go there. I don't know if it would've worked or not, but I would've liked to have seen it cut in to make that decision. But we didn't do it. This is the world as we're presenting it, and dramatically if it's interesting the viewer will be with you, which is what you have to hang your hat on, because we're in the cab and you don't see anything out the window, but hopefully you're engaged.

LG: *Speaking for myself, I find "New York" very convincing in the show—not in the graphic sense that, for example,* The Wire *is about Baltimore, but just because it's believable that the* Mad Men *world would be so interior, that we're looking at offices, suburban homes, and trains. What interests me, though, is what happens when the show goes to L.A., where it seems to open up.*

PA: There is an Eastern sensibility of the West being like a promised land. I don't necessarily feel that way, but I understand it as a feeling. I don't know if it's a past sense of pioneering but there was something about the West, and the weather, and the sunshine. I can see it being sort of enticing. I know that even in "The Jet Set" the guys in the office say, "I want to get out there." They pine for that, and all Pete does is bring back a bag of oranges. But there is a false sense of the open frontier to a Northeasterner that L.A. might represent.

LG: *As you directed "The Jet Set," what did you want to make of the sudden brightness and sunniness of L.A.?*

PA: That was very much a part of what that episode was, and that's the way we wanted to present it. There was no question. All of a sudden we're not on Madison Avenue, and let's show that as best we can. However, I have to say that if we had that opportunity to be outside in New York in the West Village, we would show that much more than we do. Just the sheer logistics of it. I mean, if we could have a scene in the subway or something, we would do that instantly, but it's too big a deal to build it. We shoot the show in eight days now, and you're literally going from eight-day cycle to eight-day cycle, so you don't have that much time to create these things. Or the money. But in "The Jet Set" there was this sense of L.A. involving a hedonism that you don't have at home, and Joy was the embodiment of that in that episode.

LG: *And in "Souvenir," when Don and Betty travel to Italy, how did that open things up or change things?*

PA: That was a great episode. I loved it a lot. There are challenges to finding those locations in L.A. We looked at *La Dolce Vita* [1960] and *8 ½* [1963], and that's what we wanted it to feel like. But the scenes in Rome just frame what happens within the episode, and they influence the episode, but it's not like the whole episode is out there. We just wanted that feeling. We shot it outside the Dorothy Chandler Pavilion in L.A. We really created that space. We put cars in an interior walkway. It was a little bit of a production number. But the aim was just to present something different that we don't usually get to see on the show.

LG: *What about the flashbacks in episodes like "The Hobo Code"? That must have felt so different. Suddenly you're on a farm in Illinois.*

PA: Yeah, but to me a flashback is such a motion picture device. I'm sure there's a novelistic precedent for it as well. It did feel very different, and it's important to cast these people just correctly. Who are his parents? And we're beginning to tell that story. Formally, I certainly shot it in a different way. There were certain images that came into my mind. There's that image when we first reveal the hobo, and I come out over him, and it was an image that was repeated throughout *The Searchers* [1956]. It's a very John Ford kind of image, and I had that in mind. But one of the great things for me in that episode was how the hobo marked that the father was a dishonest man. And at the end of the show I follow Don into his door and the door closes and there's Don Draper. That was something that was not scripted. I don't know where the idea actually came to me, but I enjoyed that it worked so well.

JV: *Since you can't shoot outdoors in New York where most of the action is set, does that structural constraint affect the texture of the show? Toward the later part of the 1960s the action is in the streets, metaphorically and physically. So how do you open that up if you can't get into the streets? Can certain stories be told from the interior?*

PA: That's a good question. The show has yet to discover how they're going to do that. The show at most has three more seasons, probably just two. So where will it take us in time? I don't know. We've always talked about it going into the 1970s, so maybe that's what it will do. But I don't know what's in store for it, but Matt has been very smart about where he sets these scenes and how he tells the story in its setting, and there are certain things that are very important to him where they might be. Of course he understands the limitations, and that is what it is. We'll find a little corner of the street and that'll be the street, and we've done some effects stuff where we have Don walking down the block and we'll put stuff in behind him or we'll digitally remove palm trees. But will it ever get to the point of that sort of unrest and taking to the streets? I don't know, but if we need to I think the show will find its way to do that.

LG: *If you could do anything, add any character, any setting, any location, any situation, what would it be?*

PA: For some reason, I've always wanted to do a scene on the subway. To me, that is the quintessential New York experience. So maybe one day we'll do it. We've been on commuter trains and we've been on airplanes, but to be on a subway is visually a cool thing. It's so New York. But that's ephemera, little things that you'd like to do. I haven't really thought that much about it. Really, as a director, especially a director on television, once you're given that script, that becomes your blueprint for your work, and you might see opportunities in there and you go to Matt and say, "What if we could do this or that," or "I found this location so instead of setting it here could we do it here?" Those are the things that I get invested in. But I don't know if I just abstractly think, "Gee, I wish we could . . ." Personally, I wish we could be out more. I appreciate the interior, internal quality to the show, but I would love to be out on the streets a little bit more.

LG: *Do you have a particular character that you feel strongly about that you'd like to put in a different situation?*

PA: I have certain characters who are great, who I love. I've done a bunch of shows with Pete, and I like him as a character because I think, as a dramatic lead, he's just very interesting in terms of how he navigates that world. And he's changed in how he relates to Don and Roger and being at Sterling Cooper. He's "owning it" more, and he's more self-assured than he was when we first met him. Because of this interview I started going back and I looked at some older shows because I never go back and look at old shows. But I did because you were asking specifically about "Maidenform" and "The Jet Set." I looked a little bit at "Marriage of Figaro" [1.3] and I saw Pete in that and how, him coming back from his honeymoon, it really felt like this character has changed a lot just in terms of the way he deals with Don and the way he deals with everyone in the office. The show has changed a lot. The characters have changed a lot over that period of time, as they get to know each other better and as we get to know them better. I like the minor characters a lot. Harry and Ken, I like those guys, and I love it when they get some juicy bit of business to do because it's fun to explore that with them.

LG: *Do you miss Paul?*
PA: [hesitates] At times.

LG: *Sal?*
PA: You know, Sal . . . Do I miss them? No, not really. Do I miss them as a fan of the show or as a director — "Oh, I wish I had a scene to do with Sal"? No, not really. I like them all individually as people. So I'm sorry that we're not all together, but you know what, dramatically you kind of have to let characters go sometimes. At least on *Mad Men* there is always the chance that they will come back down the road — you never know. On *The Sopranos* when we let a character go it was usually more permanent. [Paul] was an interesting character in terms of where he took us historically: his black girlfriend and the civil rights movement was interesting. But I don't think that those aspects of society are something that Matt is just cutting loose by losing Paul. I think we'll find other ways to get there.

LG: *At least in my generation, thinking about "the 1960s" meant feminism and Jim Morrison, and those sorts of countercultural figures and events. Whereas the early years of the decade seemed to be lost to cultural consciousness. Now that the last season has ended in the summer of 1965, what challenges do you think the imminent arrival of "those 1960s" are going to pose?*

PA: I can't wait. I've talked about seeing Don Draper into the early 1970s, with the sideburns and the long hair. I think that would be fantastic. But I don't know what makes that earlier period "lost," as you described it. What makes it lost in terms of the collective consciousness? And has *Mad Men* resurrected it and has that vision that the show is portraying now clouded our own view as a culture, thinking, "Oh, *that's* what it was like, I didn't really know." Anymore than the 1950s were like *Leave It to Beaver* or *Father Knows Best* or those kinds of shows. Was that representative of what the culture really was at that time, or was it just the TV version of that?

LG: *I think those are two separate questions. One of them is, is the TV version of any-thing—1950s, 1960s, or otherwise—an accurate reflection of what was going on? But another is, prior to* Mad Men, *was the 1960s in some sense a truncated decade in terms of what was remembered? People remember* Camelot, *and Jackie, and JFK—*

PA: And the assassination, and the Bay of Pigs. There are a lot of historical associa-tions and touchstones there . . . but I never thought of it as a period that was forgotten. I never did, maybe because I was born right then.

JV: *But it does push to the margins a lot of important stuff in the 1960s, like the civil rights movement. These guys in* Mad Men *are in a bubble—*

PA: They are totally in a bubble.

JV: *They're not curious, they're racists. Peggy is bringing in feminism, but in a very halt-ing way. You asked, is this depiction making the picture of the 1960s more cloudy? There is perhaps a danger that some of the things we commonly associate with the decade are so pushed to the side that that important history in some sense gets lost and is minimized in the effort to show that not everyone was on the barricades or in a sit-in.*

PA: Right. Well, we're not making a documentary. So, yes, there are going to be people who say—I mean, there's a certain innocence when Pete goes into the elevator in "The Fog" with Hollis, and they're talking about televisions, and he stops the elevator and asks, do black people buy . . . ? [*Hesitates, trying to remem-ber the brand.*]

LG: *Admiral. It's a great scene*

JV: *It is, and we do judge Pete, but Hollis never really gets to come into his own as a char-acter. Have you thought of having an African American character of some substance and dimension?*

PA: We have talked about it, and Matt knows that he gets grief for not having African Americans in the show, but truthfully, in that time, they were working as custodians and elevator men in that environment. Were they having peers on Madison Avenue in 1963 in the inner office? As far as he's saying, no, that wasn't really happening. Maybe there was one or two guys, but then I think dramatically if you say out of a pool of a thousand people there were two African American account execs, and we're going to have one of them on our show, it becomes the homogenized TV version of, "Oh, we're representing everybody." In a way, I think it's a little more truthful when you do have African Americans on the show, you have them in the way they *are* in the period and that's the way we're doing it. I think it will change. As the time progresses forward there's no doubt that Matt will be more true to what that time was doing. I think that's the intention at least. It's not unnoticed.

LG: *Could you imagine how the show might be if, say—and I realize this could be a completely different show—we met Carla's husband and her kids in one episode?*

PA: No, I think that would be cool. I don't think that would be beyond what the show currently is and wants to be. There could be something that happens where Carla has to take the kids home and you have a moment there and you see that.

JV: *I mean, you can put African Americans into the executive world in an artificial way, and that violates a kind of realism, or you could do what we're discussing now, opening up a world that you don't yet show, and then you have a tension of two different communities experiencing the same times differently.*

PA: Yes, but you know these are choices that are made. I don't think that you're wrong, but I think that there may be a feeling from Matt that to do that would be considered sort of—

JV: *Pandering to a kind of pressure?*

PA: Or being this progressive television writer who is looking at things progressively and not being so on the nose about how things really were. In fact, it's very pointed not to have African American executives, and that makes the subject and the discussion in a way even more lively. So there are many ways of looking at that.

LG: *You haven't said anything about Peggy or Joan. I'm curious how you relate to those characters.*

PA: Well, Peggy is probably the best character on the show. She's just so fantastic. I sort of struggle with Joan a little bit more as a character, or maybe as an actor. When you're directing these people, and I know them all well, sometimes either the real person's personality speaks to you in that personal way or it doesn't. For whatever reason, Christina [Hendricks] and I—we don't talk the same language as people—maybe it's because we're both redheads. I feel badly because

I know sometimes I've confused her about what she's doing—which is exactly the opposite of what you want to be doing as a director. But I think that's where people's real personality comes into play, and your job as a director is to find the bit of explanation or direction that will work for that particular actor.

LG: *I'm thinking back to the episodes you directed—*

PA: I haven't done a lot with her, but on this last season in "The Summer Man," where Joan confronts Stan and Joey in the Creative Lounge as they're laughing about the drawing they taped on her glass wall. She lays into them in this cold, emotionless way about how she'll have the last laugh when they're knee deep in a rice paddy in Vietnam, and I wanted to nuance her delivery of that speech— which she did really well. I was trying to explain to her that just being able to deliver it in this cold, unemotional way is a very emotional thing, and could we see hints of that toll it's actually taking on her to stand up to them like that? Well, I guess I wasn't explaining myself and it served to confuse her, which I feel badly about. In the end I think it turned out well, but if I had been better at my job there might have been an additional moment where we could see how this really affected Joan.

JV: *You speak about characters in* Mad Men *almost like real people, and at this level of involvement in constructing them, do they almost seem real?*

PA: Totally. Yes.

JV: *What's it like having a show with no protagonist in a classic sense?*

PA: Well, there's always a protagonist for the episode. What I always try to do is ask, what is this episode about? Once I understand that, then formally I try to figure out how to visually set up—whatever it's about. I want it to influence every decision I make. You can't always do that, but if you try to, sometimes you get to. But in terms of characters, the beauty of the show for me is the rotating group of characters. We go to Pete and Trudy, and we see Peggy and her misadventures, and Roger, and then Don. And there are threads that bind them all together. Dramatically, those are the things that—without there being what you call real self-introspection—bind everything together so that collectively the viewer gets a sense of introspection. That's a crucial thing dramatically; the viewer feels the very thing that the character's feeling, even though the character may not be intellectualizing it.

JV: *Do you find yourself rooting for them, where there's disappointment when they fall and happiness when they rise?*

PA: Of course. Absolutely. That's actually very present in my feeling. The people who work on the show are huge fans of the show. We're living it with them.

JV: *Do you want things for the characters?*

PA: Certainly for Peggy. Peggy is the most—you want everything for her.

LG: *Is she getting the things that you want for her?*

PA: Is she? Never quite. There's always that feeling of falling short—you know, poor Peggy. Like she even says, "I knew things were going too well." In "Chinese Wall," where she finally has this fling with this guy, and she comes down and they're having a whole meeting about how they're cutting back because they lost Lucky Strike. So she's whistling her way down the hallway, just having her affair with her new boyfriend, only to be confronted with bad news. So Peggy is always getting that comeuppance. As are most people in the show, which is what life is like.

LIST OF *MAD MEN* EPISODES

SEASON 1

1.1
"Smoke Gets in Your Eyes." AMC. Dir. Alan Taylor. Writ. Matthew Weiner. 19 July 2007.

1.2
"Ladies Room." AMC. Dir. Alan Taylor. Writ. Matthew Weiner. 26 July 2007.

1.3
"Marriage of Figaro." AMC. Dir. Ed Bianchi. Writ. Tom Palmer. 2 Aug. 2007

1.4
"New Amsterdam." AMC. Dir. Tim Hunter. Writ. Lisa Albert. 9 Aug. 2007.

1.5
"5G." AMC. Dir. Lesli Linka Glatter. Writ. Matthew Weiner. 16 Aug. 2007.

1.6
"Babylon." AMC. Dir. Andrew Bernstein. Writ. Andre Jacquemetton and Maria Jacquemetton. 23 Aug. 2007.

1.7
"Red in the Face." AMC. Dir. Tim Hunter. Writ. Bridget Bedard. 30 Aug. 2007.

1.8
"The Hobo Code." AMC. Dir. Phil Abraham. Writ. Chris Provenzano. 6 Sept. 2007.

1.9
"Shoot." AMC. Dir. Paul Feig. Writ. Chris Provenzano and Matthew Weiner. 13 Sept. 2007.

1.10
"Long Weekend." AMC. Dir. Tim Hunter. Writ. Bridget Bedard, Andre Jacquemetton, Maria Jacquemetton, and Matthew Weiner. 27 Sept. 2007.

1.11
"Indian Summer." AMC. Dir. Tim Hunter. Writ. Tom Palmer and Matthew Weiner. 4 Oct. 2007.

1.12
"Nixon vs. Kennedy." AMC. Dir. Alan
Taylor. Writ. Lisa Albert, Andrew
Jacquemetton, and Maria Jacque-
metton. 11 Oct. 2007.

1.13
"The Wheel." AMC. Dir. Matthew
Weiner. Writ. Matthew Weiner and
Robin Veith. 18 Oct. 2007.

SEASON 2

2.1
"For Those Who Think Young." AMC.
Dir. Tim Hunter. Writ. Matthew
Weiner. 27 July 2008.

2.2
"Flight 1." AMC. Dir. Andrew Bernstein.
Writ. Lisa Albert and Matthew Weiner.
3 Aug. 2008.

2.3
"The Benefactor." AMC. Dir. Lesli Linka
Glatter. Writ. Matthew Weiner and Rick
Cleveland. 10 Aug. 2008.

2.4
"Three Sundays." AMC. Dir. Tim
Hunter. Writ. Andre Jacquemetton and
Maria Jacquemetton. 17 Aug. 2008.

2.5
"The New Girl." AMC. Dir. Jennifer
Getzinger. Writ. Robin Veith. 24 Aug.
2008.

2.6
"Maidenform." AMC. Dir. Phil Abraham. Writ. Matthew Weiner. 31 Aug.
2008.

2.7
"The Gold Violin." AMC. Dir. Andrew
Bernstein. Writ. Jane Anderson, Andre
Jacquemetton, and Maria Jacque-
metton. 7 Sept. 2008.

2.8
"A Night to Remember." AMC. Dir.
Lesli Linka Glatter. Writ. Robin Veith
and Matthew Weiner. 14 Sept. 2008.

2.9
"Six Month Leave." AMC. Dir. Michael
Uppendahl. Writ. Andre Jacquemetton,
Maria Jacquemetton, and Matthew
Weiner. 28 Sept. 2008.

2.10
"The Inheritance." AMC. Dir. Andrew
Bernstein. Writ. Lisa Albert, Marti
Noxon, and Matthew Weiner. 5 Oct.
2008.

2.11
"The Jet Set." AMC. Dir. Phil Abraham.
Writ. Matthew Weiner. 12 Oct. 2008.

2.12
"The Mountain King." AMC. Dir. Alan
Taylor. Writ. Matthew Weiner and
Robin Veith. 19 Oct. 2008.

2.13
"Meditations in an Emergency." AMC.
Dir. Matthew Weiner. Writ. Matthew
Weiner and Kater Gordon. 26 Oct.
2008.

SEASON 3

3.1
"Out of Town." AMC. Dir. Phil Abraham. Writ. Matthew Weiner. 16 Aug. 2009.

3.2
"Love among the Ruins." AMC. Dir. Lesli Linka Glatter. Writ. Cathryn Humphris and Matthew Weiner. 23 Aug. 2009.

3.3
"My Old Kentucky Home." AMC. Dir. Jennifer Getzinger. Writ. Dahvi Waller and Matthew Weiner. 30 Aug. 2009.

3.4
"The Arrangements." AMC. Dir. Michael Uppendahl. Writ. Andrew Colville and Matthew Weiner. 6 Sept. 2009.

3.5
"The Fog." AMC. Dir. Phil Abraham. Writ. Kater Gordon. 13 Sept. 2009.

3.6
"Guy Walks into an Advertising Agency." AMC. Dir. Lesli Linka Glatter. Writ. Robin Veith and Matthew Weiner. 20 Sept. 2009.

3.7
"Seven Twenty Three." AMC. Dir. Daisy von Scherler Mayer. Writ. Andre Jacquemetton, Maria Jacquemetton, and Matthew Weiner. 27 Sept. 2009.

3.8
"Souvenir." AMC. Dir. Phil Abraham. Writ. Lisa Albert and Matthew Weiner. 4 Oct. 2009.

3.9
"Wee Small Hours." AMC. Dir. Scott Hornbacher. Writ. Dahvi Waller and Matthew Weiner. 11 Oct. 2009.

3.10
"The Color Blue." AMC. Dir. Michael Uppendahl. Writ. Kater Gordon and Matthew Weiner. 18 Oct. 2009.

3.11
"The Gypsy and the Hobo." AMC. Dir. Jennifer Getzinger. Writ. Marti Noxon, Cathryn Humphris, and Matthew Weiner. 25 Oct. 2009.

3.12
"The Grown-Ups." AMC. Dir. Barbet Schroeder. Writ. Brett Johnson and Matthew Weiner. 1 Nov. 2009.

3.13
"Shut the Door. Have a Seat." AMC. Dir. Matthew Weiner. Writ. Matthew Weiner and Erin Levy. 8 Nov. 2009.

SEASON 4

4.1
"Public Relations." AMC. Dir. Phil Abraham. Writ. Matthew Weiner. 25 July 2010.

4.2
"Christmas Comes but Once a Year." AMC. Dir. Michael Uppendahl. Writ. Tracy McMillan and Matthew Weiner. 1 Aug. 2010.

4.3
"The Good News." AMC. Dir. Jennifer Getzinger. Writ. Jonathan Abrahams and Matthew Weiner. 8 Aug. 2010.

4.4
"The Rejected." AMC. Dir. John Slattery. Writ. Keith Huff and Matthew Weiner. 15 Aug. 2010.

4.5
"The Chrysanthemum and the Sword." AMC. Dir. Lesli Linka Glatter. Writ. Erin Levy. 22 Aug. 2010.

4.6
"Waldorf Stories." AMC. Dir. Scott Hornbacher. Writ. Brett Johnson and Matthew Weiner. 29 Aug. 2010.

4.7
"The Suitcase." AMC. Dir. Jennifer Getzinger. Writ. Matthew Weiner. 5 Sept. 2010.

4.8
"The Summer Man." AMC. Dir. Phil Abraham. Writ. Lisa Albert, Janet Leahy, and Matthew Weiner. 12 Sept. 2010.

4.9
"The Beautiful Girls." AMC. Dir. Michael Uppendahl. Writ. Dahvi Waller and Matthew Weiner. 19 Sept. 2010.

4.10
"Hands and Knees." AMC. Dir. Lynn Shelton. Writ. Jonathan Abrahams and Matthew Weiner. 26 Sept. 2010.

4.11
"Chinese Wall." AMC. Dir. Phil Abraham. Writ. Erin Levy. 3 Oct. 2010.

4.12
"Blowing Smoke." AMC. Dir. John Slattery. Writ. Andre Jacquemetton and Maria Jacquemetton. 10 Oct. 2010.

4.13
"Tomorrowland." AMC. Dir. Matthew Weiner. Writ. Jonathan Igla and Matthew Weiner. 17 Oct. 2010.

Adorno, Theodor W. *Aesthetic Theory*. Trans. Robert Hullot-Kentor. Minneapolis: University of Minnesota Press, 1997.

Adorno, Theodor W., and Max Horkheimer. *The Dialectic of Enlightenment*. 1944. Trans. John Cumming. London and New York: Verso, 1997.

AlSayyad, Nezar. *Cinematic Urbanism: A History of the Modern from Reel to Real*. New York: Routledge, 2006.

Alvey, Mark. "The Defenders." *The Encyclopedia of Television*, 2nd ed., ed. Horace Newcomb, 672–74. Chicago: Taylor and Francis, 2004.

Aminosharei, Nojan, and Malina Joseph. "Mad Men Fashion! How to Dress Like Betty, Peggy and Joan." *Elle*, 3 September 2009. Web. Accessed 22 April 2011.

Anderson, Jervis. *A. Philip Randolph: A Biographical Portrait*. New York: Harcourt, 1973.

Anderson, Steve. "Loafing in the Garden of Knowledge: History TV and Popular Memory." *Film and History* 30.1 (2000): 14–23.

Anderson, Terry. *The Movement and the Sixties: Protest America from Greensboro to Wounded Knee*. London: Oxford University Press, 1996.

Andreeva, Nellie. "Ratings Rat Race: Season 3 Premiere of HBO's 'True Blood' Scores Big on Sunday." *Deadline Hollywood*, 15 June 2010. Web. Accessed 28 May 2011.

Ang, Ien. *Desperately Seeking the Audience*. London: Routledge, 1991.

Armstrong, Jennifer. "Hey, 'Mad Men' Fans, Can We Borrow a Few Bucks?" *Popwatch* (blog), *Entertainment Weekly*, 26 July 2010. Web. Accessed 28 May 2011.

Associated Press. "'Sopranos' Ratings Beat Most Network Shows." *Today*, 15 June 2007. Web. Accessed 28 May 2011.

Auslander, Philip. *Liveness: Performance in a Mediatized Culture*. London: Routledge, 1999.

Bacon-Smith, Camille. *Enterprising Women: Television Fandom and the Creation of Popular Myth*. Philadelphia: University of Pennsylvania Press, 1992.

Baehr, Helen, and Gillian Dyer, eds. *Boxed In: Women and Television*. London: Pandora, 1987.

Baker, Houston A., Jr. *Blues, Ideology, and Afro-American Literature: A Vernacular Theory*. Chicago: University of Chicago Press, 1984.

Baldwin, James. *The Fire Next Time*. New York: Dell, 1964.

———. *Notes of a Native Son*. Boston: Beacon, 1955.

———. *The Price of the Ticket: Collected Nonfiction, 1948–1985*. New York: St. Martin's, 1985.

Baraka, Amiri (LeRoi Jones). *Blues People: Negro Music in White America*. New York: William Morrow, 1963.

Barthes, Roland. *Camera Lucida: Reflections on Photography*. Trans. Richard Howard. New York: Hill and Wang, 1981.

Battaglio, Stephen. "Old-Movie Channels Nearing Showdown." *New York Daily News*, 28 June 2002. Web. Accessed 12 April 2012.

Baudelaire, Charles. "The Painter of Modern Life." 1859. *The Painter of Modern Life and Other Essays*. Trans. and ed. Jonathan Mayne, 1–40. New York: Da Capo, 1964.

Beauchamp, Cari, and Judy Balban. "Cary in the Sky with Diamonds." *Vanity Fair*, August 2010. Web. Accessed 29 May 2011.

Becker, Ron. *Gay TV and Straight America*. New Brunswick: Rutgers University Press, 2006.

Bellafante, Ginia. "Abortion in the Eyes of a Girl from Dillon." *New York Times*, 9 July 2010. Web. Accessed 15 July 2010.

———. "'Mad Men' Watch: A Mood of Desperation." *New York Times*, 11 October 2010. Web. Accessed 31 May 2011.

Benjamin, Walter. "The Author as Producer." *New Left Review* 1.62 (July/August 1970).

———. "Paris of the Second Empire in Baudelaire." *Selected Writings, 1938–1940*. Ed. Howard Eiland and Michael W. Jennings, 3–92. Cambridge: Harvard University Press, 2003.

Bennett, Mark. *TV Sets: Fantasy Blueprints of Classic TV Homes*. New York: Black Dog, 2000.

Benton, Joshua. "'Mad Men' Ads Keep You on Your Couch." *Nieman Journalism Lab*, 23 October 2008.

Berger, John. *Ways of Seeing*. New York: Penguin, 1972.

Bérubé, Michael. *What's Liberal about the Liberal Arts? Classroom Politics and "Bias" in Higher Education*. New York: Norton, 2006.

Biondi, Martha. *To Stand and Fight: The Struggle for Civil Rights in Postwar New York City*. Cambridge: Harvard University Press, 2003.

Bondanella, Peter. *Italian Cinema: From Neorealism to the Present*. 3rd ed. New York: Continuum, 2001.

Bonilla-Silva, Eduardo. *Racism without Racists: Color-Blind Racism and Racial*

Inequality in Contemporary America. 3rd ed. Lanham, Md.: Rowman and Littlefield, 2010.

Bornstein, George. "The Colors of Zion: Black, Jewish, and Irish Nationalisms at the Turn of the Century." *Modernism/Modernity* 12.3 (2005): 369–84.

Bowden, Mark. "The Angriest Man on Television." *Atlantic Monthly*, January/February 2008, 50–57.

Boyarin, Jonathan. "Reading Exodus into History." *Palestine and Jewish History: Criticism at the Borders of Ethnography*, 40–67. Minneapolis: University of Minnesota Press, 1996.

Braxton, Greg. "A White, White World on TV's Fall Schedule." *Los Angeles Times*, 28 May 1999. Web. Accessed 12 April 2011.

Braxton, Joanne M., ed. *The Collected Poetry of Paul Laurence Dunbar.* Charlottesville: University Press of Virginia, 1993.

Breward, Christopher. "The Dandy Laid Bare: Embodying Practices and Fashion for Men." *Fashion Cultures: Theories, Explorations and Analysis*, ed. Stella Bruzzi and Pamela Church Gibson, 221–38. New York: Routledge, 2000.

Brodkin, Karen. *How Jews Became White Folks and What That Says about Race in America.* New Jersey: Rutgers University Press, 2000.

Brown, Bill. "Now Advertising: Late James." *Henry James Review* 30.1 (winter 2009): 10–21.

Brown, Claude. *Manchild in the Promised Land.* New York: Signet, 1965.

Brown, Helen Gurley. *Sex and the Single Girl.* 1962. New York: Barnes and Noble, 2004.

Brunsdon, Charlotte, Julie D'Acci, and Lynn Spigel, eds. *Feminist Television Criticism: A Reader.* 2nd ed. Buckingham: Open University Press, 2007.

Bruzzi, Stella. *Undressing Cinema: Clothing and Identity in the Movies.* London: Routledge, 1997.

Bryant, Janie, with Monica Corcoran Harel. *The Fashion File: Advice, Tips and Inspiration from the Costume Designer of "Mad Men."* New York: Grand Central, 2010.

Bryer, Marjorie Lee. "Representing the Nation: Pinups, Playboy, Pageants and Racial Politics, 1945–1966." Diss., University of Minnesota, 2003.

Bulk, Beth Snyder. "You Are What You Watch, Market Data Suggest." *Advertising Age*, 1 November 2010. Web. Accessed 28 May 2011.

Bury, Rhiannon. *Cyberspaces of Their Own: Female Fandoms Online.* New York: Peter Lang, 2005.

Buscombe, Edward. "Cary Grant." *Fashion Cultures: Theories, Explorations and Analysis*, ed. Stella Bruzzi and Pamela Church Gibson, 201–4. New York: Routledge, 2000.

Butler, Jeremy. "The Oppressive Rectangularity of the Fluorescent Light." *In Media Res*, Media Commons, 22 April 2009. Web. Accessed 12 April 2011.

Butler, Judith. *Gender Trouble: Feminism and the Subversion of Identity*. New York: Routledge, 1990.

Buzard, James. "'Anywhere's Nowhere': *Bleak House* as Autoethnography." *Yale Journal of Criticism* 12.1 (1999): 7–39.

Caddell, Bud. "Becoming a Mad Man." *We Are Sterling Cooper*, 2009. Web. Accessed 12 April 2011.

Caldwell, John Thornton. *Production Culture: Industrial Reflexivity and Critical Practice in Film and Television*. Durham: Duke University Press, 2008.

———. *Televisuality: Style, Crisis, and Authority in American Television*. New Brunswick: Rutgers University Press, 1995.

Calhoun, Ada. "*I Didn't Know I Was Pregnant*: Travesty or Guilty Pleasure?" *Time Entertainment*, 12 Jan 2010. Web. Accessed 3 July 2012.

Carlin, Diana B. "Lady Bird Johnson: The Making of a Public First Lady with Private Influence." *Inventing a Voice: The Rhetoric of American First Ladies of the Twentieth Century*, ed. Molly Meijer Wertheimer, 273–95. Oxford: Rowman and Littlefield, 2004.

Cawthorne, Nigel. *The New Look: The Dior Revolution*. Edison, N.J.: Welfleet, 1996.

Cha-Jua, Sundiata Keita, and Clarence Lang. "The 'Long Movement' as Vampire: Temporal and Spatial Fallacies in Recent Black Freedom Studies." *Journal of African American History* 92.2 (2007): 265–88.

Chambers, Jason. *Madison Avenue and the Color Line: African Americans in the Advertising Industry*. Philadelphia: University of Pennsylvania Press, 2008.

Chambers, Samuel A. *The Queer Politics of Television*. London: I. B. Tauris, 2006.

Chatman, Seymour. *Antonioni, or, The Surface of the World*. Berkeley: University of California Press, 1985.

Cheever, John. *The Stories of John Cheever*. New York: Knopf, 1978.

Cheyette, Bryan. *Constructions of "the Jew" in English Literature and Society: Racial Representations, 1875–1945*. Cambridge: Cambridge University Press, 1995.

Cheyette, Bryan, and Nadia Valman. *The Image of the Jew in European Liberal Culture, 1789–1914*. Edgware, UK: Vallentine Mitchell, 2004.

Childress, Alice. *Like One of the Family: Conversations from a Domestic's Life*. 1956. Boston: Beacon, 1986.

Clark, Amy S. "Detox for Video Game Addiction?" CBS *News*, 3 July 2006. Web. Accessed 30 December 2010.

Clarke, Steve. "BBC Finds Time for 'The Hour.'" *Variety*, 10 November 2010. Web. Accessed 5 December 2010.

Clover, Carol J. "The Eye of Horror." *Viewing Positions: Ways of Seeing Film*, ed. Linda Williams, 184–230. New Brunswick: Rutgers University Press, 1995.

———. *Men, Women and Chain Saws: Gender in the Modern Horror Film*. Princeton: Princeton University Press, 1992.

Coates, Ta-Nehisi. "The Negro Donald Draper." *Atlantic Monthly*, October 2008. Web. Accessed 15 August 2011.

———. "Race and Mad Men" (blog post). *Atlantic*, August 17, 2009. Web. Accessed 21 January 2011.

Cohan, Steven, and Ina Rae Hark. *Screening the Male: Exploring Masculinities in Hollywood Cinema*. New York: Routledge, 1993.

Cohen, Lizabeth. *A Consumer's Republic: The Politics of Mass Consumption in Postwar America*. New York: Knopf, 2003.

Collins, William J. "The Political Economy of State-Level Fair Employment Laws, 1940–1964." *Explorations in Economic History* 40.1 (2003): 24–51.

Conley, Jim, and Arlene Tigar McLaren. *Car Troubles: Critical Studies of Automobility and Auto-Mobility*. Farnham: Ashgate, 2009.

Cook, Pam. "Masculinity in Crisis?" *Screen* 23.3–4 (1982): 39–46.

Countryman, Matthew J. *Up South: Civil Rights and Black Power in Philadelphia*. Philadelphia: University of Pennsylvania Press, 2006.

Coward, Rosalind. *Female Desire*. London: Paladin, 1983.

Craik, Jennifer. *The Face of Fashion: Cultural Studies in Fashion*. London: Routledge, 1994.

Curtis, William J. R. *Modern Architecture since 1900*. 3rd ed. London: Phaidon, 1996.

D'Acci, Julie. *Defining Women: Television and the Case of "Cagney and Lacey."* Chapel Hill: University of North Carolina Press, 1994.

———. "Television, Representation, and Gender." *The Television Studies Reader*, ed. Robert C. Allen and Annette Hill, 373–88. New York: Routledge, 2004.

Dames, Nicholas. *The Physiology of the Novel: Reading, Neural Science, and the Form of Victorian Fiction*. Oxford: Oxford University Press, 2007.

Davis, Glyn, and Gary Needham, eds. *Queer TV: Theories, Histories, Politics*. New York: Routledge, 2009.

Davis, James A. "Cultural Factors in the Perception of Status Symbols." *Midwest Sociologist* 21 (1958): 5–10.

Davis, Kathy. *The Making of "Our Bodies, Ourselves": How Feminism Travels across Borders*. Durham: Duke University Press, 2007.

Davis, Maxine. "'Most Women Can Have Babies.'" *Good Housekeeping*, September 1940, 30–31, 66.

Dayan, Daniel, and Elihu Katz. *Media Events: The Live Broadcasting of History*. Cambridge: Harvard University Press, 1992.

Dean, Will. "The Last of the Madison Avenue Mavericks of Mad Men." *Guardian*, 17 July 2010. Web. Accessed 21 May 2011.

de Certeau, Michel. *The Practice of Everyday Life*. Trans. Steven Rendall. Berkeley: University of California Press, 1988.

Delaney, Sam. "HBO: Television Will Never Be the Same Again." *Telegraph*, 25 February 2009. Web. Accessed 30 December 2010.

DeLong, Marilyn, Barbara Heinemann, and Kathryn Reily. "Hooked on Vintage!" *Fashion Theory* 9.1 (2005): 23–43.

Dempsey, John. "AMC Unveils More Contemporary Slate, Extra Ads." *Variety*, 13 May 2002. Web. Accessed 12 April 2012.

Dickinson, Greg. "The Pleasantville Effect: Nostalgia and the Visual Framing of (White) Suburbia." *Western Journal of Communication* 70.3 (2006): 212–33.

Dienst, Richard. *Still Life in Real Time: Theory after Television*. Durham: Duke University Press, 1994.

Doane, Mary Ann. "Film and Masquerade: Theorizing the Female Spectator." *Screen* 23.3–4 (1982): 74–88.

———. "Information, Crisis, Catastrophe." *Logics of Television: Essays in Cultural Criticism*, ed. Patricia Mellencamp, 222–39. Bloomington: Indiana University Press, 1990.

Doty, Alexander. *Making Things Perfectly Queer: Interpreting Mass Culture*. Minneapolis: University of Minnesota Press, 1993.

Doyle, Sady. "Mad Men's Very Modern Sexism Problem." *Atlantic Monthly*, 2 August 2010. Web. Accessed 29 May 2011.

Duménil, Gérard, and Dominique Lévy. "The Nature and Contradictions of Neoliberalism." 20 December 2004. Web. Accessed 15 August 2011.

Dyer, Richard. "Don't Look Now — The Male Pin-Up." *Screen* 23.3–4 (1982): 61–73.

———. *White: Essays on Race and Culture*. London: Routledge, 1997.

Eagleton, Terry. *Criticism and Ideology: A Study in Marxist Literary Theory*. 1976. London: Verso, 1998.

Early, Gerald. "The Art of the Muscle: Miles Davis as American Knight and American Knave." *Miles Davis and American Culture*, ed. Gerald Early, 2–23. St. Louis: Missouri Historical Society, 2001.

Easthope, Antony. *What a Man's Gotta Do: The Masculine Myth in Popular Culture*. New York: Routledge, 1990.

Edgerton, Gary. "Falling Man and Mad Men (1:54)." *In Media Res*, Media Commons, 14 April 2009. Web. Accessed 12 April 2012.

———. "The Selling of *Mad Men*: A Production History." *Mad Men*, ed. Gary Edgerton, 3–24. New York: I. B. Tauris, 2011.

———. "Television as Historian: A Different Kind of History Altogether." *Television Histories: Shaping Collective Memory in the Media Age*, ed. Gary R. Edgerton and Peter C. Rollins, 1–16. Lexington: University Press of Kentucky, 2001.

Edgerton, Gary R., and Peter C. Rollins, eds. *Television Histories: Shaping Collective Memory in the Media Age*. Lexington: University Press of Kentucky, 2001.

Egner, Jeremy. "Seeing History in 'Mad Men.'" 16 July 2010. Web. Accessed 21 May 2011.

Ehrenreich, Barbara, and John Ehrenreich. "The Professional-Managerial Class." *Between Capital and Labor: The Professional-Managerial Class*, ed. Pat Walker, 5–46. Boston: South End, 1999.

Eliot, Marc. *Cary Grant: A Biography*. New York: Three Rivers Press, 2004.

Elliot, Stuart. "A Blitz That Has Don Draper Written All Over It." *New York Times*, 9 July 2009, B5.

———. "'Mad Men' Dolls in a Barbie World, but the Cocktails Must Stay Behind." *New York Times*, 9 March 2010, B3.

———. "What Was Old Is New as TV Revisits Branding." *New York Times*, 13 June 2007, C5.

Ellis, John. *Visible Fictions*. London: Routledge and Kegan Paul, 1982.

Ellison, Ralph. *Invisible Man*. New York: Signet, 1952.

———. *Shadow and Act*. 1964. New York: Vintage, 1972.

Estes, Steve. *I Am a Man! Race, Manhood, and the Civil Rights Movement*. Chapel Hill: University of North Carolina Press, 2005.

Faulkner, William. *Requiem for a Nun*. New York: Vintage, 1951.

Feld, Rob, Jean Oppenheimer, and Ian Stasukevich. "Tantalizing Television." *American Cinematographer* 89.3 (2008): 46–50.

Ferguson, Frances. *Pornography, the Theory: What Utilitarianism Did to Action*. Chicago: University of Chicago Press, 2004.

Feuer, Jane. "The Concept of Live Television: Ontology as Ideology." *Regarding Television: Critical Approaches*, ed. E. Ann Kaplan, 12–22. Frederick, Md.: University Publications of America, 1983.

———. "MTM Enterprises: An Overview." *MTM: "Quality Television,"* ed. Jane Feuer, Paul Kerr, and Tise Vahimagi, 1–31. London: BFI, 1984.

Finney, Gail. "What's Happened to Feminism?" *Comparative Literature in an Age of Globalization: The American Comparative Literature Association 2004 Report on the Discipline*, ed. Haun Saussy, 114–26. Baltimore: Johns Hopkins University Press, 2006.

Fiske, John. *Understanding Popular Culture*. London: Routledge, 1989.

Fitzpatrick, Kevin. "Matriarch-Nemesis: TV's Most Undeniably Horrible Mothers." *UGO*, 9 May 2011. Web. Accessed 29 May 2011.

Flaherty, Mike. "AMC Introduces 'Mad-vertising': Blurbs Reference Products and Theme of 'Men,'" *Variety*, 22 August 2008. Web. 12 April 2012.

Flaubert, Gustave. *Madame Bovary*. 1857. Ed. Margaret Cohen. Trans. Eleanor Marx Aveling and Paul de Man. 2nd ed. New York: Norton, 2004.

Fogelson, Robert M. *Bourgeois Nightmares: Suburbia, 1870–1930*. New Haven: Yale University Press, 2005.

Foster, John Bellamy, and Fred Magdoff. *The Great Financial Crisis: Causes and Consequences*. New York: Monthly Review, 2009.

Fox, Stephen. *The Mirror Makers: A History of American Advertising and Its Creators*. Urbana: University of Illinois Press, 1997.

Frampton, Kenneth. *Modern Architecture: A Critical History*. 3rd ed. London: Thames and Hudson, 1992.

Frank, Thomas. *The Conquest of Cool: Business Culture, Counterculture, and the Rise of Hip Consumerism*. Chicago: University of Chicago Press, 1997.

Fraterrigo, Elizabeth. *Playboy and the Making of the Good Life in Modern America*. New York: Oxford University Press, 2009.

Fredericks, Elizabeth. "The Mad Men of Remember WENN: Comparing the Original Period Series of AMC." *Suite101.com*, 5 March 2009. Web. Accessed 12 April 2011.

Freud, Sigmund. "The Uncanny." 1919. *The Standard Edition of the Complete Works of Sigmund Freud*. 24 vols. Ed. James Strachey et al., 17: 217–52. London: Hogarth, 1953–74.

Freund, David M. P. *Colored Property: State Policy and White Racial Politics in Suburban America*. Chicago: University of Chicago Press, 2007.

Friedan, Betty. *The Feminine Mystique*. New York: Dell, 1963.

Friedman, Diana. *Sitcom Style: Inside America's Favorite TV Homes*. New York: Clarkson Potter, 2005.

Gamson, Joshua. *Freaks Talk Back: Tabloid Talk Shows and Sexual Nonconformity*. Chicago: University of Chicago Press, 1998.

Gant, Margaret Elizabeth. *The Raven's Story*. Glen Raven, N.C.: Glen Raven, 1979.

Gilbert, Matthew. "Slick *Mad Men* Visits Madison Ave. at Dawn of the '60s." *Boston Globe*, 19 July 2007. Web. Accessed 8 April 2011.

Gilbert, Sandra M., and Susan Gubar. *The Madwoman in the Attic: The Woman Writer and the Nineteenth-Century Literary Imagination*. New Haven: Yale University Press, 1979.

Ginsberg, Allen. *Howl and Other Poems*. San Francisco: City Lights, 1956.

Gitlin, Todd. *The Sixties: Years of Hope, Days of Rage*. New York: Bantam, 1987.

Givhan, Robin. "A Rough Reality beneath a Slick Surface." *Washington Post*, 27 July 2008, M1. Web. Accessed 12 April 2011.

Glaude, Eddie S., Jr. *In a Shade of Blue: Pragmatism and the Politics of Black America*. Chicago: University of Chicago Press, 2007.

Glick, Elisa. *Materializing Queer Desire: Oscar Wilde to Andy Warhol*. Albany: SUNY Press, 2009.

Goffman, Erving. *Stigma: Notes on the Management of Spoiled Identity*. New York: Simon and Schuster, 1963.

Goldman, Peter. *The Death and Life of Malcolm X*. 2nd ed. Urbana: University of Illinois Press, 1979.

Gomery, Douglas. "American Movie Classics." *The Encyclopedia of Television*, 2nd ed., ed. Horace Newcomb, 93. Chicago: Taylor and Francis, 2004.

Goodlad, Lauren M. E. "Trollopian 'Foreign Policy': Rootedness and Cosmopolitanism in the Mid-Victorian Global Imaginary." *PMLA* 124 (2009): 437–54.

———. "Why We Love *Mad Men*." *Chronicle of Higher Education*, 31 August 2009. Web. Accessed 4 January 2010.

Goodlad, Lauren M. E., and Caroline Levine. "You've Come a Long Way, Baby." *Kritik*. 11 June 2012. Web. Accessed 5 July 2012.

Goodlad, Lauren M. E., and Rob Rushing. "Groundhog Day." *Kritik*, 18 October 2010. Web. Accessed 29 December 2010.

Goodman, Tim. "New York in 1960, when the 'Mad Men' Were In Charge — and Everything Was About to Change." *San Francisco Chronicle*, 18 July 2007. Web. Accessed 8 April 2011.

Gould, Jack. "TV: Drama Used as Editorial Protest." *New York Times*, 30 April 1962.

Grad, Rachel. "The Drapers' New Living Room Decor." *Apartment Therapy*, 28 September 2009. Web. Accessed 29 May 2011.

Graff, Amy. "Betty Draper: Is She as Bad as She Seems?" *The Mommy Files, San Francisco Chronicle*, 26 July 2010. Web. Accessed 29 May 2011.

Graham, Dan. "Homes for America: Early 20th-Century Possessable House to the Quasi-Discrete Cell of '66." *Arts Magazine*, December/January 1966–67, 21–22.

Gray, Herman. "Remembering Civil Rights: Television, Memory and the 1960s." *The Revolution Wasn't Televised: Sixties Television and Social Conflict*, ed. Lynn Spigel and Michael Curtin, 349–58. New York: Routledge, 1997.

———. *Watching Race: Television and the Struggle for Blackness*. Minneapolis: University of Minnesota Press, 1995.

Gray, Jonathan, Cornel Sandvoss, and C. Lee Harrington, eds. *Fandom: Identities and Communities in a Mediated World*. New York: New York University Press, 2007.

Green, Adam. *Selling the Race: Culture, Community, and Black Chicago, 1940–1955*. Chicago: University of Chicago Press, 2007.

Greenberg, Clement. "The Feeling Is All." *Clement Greenberg: The Collected Essays and Criticism*. Vol. 3, *Affirmations and Refusals, 1950–1956*. Ed. John O'Brian, 99–106. Chicago: University of Chicago Press, 1986.

———. "Modernist Painting." *Clement Greenberg: The Collected Essays and Criticism*. Vol. 4, *Modernism with a Vengeance, 1957–1969*. Ed. John O'Brian, 85–93. Chicago: University of Chicago Press, 1986.

Gregory, Dick. *From the Back of the Bus*. Ed. Bob Orben. New York: Dutton, 1962.

Gregory, Dick, with Robert Lipsyte. *Nigger: An Autobiography*. New York: Washington Square, 1964.

Gregory, Dick, with James R. McGraw. *Up from Nigger*. New York: Stein and Day, 1976.

Greif, Mark. "You'll Love the Way It Makes You Feel." *London Review of Books*, 23 October 2008. Web. Accessed 5 January 2010.

Gripsrud, Jostein. "Television, Broadcasting, Flow: Key Metaphors in TV Theory." *The Television Studies Book*, ed. Christine Geraghty and David Lusted, 11–32. London: Arnold, 1998.

Gross, Larry. "Out of the Mainstream: Sexual Minorities and the Mass Media." *Remote Control: Television, Audiences and Cultural Power*, ed. Ellen Seiter,

Hans Borchers, Gabriele Kreutzner, and Eva-Maria Warth, 130–49. New York: Routledge, 1989.

Hall, Jacquelyn Dowd. "The Long Civil Rights Movement and the Political Uses of the Past." *Journal of American History* 91.4 (2005): 1233–63.

Hamilton, Charles V. *Adam Clayton Powell, Jr.: The Political Biography of an American Dilemma*. New York: Atheneum, 1991.

Hansberry, Lorraine. *A Raisin in the Sun: A Drama in Three Acts*. New York: Random House, 1959.

Hansen, Jim. "The Coolest Medium." *Kritik*, 18 August 2010. Web. Accessed 6 December 2010.

Haralovich, Mary Beth, and Lauren Rabinovitz, eds. *Television, History, and American Culture: Feminist Critical Essays*. Durham: Duke University Press, 1999.

Harris, Cheryl, and Alison Alexander, eds. *Theorizing Fandom: Fans, Subculture, and Identity*. Cresskill, N.J.: Hampton, 1998.

Harris, Dianne, and D. Fairchild Ruggles. "Landscape and Vision." *Sites Unseen: Landscape and Vision*, ed. Dianne Harris and D. Fairchild Ruggles, 5–29. Pittsburgh: University of Pittsburgh Press, 2007.

Harris, Trudier. *From Mammies to Militants: Domestics in Black American Literature*. Philadelphia: Temple University Press, 1982.

Haug, Wolfgang. *Critique of Commodity Aesthetics: Appearance, Sexuality, and Advertising in Capitalist Society*. Trans. Robert Bock. Cambridge: Polity, 1986.

Hayden, Dolores. *Building Suburbia: Green Fields and Urban Growth, 1820–2000*. New York: Pantheon, 2003.

Heath, Stephen, and Gillian Skirrow. "Television: A World in Action." *Screen* 18.2 (1977): 7–60.

Heidkamp, Bernie. "Television Under the Radar: 'Mad Men' and the Allegorical Past." *PopPolitics*, August 2008. Web. Accessed 15 May 2010.

Hellekson, Karen, and Kristina Busse, eds. *Fan Fiction and Fan Communities in the Age of the Internet*. Jefferson, N.C.: McFarland, 2006.

Hill, C. P. *British Economic and Social History, 1700–1982*. London: Edward Arnold, 1985.

Hill, Herbert. "Twenty Years of State Fair Employment Practices Commissions: A Critical Analysis with Recommendations." *Negroes and Jobs: A Book of Readings*, ed. Louis A. Ferman, Joyce L. Kornbluh, and J. A. Miller, 496–522. Ann Arbor: University of Michigan Press, 1968.

Hills, Matt. *Fan Cultures*. London and New York: Routledge, 2002.

Hine, Darlene Clark. "Rape and the Inner Lives of Black Women in the Middle West: Preliminary Thoughts on the Culture of Dissemblance." *Signs* 14.4 (1989): 912–20.

Hollander, Anne. *Sex and Suits: The Evolution of Modern Dress*. New York: Knopf, 1994.

hooks, bell. *Black Looks: Race and Representation*. Boston: South End, 1992.

Horowitz, Daniel. *Betty Friedan and the Making of "The Feminine Mystique": The American Left, the Cold War, and Modern Feminism*. Amherst: University of Massachusetts Press, 1998.

————, ed. *Selections from Vance Packard's "The Status Seekers."* Boston: Bedford St. Martin's, 1995.

Hughes, Linda K., and Michael Lund. *The Victorian Serial*. Charlottesville: University of Virginia Press, 1991.

Hughey, Matthew. "Cinethetic Racism: White Redemption and Black Stereotypes in 'Magical Negro' Films." *Social Problems* 3 (2009): 543–77.

Hunt, Darnell M., ed. *Channeling Blackness: Studies on Television and Race in America*. New York: Oxford University Press, 2004.

Isakson, Paul. "Confessions of a (Fake) Mad Man." *Paul Isakson*, 16 November 2008. Web. Accessed 12 April 2012.

Isenstadt, Sandy. *The Modern American House: Spaciousness and Middle Class Identity*. New York: Cambridge University Press, 2006.

Itzkoff, Dave. "Matthew Weiner Closes the Books on Season 4 of *MadMen*." Arts Beat, *New York Times*, 17 October 2010. Web. Accessed 29 December 2010.

Ivy Horsemen. "'Mad Men' Doesn't Have to Care about Black People." 20 August 2009. Web. Accessed 14 May 2011.

Jackson, Charles. *The Lost Weekend*. 1944. Syracuse: Syracuse University Press, 1996.

Jackson, Kenneth. *Crabgrass Frontier: The Suburbanization of the United States*. New York: Oxford University Press, 1985.

James, Henry. *Notes on Novelists with Some Other Notes*. New York: Scribners, 1914.

Jameson, Fredric. "Cognitive Mapping." *Marxism and the Interpretation of Culture*, ed. Cary Nelson and Lawrence Grossberg, 347–58. Urbana: University of Illinois Press, 1988.

————. "The Cultural Logic of Late Capitalism." *Postmodernism, or, The Cultural Logic of Late Capitalism*, 1–54. Durham: Duke University Press, 1991.

————. *The Geopolitical Aesthetic: Cinema and Space in the World System*. Bloomington: Indiana University Press, 1995.

————. "Introduction." *The Historical Novel*, by Georg Lukács, trans. Hannah Mitchell and Stanley Mitchell, 1–8. Lincoln: University of Nebraska Press, 1983.

————. "Postmodernism and Consumer Society." *The Anti-aesthetic: Essays on Postmodern Culture*, ed. Hal Foster, 111–25. Townsend: Bay Press, 1983.

Jeffers, Tamar. "*Pillow Talk*'s Repackaging of Doris Day: 'Under all those dirndls . . .'" *Fashioning Film Stars: Dress, Culture, Identity*, ed. Rachel Moseley, 50–61. London: BFI, 2005.

Jenkins, Henry. *Convergence Culture: Where Old and New Media Collide*. New York: New York University Press, 2006.

————. *Fans, Bloggers, and Gamers: Exploring Participatory Culture*. New York: New York University Press, 2006.

———. *Textual Poachers: Television Fans and Participatory Culture.* New York: Routledge, 1992.

Jhally, Sut, and Justin Lewis. *Enlightened Racism: "The Cosby Show," Audiences, and the Myth of the American Dream.* Boulder: Westview, 1992.

Joffe, Carol. *Dispatches from the Abortion Wars: The Costs of Fanaticism to Doctors, Patients, and the Rest of Us.* Boston: Beacon, 2009.

Johnson, Merri Lisa, ed. *Third Wave Feminism and Television: Jane Puts It in a Box.* London: I. B. Tauris, 2007.

Jones, LeRoi. *Blues People: Negro Music in America.* 1963. New York: William Morrow, 1999.

Jones, Patrick D. *The Selma of the North: Civil Rights Insurgency in Milwaukee.* Cambridge: Harvard University Press, 2009.

Jones, Sara Gwenllian. "The Sex Lives of Cult Television Characters." *Screen* 43.1 (2002): 79–90.

Joselit, David. "Notes on Surface: Toward a Genealogy of Flatness." *Art History* 23.1 (2000): 19–34.

Joseph, Peniel E. "Waiting till the Midnight Hour: Reconceptualizing the Heroic Period of the Civil Rights Movement, 1954–1965." *Souls* 2.2 (2000): 6–17.

Joseph, Ralina. "'Tyra Banks Is Fat': Reading (*Post-*)Racism and (*Post-*)Feminism in the New Millennium." *Critical Studies in Media Communication* 26.3 (2009): 237–54.

Joyrich, Lynne. "Epistemology of the Console." *Critical Inquiry* 27.3 (2001): 439–67.

———. "Feminist Enterprise? *Star Trek: The Next Generation* and the Occupation of Femininity." *Cinema Journal* 35.2 (1996): 61–84.

———. *Re-viewing Reception: Television, Gender, and Postmodern Culture.* Bloomington: Indiana University Press, 1996.

Jurca, Catherine. "The Sanctimonious Suburbanite: Sloan Wilson's *The Man in the Gray Flannel Suit.*" *American Literary History* 11.1 (1999): 82–106.

Kael, Pauline. "The Man from Dream City." *New Yorker,* 14 July 1975, 40–68.

Kaplan, Amy. "Exodus and the Americanization of Zionism." Lecture, CAS/MillerComm series, University of Illinois, Urbana-Champaign, 8 November 2010.

Kaplan, E. Ann. "Feminist Criticism and Television." *Channels of Discourse, Reassembled,* 2nd ed., ed. Robert C. Allen, 186–213. Chapel Hill: University of North Carolina Press, 1992.

Kapsalis, Terri. *Public Privates: Performing Gynecology from Both Ends of the Speculum.* Durham: Duke University Press, 1997.

kasviel. "Portrait of a One Night Stand." *Fanfiction.net,* 31 October 2009. Web. Accessed 29 May 2011.

Katzman, David M. *Seven Days a Week: Women and Domestic Service in Industrializing America.* 1978. Urbana: University of Illinois Press, 1981.

Keane, Maribeth, and Jessica Lewis. "An Interview with Scott Buckwald, Prop

Master for the Hit TV Show Mad Men." *Collectors Weekly*, 15 October 2009. Web. Accessed 5 January 2010.

Keane, Meghan. "How Did AMC's Mad Men Yourself Get Everywhere?" *Econsultancy*, 5 October 2009. Web. Accessed 12 April 2012.

Kelley, Robin D. G. *Race Rebels: Culture, Politics, and the Black Working Class*. New York: Free Press, 1996.

Kelner, Anna. "The 'Mad Men' Effect: Bringing Back Sexism with Style." *Ms. Blog*, 22 July 2010. Web. Accessed 28 May 2011.

Kendrick, Walter. "The Eustace Diamonds: The Truth of Trollope's Fiction." ELH 46.1 (1979): 136–57.

Kermode, Frank. *The Sense of an Ending: Studies in the Theory of Fiction*. 1967. New York: Oxford University Press, 2000.

Kerouac, Jack. *On the Road*. New York: Viking, 1957.

King, Lindy. "'Mad Men Twitter' Reaches Semi-finals in SAMMY Award Competition." *Examiner.com*, 19 September 2009. Web. Accessed 12 April 2012.

K'Meyer, Tracy E. *Civil Rights in the Gateway to the South: Louisville, Kentucky, 1945–1980*. Lexington: University Press of Kentucky, 2009.

Kondolojy, Amanda. "Season Five Premiere Is Most Watched 'Mad Men' Episode Yet." *TV by the Numbers*, 26 March 2012. Web. Accessed 7 July 2012.

Krentcil, Faran. "The *Mad Men* Fashion File — How to Dress Like a *Mad* Woman." *AMCtv.com*, 1 December 2009. Web. Accessed 24 January 2010.

———. "The *Mad Men* Fashion File — The Blues Never Felt So Good." *AMCtv.com*, 29 July 2010. Web. Accessed 28 November 2010.

———. "The *Mad Men* Fashion File — The Frills, The Chills, The Thrills." *AMCtv.com*, August 2008. Web. Accessed 24 January 2010.

Lacan, Jacques. "The Mirror Stage as Formative of the *I* Function as Revealed in Psychoanalytic Experience." *Écrits: The First Complete Edition in English*. Trans. Bruce Fink, 75–81. New York: Norton, 2007.

LaCapra, Dominick. *History and Memory after Auschwitz*. Ithaca: Cornell University Press, 1998.

———. *"Madame Bovary" on Trial*. Ithaca: Cornell University Press, 1986.

———. *Writing History, Writing Trauma*. Baltimore: Johns Hopkins University Press, 2000.

Lafayette, Jon. "AMC Tinkers with Advertising in 'Mad Men.'" *Television Week*, 11 June 2007, 35.

Lamster, Mark, ed. *Architecture and Film*. New York: Princeton Architectural Press, 2000.

Lander, Christian. "Mad Men." *Stuff White People Like*, 11 March 2009. Web. Accessed 25 June 2010.

Lang, Clarence. "Between Civil Rights, Black Power, and the Mason-Dixon Line: A Case Study of Black Freedom Movement Militancy in the Gateway City."

Race Struggles, ed. Theodore Koditschek, Sundiata Keita Cha-Jua, and Helen A.
Neville, 231–59. Urbana: University of Illinois Press, 2009.

———. Grassroots at the Gateway: Class Politics and Black Freedom Struggle in St.
Louis, 1936–75. Ann Arbor: University of Michigan Press, 2009.

Lassiter, Matthew D., and Joseph Crespino, eds. The Myth of Southern
Exceptionalism. New York: Oxford University Press, 2010.

Law, Graham. Serializing Fiction in the Victorian Press. Basingstoke: Palgrave, 2000.

Lawson, Mark. "Mark Lawson Talks to David Chase." Quality TV: Contemporary
American Television and Beyond, ed. Janet McCabe and Kim Akass, 185–220. New
York: I. B. Tauris, 2007.

Leavitt, Judith Walzer. Make Room for Daddy: The Journey from Waiting Room to
Birthing Room. Chapel Hill: University of North Carolina Press, 2009.

Leiss, William, Stephen Kline, Sut Jhally, and Jackie Botterill, eds. Social
Communication in Advertising: Consumption in the Mediated Marketplace. 3rd ed.
New York: Routledge, 2005.

Leland, John. Hip: The History. New York: Ecco, 2004.

Lentz, Kirsten Marthe. "Quality versus Relevance: Feminism, Race, and the
Politics of the Sign in 1970s Television." Camera Obscura 15.1 (2000): 45–93.

Lerner, Barron H. The Breast Cancer Wars: Hope, Fear, and the Pursuit of a Cure in
Twentieth-Century America. New York: Oxford University Press, 2001.

Lerner, Gerda. Black Women in White America: A Documentary History. New York:
Random House, 1972.

———. The Majority Finds Its Past: Placing Women in History. New York: Oxford
University Press, 1979.

Levine, Andrea. "The (Jewish) White Negro: Norman Mailer's Racial Bodies."
MELUS 28.2 (2003): 59–81.

Levine, Caroline. "Historicism at Its Limits: An Antislavery Sonnet, Bleak House,
and The Wire." Presentation, Columbia University, New York, 8 November 2007.

Levy, Peter B. Civil War on Race Street: The Civil Rights Movement in Cambridge,
Maryland. Gainesville: University Press of Florida, 2003.

Lewis, Carolyn Herbst. "Waking Sleeping Beauty: The Pre-marital Pelvic
Exam and Heterosexuality in the Cold War." Journal of Women's History 17.4
(December 2005): 86–110.

Lewis, Lisa A., ed. The Adoring Audience: Fan Culture and Popular Media. New
York: Routledge, 1992.

Lincoln, C. Eric. The Black Muslims in America. Boston: Beacon, 1961.

Lipp, Deborah. "Open Thread: Question of the Week." Basket of Kisses. 19
December 2010. Web. Accessed 29 May 2011.

Lipp, Deborah, and Roberta Lipp. "1960s Earnings and Spendings." Basket of Kisses.
Web. Accessed 18 February 2010.

Lipsitz, George. The Possessive Investment in Whiteness: How White People Profit from
Identity Politics. Philadelphia: Temple University Press, 1998.

Little, Ann M. "Mad Men: Cutting-Edge TV, or an Excuse to Let Racism and Sexism Run Free?" *Historiann*, 16 August 2008. Web. Accessed 15 May 2010.

Living Age. "Our Sensation Novelists." 22 August 1863, 353–54.

Lomax, Louis E. *The Negro Revolt.* New York: Harper, 1962.

Longstreth, Richard. "The Levitts, Mass-Produced Houses, and Community Planning in the Mid-Twentieth Century." *Second Suburb: Levittown, Pennsylvania*, ed. Dianne Harris, 123–74. Pittsburgh: University of Pittsburgh Press, 2010.

Lorts, Justin T. "Black Laughter/Black Protest: Civil Rights, Respectability, and the Cultural Politics of African American Comedy, 1934–1968." Diss., Rutgers University, 2008.

Los Angeles Times. "Boston Bans Defenders — 10 Other Cities, Too." 28 April 1962, B3.

Loshitzky, Yosefa. "National Rebirth as a Movie: Otto Preminger's *Exodus.*" *National Identities* 4.2 (2002): 119–31.

Lott, Eric. *Love and Theft: Blackface Minstrelsy and the American Working Class.* New York: Oxford University Press, 1993.

Lukács, Georg. "Hegel's *Aesthetics.*" 1951. Trans. David Taffel. *Graduate Faculty Philosophy Journal* 23.2 (2002): 87–124.

———. *The Historical Novel.* Trans. Hannah Mitchell and Stanley Mitchell. Lincoln: University of Nebraska Press, 1983.

———. "Realism in the Balance." 1938. *Aesthetics and Politics: Theodor Adorno, Walter Benjamin, Ernst Bloch, Bertolt Brecht, Georg Lukács.* Afterword by Fredric Jameson. Ed. Ronald Taylor, 28–59. New York: Verso, 1988.

———. *Studies in European Realism: A Sociological Survey of the Writings of Balzac, Stendhal, Zola, Tolstoy, Gorki and Others.* Trans. Edith Bone. London: Hillway, 1950.

Lull, James, and Stephen Hinerman, eds. *Media Scandals: Morality and Desire in the Popular Culture Marketplace.* New York: Columbia University Press, 1997.

Lusher, Tim. "The Top 50 TV Dramas of All Time." *TV and Radio Blog, Guardian,* 12 January 2010. Web. Accessed 12 January 2010.

MacDonald, J. Fred. *Blacks and White TV: Afro-Americans in Television since 1948.* Chicago: Nelson-Hall, 1992.

Macherey, Pierre. *Pour une théorie de la production littéraire.* Paris: Editions Maspéro, 1966.

Mailer, Norman. *Advertisements for Myself.* New York: Putnam, 1959. Repr. Cambridge: Harvard University Press, 1992.

Malcolm X, as told to Alex Haley. *The Autobiography of Malcolm X.* New York: Ballantine, 1965.

Mann, Denise. "It's Not TV, It's Brand TV: The Collective Author(s) of the *Lost* Franchise." *Production Studies: Cultural Studies of Media Industries*, ed. Vicki Mayer, Miranda J. Banks, and John Caldwell, 99–114. New York: Routledge, 2009.

Mapes, Diane. "'Mad Men' Characters Abound on Twitter: Microblogging

Site Popular for Those Taking On the Characters' Personae." *MSNBC.com*, 28 September 2009. Web. Accessed 12 April 2012.

Marc, David. *Demographic Vistas: Television in American Culture*. Philadelphia: University of Pennsylvania Press, 1984.

Marie Claire. "Mad Men Fashion: Get the Ladylike Look." 23 October 2008. Web. Accessed 22 April 2011.

Marks, Lara. *Sexual Chemistry: A History of the Contraceptive Pill*. New Haven: Yale University Press, 2010.

Marling, Karal Ann. *As Seen On TV: The Visual Culture of Everyday Life in the 1950s*. Cambridge: Harvard University Press, 1994.

Martin, John Bartlow. "Abortion." *Saturday Evening Post*, 20 May 1961, 19–21, 72–74.

Martin, Waldo E., Jr. *No Coward Soldiers: Black Cultural Politics and Postwar America*. Cambridge: Harvard University Press, 2005.

Marx, Karl. *Capital: A Critique of Political Economy*. Vol. 1. Trans. Ben Fowkes. New York: Penguin, 1992.

Masket, Seth. "The Mad Men Cake." *Enik Rising*, 9 March 2010. Web. Accessed 29 May 2011.

Maynard, Micheline. "Reliving a 1962 Crash on 'Mad Men.'" *New York Times*, 4 August 2008. Web. Accessed 21 May 2011.

McCarthy, Anna. "*Mad Men's* Retro Charm." *The Nation*, 10 September 2007. Web. Accessed 30 December 2010.

———. "Must See Queer TV: History and Serial Form in *Ellen*." *Quality Popular Television*, ed. Mark Jancovich and James Lyons, 88–102. London: BFI, 2003.

McEwen, Todd. "Cary Grant's Suit." *Granta* 94 (2006): 117–26.

McLean, Jesse. *Kings of Madison Avenue: The Unofficial Guide to Mad Men*. New York: ECW, 2009.

McPherson, Tara. "Reload: Liveness, Mobility, and the Web." *New Media, Old Media: A History and Theory Reader*, ed. Wendy Hui Kyon Chun and Thomas Keenan, 199–208. New York: Routledge, 2006.

McWhorter, John. *All about the Beat: Why Hip-Hop Can't Save Black America*. New York: Gotham, 2008.

Mendelsohn, Daniel. "The Mad Men Account." *New York Review of Books*, 24 February 2011.

Merritt, Pamela. "'Mad Men' Salon: America's Struggle with Race, Shaken Not Stirred." *RHRealityCheck.org*, 14 August 2009. Web. Accessed 21 January 2011.

Miller, Toby. "Foreword: It's Television. It's HBO." *It's Not TV: Watching HBO in the Post-television Era*, ed. Marc Leverette, Brian Ott, and Cara Louise Buckley, ix–xii. New York: Routledge, 2008.

Mitchell, W. J. T., ed. *Landscape and Power*. 2nd ed. Chicago: University of Chicago Press, 2002.

Mittell, Jason. "On Disliking *Mad Men*." *Just TV*, 29 July 2010. Web. Accessed 1 September 2010.

————. "Serial Boxes: The Cultural Value of Long-Form American Television." *Just TV*, 29 December 2010. Web. Accessed 10 January 2009.

Molitor, Emily. "Mad Men Yourself: The Beauty of Putting Fans to Work." *SmartBlog on Social Media e-Newsletter*, 8 April 2010. Web. Accessed 12 April 2011.

Morley, David. *Family Television: Cultural Power and Domestic Leisure*. London: Comedia, 1986.

Morse, Margaret. "The Television News Personality and Credibility: Reflections on the News in Transition." *Studies in Entertainment: Critical Approaches to Mass Culture*, ed. Tania Modleski, 55–79. Bloomington: Indiana University Press, 1986.

Mufti, Amir R. *Enlightenment in the Colony: The Jewish Question and the Crisis of Postcolonial Culture*. Princeton: Princeton University Press, 2007.

Mullen, Megan. "Surfing through 'TV Land': Notes toward a Theory of 'Video Bites' and Their Function on Cable TV." *Velvet Light Trap* 36 (1995): 60–67.

Mulvey, Laura. "Some Afterthoughts on 'Visual Pleasure and Narrative Cinema.'" *Framework* 15–17 (1981): 12–15.

————. "Visual Pleasure and Narrative Cinema." *Screen* 16.3 (1975): 6–18.

Mumford, Eric. *The CIAM Discourse on Urbanism, 1928–1960*. Cambridge: MIT Press, 2000.

Mumford, Laura Stempel. "Feminist Theory and Television Studies." *The Television Studies Book*, ed. Christine Geraghty and David Lusted, 114–30. London: Arnold, 1998.

Murray, Albert. *The Hero and the Blues*. Columbia: University of Missouri Press, 1973.

Nead, Lynda. *Victorian Babylon: People, Streets and Images in Nineteenth-Century London*. New Haven: Yale University Press, 2005.

Neuman, Clayton. "Q&A: Christina Hendricks (Joan Holloway)." *AMCtv.com*, 26 August 2008. Web. Accessed 9 January 2010.

Neumann, Dietrich, ed. *Film Architecture: Set Designs from Metropolis to Blade Runner*. Munich: Prestel, 1996.

Newcomb, Horace, and Robert Alley. *The Producer's Medium: Conversations with the Creators of American TV*. New York: Oxford University Press, 1983.

New York Times. "Mad Men City: The Story behind the Stories." 25 July 2010, MB9.

————. "Plenty of Smoke, Fewer Martinis." 25 July 2010, MB9.

Nicholls, Brendon. "The Melting Pot That Boiled Over: Racial Fetishism and the Lingua Franca of Jack Kerouac's Fiction." *Modern Fiction Studies* 49.3 (2003): 524–49.

Nickles, Shelley. "More Is Better: Mass Consumption, Gender, and Class Identity in Postwar America." *American Quarterly* 54.4 (2002): 581–623.

Nielsenwire. "Top Trends for 2010." 22 December 2010. Web. Accessed 28 May 2011.

Nora, Pierre. "Between Memory and History: *Les Lieux de Mémoire*." Trans. Marc Roudebush. *Representations* 26 (1989): 7–25.

O'Connor, John E., ed. *American History/American Television: Interpreting the Video Past*. New York: Frederick Ungar, 1983.

Oei, Lily. "Q&A—Dyna Moe (Freelance Illustrator)." *AMCtv.com*, 19 May 2009. Web. 12 April 2012.

Ogilvy, David. *Confessions of an Advertising Man*. New York: Athenaeum, 1963.

Ono, Kent A. "Postracism: A Theory of the 'Post-' as Political Strategy." *Journal of Communication Inquiry* 34.3 (2011): 227–33.

O'Sullivan, Sean. "Old, New, Borrowed, Blue: *Deadwood* and Serial Fiction." *Reading Deadwood: A Western to Swear By*, ed. David Lavery, 115–32. London: I. B. Tauris, 2006.

Packard, Vance. *The Hidden Persuaders*. 1957. New York: Penguin, 1991.

Panetta, George. *Viva Madison Avenue!* New York: Harcourt Brace, 1957.

Parker, Mary Jane. "The Name on the Door." *Fanfiction.net*, 1 January 2011. Web. Accessed 29 May 2011.

Paulicelli, Eugenia. "Framing the Self, Staging Identity: Clothing and Italian Style in the Films of Michelangelo Antonioni." *The Fabric of Cultures: Fashion, Identity, and Globalization*, ed. Eugenia Paulicelli and Hazel Clark, 53–72. Florence, Ky.: Routledge, 2008.

Pearson, Roberta E., and Sara Gwenllian-Jones, eds. *Cult Television*. Minneapolis: University of Minnesota Press, 2004.

Penley, Constance, ed. *Feminism and Film Theory*. New York: Routledge, 1988.

———. *NASA/Trek: Popular Science and Sex in America*. New York: Verso, 1997.

Penley, Constance, and Sharon Willis, eds. *Male Trouble*. Minneapolis: University of Minnesota Press, 1993.

Petchesky, Rosalind Pollack. *Abortion and Woman's Choice: The State, Sexuality, and Reproductive Freedom*. Boston: Northeastern University Press, 1983.

Peterson, Latoya. "Why 'Mad Men' Doesn't Care about Black People." *The Root*, 13 August 2009. Web. Accessed 30 December 2010.

———. "Why 'Mad Men' Is Afraid of Race." *Slate*, 13 August 2009. Web. Accessed 8 April 2011.

Pettigrew, Thomas F. "Post-racism? Putting President Obama's Victory in Perspective." *DuBois Review* 6.2 (2009): 279–92.

Pfeffer, Paula A. *A. Philip Randolph, Pioneer of the Civil Rights Movement*. Baton Rouge: Louisiana State University Press, 1990.

Pleck, Elizabeth. *Not Just Roommates: Cohabitation after the Sexual Revolution*. Chicago: University of Chicago Press, 2012.

Polan, Dana. "Invisible City." *Museum of the Moving Image*, 28 July 2008. Web. Accessed 29 December 2010.

———. *The Sopranos*. Durham: Duke University Press, 2009.

Poovey, Mary. *Making a Social Body: British Cultural Formation, 1830–1864*. Chicago: University of Chicago Press, 1995.

Porter, Eric. *What Is This Thing Called Jazz? African American Musicians as Artists, Critics, and Activists*. Berkeley: University of California Press, 2002.

Potter, Claire B. "The Moonlight and Magnolias School of Women's History: Katie

Roiphe's Take on *Mad Men*." *Tenured Radical*, 1 August 2010. Web. Accessed 29 May 2011.

Purnell, Brian. "'Drive Awhile for Freedom': Brooklyn CORE's 1964 Stall-In and Public Discourses of Protest Violence." *Groundwork: Local Black Freedom Movements in America*, ed. Jeanne Theoharis and Komozi Woodard, 45–75. New York: New York University Press, 2005.

———. "'Taxation without Sanitation Is Tyranny': Civil Rights Struggles over Garbage Collection in Brooklyn, New York during the Fall of 1962." *Afro-Americans in New York Life and History* 31.2 (2007): 61–88.

Radway, Janice. *Reading the Romance*. Chapel Hill: University of North Carolina Press, 1984.

Ragussis, Michael. *Figures of Conversion: "The Jewish Question" and English National Identity*. Durham: Duke University Press, 2005.

Ransby, Barbara. *Ella Baker and the Black Freedom Movement: A Radical Democratic Vision*. Chapel Hill: University of North Carolina Press, 2003.

Reagan, Leslie J. "Crossing the Border for Abortions: California Activists, Mexican Clinics, and the Creation of a Feminist Health Agency in the 1960s." *Feminist Studies* 26.2 (2000): 323–48.

———. *Dangerous Pregnancies: Mothers, Disabilities, and Abortion in Modern America*. Berkeley: University of California Press, 2010.

———. *When Abortion Was a Crime: Women, Medicine, and Law, 1867–1973*. Berkeley: University of California Press, 1997.

Reagan, Leslie J., Nancy Tomes, and Paula A. Treichler. "Introduction: Medicine, Health, and Bodies in American Film and Television." *Medicine's Moving Pictures: Medicine, Health, and Bodies in American Film and Television*. Rochester: University of Rochester Press, 2007.

Reed, Ishmael. *Mixing It Up: Taking On the Media Bullies and Other Reflections*. Philadelphia: Da Capo, 2008.

Reeves, Rosser. *Reality in Advertising*. New York: Knopf, 1961.

Riesman, David, Nathan Glazer, and Reuel Denney. *The Lonely Crowd: A Study of the Changing American Character*. 1950. New Haven: Yale University Press, 2001.

Roberts, Dorothy. *Killing the Black Body: Race, Reproduction, and the Meaning of Liberty*. New York: Random House, 1997.

Robertson, Lindsay. "That Decemberists Montage from *Mad Men* That Everyone's Talking About." *Videogum*, 2 September 2008. Web. Accessed 20 April 2011.

Roediger, David R., ed. *Black on White: Black Writers on What It Means to Be White*. New York: Schocken, 1998.

Rogers, Mark C., Michael Epstein, and Jimmie L. Reeves. "*The Sopranos* as HBO Brand Equity: The Art of Commerce in the Age of Digital Reproduction." *This Thing of Ours: Investigating The Sopranos*, ed. David Lavery, 42–59. New York: Columbia University Press, 2002.

Rogin, Michael. *Blackface, White Noise: Jewish Immigrants in the Hollywood Melting Pot*. Berkeley: University of California Press, 1996.

Rohdie, Sam. *Antonioni*. London: BFI, 1990.

Roiphe, Katie. "On 'Mad Men,' the Allure of Messy Lives." *New York Times*, 1 August 2010, ST1.

———. "A Real Mad Man." *Financial Times*, 16 July 2010. Web. Accessed 21 May 2011.

Rosenberg, Bernard, and David Manning White, eds. *Mass Culture: The Popular Arts in America*. New York: Free Press, 1957.

Roxborough, Scott. "'Mad Men' Stars Nab THR Award." *Hollywood Reporter*, 14 October 2010. Web. Accessed 31 May 2011.

Russo, Julie Levin. "Indiscrete Media: Television/Digital Convergence and Economies of Online Lesbian Fan Communities." Diss., Brown University, 2010.

Salzinger, Leslie. "Manufacturing Sexual Subjects: 'Harassment,' Desire, and Discipline on a Maquiladora Shopfloor." *Ethnography* 1.1 (2000): 5–27.

Sandvoss, Cornel. *Fans: The Mirror of Consumption*. Cambridge: Polity, 2005.

Santo, Avi. "Para-television and Discourses of Distinction: The Culture of Production at HBO." *It's Not TV: Watching HBO in the Post-television Era*, ed. Marc Leverette, Brian Ott, and Cara Louise Buckley, 19–45. New York: Routledge, 2008.

Saul, Scott. *Freedom Is, Freedom Ain't: Jazz and the Making of the Sixties*. Cambridge: Harvard University Press, 2003.

Scanlon, Jennifer. "Sexy from the Start: Anticipatory Elements of Second Wave Feminism." *Women's Studies* 38 (2009): 127–50.

Schiffren, Lisa. "*Mad Men* and Its Discontents." *National Review*, 23 October 2009. Web. Accessed 21 May 2011.

Schleier, Merrill. *Skyscraper Cinema: Architecture and Gender in American Film*. Minneapolis: University of Minnesota Press, 2009.

Schlessinger, Laura. *In Praise of Stay-at-Home Moms*. New York: Harper, 2009.

———. "The Mommy Wars: Dr. Laura on Stay-at-Home Moms." Interview by Michelle Kung. *Wall Street Journal*, 8 April 2009. Web. Accessed 30 December 2010.

Schneider, John. *The Golden Kazoo*. New York: Rinehart, 1956.

Schudson, Michael. *Advertising, the Uneasy Persuasion: Its Dubious Impact on American Society*. New York: Basic Books, 1984.

Schulman, Sam. "The Television Show That Says You're Better Than Your Parents." *Commentary*, February 2009, 46–48.

Schwarz, Benjamin. "Mad about *Mad Men*: What's Wrong—and What's Gloriously Right—with AMC's Hit Show." *Atlantic Monthly*, November 2009. Web. Accessed 21 May 2011.

Sedgwick, Eve. *Epistemology of the Closet*. Berkeley: University of California Press, 1991.

Self, Robert O. *American Babylon: Race and the Struggle for Postwar Oakland.* Princeton: Princeton University Press, 2003.

Shaw, Harry E. *Narrating Reality: Austen, Scott, Eliot.* Ithaca: Cornell University Press, 1999.

Shohat, Ella. *Israeli Cinema: East/West and the Politics of Representation.* Austin: University of Texas Press, 1989.

Silliman, Jael, Marlene Gerber Fried, Loretta Ross, and Elena R. Gutiérrez. *Undivided Rights: Women of Color Organize for Reproductive Justice.* Cambridge, Mass.: South End, 2004.

Silverman, Kaja. "Fragments of a Fashionable Discourse." *Studies in Entertainment,* ed. Tania Modleski, 139–52. Bloomington: Indiana University Press, 1986. Rpt. *On Fashion,* ed. Shari Benstock and Susanne Ferris, 183–96. New Brunswick: Rutgers University Press, 1994.

———. *Male Subjectivities at the Margins.* New York: Routledge, 1992.

Simon, David. "Introduction." *"The Wire": Truth Be Told,* ed. Ralph Alvarez. New York: Simon and Schuster, 2004.

Simon, David R. *Tony Soprano's America: The Criminal Side of the American Dream.* Boulder: Westview, 2004.

Simone, Nina, with Stephen Cleary. *I Put a Spell on You: The Autobiography of Nina Simone.* New York: Da Capo, 1991.

Simons, Natasha. "Mad Men and the Paradox of the Past." *National Review,* 19 July 2010. Web. Accessed 21 May 2011.

Singh, Nikhil Pal. *Black Is a Country: Race and the Unfinished Struggle for Democracy.* Cambridge: Harvard University Press, 2004.

Smethurst, James Edward. *The Black Arts Movement: Literary Nationalism in the 1960s and 1970s.* Chapel Hill: University of North Carolina Press, 2005.

Solinger, Rickie. *Wake Up Little Susie: Single Pregnancy and Race before Roe v. Wade.* New York: Routledge, 1992.

Spain, Daphne. *Gendered Spaces.* Chapel Hill: University of North Carolina Press, 1992.

Spigel, Lynn. "From the Dark Ages to the Golden Age: Women's Memories and Television Reruns." *Screen* 36.1 (1995): 16–33.

———. *Make Room for TV.* Chicago: University of Chicago Press, 1992.

Spigel, Lynn, and Michael Curtin, eds. *The Revolution Wasn't Televised: Sixties Television and Social Conflict.* New York: Routledge, 1997.

Spin. "The Cold-Rock Stuff: These Are a Few of Our Favorite Things." October 1989, 25.

Stanley, Alessandra. "Back to Work." *New York Times,* 18 July 2010. Web. Accessed 21 May 2011.

Steele, Valerie. "Dressing for Work." *Men and Women: Dressing the Part,* ed. Claudia Brush Kidwell and Valerie Steele, 64–91. Washington: Smithsonian, 1989.

Stein, Jeannine. "Watching Television Shortens Life Span, Study Finds." *Los Angeles Times*, 12 January 2010. Web. Accessed 30 December 2010.

Sturken, Marita. *Tangled Memories: The Vietnam War, the AIDS Epidemic, and the Politics of Remembering.* Berkeley: University of California Press, 1997.

Sugrue, Thomas J. "Jim Crow's Last Stand: The Struggle to Integrate Levittown." *Second Suburb: Levittown, Pennsylvania*, ed. Dianne Harris, 175–99. Pittsburgh: University of Pittsburgh Press, 2010.

———. *Sweet Land of Liberty: The Forgotten Struggle for Civil Rights in the North.* New York: Random House, 2008.

Sunday Gazette Mail. "'Defenders' Star Likes Controversy." N.d. [1964]. Folder 7, box 22. Reginald Rose Papers, Wisconsin State Historical Society, Madison.

Szalay, Michael. *Hip Figures: A Literary History of the Democratic Party.* Palo Alto: Stanford University Press, 2012.

———. "Mad Style: Market Segmentation and the Birth of Cool." Presentation, "Mad World: Sex, Politics, Style and the 1960s," Unit for Criticism and Interpretive Theory, University of Illinois, Urbana-Champaign, Levis Faculty Center, Urbana, 19 February 2010.

Taylor, Clarence. "Robert Wagner, Milton Galamison and the Challenge to New York City Liberalism." *Afro-Americans in New York Life and History* 31.2 (July 2007): 121–37.

Taylor, Diana. *The Archive and the Repertoire: Performing Cultural Memory in the Americas.* Durham: Duke University Press, 2003.

Theoharis, Jeanne. "Black Freedom Struggles: Re-imagining and Redefining the Fundamentals." *History Compass* 4.2 (2006): 348–67.

Theoharis, Jeanne F., and Komozi Woodard, eds. *Freedom North: Black Freedom Struggles Outside the South, 1940–1980.* New York: Palgrave Macmillan, 2003.

Thompson, Heather Ann. *Whose Detroit? Politics, Labor, and Race in a Modern American City.* Ithaca: Cornell University Press, 2001.

Thompson, Howard. "Office Romances." *New York Times*, 9 October 1959. Web. Accessed 29 May 2011.

Tillich, Hannah. *From Time to Time.* New York: Stein and Day, 1974.

Tillich, Paul. *Systematic Theology.* Vol. 2, *Existence and Christ.* Chicago: University of Chicago Press, 1975.

———. "You Are Accepted." *The Shaking of the Foundations*, 153–63. New York: Scribner, 1948.

Time. "Advertising: It's Toasted." 5 December 1938. Web. Accessed 12 April 2011.

———. "Advertising: Toasted." 9 July 1951. Web. Accessed 12 April 2011.

Todd, Drew. "Decadent Heroes: Dandyism and Masculinity in Art Deco Hollywood." *Journal of Popular Film and Television* 32.4 (2005): 168–81.

Torres, Sasha. *Black, White, and In Color: Television and Black Civil Rights.* Princeton University Press, 2003.

————, ed. *Living Color: Race and Television in the United States*. Durham: Duke University Press, 1998.

————. "Television/Feminism: *HeartBeat* and Prime Time Lesbianism." *The Lesbian and Gay Studies Reader*, ed. Henry Abelove, Michele Aina Barale, and David M. Halperin, 176–85. New York: Routledge, 1993.

Treib, Marc, ed. *An Everyday Modernism: The Houses of William Wurster*. Berkeley: University of California Press, 1995.

Trollope, Anthony. *The Prime Minister*. 1875–76. Ed. Jennifer Uglow. London: Oxford University Press, 2009.

Turow, Joseph. *Playing Doctor: Television, Storytelling, and Medical Power*. New York: Oxford University Press, 1989.

Turow, Joseph, and Rachel Gans-Boriskin. "From Expert in Action to Existential Angst: A Half Century of Television Doctors." *Medicine's Moving Pictures: Medicine, Health, and Bodies in American Film and Television*, ed. Leslie J. Reagan, Nancy Tomes, and Paula A. Treichler, 263–81. Rochester: University of Rochester Press, 2007.

Twitchell, James. *Adcult USA*. New York: Columbia University Press, 1997.

Umansky, Lauri. *Motherhood Reconceived: Feminism and the Legacies of the Sixties*. New York: New York University Press, 1996.

Upton, Dell. *Another City: Urban Life and Urban Spaces in the New American Republic*. New Haven: Yale University Press, 2008.

————. "Sound as Landscape." *Landscape Journal* 26.1 (2007): 24–35.

USA Today. "Veteran Ad Exec Says 'Mad Men' Were Really about Sex, Booze." 31 August 2009. Web. Accessed 21 May 2011.

Van Grove, Jennifer. "MadMenYourself: Create a Mad Men Inspired Avatar for Twitter, Facebook, and iPhone." *Mashable*, 30 July 2009. Web. Accessed 12 April 2012.

Vargas-Cooper, Natasha. *Mad Men Unbuttoned: A Romp through 1960s America*. New York: Collins Design, 2010.

Varon, Jeremy, Michael S. Foley, and John McMillian. "Time Is an Ocean: The Past and Future of the Sixties." *The Sixties* 1.1 (2008): 1–7.

Vulture. "Don Draper's 'Mad Men' Bookshelf." 24 July 2008. Web. Accessed 29 May 2011.

Waldman, Allison. "The *Mad Men–Twilight Zone* Connection—Videos." *TV Squad*, 25 August 2008. Web. Accessed 12 April 2012.

————. "Matt Weiner of *Mad Men*: The TV Squad Interview." *TV Squad*, 8 August 2008. Web. Accessed 12 April 2012.

Wales, Anne. "Television as History: History as Television." *Television and Criticism*, ed. Solange Davin and Rhona Jackson, 49–60. Bristol: Intellect, 2008.

Walker, Juliet E. K. *The History of Black Business in America: Capitalism, Race, Entrepreneurship*. New York: Twayne, 1998.

Wallace, Kelsey. "Mad Men's Portrayal of Sexism Seeps Unironically into Its Commercial Breaks." *BitchMedia*, 31 August 2009. Web. Accessed 12 April 2012.

Ward, Jule Dejager. *La Leche League: At the Crossroads of Medicine, Feminism, and Religion.* Chapel Hill: University of North Carolina Press, 2000.

Warhol, Robyn R. *Having a Good Cry: Effeminate Feelings and Pop-Culture Forms.* Columbus: Ohio State University Press, 2003.

Warner, Michael. "Publics and Counterpublics." *Publics and Counterpublics*, 65–124. New York: Zone Books, 2005.

Weems, Robert E., Jr. *Desegregating the Dollar: African American Consumerism in the Twentieth Century.* New York: New York University Press, 1998.

Weinman, Jaime. "Friday Night Lights and Matter-of-Factness." *Maclean's*, 12 July 2010. Web. Accessed 15 July 2010.

Weissbrod, Rachel. "*Exodus* as a Zionist Melodrama." *Israel Studies* 4.1 (1999): 129–52.

White, Mimi. "Television: A Narrative — A History." *Cultural Studies* 3.3 (1989): 282–300.

———. "Television Liveness: History, Banality, Attractions." *Spectator* 20 (1999/2000): 39–56.

Whitehead, Colson. *The Intuitionist.* New York: Doubleday, 1999.

Wicke, Jennifer. *Advertising Fictions: Literature, Advertisement, and Social Reading.* New York: Columbia University Press, 1988.

Wilde, Oscar. *The Importance of Being Earnest. The Complete Works of Oscar Wilde*, 321–84. New York: Harper Perennial, 1989.

———. *The Picture of Dorian Gray. The Complete Works of Oscar Wilde*, 17–167. New York: Harper Perennial, 1989.

———. "The Soul of Man under Socialism." *The Complete Works of Oscar Wilde*, 1079–104. New York: Harper Perennial, 1989.

Williams, Alex. "It's an Easy Sell." *New York Times*, 13 July 2008. Web. Accessed 8 April 2011.

Williams, Linda. "Introduction." *Viewing Positions: Ways of Seeing Film*, ed. Linda Williams, 1–20. New Brunswick: Rutgers University Press, 1995.

———, ed. *Viewing Positions: Ways of Seeing Film.* New Brunswick: Rutgers University Press, 1995.

Williams, Raymond. "Advertising: The Magic System." *Advertising and Society Review* 1.1 (2000). Web.

———. *Television: Technology and Cultural Form.* London: Fontana, 1974.

Willis, Susan. "I Shop Therefore I Am: Is There a Place for Afro-American Culture in Commodity Culture?" *Changing Our Own Words*, ed. Cheryl Wall, 173–95. New Brunswick: Rutgers University Press, 1989.

Wilson, Elizabeth. *Adorned in Dreams: Fashion and Modernity.* 1987. New Brunswick: Rutgers University Press, 2003.

Wilson, Sloan. *The Man in the Gray Flannel Suit*. New York: Simon and Schuster, 1955.

Witchel, Alex. "Mad Men Has Its Moment." *New York Times Magazine*, 22 June 2008. Web. Accessed 21 June 2010.

Witkowski, Melissa. "It's Still a Mad Men World." *Guardian*, 2 February 2010. Web. Accessed 30 December 2010.

Wojcik, Pamela Robertson. *The Apartment Plot: Urban Living in American Film and Popular Culture, 1945 to 1975*. Durham: Duke University Press, 2010.

Wolf, Jacqueline H. *Deliver Me from Pain: Anesthesia and Birth in America*. Baltimore and London: Johns Hopkins University Press, 2009.

Wrayle, Matt, and Annalee Newitz, eds. *White Trash: Race and Class in America*. New York: Routledge, 1997.

Wright, Gwendolyn. *USA: Modern Architectures in History*. London: Reaktion Books, 2008.

Wright, Lee. "Objectifying Gender: The Stiletto Heel." *Fashion Theory: A Reader*, ed. Malcolm Barnard, 197–208. London: Routledge, 2007.

Yates, Richard. *Revolutionary Road*. New York: Vintage, 1961.

Zimmer, Ben. "Mad Men-ese." *New York Times*, 19 July 2010. Web. Accessed 28 December 2010.

Žižek, Slavoj. "Courtly Love, or, Woman as Thing." *The Metastases of Enjoyment: Six Essays on Woman and Causality*, 89–112. New York: Verso, 1994.

———. *Enjoy Your Symptom!* New York: Routledge, 1992.

———. *The Plague of Fantasies: Six Essays on Woman and Causality*. New York: Verso, 1998.

Zola, Emile. *Le Roman expérimental. Œuvres complètes*. Ed. Henri Mitterand. Paris: Cercle du Livre Précieux, Tome 10, 1968.

MICHAEL BÉRUBÉ is the director of the Institute for the Arts and Humanities at Pennsylvania State University. His most recent book is *The Left at War* (2009). He is the president of the Modern Language Association for 2012–13.

ALEXANDER DOTY was the author of two influential books, *Making Things Perfectly Queer: Interpreting Mass Culture* (1993) and *Flaming Classics: Queering the Film Canon* (2000), as well as numerous essays on topics including queer authorship, Hollywood stars, and queer representation in mainstream media. He also edited two special issues of *Camera Obscura* on divas (2007 and 2008), and coedited (with Corey K. Creekmur) *Out in Culture: Gay, Lesbian, and Queer Essays on Popular Culture* (Duke University Press, 1995). He served on the editorial board of many journals, including *Camera Obscura*, *Quarterly Review of Film and Video*, *Velvet Light Trap*, and GLQ: *A Journal of Gay and Lesbian Studies*. Among the first generation of "male feminist" and gay film scholars to embrace and elaborate the theoretical implications of "queerness," in his work and teaching, Doty not only embraced alternative challenges to mainstream media from queer artists, but located queerness at the heart of mainstream culture through his dazzlingly original readings of seemingly heteronormative films and television programs.

LAUREN M. E. GOODLAD is University Scholar, associate professor of English, and director of the Unit for Criticism and Interpretive Theory at the University of Illinois, Urbana-Champaign. Her books include the coedited *Goth: Undead Subculture* (2007) and *The Victorian Geopolitical Aesthetic: Realism, Sovereignty, and Transnational Experience* (forthcoming). Her articles have appeared in journals such as *American Literary History*, *Cultural Critique*, ELH, *Journal of Human Rights*, *Literature Compass*, *Novel: A Forum on Fiction*, PMLA, and *Victorian Studies*.

JIM HANSEN is associate professor of English and critical theory at the University of Illinois. He is author of *Terror and Irish Modernism: The Gothic Tradition from Burke to Beckett* (2009) and coeditor with Matthew Hart of *Contemporary Literature and the State* (2008). His articles have appeared in *Contemporary Literature, New Literary History,* and *Studies in Romanticism.* He is currently working on a book titled *The Adorno Problematic: Formalism and the End of Politics.*

DIANNE HARRIS is director of the Illinois Program for Research in the Humanities and professor of landscape architecture, architecture, art history, and history at the University of Illinois, Urbana-Champaign. Her most recent publications include the edited volume *Second Suburb: Levittown, Pennsylvania* (2010), and *Little White Houses: How the Postwar Home Constructed Race in America* (forthcoming). She is a past president for the Society of Architectural Historians.

LYNNE JOYRICH is associate professor of modern culture and media at Brown University. She is author of *Re-viewing Reception: Television, Gender, and Postmodern Culture* (1996). Her articles on film, television, feminist, queer, and cultural studies have appeared in *Camera Obscura, Cinema Journal, Critical Inquiry, differences, Discourse, Journal of Visual Culture,* and *Transformative Works and Cultures* and in such volumes as *Logics of Television* (1990), *Private Screenings: Television and the Female Consumer* (1992), *New Media, Old Media: A History and Theory Reader* (2005), *Inventing Film Studies* (2008), and *Queer TV: Theories, Histories, Politics* (2009). She has been a member of the editorial collective of *Camera Obscura* since 1996.

LILYA KAGANOVSKY is associate professor of Slavic, comparative literature, and media and cinema studies at the University of Illinois, Urbana-Champaign. She is author of *How the Soviet Man Was Unmade* (2008), articles on gender and masculinity in Russian cinema, and, together with Masha Salazkina, an edited volume on sound, music, and speech in Soviet and post-Soviet audiovisual media. She serves on the editorial board of the journal *Studies in Russian and Soviet Cinema* and reviews films for the online journal *KinoKultura.*

CLARENCE LANG is associate professor of African and African-American studies at the University of Kansas, where he was a Langston Hughes Visiting Professor. He is author of *Grassroots at the Gateway: Class Politics and Black Freedom Struggle in St. Louis, 1936–75* (2009), and coeditor with Robbie Lieberman of *Anticommunism and the African American Freedom Movement: "Another Side of the Story"* (2009). He has published articles and essays in *Against the Current, The Black Scholar, Journal of African American History, Journal of Social History, Journal of Urban History, New Politics, Race and Society,* and *Trans-Scripts.*

CARL LEHNEN earned a Ph.D. in English from the University of Illinois. His dissertation, "Sex, Aesthetics, and Modernity in the British Romance of Italy, 1870–1914," examines how British narratives of travel to Italy articulate queer sexualities in terms of space, temporality, and genre.

CAROLINE LEVINE is professor of English at the University of Wisconsin, Madison. She is author of *The Serious Pleasures of Suspense* (2003) and *Provoking Democracy: Why We Need the Arts* (2007). She is currently the nineteenth-century editor for the *Norton Anthology of World Literature* and is completing a book called *Strategic Formalism: Shape, Rhythm, Hierarchy, Network*.

KENT ONO is professor and chair of the Department of Communication at the University of Utah. He has contributed essays to numerous journals, including *Amerasia Journal, Communication and Critical/Cultural Studies, Communication Monographs, Cultural Studies, Journal of Asian American Studies, Philosophy and Rhetoric*, and *Western Journal of Communication*. He is author of *Contemporary Media Culture and the Remnants of a Colonial Past* (2009) and coauthor of *Asian Americans and the Media* (with Vincent Pham, 2009) and *Shifting Borders: Rhetoric, Immigration, and California's Proposition 187* (with John Sloop, 2002). He is coeditor of *Critical Rhetorics of Race* (with Michael Lacy, 2011) and *Enterprise Zones: Critical Positions on "Star Trek"* (with Taylor Harrison, Sarah Projansky, and Elyce Helford, 1996) and editor of *Asian American Studies after Critical Mass* (2005) and *A Companion to Asian American Studies* (2005). He coedits the book series Critical Cultural Communication with Sarah Banet-Weiser. He is also coeditor of the journal *Critical Studies in Media Communication* with Ronald Jackson. He is now working on a book titled *Critical Intercultural Communication* with Etsuko Kinefuchi.

DANA POLAN is professor of cinema studies at New York University. He is the author of eight books including, most recently, *Julia Child's "The French Chef"* (2011). He has done commentary tracks for eight DVDs.

LESLIE J. REAGAN is professor of history at the University of Illinois, Urbana-Champaign. She also has affiliations with the Department of Gender and Women's Studies, the College of Law, the College of Medicine, and Media and Cinema Studies in the College of Media. She is author of *Dangerous Pregnancies: Mothers, Disabilities, and Abortion in Modern America* (2010) and *When Abortion Was a Crime: Women, Medicine, and Law in the United States, 1867–1973* (1997), and coeditor of *Medicine's Moving Pictures: Medicine, Health, and Bodies in American Film and Television* (2007) with Nancy Tomes and Paula Treichler. Her recent articles include "Representations and Reproductive Hazards of Agent Orange" in the *Journal of Medicine, Law, and Ethics* (2010); "Rashes, Rights, and Wrongs in the Hospital and in the Courtroom: German Measles, Abortion, and Malpractice" in *Law and History Review* (2009); and "Law and Medicine" in *Cambridge History of Law in America* (2008).

MABEL ROSENHECK is a doctoral student in the Screen Cultures program at Northwestern University. In 2012 she directed exhibition research for the reopening of the Museum of Broadcast Communications in Chicago. She has presented research at conferences including the Society for Cinema and Media Studies, Console-ing Passions, and the American Studies Association. Her dissertation research examines public memory, media history, and local media museums.

ROBERT A. RUSHING is associate professor of Italian and comparative literature at the University of Illinois, where he holds affiliate appointments with the Unit for Criticism and Interpretive Theory, cinema studies, and the European Union Center. He works predominantly on twentieth- and twenty-first-century literature and popular culture in Italian, English, French, and Spanish. His research interests include modern Italian literature; film studies; critical theory, especially psychoanalysis; comparative literary studies; and genre. Rushing is the author of *Resisting Arrest: Detective Fiction and Popular Culture* (2007). His articles and reviews, on topics ranging from Italian bodybuilder films of the 1950s to sexual difference in De Sica, have appeared in *American Imago, American Literary History, California Italian Studies, Camera Obscura, Comparative Literature*, MLN, *Post Script, Studies in European Cinema*, and *Yale French Studies*.

IRENE V. SMALL is assistant professor of modern and contemporary art history at Princeton University. Her current book project, *Hélio Oiticica: Folding the Frame*, focuses on experimental participatory art in Brazil in the 1960s. Her research interests include historical and neo-avant-gardes; modernism in a global context, particularly Brazil and Latin America; abstraction; problems of methodology and interpretation; relationality; and the social implications of form. Her articles and criticism have appeared in several journals, including *Artforum, The Getty Research Journal, Res: Anthropology and Aesthetics*, and *Third Text*.

MICHAEL SZALAY is professor of English at the University of California, Irvine, and author of *New Deal Modernism: American Literature and the Invention of the Welfare State* (2000) and *Hip Figures: A Literary History of the Democratic Party* (2012). He writes and teaches on literature, television, film, comics, and popular music. He is also the coeditor of the Post45 book series.

JEREMY VARON is associate professor of history at the New School for Social Research. He is author of *Bringing the War Home: The Weather Underground, the Red Army Faction, and Revolutionary Violence in the Sixties and Seventies* (2004) and, most recently, "After the Fall: Politics, Representation, and the Permanence of Empire in the Cinema of Peter Whitehead" in FRAMEWORK (2011). He cofounded and edits *The Sixties: A Journal of History, Politics and Culture*. His writings have appeared in *New German Critique, Reviews in American History*, and various edited volumes.

Roiphe, Katie, 18

Rolling Stones, the, 41, 371

Romano, Salvatore, 16–17; as archetypal closeted homosexual, 280–82, 291, 293; sexual harassment of, 11–12, 225–26, 290–91

Rosenberg, Ethel, 344n7

Rothko, Mark, 185–88

Route 66 (television series), 331

Rumsen, Freddy, 292, 337

Saint, Eva Marie, 154, 331, 334

Schudson, Michael, 11, 341, 343, 353. *See also* advertising

Schwarz, Benjamin, 8

Searchers, The (film), 374

Seconds (film), 43, 46

secretarial pool, 44–45, 124; gendered space of, 5, 59–62; sexual objectification of, 59, 61–62, 243. *See also* Harris, Joan; Olson, Peggy

Sellers, Peter: *I Love You, Alice B. Toklas*, 45

seriality, 3, 24–26, 342–43; of television, 24–29, 253, 255, 321–25, 337–43

Sesame Street (television series), 213–15, 218, 230, 332

Silverman, Kaja: retro fashion, 163, 170

Simon, David. See *Wire, The*

Simone, Nina, 86

Sirk, Douglas, 7–8, 367

"slash fiction," 31n16

smoking, 44, 48, 95, 276n3, 344n12, 368–69. *See also* Freud, Sigmund: death wish

Sopranos, The (television series), 18, 21, 35, 40, 42, 92–93, 97, 111–16, 118–19, 123, 134–35, 261, 266, 271–72, 321–22, 362–63, 369–70

space age, 27–28

Star Trek (television series), 26, 31n20, 235n22

Sterling, Roger, 15, 126–27, 318n9; and Jane Sterling (née Siegel), 372; and Joan Holloway (Harris), 84, 337–38

Sterling Cooper (advertising firm in *Mad Men*), 14; spatial arrangement of, 54–62;

and transition to Sterling Cooper Draper Pryce, 90–91, 209

Stranger in a Strange Land (novel), 344n11

suburbia, 62–64, 69–70, 79, 188–89

Ted Bates (advertising firm), 12–13

television, 43, 46–47, 75, 77, 276n10; authenticity and historicism of, 2–3, 11–12, 27, 29–30n3, 39–40, 42, 70–71, 80, 93, 104, 161, 179, 218, 240, 258, 272–73, 275n1, 302, 305–6, 367–69; extratelevisual and critical responses to, 1–2, 8–10, 18–19, 27, 41, 44, 51, 52n2, 74, 97, 137–38, 214, 270, 275n1, 302–3, 345–47, 349–51, 363; novelistic qualities of, 24–26, 113, 133–34, 320–21, 370, 374; "quality" series, 18, 21, 24–25, 111–13, 115–16, 220, 320–21; self-referentiality of, 16, 113, 122, 125, 127, 180nn1–3, 190–91, 214, 220–21, 227, 353; showrunner as *auteur*, 112; use of flashback in, 44, 145, 265, 268, 289, 329, 374; use of montage in, 337–38

Tillich, Paul, 268–69

To Kill a Mockingbird (film), 4

Trollope, Anthony, 3, 25, 321–22, 326–29

uncanny, 16–17, 137, 139, 144

Vargas-Cooper, Natasha: *The Footnotes of Mad Men*, 3

Victorian literature. *See* television: novelistic qualities of

Vietnam War, 27, 37, 278n25

Warhol, Andy, 187–88, 190

Warhol, Robyn, 25–26, 321

Warner, Michael: the counterpublic, 31n18

Weiner, Matthew (showrunner of *Mad Men*), 25, 111, 113, 122–24, 126, 127, 129, 234n11, 255n2, 327–28, 363–64, 366, 369–71, 374, 376–77

Whitman, Dick. *See* Draper, Don

Wicke, Jennifer, 341–42

Wilde, Oscar, 156, 344n13; *The Importance of Being Earnest*, 148–49; *The Picture of Dorian Gray*, 145–46, 149, 270, 338

LAUREN M. E. GOODLAD is associate professor of English at the University of Illinois, Urbana-Champaign, and director of the Unit for Criticism and Interpretive Theory. She is the coeditor of *Goth: Undead Subculture* (2007) and the author of *The Victorian Geopolitical Aesthetic: Realism, Sovereignty, and Transnational Experience* (forthcoming).

LILYA KAGANOVSKY is associate professor of Slavic, comparative literature, and media and cinema studies at the University of Illinois, Urbana-Champaign. She is the author of *How the Soviet Man Was Unmade* (2008).

ROBERT A. RUSHING is associate professor of Italian and comparative literature at the University of Illinois, Urbana-Champaign. He is the author of *Resisting Arrest: Detective Fiction and Popular Culture* (2007).

Library of Congress Cataloging-in-Publication Data
Mad men, mad world : sex, politics, style, and the 1960s /
Lauren M. E. Goodlad, Lilya Kaganovsky,
and Robert A. Rushing, eds.
p. cm.
Includes bibliographical references and index.
ISBN 978-0-8223-5402-4 (cloth : alk. paper)
ISBN 978-0-8223-5418-5 (pbk. : alk. paper)
1. Mad men (Television program). 2. Television programs—
Social aspects—United States. 3. Television programs—
United States—History and criticism. I. Goodlad,
Lauren M. E. II. Kaganovsky, Lilya.
III. Rushing, Robert A.
PN1992.77.M226M337 2013
791.45′72—dc23   2012033726